A HISTORY
OF PROPHECY
IN ISRAEL

A HISTORY
OF PROPHECY
IN ISRAEL
Revised and Enlarged

Joseph Blenkinsopp

Westminster John Knox Press
LOUISVILLE • LONDON

Book design by Jennifer K. Cox
Cover design by Kevin Darst
Cover illustration: The Prophet Isaiah *by Michelangelo Buonarroti, Sistine Chapel, Vatican, Rome. Courtesy SuperStock.*

Published by Westminster John Knox Press
Louisville, Kentucky

This book is printed on acid-free paper that meets the American National Standards Institute Z39.48 standard. ∞

PRINTED IN THE UNITED STATES OF AMERICA

Library of Congress Cataloging-in-Publication Data

Blenkinsopp, Joseph, date.
    A history of prophecy in Israel / Joseph Blenkinsopp
        p.   cm.
    "Revised and enlarged."
    ISBN: 978-0-664-25639-5 (alk. paper)
    1. Prophets. 2. Bible. O.T.—Prophecies—History. I. Title.
BS1198.B53   1996
224'.06—dc20   96-21402

In memory of my father and mother

Joseph William Blenkinsopp
and
Mary Lyons

CONTENTS

PREFACE TO THE
REVISED EDITION

That a second edition of *A History of Prophecy in Israel* can claim some plausible justification after being in print only twelve years is a tribute to the quantity and quality of commentary on and analysis of prophetic texts published during that time. While not much new data have come to light, conclusions that seemed to be in secure possession of the field have been challenged and new directions taken, several of them influenced by contemporary literary theory. While I have duly taken account of these recent developments, especially the current predilection for synchronistic readings of prophetic books (conspicuously Isaiah), none of this more recent writing has given me reason to abandon more traditional methods of redactional analysis. I continue to believe that synchrony and diachrony can and should coexist.

Anyone who reads historians working with data bearing on more recent topics—a medieval Cathar village or witchcraft in eighteenth-century Auvergne, reconstructed by Emmanuel Le Roy Ladurie, for example, or apocalyptic movements of the Middle Ages, brought to life by Norman Cohn—could easily despair of writing a history of prophecy, or a history of anything else, in Iron Age Israel. The political and military vicissitudes to which that part of the world has always been subject, together with the Palestinian climate, have seen to it that practically no data of the kind available to these historians have survived from that time. I was aware of this twelve years ago, but the awareness has grown during the intervening period and will be apparent at several points in what follows. However, I persist in the view that it is possible, and therefore necessary, to make the best of what we have, to keep trying to elevate possibilities into serious probabilities, and to detect some glimmer of personalities, politics, and ideas of those times using the often uncooperative texts and artifacts at our disposal.

In addition to making changes of style and substance that seemed to be called for, rearranging the order of treatment here and there (especially with respect to Isaiah), and updating the bibliographies, I have eliminated whatever infelicities of expression, factual mistakes, or typographical errors I have noticed myself, as well as those brought to my attention by colleagues, students, and reviewers. My thanks to them, to my assistant, Shaun Longstreet, for valuable help with bibliographies, computer-related matters, and indexing, and to the staff of Westminster John Knox Press for their unfailing courtesy and cooperation.

South Bend, Indiana
December 1995

ABBREVIATIONS

ABD	*The Anchor Bible Dictionary*, 6 volumes (New York: Double-day, 1992)
AcOr	*Acta Orientalia*
AfO	*Archiv für Orientforschung*
AJSL	*American Journal of Semitic Languages and Literatures*, Chicago
ALUOS	*Annual of the Leeds University Oriental Society*, Leeds
ANET	*Ancient Near Eastern Texts relating to the Old Testament*, J. B. Pritchard, ed. (Princeton: Princeton University Press, 1950, 1995², 1969³)
Ant	Flavius Josephus, *Antiquities of the Jews*
ASTI	*Annual of the Swedish Theological Institute*, Jerusalem/Leiden
BA	*The Biblical Archaeologist*, Cambridge, Mass.
BDB	F. Brown, S. R. Driver, and C. A. Briggs, eds., *A Hebrew and English Lexicon of the Old Testament* (Oxford University Press, 1906; rev. ed. 1957)
Bib	*Biblica*, Rome
BibOr	*Bibliotheca Orientalis*, Leiden
BJRL	*Bulletin of the John Rylands Library*, Manchester
BN	*Biblische Notizen*, Munich
BTB	*Biblical Theology Bulletin*, Jamaica, N.Y.
BWANT	Beiträge zur Wissenschaft vom Alten und Neuen Testament (Stuttgart: W. Kohlhammer)
BZ	*Biblische Zeitschrift*, Paderborn
BZAW	Beiheft zur *Zeitschrift für die alttestamentliche Wissenschaft*, Berlin
CAH	*The Cambridge Ancient History*
CBQ	*The Catholic Biblical Quarterly*, Washington
Dtr	Deuteronomistic History

EJ	*Encyclopedia Judaica* (Jerusalem: Keter Publishing House)
ETL	*Ephemerides Theologicae Lovanienses*, Leuven/Louvain
EvQ	*Evangelical Quarterly*, Exeter
EvTh	*Evangelische Theologie*, Munich
ExpT	*The Expository Times*, Edinburgh
HAR	*Hebrew Annual Review*, Columbus, Ohio
HeyJ	*Heythrop Journal*, London
HTR	*Harvard Theological Review*, Cambridge, Mass.
HUCA	*The Hebrew Union College Annual*, Cincinnati
IB	*The Interpreter's Bible*, G. A. Buttrick, ed. (Nashville: Abingdon Press, 1951–57)
IDB	*The Interpreter's Dictionary of the Bible*, G. A. Buttrick, ed. (Nashville: Abingdon Press, 1962)
IDBS	*The Interpreter's Dictionary of the Bible, Supplementary Volume*, K. Crim, ed. (Nashville: Abingdon Press, 1976)
IEJ	*Israel Exploration Journal*, Jerusalem
Int	*Interpretation*, Richmond, Virginia
JAAR	*Journal of the American Academy of Religion*, Atlanta, Georgia
JBL	*Journal of Biblical Literature*, Atlanta, Georgia
JCS	*Journal of Cuneiform Studies*, Atlanta, Georgia
JJS	*Journal of Jewish Studies*, London
JNES	*Journal of Near Eastern Studies*, Chicago
JNSL	*Journal of Northwest Semitic Languages*, Stellenbosch, Republic of South Africa
JQR	*Jewish Quarterly Review*, Philadelphia
JRE	*Journal of Religious Ethics*
JSOT	*Journal for the Study of the Old Testament*, Sheffield
JSS	*Journal of Semitic Studies*, Manchester
JTS	*Journal of Theological Studies*, Oxford
LXX	Septuagint
MT	Masoretic text
NEB	New English Bible (1970, 1989)
NRSV	New Revised Standard Version (1989)
NTT	*Nieuw theologisch Tijdschrift*, Haarlem
OA	*Oriens Antiquus*
OG	Old Greek version (LXX)
OTS	*Oudtestamentische Studiën*, Leiden
PJB	*Palästina Jahrbuch*, Berlin
RA	*Revue d'Assyriologie et d'archéologie orientale*, Paris
RB	*Revue Biblique*, Paris
RHPR	*Revue d'histoire et de philosophie religieuses*, Strasbourg
RSR	*Recherches de science religieuse*, Paris

RSV	Revised Standard Version
RTP	*Revue de théologie et de philosophie*, Lausanne
SBL	Society of Biblical Literature
SDB	*Supplément au Dictionnaire de la Bible*, L. Pirot, A. Robert, H. Cazelles, eds. (Paris, 1928–)
SEÅ	*Svensk Exegetisk Årsbok*, Lund
SJOT	*Scandinavian Journal of Theology*, Oslo
SJT	*Scottish Journal of Theology*, Edinburgh
StTh	*Studia Theologica*, Lund
SVT	Supplements to *Vetus Testamentum*, Leiden
TB	*Tyndale Bulletin*, Cambridge
TDNT	*Theological Dictionary of the New Testament*, G. Kittel and G. Friedrich, eds. (Grand Rapids: Wm. B. Eerdmans, 1964–76)
TDOT	*Theological Dictionary of the Old Testament*, G. J. Botterweck & H. Ringgren, eds. (Grand Rapids: Wm. B. Eerdmans, 1977–)
TGUOS	*Transactions of the Glasgow University Oriental Society*, Glasgow
TLZ	*Theologische Literaturzeitung*, Leipzig
TR	*Theologische Rundschau*, Tübingen
TZ	*Theologische Zeitschrift*, Basel
UF	*Ugaritforschungen*, Munich
VT	*Vetus Testamentum*, Leiden
VTS	Supplements to *Vetus Testamentum*, Leiden
WO	*Die Welt des Orients*, Göttingen
ZAW	*Zeitschrift für die alttestamentliche Wissenschaft*, Berlin
ZDMG	*Zeitschrift der Deutschen Morgenländischen Gesellschaft*, Leipzig
ZDPV	*Zeitschrift des Deutschen Palästinavereins*, Wiesbaden
ZTK	*Zeitschrift für Theologie und Kirche*, Tübingen

INTRODUCTION

Over the past two centuries or so the interpretation of prophetic texts has described an extremely broad arc. One has only to contrast millenarian and apocalyptic interpretations with the rabbinic view, which aimed at blunting the disruptive and destabilizing effect of prophecy, to see how different situations, with their own demands and constraints, produce different readings of prophetic texts. Modern critical scholarship, the course of which over the last century and a half is outlined briefly in chapter 1, broke decisively with traditional understandings of prophecy in Christianity and Judaism. Yet in spite of significant advances we are still some way from a consensus on several crucial issues, for example, the institutional and social connections and locations of different kinds of prophecy, the relation between prophetic experience and tradition, and the dating and editorial history of prophetic material. Also, only recently has the study of Israelite prophecy begun to free itself from theories of development inspired by philosophical or denominational perspectives that colored much of what was written on prophecy in the nineteenth and early twentieth centuries.

The best way to get beyond this situation is to keep our attention fixed on the actual phenomenon of prophecy in Israel, which involves us in an attempt to make sense of its development over a long period, a millennium more or less, whole sections of which are poorly documented. It would be easier, and certainly safer for one's reputation, to eschew the attempt at a comprehensive overview and to limit oneself to detailed work on specific texts and problems the results of which are much easier to assess. But from time to time anyone engaged in this study will feel the need to stand back and take stock, to regain perspective on the phenomenon of prophecy as a whole. This was the goal I had in mind in writing.

My justification for adding to the bibliographical mountain on prophecy is that one can find many thematic and theological studies of

Israelite prophecy but few critical histories, and those that are available rarely attempt to cover the entire span of the biblical period. In most cases attention is concentrated almost exclusively on the period of "classical" prophecy, meaning the two centuries from Amos to the "Isaiah" of the Babylonian exile. Yet the earliest of these "classical" prophets, Amos and Hosea, refer to a prophetic tradition extending back over some three centuries, a tradition that had by their time reached a fairly mature stage of consolidation. To ignore or pass rapidly over this early stage puts us at risk of misunderstanding some crucial aspects of prophetic activity during the much better-known period of Assyrian and Babylonian hegemony (eighth to sixth century B.C.E.).

Even more problematic is the tendency for historical surveys of prophecy to either peter out or reach a grand finale with the Babylonian exile in the sixth century B.C.E. The effect, if not the intent, is to perpetuate the idea, widespread in the last century, that later developments, with their quite different forms of religious expression, represent a falling away from the high plateau of prophetic religion and a surrender to institutional paralysis. Bringing the history of prophecy to an end at the Babylonian exile also leads to neglect of the interesting transformations that prophecy underwent during the time of the Second Temple. This, after all, was the epoch that witnessed not only the rise and consolidation of Judaism in the Diaspora and the Judean homeland at the beginning of the period but also the emergence of Christianity with its own forms of prophetic activity at the end.

I have aimed therefore at a historical overview that treats with skepticism the distinctions between "primitive" and "classical" prophecy and assertions about the "drying up" of prophetic inspiration at the time of the Babylonian exile or shortly thereafter. It would have been appropriate, and was in fact originally intended, to take the survey down to the end of the Second Temple period. But considerations of space, as well as common sense (given the formidable problems involved), dictated otherwise, and that part of the task is left to others.[1]

If a history of prophecy is not to be merely a series of sketches of individual prophetic figures, the lines of continuity throughout the history must be identified and followed up. In this respect our task would have been made much easier if prophets had explicitly acknowledged borrowings from their predecessors or contemporaries. Yet despite the fact that prophets never refer to one another by name, we can certainly speak of a prophetic *tradition*. Jeremiah's complaint that his prophetic contemporaries were stealing sayings from one another (Jer. 23:30) may perhaps be interpreted in this sense, and we have just seen that Amos and Hosea align themselves with a tradition of prophetic protest already in place.

Hosea appears to have been familiar with the public pronouncements of his near-contemporary Amos, and both announce the end of the special relationship between Israel and Israel's God Yahweh. In an early stage of his career, Isaiah applied the message of Amos to his own contemporaries in the kingdom of Judah. Isaiah and Micah have much in common, Jeremiah's debt to Hosea is easily verifiable, Ezekiel borrows from his older contemporary Jeremiah and composes a sermon using one of the visions of Amos as his text (Ezek. 7:1–27; cf. Amos 8:1–3), and so on.

In reading through the prophetic books, therefore, we experience a cumulative process of appropriation, assimilation, and adaptation that, as we move into the time of the Second Temple, shades off into an increasingly frequent recycling and reinterpreting of older prophetic material. This inner-biblical process provides a valuable indication of changes in the understanding of prophecy itself, and especially the shift from direct inspiration to the inspired interpretation of earlier prophecy. It leads, eventually, to the point where the prophetic books, having achieved canonical fixity, generate their own distinct commentaries.

We can therefore speak of a prophetic tradition, but we must add that this tradition follows different lines and involves different kinds of prophetic roles and personalities. We have to bear in mind that the sources at our disposal, almost exclusively biblical sources, have been selected, edited, and presented according to very definite criteria, quite apart from the question of how much prophetic material actually survived down to the time when the selecting, editing, and presenting was going on. It follows that those whom we refer to as *the* prophets formed only a small, and in some respects anomalous, minority of prophets in Israel at any given time. If by "the religion of Israel" we mean to refer to the beliefs and activities of the population as a whole, we would have to conclude that many of the prophets whose stories and sayings have survived were more often than not at odds with it. They played, in other words, a destabilizing rather than a validating role in the religious life of their contemporaries. But there were also prophets more closely tied to established institutions, especially the cult, and it is possible that their sayings, like those of similar figures elsewhere in the Near East, were preserved and transmitted by these institutions. These cultic prophets form a distinct class and have a fairly well-defined role, though we shall see that the task of deciding who belongs to this category is by no means simple.

Prophets, then, could play either a supportive or a destabilizing role, and they could operate either within recognized and approved institutions or outside of them. Another approach to multiple prophetic traditions that has been suggested is along geographical lines of demarcation. Some attention has been given in recent English-language scholarship (especially by A. W. Jenks and R. R. Wilson[2]) to Ephraimite or Northern prophecy as a special type preserving its own distinctive characteristics over several centuries. According to this view the line runs from the Elohist narrative strand in the Pentateuch, deemed to have originated in the kingdom of Samaria, through prophetic and Levitical groups that opposed the monarchy throughout the history of the same kingdom, then to Hosea, Jeremiah, and the Deuteronomic program as embodying elements of what might be called an Ephraimite prophetic theology. Judean prophecy, it is claimed, moved along a quite different trajectory. First attested during the reign of David in the persons of Gad and Nathan, it was taken up by Amos, Isaiah, and the other preexilic, exilic, and postexilic figures in Latter Prophets with the exception of Hosea and Jeremiah. The Ephraimite tradition, it is claimed, had its own characteristic speech forms, its own way of describing the process of prophetic mediation, and gave pride of place to Moses as the first and paradigmatic prophetic mediator.

While it is plausible to suggest that prophecy as an institution will reflect cultural conditions characteristic of different regions, the regional factor should not be overstated. Even if the elusive Elohist (E) constitutes an identifiable and independent source, which many scholars would no longer be prepared to grant, its "northern" provenance is simply assumed rather than demonstrated. It is worth noting, for example, that the three narratives presented as major evidence for an independent E source (Gen. 20:1–17; 21:8–21, 22–34) are all set in the Negev, and the Reuben-Midianite strand in the Joseph story, deemed to be Elohistic, also points toward the south rather than the north. Furthermore, the hypothesis of a prophetic-Levitical axis among the Joseph tribes (Ephraim, Manasseh) is also unsupported by evidence and clouded by anachronistic assumptions deriving from the author of 1 and 2 Chronicles. There are certainly links between the Ephraimite Hosea and Deuteronomy, but we must add that the social legislation of Deuteronomy owes nothing to Hosea and, as I will argue in due course, a great deal to Judean prophecy, especially Micah. This is not to deny the existence of distinctive Ephraimite prophetic features, but the distinctiveness should not be overstated.

At appropriate points in the historical overview I will suggest that the distinction between Jerusalemite and Judean, or metropolitan and provincial, prophecy may be noteworthy. Arguably the most angry, radical, and detailed critique of contemporary society, and especially of the state bureaucracy, is to be found in Micah, from the provincial center of Moresheth southwest of Jerusalem. It also will be proposed that Micah and his "school" represent the ethos and interests of the traditionalist so-

cial class known as "the people of the land," and that their teaching notably influenced the social program set out in the Deuteronomic lawbook. Enough has been said, for the time being at any rate, to make the
point that prophecy developed in different directions and with different
emphases, drawing on religious traditions that were often radically reinterpreted in the process.[3]

Protest on behalf of the poor and disadvantaged, those least equipped
to survive the transition from a traditional way of life based on the kinship network to a state system, is one of the most powerful strands in
prophetic preaching. Beginning with Amos, it is taken up in different
ways by Isaiah and Micah, developed further by the disciples or editors
of the latter and also, to a lesser extent, by Zephaniah during the last century of Judean independence. It is not nearly so prominent in Hosea and
Jeremiah, whose concerns focus more on syncretic cults and the foreign
policy pursued by ruler and court. Linked with this critique of the encroaching state apparatus is the fundamental prophetic concern for
community. On this point the difference between the optimistic and the
critical prophet is that the latter, unlike the former, refuses to validate
unconditionally the contemporary institutional form assumed by the
community that calls itself Israel. When the critical prophet speaks of
"the remnant," he (less commonly she) implies that there will indeed be
a future for that community even though the form it currently assumes—
that is, an independent state system—will be swept away in the destructive flow of historical events. According to this predominantly Judean
prophetic tradition, the fundamental reason for this state of affairs is dis-
regard for justice and righteousness (Amos 5:7, 24; 6:12; Isa. 5:7; etc.).
These twinned concepts (Hebrew *mišpāṭ, ṣedaqâ*) connote the maintenance of right order, of societal structures, and of judicial procedures re-
spectful of the rights of all classes. The critical prophet is saying that a society that neglects that order, even one in which the practice of religion
flourishes (cf. Amos 5:21–24; Isa. 1:12–17), does not deserve to survive.

While we hear nothing about a group of disciples that gathered
around Amos, the victims of injustice on whose behalf he spoke would
have been presumbably the most receptive to his message. That they are
also described as "righteous" (Amos 2:6; 5:12; cf. Isa. 5:23) may perhaps
be taken as a move toward the idea that the nucleus of the new or renewed community is to be found among those who adhere to the
prophet's teaching and who strive to embody the alternative vision proclaimed by the prophet in their lives. The question then arises, and is still
relevant, whether that alternative vision can find embodiment at the center of society, even of the ecclesiastical community, or only at the periphery. Our study suggests that there is no clear-cut answer to this

question. On the one hand, prophetic protest against injustice and exploitation was given "official" sanction and expression in a state document, Deuteronomy, and it continued thereafter as a powerful force for social renewal in mainline Judaism and Christianity. On the other hand, we have to reckon as early as the exilic period or shortly thereafter with the formation of prophetic groups around a charismatic figure—groups that betray some of the characteristics of the well-known sects of the Hasmonaean period. For this reason I take the passages referring to the Servant of Yahweh in the exilic Isaian material and to the servants of Yahweh in the last eleven chapters of Isaiah as marking an important stage in the historical development of prophecy.

A theological assessment of prophecy does not require us to follow the lead of those nineteenth-century pioneers who contrasted other forms of religious life unfavorably with it. Prophecy is only one of several such forms, and it seems that its fate is to be always necessary but never by itself sufficient. Concluding the survey with Jonah, which contains a shrewd theological critique of prophecy, is meant to suggest precisely that, and to recall the unsolved and perhaps insoluble problems endemic to prophecy we will be noting at different points throughout the history. On the other hand, no writings in the scriptures more than these confront the serious reader so directly with the need to question the perceptions, mundane and religious, that tend to control our lives.

To end this introduction on a practical note, it may be necessary to warn some readers that we will be engaged in a critical study, and in the critical study of prophecy there are very few "assured results of modern scholarship." It follows, therefore, that few solutions to outstanding problems or interpretations of texts offered in this book will pass unchallenged. While obvious limitations of space have not permitted me to present adequately all alternatives worthy of serious attention, I have at least tried to acknowledge their existence while presenting my own views as clearly as possible. The bibliographies are intended to help the reader put the conclusions reached into the context of contemporary scholarly discussion where they belong. Here, too, choices had to be made, and it seemed to make sense to give preference, where possible, to recent studies available in English. (For works translated from foreign languages, the original date of publication is added in parentheses.) If, with their help, the reader will be in a position to draw his or her own conclusions, even if they differ from the ones proposed in the book, my purpose in writing it will have been achieved.

I

PROLEGOMENA:
DEFINING THE OBJECT
OF STUDY

1. SOURCES FOR THE STUDY
OF ISRAELITE PROPHECY

J. **Barr,** *Holy Scripture: Canon, Authority, Criticism,* Philadelphia: Westminster Press, 1983; J. **Barton,** *Oracles of God: Perceptions of Ancient Prophecy in Israel after the Exile,* Oxford: Oxford University Press, 1986; C. T. **Begg,** "The 'Classical Prophets' in Josephus' *Antiquities,*" *Louvain Studies* 13 (1988): 341–57; J. **Blenkinsopp,** *Prophecy and Canon,* Notre Dame: University of Notre Dame Press, 1977; M. C. **Brett,** *Biblical Criticism in Crisis? The Impact of the Canonical Approach on Old Testament Studies,* Cambridge: Cambridge University Press, 1991; H. **von Campenhausen,** *The Formation of the Christian Bible,* Philadelphia: Fortress Press, 1972; B. S. **Childs,** "The Canonical Shape of the Prophetic Literature," *Int* 32 (1978): 46–55; *Introduction to the Old Testament as Scripture,* Philadelphia: Fortress Press, 1979; G. W. **Coats** and B. O. **Long,** eds., *Canon and Authority,* Philadelphia: Fortress Press, 1977; O. **Eissfeldt,** *The Old Testament: An Introduction,* New York: Harper & Row, 1965, 562–71; D. N. **Freedman,** "The Law and the Prophets," *SVT* 9 (1963): 250–65; "Son of Man, Can These Bones Live?" *Int* 29 (1975): 171–86; S. Z. **Leiman** ed., *The Canonization of Hebrew Scripture,* Hamden, Conn.: Archon Books, 1976; R. H. **Pfeiffer,** "Canon of the Old Testament," *IDB* 1 (1962): 498–520; G. **von Rad,** *Old Testament Theology,* New York: Harper & Row, 1965, 2:3–5, 388–409; R. **Rendtorff,** *Canon and Theology,* Minneapolis: Fortress Press, 1993; A. C. **Sundberg,** Jr., *The Old Testament of the Christian Church,* Cambridge, Mass.: Harvard University Press, 1964; G. M. **Tucker,** D. L. **Petersen,** R. R. **Wilson,** eds., *Canon, Theology and Old Testament Interpretation,* Philadelphia: Fortress Press, 1988; J. **Wellhausen,** *Prolegomena to the History of Ancient Israel,* Atlanta: Scholars Press, 1994 [1883]; W. **Zimmerli,** *The Law and the Prophets,* Oxford: Basil Blackwell, 1965.

Apart from the biblical texts, the only direct reference to Israelite prophecy, and a very meager one at that, occurs on inscribed potsherds (ostraca) discovered during the excavation of Tell ed-Duweir (Lachish) in the 1930s. These were written during the Babylonian campaign that ended with the destruction of Jerusalem in 586 B.C.E. One of them (#3), a letter written by a certain Hoshaiah (Hosea), refers to an earlier letter containing a dire warning sent from one royal official to another by means of a prophet (*nābî'*), and another (#16) mentions a prophet, not necessarily the same one, the last part of whose name, unfortunately the only part extant, is identical with the last part of Jeremiah's name (*Yirmeyahu* in Hebrew). Yet a third (#6) speaks of someone (there is a lacuna at this point) whose words are demoralizing people; some scholars supply the word "prophet" (*nābî'*) and refer it to Jeremiah since the same accusation, using the same idiom, is leveled against him during the Babylonian siege of Jerusalem (Jer. 38:4). This is possible but uncertain; and all we are left with is confirmation of some degree of political involvement on the part of contemporary prophets like Jeremiah and others whose names are known to us from the book that bears his name (Jer. 26:20–23; 28:1–17; 29:21–23, 31).[1]

These letters and lists were written on broken-off pieces of pottery, but texts of any length would have been written on papyrus, and the Palestinian weather with its rainy winters has seen to it that, so far, we have only one papyrus from the time of the kingdoms. The only other non-biblical text dealing directly with our subject is an inscription written in ink on plaster discovered east of the Jordan at Deir 'Alla in 1967, which speaks of Balaam the seer (cf. Numbers 22—24). But since Balaam is a foreign seer, we postpone comment on this text to the appropriate point in the following chapter. Postbiblical sources that retell the biblical story, conspicuously the *Antiquities* of Josephus, rarely if ever contain any independent historical information on the subject.

Comparativist approaches to Israelite prophecy have appealed to a variety of phenomena, social roles, and personalities in a wide range of cultures from the Nuer of southern Sudan to the Plains Indians.[2] Such comparative studies can lead to useful generalizations about religious intermediaries and stimulate new ways of thinking about familiar biblical figures, but the differences are often more in evidence than the similarities. They also raise the question to what extent ancient Israel is really comparable to traditional societies that have survived into the modern world. For these reasons, and the practical demands of space and time, we will confine ourselves—in the following section—to "prophetic" phenomena in societies in the ancient Near East and Levant.

This brings us to the biblical sources. For the reader of the Bible, "prophecy" connotes the fifteen books attributed to prophetic authors in the midsection of the Hebrew Bible. Yet these books by no means exhaust the phenomenon of prophecy in Israel. According to a rabbinic dictum (*b. Meg.* 14a) there were forty-eight prophets and seven prophetesses in Israel, a conclusion no doubt based on a head count over the entire Hebrew Bible. None of the books accepted as canonical is ascribed to a prophet who lived before the eighth century B.C.E., yet the earliest of these canonical prophets, Amos and Hosea, knew of prophetic predecessors and stood quite consciously within a prophetic tradition (Amos 2:11–12; Hos. 6:5; 9:7–8; 12:10, 13). By the eighth century, in fact, Israelite prophecy had a history of some three centuries behind it.

It is also noteworthy that the canonical prophets refer often, and almost always disparagingly, to a class of people they themselves called "prophets" (*nebî'îm*), leaving us wondering whether they would have wished to be known by that title. One of them, Amos, appears to disavow it, though the passage in question has been interpreted otherwise (Amos 7:14). One explanation is that prophecy, in Israel as elsewhere, corresponded to an acknowledged institution and one that functioned within either royal court or temple. Hence the problem, which still awaits a satisfactory solution, of the relation of canonical prophets like Amos and Micah to Israelite institutions. We are reminded, at any rate, that the people we call *the* prophets formed only a small minority among prophets at any given time. Furthermore, the prophetic material in the Hebrew Bible has been chosen for inclusion and edited according to specific ideological criteria. The final editors were no more anxious to preserve sayings of those who did not meet these criteria, those they considered false prophets, than early ecclesiastical writers were to preserve the writings of those they considered heretics. This fairly obvious fact must be borne in mind by anyone using the Bible as a historical source for prophecy or anything else.

One of the most notable and, for some, disturbing tendencies in recent Old Testament scholarship is that of low or late dating of biblical texts. One aspect of this tendency relevant to the present study is the contention that the prophetic books are essentially or even entirely post-exilic compositions.[3] Few critical scholars doubt that, *in their final form,* many of the prophetic books (e.g., Amos, Isaiah, Jeremiah) date from the Persian period or later. Also, no one would underestimate the difficulty of identifying an early nucleus of material in the individual books. But the comparative material available, as exiguous as it is, gives at least initial credence to the existence of similar phenomena, and the production of similar texts, in Israel during the time of the kingdoms, even if the prophetic designation was added at a later time. An instructive parallel might be the passages in verse predicting disaster consequent on social injustice attributed to Solon. These come to us from authors (Demosthenes and Diodorus Siculus) later than the time of Solon (early sixth century B.C.E.). They may well have been edited and expanded, but as far as I know no one doubts Solon's substantial authorship.[4]

Before looking more closely at the biblical sources for Israelite prophecy, a brief note on the formation of the Hebrew-Aramaic Bible may be useful. The first section of the tripartite Hebrew canon, the "five-fifths of the law" or Torah, contains a narrative of founding events from creation to the death of Moses together with a great deal of legal material. According to the traditional view, the Pentateuch was written by Moses and promulgated by Ezra and a learned body known in Jewish tradition as the Great Assembly. This entity was thought to be composed of Ezra himself, Nehemiah, the last three prophets (Haggai, Zechariah, Malachi) and other worthies, one hundred and twenty in all. The second section, Prophets (*Nebi'im*), takes in the historical books Joshua through Kings and the fifteen books ascribed to prophetic authors. These are known, respectively, as Former Prophets and Latter Prophets, a distinction unknown to Judaism of the biblical period. Latter Prophets includes the three lengthy scrolls of Isaiah, Jeremiah, and Ezekiel and a collection of twelve shorter books on a separate scroll of comparable length. The further distinction into Major and Minor is even later, indicates length rather than relative importance, and can be safely ignored. The third section, the Writings (*Ketuvim*), comprises all the remaining books in the Hebrew Bible, and an even greater number in the Old Greek translation known as the Septuagint (LXX).

Recent decades have witnessed a revival of interest in the canon, including the process leading to its final definition, the way it is structured, and the nature of the claims implied in the shaping of the tradition in its final stages of development (Blenkinsopp, Childs, Rendtorff). While there is much that is problematic about recent essays in "canonical criticism," not least the impatience of some of its practitioners with historical-critical approaches to biblical texts, they have helped to show how the process leading to a canonical collection corresponds to a cumulative effort to give shape and significant form to a common tradition. But the process of forming such a tradition also involved reconciling, or simply juxtaposing, quite different and sometimes mutually exclusive interpretations and points of view. Critical attention to the formation of the tradition, therefore, has raised the issue of a plurality of interpretations and the need to resolve or mediate conflicting authority claims in the religious sphere. Given the peremptory and sharply divisive claims advanced by prophets, or by others on their behalf, prophecy was bound to play a decisive role in this ongoing process.

One of the principal stages in the emergence of a Torah canon was the promulgation of a lawbook allegedly found during repair work on the Jerusalem temple during the reign of Josiah (640–609 B.C.E. *passim*) as described in 2 Kings 22. Modern scholarship has concurred in identifying this book with Deuteronomy, though perhaps not exactly as we have it today. Deuteronomy for the first time uses the language of *tôrâ* in the sense of a comprehensive body of law and instruction. It presents itself as an official public document not to be tampered with (Deut. 4:2; 12:32) and represents the first attempt to impose an official state religion, an orthodoxy. About two centuries later the priest-scribe Ezra was sent on an official mission to the province of Judah, now under Iranian rule, by either Artaxerxes I, nicknamed Long Hand, or Artaxerxes II, nicknamed Memory Man, with the task of seeing that "the law of the God of heaven" was enforced among Jews in the Trans-Euphrates satrapy of the Persian empire (Ezra 7). While this law cannot simply be identified with our Pentateuch, it provides one of several indications that the Persian period was decisive for the formation of the legal traditions in their final written form.

Attempts to impose orthodoxies and enforce legislation are not, however, invariably successful. We should therefore not be surprised to find, in the Greco-Roman period, a variety of different approaches to the legal tradition, for example in *Jubilees* and the *Temple Scroll*. It was probably in the same period that the Pentateuch was divided into five books, the division being first explicitly attested in Josephus writing at the end of the first century C.E. ("Five are the books of Moses, comprising the laws and the traditional history from the birth of man down to the death of the lawgiver," *Against Apion* 1:39.)

The phrase "the Law and the Prophets," familiar to readers of the New Testament, first occurs in writings of the second century B.C.E. (Prologue to Sir.; 2 Macc. 15:9), but without the distinction between Former and Latter Prophets, that is, between historical books and prophetic books properly so called. Writing about 180 B.C.E., Jesus ben Sira traced the course of prophecy from Joshua, "the successor of Moses in prophesying" (Sir. 46:1), to Isaiah, Jeremiah, Ezekiel, and the Twelve, again covering both historical and prophetic books without distinction. Thus the historical and prophetic books were always closely associated. The present consensus is that the historical books from Joshua to 2 Kings form a continuous history written according to the ideology of Deuteronomy, therefore known somewhat inelegantly as the Deuteronomistic History (hereafter Dtr). There is broad agreement that this history was composed toward the end of the monarchy and was revised and expanded during the exilic period, around the middle of the sixth century B.C.E.

While it must have enjoyed great authority from the moment of its appearance on account of its connections with the Deuteronomic lawbook, it had to survive the challenge of later essays in historiography, including 1 and 2 Chronicles composed about two centuries later.

The rabbinic text dealing with the order and authorship of biblical books (*b. B. Bat.* 14b-15a) attributes the book of Joshua to Joshua; Judges, Ruth, and Samuel to Samuel; and Kings to Jeremiah. Thus the designation "Former Prophets" was due not to content but to the tradition of prophetic authorship. Josephus (*Against Apion* 1:37) also viewed the writing of sacred history as a prophetic prerogative, which had the advantage of advertising his own career as historian and his own claim to prophetic gifts providentially discovered or activated as he awaited capture and possible execution in the cave of Jotapata.[5] More than four centuries earlier, the author of Chronicles named so many seers and prophets among his sources as to leave little doubt that even then the idea of the prophetic historian was well established. This transformation of the prophet into the historian is only one aspect of a gradual semantic expansion in the use of the term *nābî'*, to the point where practically any significant figure in the historical tradition (e.g., Abraham, Moses) could be described as prophetic (Barton).

Former Prophets (Dtr) traces the history of prophecy from Moses, prophet par excellence, to Joshua, who received a share in his charisma (Num. 27:18–23; Deut. 34:9), thence through a series of prophetic successors referred to as "his (God's) servants the prophets" to the final disaster predicted by these servants as the consequence of neglecting the (Deuteronomic) law. The authors of Deuteronomy had their own theory about prophecy which dictated the role Dtr assigned to prophets throughout the history. In Deut. 18:15–19, the passage about the "prophet like Moses," prophecy is, in effect, redefined as a way of continuing the work of Moses throughout history; it is therefore understood in terms of urging law observance and transmitting the same message to posterity. This redefined prophetic role will be detected in the historian's comment on the conquest of Samaria by the Assyrians (722 B.C.E.):

> Yahweh had warned Israel (and Judah) by means of every prophet and seer: turn from your evil ways and observe the commandments and statutes as found in all of the law which I prescribed for your forebears and which I also sent to you through my servants the prophets. (2 Kings 17:13)

The view is retrospective, and therefore hints that prophecy, or at least this kind of prophecy, is considered to be essentially a thing of the past. That many, including the historian, held such a view in the last decades of Judah's independence is hardly surprising in view of the crisis of confidence in prophecy to which the biblical sources from that time attest (see parts 4 and 5).

An odd feature of Dtr is that it mentions many prophets, and speaks at length about several of them (e.g., Samuel, Elijah, Elisha), yet it has practically nothing to say about the canonical prophets, that is, the prophets to whom books are attributed. Second Kings 18:13–20:19 contains mostly legendary narrative about Isaiah in his dealings with King Hezekiah, which has been copied into the book of Isaiah (chapters 36—39), but this Isaiah is a very different figure from the author of the sayings in Isaiah 1—39. The anomalous Jonah is the only other one of the Latter Prophets mentioned in Dtr. He is assigned a role supportive of Jeroboam II of Israel (2 Kings 14:25) even though Amos, active during the same reign, is passed over in silence.[6] Since it is unlikely that the historian was unfamiliar with the ones unnamed—Amos, Hosea, Micah, and the rest—it seems that the omission was deliberate, perhaps because he considered their message, largely condemnatory as it was, inappropriate for the needs of his contemporaries.

An alternative explanation that has been offered to explain the historian's failure to mention major preexilic prophetic figures is that the nucleus of Latter Prophets was put together by adherents of the Deuteronomistic school as a supplement to the History during the Babylonian exile (Freedman). The Deuteronomists may therefore have thought in terms of a prophetic succession from Moses the protoprophet (Deut. 18:15–18; 34:10) to Jeremiah, last of "his servants the prophets." The call of Moses (Ex. 3:1–4:17) has much in common with that of Jeremiah (Jer. 1:4–19), and the forty years prophetic activity editorially assigned to Jeremiah (Jer. 1:2–3, corresponding to the period 627–587 B.C.E.) points toward the same conclusion. We will be in a better position to evaluate this hypothesis after our study of Jeremiah in part 4.

This brings us to the question of how prophetic books were put together. It is reasonable to conclude that small collections of sayings were assembled during the prophet's lifetime, by the prophet or by disciples, as seems to have been the case in contemporary Assyria. When such sayings came to the attention of the civil or religious authorities they must have been widely reported. Amaziah, priest-in-charge at Bethel, was able to quote a saying of Amos as grounds for extraditing him (Amos 7:11), and at his trial for sedition in 609 B.C.E. Jeremiah was saved from death by the timely citing of an oracle of Micah delivered a century earlier (Jer. 26:17–19; Micah 3:12). A scribe wrote down Jeremiah's sayings in 605 B.C.E., read them in public, and rewrote them from dictation when the first copy was destroyed (Jeremiah 36). In some cases sayings and stories would have circulated in a group of disciples, to be consigned to writing only when memories began to fade. Utterances of professional prophets would presumably have been preserved among the temple and court records. Several of these have survived from the kingdom of Mari in northern Mesopotamia from the eighteenth century B.C.E., but none, unfortunately, at least none recognizable as such, from Israel.

The political disasters of the early sixth century B.C.E. (the fall and destruction of Jerusalem and subsequent deportations) would have provided a powerful stimulus to the preservation of prophetic sayings, and we have seen that the first compilation of prophetic material probably dates from that time. The process of recycling and expanding earlier sayings and composing new ones continued on into the Second Temple period. By the early second century B.C.E. at the latest the three plus twelve division was in place (Sir. 48:20–49:10), and not much later we begin to hear allusions to "the Law and the Prophets" (Prologue to Sir.; 2 Macc. 15:9; cf. Dan. 9:2). The complete Isaiah scroll from Qumran (1QIsa^a), presumed to have been written in the second century B.C.E., shows that the fixing of the text of biblical books was well advanced by that time. From a not-much-later date we have the first independent commentaries on prophetic books, the Qumran *p̆šārîm* on Isaiah, Hosea, Micah, Nahum, and Habbakuk.

The Deuteronomic redefinition of prophecy mentioned earlier raises a broader issue, of central concern to the discipline since the nineteenth century at least, that of the relation between law and prophecy. The traditional Jewish view is stated succinctly in the opening sentence of the Mishnaic treatise *Pirke Avot* (The Sayings of the Fathers):

> Moses received Torah from Sinai and delivered it to Joshua; then Joshua delivered it to the elders, the elders to the prophets, and the prophets delivered it to the men of the Great Assembly.

On this showing, the function of the prophet was to bridge the historical gap between the primordial revelation at Sinai and the rabbinic leadership. The prophets, therefore, had essentially the same function as the sages who followed them, namely, that of custodians and tradents of Torah. Critical scholarship in the nineteenth century subverted this traditional construct by arguing that the bulk of the laws, especially the ritual laws, date from the beginning not of Israel but of Judaism. Summing up the scholarly work of many predecessors, Julius Wellhausen argued in his landmark *Prolegomena to the History of Israel* (1883) that the prophets antedated the law codes and therefore could not have discharged the function assigned to them by the tradition. On the contrary, it was the ethical and spiritual religion of the prophets that made the law codes possible. It was also, according to Wellhausen, precisely the codification of the laws that created a situation fatal to the exercise of prophecy.

While much of the exegetical work of Wellhausen has held up remarkably well, the overall understanding of the religious history of Israel and early Judaism looks very different after the passage of more than a century. Discovery of several collections of laws from the ancient Near East, beginning with the Code of Hammurabi in the winter of 1901–02, has opened up the form-critical study of legal material and obliged us to distinguish more carefully between the age of individual laws and that of the collections to which they belong. Form criticism also has given us a more precise understanding of different types of prophetic sayings and the social situations that generated them. It has shown, for example, that many literary genres used by prophets are rooted in ancient institutions, especially warfare, law, and worship. Specific prophetic indictments often will be found to correspond to legal stipulations, and verdicts of condemnation to curses attached routinely to ancient law codes. All this has obliged us to reconsider common assumptions about the prophet as radical innovator preaching a radically innovative ethic.

The relation between law and prophecy is therefore too complex to be decided solely in terms of which came first. The earliest Israelite compilation, the so-called Covenant Code (Ex. 20:23–23:19), probably dates from about the time of Elijah and Elisha. The Deuteronomic law or program (Deut. 12–26), the first draft of which was composed and perhaps also promulgated toward the end of the Judean monarchy, was clearly influenced by prophetic preaching, especially Hosea and Micah. Most of the compilations of ritual laws were put together in the postexilic period, though some of the practice they reflect is probably quite ancient. And in general, as Max Weber pointed out, we may expect tension to arise between "a stratum of those ritually oriented to a law book" and "prophetic charismatics."[7] Jeremiah's attack on those who claimed to be wise on account of their possession or control of the law, and who at the same time neglected the prophetic word (Jer. 8:8), is one of several indications of conflict between different claims to authority in the religious sphere. It may also suggest that one reason for the redaction and promulgation of law codes was precisely to neutralize the disconcerting and often contradictory claims advanced by prophets. The definition of a certain epoch in the past as normative could be seen as part of the same polemic. The postscript or coda to the Pentateuch (Deut. 34:10–12) establishes a clear line of demarcation at the death of Moses and denies parity between the Mosaic age and that of the prophets that followed. This move notwithstanding, both Rabbinic Judaism and early Christianity accepted

Prophets alongside Law, if with very different emphases. Both faiths, therefore, found themselves caught up in an ongoing mediation between tradition and situation, the claims of the past and those of the present and the future.

2. MODERN CRITICAL STUDY OF PROPHECY

H. M. **Barstad,** "No Prophets? Recent Developments in Biblical Prophetic Research and Ancient Near Eastern Prophecy," *JSOT* 57 (1993): 39–60; M. J. **Buss,** "Prophecy in Ancient Israel," *IDBS* (1976): 694–97; P. R. **Davies** and D.J.A. **Clines,** eds., *Among the Prophets: Language, Image and Structure in the Prophetic Writings,* Sheffield: JSOT Press, 1993; F. E. **Deist,** "The Prophets: Are We Heading for a Paradigm Shift?" in V. Fritz et al., *Prophet und Prophetenbuch: Festschrift für Otto Kaiser zum 65. Geburtstag,* Berlin: W. de Gruyter, 1989, 1–18; O. **Eissfeldt,** in H. H. Rowley, ed., *The Old Testament and Modern Study,* Oxford: Clarendon Press, 1951, 115–61; G. **Fohrer,** "Neuere Literatur zur alttestamentlichen Prophetie," *TR* 19 (1951): 277–346; 20 (1952): 192–271, 295–361; "Zehn Jahre Literatur zur alttestamentlichen Prophetie," *TR* 28 (1961): 1–75, 235–97, 301–74; "Neue Literatur zur alttestamentlichen Prophetie," *TR* 40 (1975): 337–77; 41 (1976): 1–12; J. H. **Hayes,** "The History of the Form-Critical Study of Prophecy," *SBL Seminar Papers* 1 (1973): 60–99; D. A. **Knight,** "Wellhausen and the Intepretation of Israel's Literature," *Semeia* 25 (1982): 21–36; H.-J. **Kraus,** *Geschichte der historisch-kritischen Erforschung des Alten Testaments von der Reformation bis zur Gegenwart,* Neukirchen-Vluyn: Verlag der Buchhandlung des Erziehungsvereins, 1956; W. E. **March,** "Prophecy," in J. H. Hayes, ed., *Old Testament Form Criticism,* San Antonio: Trinity University Press, 1974, 141–77; B. D. **Napier,** "Prophet, Propheticism," *IDB* 3 (1962): 896–919; P.H.A. **Neumann,** *Das Prophetenverständnis in der deutschsprachigen Forschung seit Heinrich Ewald,* Darmstadt: Wissenschaftliche Buchgesellschaft, 1979; M. X. **Ramlot,** "Prophétisme," *SDB* 8 (1972): 811–1222; H. Graf **Reventlow,** *The Authority of the Bible and the Rise of the Modern World,* Philadelphia: Fortress Press, 1985; H. H. **Rowley,** "The Nature of Old Testament Prophecy in the Light of Recent Study," in *The Servant of the Lord and Other Essays,* London: Lutterworth Press, 1952, 89–128; J.F.A. **Sawyer,** "A Change of Emphasis in the Study of the prophets," in R. Coggins et al., eds., *Israel's Prophetic Heritage,* Cambridge: Cambridge University Press, 1982, 233–49; G. M. **Tucker,** "Prophecy and the Prophetic Literature," in D. A. Knight and G. M. Tucker, eds., *The Hebrew Bible and Its Modern Interpreters,* Chico, Calif.: Scholars Press, 1985, 325–68; C. **Westermann,** *Basic Forms of Prophetic Speech,* Philadelphia: Westminster Press, 1967, 13–89; *Prophetic Oracles of Salvation in the Old Testament,* Louisville: Westminster/John Knox Press, 1991 (1987); R. R. **Wilson,** "Form-Critical Investigation of the Prophetic Literature: The Present Situation," *SBL Seminar Papers* 1 (1973): 100–121.

One of the most significant achievements of biblical scholarship in the nineteenth century was the rediscovery of prophecy as a distinctive

religious category. The traditional Christian view, represented at that
time by conservative and apologetic theologians like E. W. Hengstenberg
and J.C.K. Hofmann, saw the prophets as forerunners and foretellers of
Christ. Wellhausen, on the other hand, argued that Christ, who inherited the religion and ethic of the prophets, was betrayed by the institutional church in much the same way as the prophets had been betrayed
by the ritualistic-legalistic system of early Judaism. The critical approach
to biblical prophecy also broke with the traditional Jewish view according to which the prophet was essentially a tradent of law, both written
and oral. Since, according to this view, everything necessary for Israel's
life had been revealed at Sinai, the prophetic message could not contain
anything new. At most, it could spell out what was only implicitly contained in the Sinaitic revelation. In this broader sense, the epoch of
Mosaic-prophetic revelation came to an end with the death of the last
prophet (*b. Sanh.* 11a; *b. Yoma* 9b; *b. Soṭa* 48b) just as, according to a traditional dogmatic topos, the Christian revelation came to an end with
the death of the last apostle.

Modern critical scholarship, which did not derive its mandate from
ecclesiastical authority, studied the prophets independently of such traditional beliefs. Applying literary criticism to the task of identifying the
actual words of the prophets, their "authentic" message as distinct from
the many "secondary" editorial accretions, critical scholarship claimed
to rediscover the true lineaments of the prophet as a unique type of religious individualist with a message addressed to the contemporary world
rather than one concerned with the past or the future. By means of the
critical analysis of the texts, therefore, it seemed possible to get back to
the real, historical figure and his (less commonly her) message; from
which point one arrived at a highly distinctive prophetic religion, at once
spiritual and ethical, which could then be contrasted with the magical
and materialistic propensities of popular and priestly religion centered
on the sacrificial cult. Prophetic religion could therefore be seen as the
high point of Israel's developing religious consciousness, and the post-
prophetic period as a falling away from this high point, a surrender to le-
galism and ritualism. We should add that only in recent years has the neglect or misrepresentation of Second Temple Judaism consequent on
this prejudicial view of development been to some extent overcome.[8]

Critical study in the nineteenth century, therefore, shifted the center
of gravity decisively from the Pentateuch to the Prophets, and this move
undeniably had a strong and, in many respects, positive impact on Christian theology and Christian living. It contributed, for example, to a new
emphasis on the religious interpretation of history, along lines quite different from those of *Heilsgeschichte* (salvation history) as expounded by

J.C.K. Hofmann and others. It also led to an enhanced appreciation for the social responsibility of the churches, for example, in its impact on the social gospel movement, the teaching and writing of the Niebuhrs and Martin Luther King and, most recently, liberation theology. These were real advances, but they were accompanied by severe limitations arising out of the presuppositions that colored much of the work done at that time. So, for example, the portrait of the prophet as "religious genius" generally went with a low esteem for religious institutions and ritual in particular. Deriving in part from Herder and the Romantics, in part from the presuppositions of liberal Protestantism, this one-sided view has since been rendered obsolete by progress in anthropology and the history of religions. Emphasis on the ethical and spiritual aspects of prophetic religion, while justified in principle, was too closely tied to such unexamined assumptions and associated polemic, for example, in the debate about prophetic opposition to the sacrificial cult.

The new critical perspective on prophecy can be conveniently dated to *Die Theologie der Propheten*, published by Bernhard Duhm at the age of twenty-eight in 1875. The full title of this book is significant: *The Theology of the Prophets as Foundation for the Inner Historical Development of Israelite Religion*. Suspicion that the ghost of Hegel is hovering nearby is confirmed by the author's tripartite division of the history into Mosaism, prophetism, and Judaism. Duhm's thesis was that the ethical idealism of the prophets represents the essence of true religion stemming from their direct and intensely personal experience of God. The emphasis, therefore, was on the prophetic commissioning, the visions, and other extraordinary experiences of these chosen intermediaries. In his commentary on Isaiah, published seventeen years later, he went on to demonstrate the method by which these conclusions were reached, and especially the exegetical procedures by which the genuine words of the prophet were sifted out from the bulk of editorial expansions. It was this method, applied with great skill, which makes his work the first genuinely modern commentary on a prophetic book.[9]

Duhm's publications did not, of course, constitute an absolute beginning, if there is such a thing in the history of literature. His idealistic portrait of the prophet had already been sketched out in the work of Heinrich Ewald (1803–1875), a leading biblical scholar of the midcentury with whom both Budde and Wellhausen had studied at Göttingen. In his *Propheten des Alten Bundes* (1840) Ewald described the prophet, in Israel as elsewhere, as proclaiming and interpreting the thoughts of God, the eternal truths destined to prevail in history but which, for the most part, remained dormant in the human consciousness. The prophet of Israel not only proclaimed these truths fearlessly to his contemporaries as an apostle of spiritual renewal but embodied them in his own intense involvement in the political events of his time. Unlike many of his academic colleagues in theological faculties at that time, Ewald practiced what he taught, and did so with such conviction that he was removed from his teaching post at the University of Göttingen for refusing to take the Prussian oath of loyalty and ended up, for a time, in one of Bismarck's prisons.

During much of the nineteenth century the study of prophecy was carried out under the influence of the philosophical currents of the time, especially romanticism (Herder, Eichhorn), idealism (Ewald, Duhm), and rationalism (Kuenen, Cornill). Common to all these approaches was an ignorance of, or indifference to, the broader political and cultural context of the history of Israel and the writings through which it was known. Knowledge of that context, which accumulated rapidly after the decipherment of cuneiform and hieroglyphic scripts around the middle of the century, inevitably called into question reconstructions and periodizations based on idealistic premises. In those early decades, however, attention was focused almost exclusively on how the new discoveries affected the understanding of the biblical account of origins (Genesis 1—11).

The impact of new data on the study of prophecy was not appreciated until 1914 when Gustav Hölscher published an important monograph on Israelite prophecy that attempted to incorporate new data and approaches in a controlled way.[10] As the subtitle *Investigations in the History of the Religion of Israel* indicates, Hölscher set out to apply the methods of the History of Religions school to the study of prophetic phenomena in Israel. He also was deeply impressed by the pioneering study of Wilhelm Wundt on the social psychology of religious phenomena in general and ecstatic phenomena in particular. Hölscher argued that ecstatic propheticism was characteristic not of nomadic societies, such as he supposed Israel to have been before the settlement in the land, but of the agrarian culture of Asia Minor, Syria, and Palestine. It could therefore be assumed that the kind of ecstatic prophecy attested most frequently in the early period of Israelite history and among the central and northern tribes was taken over from Canaanite practice. Examination of the relevant descriptions of these phenomena in the Hebrew Bible, helped out with the account of Wen-Amon's visit to Byblos (to be discussed in the next part) and other accounts in authors of late antiquity (Heliodorus, Lucian, Apuleius) dealing with prophetic phenomena, also suggested the conclusion that ecstatic prophecy generally occurred in connection with cultic acts, especially sacrifice, and in holy places dedicated to the vegetation deities. It was also, for the most part, a communal phenomenon, with bands of ecstatics under a leader similar to the organization of the Dervish *tawaf* (conventicle) of a later time. It happened, however, that from time to time these groups produced an extraordinary figure, someone like Samuel, Elijah, or perhaps one or other of the classical prophets, who detached himself from the group and acted on his own. At any event, orgiastic traits tended to recede with the passing of time, though they never entirely disappeared. Hölscher also argued that the poetry in the prophetic books arose as a spontaneous expression of the prophet's transformed consciousness, rather than a late attempt to capture the moment of inspiration, and it could therefore serve as a reliable criterion for distinguishing genuine prophetic sayings from editorial additions and embellishments.[11]

This somewhat new approach was apparent also in the early work of Hermann Gunkel (1862–1932), who combined the methods of the History of Religions school with a knowledge of and sensitivity to literature exceptional for Old Testament scholars then or since. While Gunkel concentrated primarily on the Genesis narratives and the Psalms, he was able to show that the prophets made use of many literary types, or *Gattungen,* originating in different social and institutional settings, including and especially worship.[12] Unlike many later practitioners of form criticism, however, Gunkel did not fall into the trap of invariably locating the prophet in the setting to which the literary type could be traced. On the contrary, he made a clear distinction between forms of speech and genres used by prophets for literary and rhetorical effect and forms peculiar to prophecy. For Gunkel, the most important of these were the prophetic indictment or commination and the pronouncement of judgment made in the name of God. The latter, which was invariably in the form of a brief oracular saying, was *the* characteristic prophetic speech form, though the former increased in length and importance with the passing of time. Prophetic utterance of this kind proceeded from what Gunkel called the prophet's mysterious experience of oneness with God and identification with his purposes in history.[13] This incommunicable and ultimately inexplicable experience constituted, for Gunkel, the essence of prophecy.

Hölscher and Gunkel moved the study of prophecy away from the Idealist and Romanticist perspective that had dominated most of the critical work done since Herder and Eichhorn in the late eighteenth and early nineteenth centuries. This change in direction did not come about primarily from the discovery of new material, as was the case with the Genesis narratives (especially Genesis 1—11) and the laws, since little apart from the Egyptian narrative of Wen-Amon, featuring an ecstatic oracle-giver, had come to light. The most significant developments were Hölscher's study of ecstasy in relation to cult and Gunkel's form-critical studies of prophecy, especially the prophetic judgment oracle. Gunkel's work was carried further by his student, the Norwegian scholar Sigmund Mowinckel (1884–1966), one of the most prolific and imaginative contributors to Old Testament studies of this century. Mowinckel began by applying Gunkel's conclusions about the original and characteristic forms of prophetic speech (brief oracular sayings in verse) to Jeremiah. In this study he distinguished between the original sayings of the prophet; poetic oracles, most of which are found in Jeremiah 1—25 (source A); stories about the prophet (B); speeches or sermons in the Deuteronomic style scattered throughout the book (C); and the so-called Book of Consolation (chapters 30—31), the last addition to the book.[14] Mowinckel, therefore, continued in the nineteenth-century tradition of source criticism, though now based on a certain understanding of the unique character of prophetic consciousness.

Right from the beginning of his career Mowinckel was never content with a merely mechanical division into sources but addressed himself, in his 1914 study of Jeremiah and in later works,[15] to the dynamic process by which the oral message of the prophet was transmitted, eventually achieving the form in which it now appears in the canon. Emphasis on the oral composition, delivery, and transmission of prophetic sayings was developed to its furthest point by Scandinavian scholars in the 1930s and 1940s. In its most extreme form, represented by the work of the Swedish scholar Ivan Engnell, we find a radical rejection of source criticism and therefore of any attempt to reconstruct, however tentatively, the editorial history of a prophetic book. Some prophetic books (Nahum, Habakkuk, Joel, Second Isaiah) were transmitted in cultic circles, written down right from the beginning, and remained unchanged thereafter. Others (Isaiah 1—39, Amos, Jeremiah) came to be written down only after the text had reached a point of fixity as a result of oral tradition. In either case there was no room for the kind of literary criticism that aimed at sorting out earlier and later compositional levels in a prophetic book.[16] A similar if rather less-rigid rejection of source criticism was expressed by Henrik Nyberg and Harris Birkeland, also from Sweden.[17] They too gave priority to schools of disciples, active over several generations, who preserved, adapted, and amplified the words of the master, but in such a way that it is now impossible to distinguish between "authentic" and "secondary" in the prophetic material that has been allowed to survive.

This strong emphasis on oral tradition and confidence in its staying power did not go unchallenged even then. Another Swedish scholar, Geo Widengren, for example, appealed to early Islamic texts in Arabic to make the point that prophetic texts could have been written shortly after they were orally delivered.[18] More recent comparativist studies in oral tradition have considerably increased the odds against an original utterance being transmitted unchanged over several centuries. As difficult and hypothetical as it no doubt is, the reconstruction of the editorial history of prophetic books remains a task of major importance both historically and theologically. In the course of our study of Israel's prophets we will have many occasions to note both the importance and the difficulty of this task.

Some of the twentieth-century studies in the transmission of prophetic material noted above were beginning to suggest a prominent place for the cult which, for most nineteenth-century Old Testament scholars, was antithetical to prophecy and therefore to "true religion." Taking off from Gunkel's form-critical and comparative method, Mowinckel identified a group of psalms (e.g., Pss. 60; 65; 82; 110) that contain what appear to be prophetic oracles of assurance delivered in the course of a service of worship.[19] This led him to a more thorough examination of the role of ecstatic prophets alongside priests in Israelite worship, and especially in the great New Year festival during which Mowinckel believed that the enthronement of Yahweh as king of Israel was somehow reenacted. Cultic prophecy was a well-established and acknowledged institution during the time of the monarchy, and Mowinckel argued that in the period of the Second Temple it was perpetuated by those Levites whose task was the composition and rendition of liturgical music, described by the Chronicler as a form of prophecy (1 Chronicles 25). While distinguishing in principle between these cultic functionaries and the classical or canonical prophets, Mowinckel was led to conclude that some of the latter (Nahum, Habakkuk, Joel) were probably Temple prophets, while First Isaiah (chapters 1—39) and Micah contained material composed by Jerusalemite cult prophets who were responsible for the transmission of these books.[20]

It was Mowinckel more than anyone else who brought the relation between prophecy and cult to prominence during the 1930s and 1940s. With the unfair advantage of hindsight we can see now that much of the work of that time, including some of Mowinckel's writing, was vitiated by the methodological error of reducing phenomena in different cultures, similar in some respects, to a unitary pattern. There was also a tendency in some quarters to follow uncritically the lead of William Robertson Smith, James Frazer, and others in deriving all myths from rituals. The "myth and ritual school," as it was called, was particularly well represented in Scandinavia and the United Kingdom, and for a time it exercised considerable influence.[21] On prophets and the cult we find a broad spectrum of opinion, from those at one end who maintained that all the canonical prophets were cultic functionaries to those at the other extremity who argued that the prophets were totally opposed to the cult in any shape or form.[22] We see now that neither of these positions was able to give a satisfactory account of the prophetic phenomenon in Israel as a whole. Arguments for close association with the cult could be made fairly convincingly for some of the canonical prophets, specifically Nahum, Habakkuk, Haggai, Zechariah, and Joel, but by no means for all of them. At any rate, it is now clear that positions defended at both ends of the spectrum have not been sustained, and so the discussion continues.

The issue of the relation of the prophet to established institutions could be approached from a different direction, that of form criticism first introduced into Old Testament studies by Gunkel (Hayes, March, Westermann). Gunkel listed several speech forms used by prophets—songs, liturgies, parables, priestly torah—but distinguished these carefully from forms specific and peculiar to prophecy, of which he believed the most ancient to be the oracle against a foreign and hostile land. At this point the error noted earlier enters into play, in that several form-critics of prophetic speech were led to assume that traditional liturgical forms, when used by prophets, could serve as evidence that these prophets held a cultic office.[23] Hans-Eberhard von Waldow, for example, concluded from the salvation oracles in Isaiah 40—55 that the author was a cult prophet, since such sayings feature in liturgies in which cult prophets participated.[24] Or, to take another example, starting out from the annual or septennial public reading of the law at a covenant festival in Israel, Henning Graf Reventlow concluded that prophets like Amos and Jeremiah, who condemned their contemporaries for failure to observe the laws, did so in the official capacity of "law speaker" or covenant mediator in the cult.[25]

Somewhat more nuanced was the position of Ernst Würthwein on the problematic relationship of Amos to the *nᵉbîʾîm*. In dealing with Amos 7:14 ("I am not a prophet nor the son of a prophet"), certainly one of the most discussed verses in the prophetic literature, Würthwein argued that Amos did not deny that he was a *nābîʾ*, that is, a professional cult prophet, but he wished to assert that, even though he held this office, and in spite of holding it, he had been called to deliver a message entirely different from what might be expected from a cult prophet. On this basis Würthwein went on to argue that the authentic nucleus of the book testifies to a decisive change having occurred in the career of Amos. As a cult prophet, he pronounced the curse on Israel's enemies (1:3–2:3) and interceded successfully for his people (7:1–6). Subsequently, however, he was called directly by God to pronounce sentence of death on Israel, and thus he put himself outside the ranks of his former colleagues.[26]

In a later study Würthwein went further and suggested that the typical prophetic judgment saying, pronounced in the divine first person, also originated in the cult. The basis for this conclusion lay in the similarity between the specific form of prophetic indictment (the so-called *rîb* or dispute pattern, as in Hos. 4:1–6 and Micah 6:1–5) and pronouncements of Yahweh as judge in some psalms (e.g., Ps. 50).[27] Würthwein did not comment on how this conclusion would affect the argument in his earlier article about Amos, but it would seem to imply that Amos could have gone through his entire career as a cult prophet.

Whatever their intrinsic merits or demerits, these essays helped to intensify study of the individual units and types of units in prophetic books (e.g., call narratives, vision narratives) and highlight problems in the use of the form-critical method. We note, at the same time, a waning of interest in the issue of the prophets' relationship to worship. More precisely focused studies on the traditions within which individual prophets stood seemed, in any case, to offer a better chance of clarifying, if not solving, this particular issue. One example would be Hans Walter Wolff's location of Hosea within a tradition of northern Levitical preaching and Amos within the sapiential tradition of the kinship network in the Judean wilderness.[28] Closely related to the prophecy-cult issue is that of "false" prophecy: the identity of those so described in the historical and prophetic books, their beliefs and practices, the criteria according to which they are so categorized.[29] How important the issue of criteria is for understanding the historical development of prophecy, and how important it remains for understanding the nature of the claims advanced by the canonical prophets, will become clear in the course of our study.

In addition to contributing to the historical-critical issues mentioned above, Jewish scholars have added a rich dimension from their own exegetical and philosophical tradition. One strand of the latter, represented by Moses Mendelsohn (1729–1786) and Hermann Cohen (1842–1918), emphasized the contribution of the prophets to the purification of religious ideas and the development of ethical monotheism, an approach not essentially different from that of Christian biblical scholars under the influence of the Enlightenment. Yehezkel Kaufmann (1889–1963), perhaps the most important Jewish biblical scholar of the twentieth century, believed that monotheism was present in Israel from the beginning and was therefore a precondition for rather than a product of classical prophecy. According to Kaufmann the prophetic contribution was to draw out the moral implications of religious ideas already in place, and to make them the basis for a kind of theology of history. In keeping with his distinctive existentialist thinking, Martin Buber (1878–1965) emphasized the element of divine-human encounter in the prophets. Buber's "God of the sufferers" is echoed in Abraham Heschel's "sympathy with the divine pathos" as the defining element of prophetic consciousness. Both Buber and Heschel represented a type of Jewish biblical scholarship which, while not hostile to historical-critical inquiry, is led by its commitments to move well beyond it.[30]

Over the last two or three decades biblical scholars in significant numbers, especially but not exclusively in North America, have expressed indifference to the historical-critical method or have even explicitly repudiated it. For several of these scholars the emphasis has shifted from text to reader, from traditional approaches to new options dictated by ideologies and interpretative systems—formalist, structuralist, deconstructionist, feminist, to name the most familiar. For these scholars the primary interest no longer lies with the circumstances of the production of the text—as with form criticism and, incidentally, Marxist literary criticism—but with the text itself as a closed system, severed from its moorings in a particular history and culture. Appreciation for the aesthetic qualities of biblical texts was certainly underrepresented during the period we have been surveying, and to a limited extent this lack has been made good in recent years.[31] It so happens, however, that neither prophetic nor legal texts have proved amenable to treatment according to these newer interpretative options. Contemporary literary criticism by biblical scholars concentrates overwhelmingly on narrative, and it is therefore not surprising that one of the few prophetic books to have merited close attention from the purely literary point of view is Jonah.[32]

Another and related development in recent years is a shift in emphasis from the smallest literary units, the stock-in-trade of form critics, to entire chapters and books, and from hypothetically reconstructed sources to the text in its finished form, as it is now. With respect to prophetic texts, this shift is especially in evidence in studies on the book of Isaiah that attempt to demonstrate a certain unity of structure and intent beyond the traditional division into preexilic, exilic, and postexilic sections (chapters 1—39, 40—55, 56—66, respectively). A theological version of this "holistic" approach, known as canonical criticism, holds that only the final form of a biblical text (e.g., a prophetic book), read within a believing and interpreting community, is the appropriate object of theological reflection (Childs, Rendtorff). This has proved to be in some respects a salutary emphasis, but one can acknowledge the value and even the necessity of interpreting the parts of a text and its internal organization in function of the whole without renouncing the attempt to reconstruct the process by which the final form was reached. If we think the reconstruction of the identity and message of the canonical prophet is a possible and worthwhile enterprise, we cannot rest content with the final form. Far from being mutually incompatible, synchronic and diachronic readings complement each other.

As things stand at the moment, we are still far from a satisfactory overview of prophecy, in the sense of "seeing it steadily and seeing it whole" (Matthew Arnold). We have moved away from the nineteenth-century portrait of the prophet with its often prejudicial implications for other forms of religious life, especially those in which law and ritual play a significant role. We are more aware of the need to relate canonical prophecy to existing institutions in Israel and the culture area of which Israel was part, and progress has been made in identifying the social co-ordinates of prophetic phenomena in Israel. Discussions of what used to be referred to as "the prophetic consciousness" have begun to take account of comparative data from other cultures and the social determinants of ecstatic phenomena. However, we still have trouble grasping what is involved in the passage from the moment of (at least occasionally ecstatic) prophetic-poetic inspiration to the production of the literature, with its clear indications of poetic craft, skillful adaptation of conventional forms of speech, and careful structuring. There is also the connected theological problem of the prophet's mediation and interpretation of traditions and symbols in the light of an intensely personal experience; and this in its turn raises the issue of conflicting claims to authority in the religious sphere and their eventual resolution.

3. LABELS AND ROLES

A. G. **Auld,** "Prophets through the Looking Glass: Between Writings and Moses," *JSOT* 27 (1983): 3–23, 41–44; J. **Blenkinsopp,** *Sage, Priest, Prophet: Religious and Intellectual Leadership in Ancient Israel,* Louisville: Westminster John Knox Press, 1995, 1–5, 123–29; R. P. **Carroll,** "Poets not Prophets: A Response to 'Prophets through the Looking Glass,'" *JSOT* 27 (1983): 25–31; F. H. **Cryer,** *Divination in Ancient Israel and Its Near Eastern Environment: A Socio-Historical Investigation,* Sheffield: JSOT Press, 1994; E. **Fascher,** *Prophetes: Eine sprach- und religionsgeschichtliche Untersuchung,* Giessen: A. Töpelmann, 1927; L. L. **Grabbe,** "Prophets, Priests, Diviners and Sages in Ancient Israel," in H. A. McKay and D.J.A. Clines, eds., *Of Prophets' Visions and the Wisdom of Sages,* Sheffield: JSOT Press, 1993, 54–62; D.L. **Petersen,** *The Roles of Israel's Prophets,* Sheffield: JSOT Press, 1981; B. **Vawter,** "Were the Prophets *nabi's?*" *Bib* 66 (1985): 206–20.

The term *prophecy* has been applied to so many quite different phenomena as to make it difficult, and perhaps also unhelpful, to begin with a definition. We can get some idea of the range of current usage by consulting any of the standard dictionaries. The word can refer to prediction, emotional preaching, social activism, the ability to enlighten and communicate insight, the founding of a new religion (Moses, Jesus, and Muhammad are all regarded as prophets), or the leadership of a cult group. The older meaning of biblical exposition, in use among Puritans of the sixteenth and seventeenth centuries, has survived among evangelicals, though here the stress is generally on millenarian and apocalyptic biblical interpretation. Sociologists of religion also tend to put apocalyptic and sectarian movements under the rubric of prophecy.[33] We shall see that none of these connotations corresponds exactly to the social reality of prophecy in ancient Israel.

Those who believe it possible to decide the issue by appeal to etymology point out that the word in English derives from the Greek *prophētēs*, meaning one who proclaims a message on behalf of another, generally a deity. While this point is useful symbolically, in that it locates prophecy in the order of communication, sign, and language, etymology is not a sure guide to meanings in the language group to which the word belongs, much less in others. In ancient Greece "prophecy" could refer to the giving of oracles either in a state of trance or in a normal rational way. Thus, the devotees of Zeus at the shrine of Dodona in Epirus or of Apollo at Delphi obtained guidance in matters of small or great moment from a member of the temple staff called "the prophet." The function of this prophetic office was to interpret the ecstatic and unintelligible utterances of the priestess of Zeus or the Pythia respectively. As in ancient Israel, "prophecy" also could refer to group ecstasy of the orgiastic kind, generally associated with the cult of Dionysos, as in the *Bacchae* of Aeschylus. There were also prophetic figures who foretold the future, of whom the best known is Cassandra. In philosophical works from Plato to Philo prophecy could, finally, be the object of theoretical inquiry as to its nature and origins, leading directly to early Christian theories of divine inspiration.

Though ecstasy and soothsaying are amply attested for ancient Israel, the Jewish scholars who translated the scriptures into Greek, beginning in the third century B.C.E., used the substantive *prophētēs* and the verb *prophēteuein*, avoiding *mantis* and *manteuomai*, which connote an ecstatic or mantic person and ecstatic behavior respectively. This usage probably reflects the translators' enlightened suspicion of the more uncontrolled aspects of religious behavior as well as their desire to emphasize the more declarative aspects of Israelite prophecy.

Usage in the Old Greek version of the scriptures is interesting and important as indicating an early understanding of biblical prophecy, but it is not an infallible guide to the meaning of the relevant Hebrew terms. Of these by far the most frequent is *nābî'* (plural *nᵉbî'îm*). The derivation of this word is disputed, but the closest cognate seems to be the Akkadian verb *nabū*, to call.[34] If we could conclude from this the meaning "the called one," it would conveniently indicate the importance of the prophetic commissioning, but we have seen that etymologies do not carry over into usage in a straightforward way. The decisive factor is context not etymology.

Hebrew verbal forms deriving from the noun occur in two conjugations, the *niphal* (roughly, the passive) and the *hithpael* (roughly, the reflexive), and it is sometimes argued, or simply asserted, that the former (*nibbā'*) refers to prophetic speech and the latter (*hitnabbē'*) to ecstatic or orgiastic behavior. The hithpael is indeed used of wild and uncontrolled behavior even where there is no question of anything prophetic. Saul, for example, is described as "prophesying" when, deranged by jealousy, he tried to pin David to the wall with his spear (1 Sam. 18:10–11). Even much later the ecstatic prophet (*mitnabbē'*) could be paired with the madman (*mᵉšuggā'*)who speaks and acts in an uncontrolled manner (Jer. 29: 24–28). But the niphal also is used of communal orgiastic ecstasy (1 Sam. 10:11; 19:20; 1 Kings 22:12), while the hithpael can refer to rational prophetic speech (1 Kings 22:8; Ezek. 37:10). There is therefore no hard and fast distinction between the two forms, though *nibbā'* came to be the standard word for prophetic utterance, just as speaking came to be considered the normal expression of what it meant to be a prophet.[35]

The term *nābî'* came to have a very inclusive range of meaning, serving as a catchall designation for all kinds of religious types. This semantic expansion greatly complicates the task of discovering the actual social role filled by such figures as Amos, Isaiah, and Jeremiah. The designation is also only one of a number of labels for religious specialists several of whose functions overlap. When Saul went searching for his straying donkeys, his servant suggested consulting—for a fee—a certain "man of God" in a nearby town (1 Sam. 9:5–8). This designation (Hebrew: *'îš 'ᵉlohîm*) underwent a process of decontextualization not unlike *nābî'*, being used eventually to characterize both Moses (Deut. 33:1) and David (2 Chron. 8:14). Originally, however, it described persons perceived to dispose of preternatural and dangerous power, like Elijah (1 Kings 17:18) and Elisha (2 Kings 4:1–37). Though religious specializations of this class were not confined to males, we do not hear of a "woman of God" (the Hebrew would be *'ēšet 'ᵉlohîm*), perhaps due to the social conditions, including itineracy, in which these individuals operated.

As we read on in the story of the missing donkeys, we learn that the "man of God" can also be described as a seer (Hebrew *rō'eh*), namely one who, like the early Arabic *kāhin*, has the gift of second sight or extrasensory perception. At this point in the story (1 Sam. 9:9) an editor has inserted a note (it should be after 9:11) to the effect that the term *rō'eh* was later displaced by *nābî'* and fell out of usage. Closely related to, and often indistinguishable from the *rō'eh* is the visionary (Hebrew *hōzeh*). This last proved more durable, remaining in use, especially in Jerusalemite circles, to the end of the Persian or the beginning of the Hellenistic period (fourth-third century B.C.E.). It too could be used interchangeably with *nābî'*, as may be seen in the account of the confrontation between Amos and Amaziah, priest of the Bethel sanctuary. We observe that Amaziah addresses Amos as *hōzeh*, and Amos responds by denying that he is a *nābî'* (Amos 7:12–15).

Narrative, legal, and prophetic texts leave us in no doubt that Israelites were familiar with an even wider range of religious or shamanistic specialists of the same order as the prophet, visionary, seer, and man of God. Deuteronomy 18:9–14 provides a list of such specialists, including diviners, soothsayers, sorcerers, mediums, wizards, and necromancers. These are all presented as the practitioners of foreign abominations in contrast to the native *nābî'*, but there can be no doubt that all of them were, and continued to be, part of the culture of both the common people and the elite. The Deuteronomic redefinition of prophecy and its function, to which we shall return at a later point, marks the first stage toward the standardization of terminology mentioned earlier. It follows, then, that occurrence of the term *nābî'* will not serve as a reliable guide to the social functions and roles of those to whom it is attached. These can be recovered, if at all, only by careful attention to the literary contexts in which language about prophecy occurs.

These contexts are of different kinds and their interpretation calls for careful attention to the literary character and genre of the passage in question. There are prophetic legends[36] in the historical books (1 Kings 17 to 2 Kings 13) and occasionally in the prophetic books themselves (Isaiah 36—39; Jonah). Much too can be learned from a form-critical study of prophetic sayings in oratio recta. Messages of Yahweh delivered through a prophet, like those of the Delphic Apollo communicated through the Pythia, are couched in the first person. The standard introductory formula "thus says Yahweh" is taken from the protocol used in official oral and written communications emanating from a royal court, which suggests that the prophets understood themselves as emissaries of Yahweh. The royal messenger was an important official, often a member of the court, whose task was to relay a message or command from the ruler verbatim, though he might add some words of an exhortatory, comminatory, or explanatory nature of his own.[37] This provides a simple but important clue to the way in which prophets conceived of their task, since several of them claimed to have access to the presence of Yahweh as divine ruler and to have been sent out on a mission by Yahweh. The claim was often accompanied by a denial of the same privilege to others whom they considered to be false prophets (1 Kings 22:19–23; Isa. 6; Jer. 23:18). The conviction of acting under such a mandate is essential for understanding how prophets thought theologically of their authority and right to a hearing. Since the claim was obviously unverifiable, it also will explain why they were usually accorded a less-than-enthusiastic reception.

4. THE SOCIAL LOCATION OF THE PROPHET

P. L. **Berger**, "Charisma and Religious Innovation: The Social Location of Israelite Prophecy," *American Sociological Review* 28 (1963): 940–50; K. **Burridge**, *New Heaven, New Earth*, Oxford: Blackwell, 1969; R. P. **Carroll**, *When Prophecy Failed: Cognitive Dissonance in the Prophetic Traditions of the Old Testament*, New York: Seabury Press, 1979; "Prophecy and Society," in R. E. Clements, ed., *The World of Ancient Israel*, Cambridge: Cambridge University Press, 1989, 203–25; M. **Eliade**, *Shamanism: Archaic Techniques of Ecstasy*, Princeton: Princeton University Press, 1964; D. **Emmett**, "Prophets and Their Societies," *Journal of the Royal Anthropological Institute* 86 (1956): 13–23; L. **Festinger** et al., *When Prophecy Fails*, New York: Harper & Row, 1964; C. **Geertz**, "Religion as a Cultural System," in M. Banton, ed., *Anthropological Approaches to the Study of Religion*, London: Tavistock Publications, 1966, 1–46; J. A. **Holstein**, "Max Weber and Biblical Scholarship," *HUCA* 46 (1975): 159–79; A. **Jepsen**, *NABI: Soziologische Studien zur alttestamentlichen Literatur und Religionsgeschichte*, Munich: C. H. Beck, 1934; K. **Koch**, "Zur Entstehung der sozialen Kritik bei den Propheten," in H. W. Wolff, ed., *Probleme biblischer Theologie*, Munich: Kaiser Verlag, 1971, 236–57; J. S. **Kselman**, "The Social World of the Israelite Prophets: A Review Article," *Religious Studies Review* 11 (1985): 120–29; I. M. **Lewis**, *Ecstatic Religion*, London and New York: Routledge, 1989[2]; B. O. **Long**, "Prophetic Authority as Social Reality," in G. W. Coats and B. O. Long, eds., *Canon and Authority*, Philadelphia: Fortress Press, 1977, 3–20; A.D.H. **Mayes**, "Prophecy and Society in Israel," in H. A. McKay and D.J.A. Clines, eds., *Of Prophets' Visions and the Wisdom of Sages*, 25–42; S. A. **Meier**, *The Messenger in the Ancient Semitic World*, Atlanta: Scholars Press, 1989; P. **Michaelsen**, "Ecstasy and Possession in Ancient Israel: A Review of Some Recent Contributions," *SJOT* 2 (1989): 28–54; T. W. **Overholt**, "Commanding the Prophets: Amos and the Problem of Prophetic Authority," *CBQ* 41 (1979): 517–32; *Channels of Prophecy: The Social Dynamics of Prophetic Activity*, Minneapolis: Fortress Press, 1989; "Prophecy in History: The Social Reality of Intermediation," *JSOT* 48 (1990): 3–29; S. B.

Parker, "Possession Trance and Prophecy in Pre-exilic Israel," *VT* 28 (1978) 271–85; T. **Parsons,** *Societies: Evolutionary and Comparative Perspectives,* Englewood Cliffs: Prentice-Hall, 1966; J. F. **Ross,** "The Prophet as Yahweh's Messenger," in B. W. Anderson and W. Harrelson, eds., *Israel's Prophetic Heritage,* New York: Harper & Row, 1962, 98–107; C. **Schäfer-Lichtenberg,** "'Josua' und 'Elischa'— ein biblische Argumentation zur Begründung der Autorität und Legitimität des Nachfolgers," *ZAW* 101 (1989): 198–222; S. L. **Thrupp,** *Millenarian Dreams in Action,* New York: Schocken Books, 1970; G. **van der Leeuw,** *Religion in Essence and Manifestation,* Gloucester, Mass.: Peter Smith, 1967, 1:191–241; J. **Wach,** *Sociology of Religion,* Chicago: University of Chicago Press, 1944, 331–74; M. **Weber,** *Ancient Judaism,* New York: The Free Press, 1952 [1917–1919]; *The Sociology of Religion,* Boston: Beacon Press, 1963 [1922]; *The Theory of Social and Economic Organization,* New York: The Free Press, 1964 [1913], 324–92; J. **Williams,** "The Social Location of Israelite Prophecy," *JAAR* 37 (1969): 153–65; R. R. **Wilson,** "Prophecy and Ecstasy: A Reexamination," *JBL* 98 (1979) 321–37; *Prophecy and Society,* Philadelphia: Fortress Press, 1980; P. **Worsley,** *The Trumpet Shall Sound,* New York: Schocken Books, 1968[2].

Discussion on prophetic identity until fairly recently has been carried on without reference to the social location of the prophet and the social determinants of prophetic states of consciousness and behavior. During most of the period surveyed in the previous section the main emphasis was on prophetic self-awareness and God-awareness; the terms of the discussions were therefore those of theology and psychology rather than sociology. The issue of social location nevertheless forced itself on the attention of scholars through form-critical study of prophetic material, an essential aspect of which was and is the relation of literary types to their social matrices. But the *Sitz im Leben* (social life situation) of a literary form occurring in a prophetic book is not an infallible guide to the social situation of the prophet who is using it. The protracted debate about the relation of the prophet to the cult came closest to raising the issue of social status and role in an explicit way. It did not, however, eventuate in a consensus, and was in any case conducted without benefit of sound sociological theory.

In recent years some interesting attempts have been made to apply role theory, reference group theory, the sociology of knowledge, and the results of fieldwork in millenarian and ecstatic cult groups to the study of Israelite prophecy and apocalyptic. It goes without saying that the presence and activity of contemporary cult groups (Jonestown, Waco) gives this line of inquiry a special immediacy and poignancy. To date, the effect of these "social world" studies has been not to solve longstanding points of dispute but to send us back to the texts with new questions or old questions formulated in a new way. For example: To what extent was

the self-awareness and behavior of the prophet determined by the expectations of the society in which the prophet functioned? What were
these expectations, and to what extent did the prophet fulfill them and
thus fill a socially supportive and corroborative role? What resources did
the society dispose of to discourage role deviance on the part of the
prophet? What was the prophet's support group? Who, if anyone, listened to the prophet and how would the audience have understood and
reacted to what he or she was saying to them?

Along a different line of inquiry we might ask: How did one become
a prophet? From what social classes were prophets recruited? Since Israelite prophecy was not gender-exclusive, what difference did the social
variable of gender make to role performance? How was the prophet
called or commissioned, and how was the prophetic status legitimated?
In addition, there is the long-debated issue of the prophet's standing vis-
à-vis those institutions that were officially understood to mediate well-
being and salvation—the monarchy, priesthood, and the complex of cultic acts carried out in the temple.

The likelihood of arriving at satisfactory answers is obviously restricted
by the nature of the sources at our disposal, none of which was designed
to impart the kind of information we are seeking. We have some stories
about prophets (prophetic legends) of very uneven value as source material. The prophetic books themselves contain some biographical and
autobiographical passages, but they consist, for the most part, of sayings
attributed to named prophets. Both kinds of material have undergone
extensive editing over a period of several centuries, with the result that
we cannot be optimistic about the chances of reconstructing the social
world in which a prophet like Amos acted and spoke. But this is what we
have, and we have to make the best of it.[38]

Since social issues will be raised at all major junctures in our survey,
we need offer only one or two illustrations and examples at this point. In
the early centuries, and to a more limited extent in the later period,
prophecy was closely connected with warfare and cult. Bands of dervish-
like ecstatics settled in close proximity to sanctuaries (e.g., Gilgal,
Bethel) under the leadership of a master-prophet or sheik. There were
also peripatetic figures like the anonymous man of God from Judah (1
Kings 13), Elijah, and Elisha. Some of these retained their links with the
prophetic communes and may have originated in them. Of their social
standing and station in life prior to embarking on a prophetic career we
know practically nothing. Some may have been recruited from the ranks
of males (perhaps especially younger sons) set adrift when the house-
holds to which they belonged fell apart as a result of economic or military pressures. Others, like Samuel, appear to have been dedicated to a

sanctuary at an early age in the manner of the monastic oblates of the Middle Ages. Since the members of these prophetic coenobia or communes were apparently not celibate (2 Kings 4:1 speaks of the wife of one of the "sons of the prophets"), some may also have belonged to them from birth. Of Elijah's origins we know only his family name and place of origin (1 Kings 17:1). Elisha seems to have worked the land prior to his call (1 Kings 19:19). All the indications are that they were low on the economic and social scale and, in the eyes of some of their contemporaries, eccentric to the point of insanity.

The problem of data is equally severe with the canonical prophets. The case of Amos is instructive because the information provided by the book (he is not mentioned elsewhere) is open to more than one interpretation. The title, probably added centuries after the time of Amos, describes him as being among the shepherds from Tekoa (Amos 1:1), and in the one brief biographical passage in the book he speaks of himself as a herdsman and dresser of sycamore figs (7:14). The Hebrew term translated as "shepherd" or "sheep rearer" (*nōqēd*) occurs only one other time in the Hebrew Bible, where it refers to a king of Moab (2 Kings 3:4). This would seem to rule out the idea of a visionary rustic or yokel, an idea that goes back to patristic exegesis. The occurrence of the same term in a Late Bronze Age Ugaritic text in association with priests (*rb khnm rb nqdm*) has also suggested the possibility of a cultic position, namely, keeper of herds destined for sacrifice in the temple. But since it is difficult to imagine how dressing sycamore figs could be a cultic activity, the cultic interpretation may be a false lead.[39] Amos also presents himself as a *bōqēr* (7:14), which suggests care for cattle (Hebrew *bāqār*), but he then goes on to say that Yahweh took him from following the sheep to make him a prophet. And if we succeed in putting all of this together, we still have to factor in the extensive knowledge of international affairs and religious traditions, and the sophisticated use of literary forms attested in the book, none of which we normally associate with sheep rearers, shepherds, cowherds, or sycamore prickers.

Little as we know about Amos, we know even less about most of the others in the collection apart from the occasional allusion to father or place of residence. We noted earlier that Micah's place of origin, Moresheth, may help to explain his attitude toward the Jerusalem elite. The situation is different again with Isaiah and Jeremiah. Information on Isaiah that can be deduced from the collections of sayings exists in uneasy tension with the biographical stories incorporated into the book (Isaiah 36—39). In these *legenda* he appears as a holy man not unlike Elijah who prays, intercedes, works miracles, and predicts the future. About his life prior to his call we know nothing, which has not prevented scholars from creating their own biographical elaborations. Jeremiah is the best known, and he was clearly the object of considerable biographical attention. Since he was raised in a Benjaminite priestly family claiming descent from the Shiloh priesthood, some commentators have concluded that he was more at home in the traditions of the Central Highlands than with those of Jerusalem. But we have no reliable information on his life prior to his embarking on a prophetic career, and the same is true of his younger contemporary Ezekiel, also a priest or a member of a priestly family (Ezek. 1:1–3).

It begins to look as if little importance was attached to the prophet's life, activity, and social status prior to the commissioning, which severely limits our ability to answer some of the questions we posed earlier. Examination of the call narratives shows that a common understanding of what was involved in being a prophet emerged at a fairly early date. Study of these passages is therefore of great importance for understanding the central issue of prophetic identity. The characteristic message formula ("thus says Yahweh") also indicates that the prophet typically saw himself or herself as intermediary between the people and their God. This usage presupposes the mythic scenario of the divine court in session presided over by Yahweh as ruler, to whose presence the designated messenger is admitted, and from which the messenger sets out to discharge a specific mission. The claim implicit in this mythic-theological *topos* was a large one indeed, and it was inevitable that it would lead to conflict with established authorities and jurisdictions in the political and religious sphere.

Few attempts at reconstructing the social context of Israelite prophecy have been as influential as that of Max Weber (1864–1920) whose earliest writing on the subject goes back to the second decade of the present century. In dealing with the earliest period of Israelite history, he stressed the importance of warrior ecstasy, reminiscent of the war-intoxicated berserks of early German history, devotion to the warrior god of the tribal federation, and the close ties between prophet, Nazirite, and Rechabite.[40] He argued that the passage from tribal federation to monarchy, and from the tribal war levy to a professional army partly composed of mercenaries, led to the demilitarization of this primitive type of orgiastic prophecy, though the hallowed language of the holy war continued in use in later oracles against foreign nations (e.g., Amos 1—2) and the prophetic struggle against the monarchy. According to Weber the prophets of this epoch, who were drawn from different social classes, were thrust into the role of demagogues and pamphleteers. The kind of public activity in which they engaged, unthinkable in the great empires of Mesopotamia and Egypt, testifies to the persistence of the archaic ideal of the tribal federation. It was on the basis of this traditional ethos that the canonical prophets passed judgment on their contemporaries and elaborated their ethical teaching.

In his more theoretical studies Weber located prophecy in the context of charismatic authority and defined the prophet as "a purely individual bearer of charisma".[41] This was taken to imply that the prophetic-charismatic figure is legitimated not by virtue of a socially acknowledged office like the priesthood, but solely through extraordinary personal qualities. The prophet is therefore neither designated by a predecessor, nor ordained, nor installed in office, but *called*. The claims staked by the prophet, or on the prophet's behalf by others, would tend inevitably to set him (less commonly her) in opposition to dominant elites dedicated to preserving the status quo. This kind of prophecy would therefore, according to Weber, play a destabilizing rather than a corroborative role in society.

Since Weber's analysis seemed to confirm the "religious genius" view of the prophet, and may in fact have been influenced by it, since he read the specialist literature, it should be noted that several critics have not been happy with what they regard as an excessive emphasis on exceptional individuals in Weber's work. Some also have complained that for Weber charisma is essentially a marginal phenomenon.[42] While there is some justification for these criticisms, it must be said that Weber stressed the importance of charismatic succession (admirably illustrated by the account of Elisha succeeding Elijah in the position of master-prophet, 2 Kings 2:9–15) and allowed for the embodiment or routinization of charisma in institutions, while emphasizing the instability and impermanence of charismatic authority. This part of his work, therefore, continues to provide an excellent theoretical context for understanding the nature and operation of prophetic authority and the conflicts in the political and religious spheres that it precipitated.

Weber's definition of the prophet in terms of charisma enabled him to distinguish this category of religious specialist from others, for example, priest, soothsayer, legislator, ethical teacher, philosopher, mystic. The further distinction that he introduced between exemplary and ethical-emissary prophecy, the former characteristic of India, the latter of the ancient Near East including Israel, is also useful as a rough guide, though both types are attested in the biblical sources.

In recent years studies have appeared in which some forms of Israelite prophecy are compared with types of mediation by religious specialists in contemporary traditional societies. Interesting issues have emerged from these studies, for example: the nature and extent of the social support required for activity of this kind; the circumstances and situations that favor the emergence of "prophetic" phenomena, especially social stress, political and military crisis, *anomie;* the role of society, or of a segment of society, in the process by which an individual assumes the position of intermediary. This is all to the good, but we must add that comparisons of this kind tend to ignore the fundamental differences between the societies in which the prophetic phenomena emerge. A prophet like Amos looks very different from (for example) the Nuer prophet Ngundeng Bong or the Indian Seneca prophet Handsome Lake because ancient Israel was fundamentally different from southern Sudan and Seneca land in New York State in the early nineteenth century.[43]

One respect in which progress has been made in "social world" studies of Israelite prophecy is that of the social determinants of what used to be called "the prophetic consciousness." The debate on the place of ecstatic states of consciousness and ecstatic behavior was, of course, well under way long before the results of anthropological fieldwork became available for comparative purposes. It had become something of an axiom in Old Testament scholarship that ecstatic behavior was characteristic of "primitive" but not "classical" prophecy; and the fact that these "classical" prophets—with the sole exception of Ezekiel—make little use of the language of spirit and spirit activity was cited in support of this proposition. Like all axioms, this one needed to be challenged; and the question still must be asked whether the states of consciousness and kinds of behavior described, for want of a better term, as ecstatic are of the essence of prophecy or are characteristic of only one type or one phase of development.

Though imprecise and unsatisfactory, the term itself seems to be unavoidable. Anthropologists tend to regard it as a variation of the physiological and behavioral condition known as trance. The term "ecstasy" is not used to describe the means by which an individual obtains, or is believed to obtain, communications from the divine world or the world of the spirits or the dead. For this process terms such as possession, or soul loss, or others current in the societies in which the phenomena are attested, are deemed more appropriate. The distinction is not merely formal, since it alerts us to the possibility that a prophet may experience spirit possession and receive communications from that other world without manifesting physiological and behavioral change. Yet there is always the expectation, in Israel as elsewhere, that such extraordinary behavior *may* indicate possession, and therefore justify the claim to speak out and be heard. The important issue then is whether the society, or some segment of it, accepts this interpretation of the phenomena, since it is clear that the prophet, shaman, or other mediumistic specialist cannot function without some degree of social support.

The condition of ecstasy or trance can assume many different forms depending on cultural and personal-psychological variables. It can manifest itself in violent and orgiastic or lethargic and catatonic states, both of which are well-attested in the biblical record. It can affect groups as well as individuals (e.g., the ecstatic coenobia called "sons of the prophets") and can be highly contagious, as Saul and his henchmen found to their cost (1 Sam. 19:18–24). It can happen spontaneously or be induced by a wide range of techniques—music, percussion, self-laceration, psychotropic chemicals, auto-suggestion, to name some of the better known among them. While some of its manifestations fall within the purview of clinical pathology—for example, aphasia, catatonia—it is less important for our purpose to investigate "prophetic psychology" than it is to grasp how such conditions were interpreted in the social contexts in which they occurred.

On this last point, work done to date permits us to hazard some generalizations that we can test as our survey gets under way. The first is that ecstatic phenomena are often attested among socially peripheral, dispossessed, or deprived groups that come together to take part in ecstatic practices, including speaking in tongues, as a kind of ritualized rebellion against the power structures of the society of which they are part. We have many examples of female cult gatherings in male-dominant (usually patrilineal) societies, for example, in sub-Saharan Africa and southern Italy, which engage in group ecstasy including glossolalia. These exercises function to provide mutual support, enhance the self-esteem and sometimes the status of the group, and give it a degree of visibility in the eyes of the ruling elite.

There also seems to be a correlation between the incidence of group ecstatic phenomena and situations of social, political, and military stress. A typical case would be invasion and occupation by a foreign power. It is therefore no surprise that so much prophetic activity of this kind is attested in Israel during the life-and-death struggle with the Philistines in the eleventh and tenth centuries, the intermittent warfare with the Syrians in the ninth, and during the more critical periods of Assyrian and Babylonian hegemony from the eighth to the sixth century.

Ecstasy, therefore, is characteristic of peripheral groups, serving to promote their interests and status in the society to which they belong. It can also serve to legitimate leadership in such groups. We see how Elisha had to validate his position as successor to Elijah vis-à-vis "the sons of the prophets" by deeds of power similar to those of his master. His first act, therefore, was to divide the waters of the Jordan with the help of Elijah's mantle (2 Kings 2:13–14, cf. v. 9). Less frequently, extraordinary behavior of this order, whether real or simulated, can serve to reinforce the authority of centrally located political and religious leaders, generally bolstered by propaganda and public relations activity. But historical experience attests that leadership, in the religious no less than in the political sphere, once firmly established, discourages ecstatic phenomena as a potential source of social disruption and heterodoxy. As I. M. Lewis puts it:

> The more strongly based and entrenched religious authority becomes, the more hostile it is towards haphazard inspiration. New faiths may announce their advent with a flourish of ecstatic revelations, but once they become securely established they have little time or tolerance for enthusiasm. For the religious enthusiast, with his direct claim to divine knowledge, is always a threat to the established order.[44]

We will probably agree that this tendency has been amply illustrated in the history of Christianity and, to a lesser extent, that of Judaism.

The close affinity between ecstatic phenomena and millenarian beliefs has moved some biblical scholars in recent years to examine the results of fieldwork in these areas—for example, Melanesian cargo cults and the so-called ghost dance of the Plains Indians—in the belief that they may have some bearing on our understanding of Israelite prophecy.[45] Interest has also been shown in the long and fascinating sequence of millenarian movements throughout Jewish and Christian history.[46] As for the first, we cannot overlook the profound difference between traditional societies that have survived into modern times and Iron Age Israel. As for the second, apocalyptic movements throughout Christian history (e.g., Anabaptists, Millerites) and the history of Judaism (e.g., Sabbatianism) are themselves indebted directly or indirectly to *biblical* prophecy and apocalyptic. In general, it has been easier to find valid points of comparison with the apocalyptic sects of the Second Temple period than with preexilic prophecy. For in these sects that arose in early Judaism, as in those of a much later time, we see a redefining and restructuring of the redemptive process by groups deprived of power in the wider society, whether state, church, or synagogue. And more often than not, such groups end up as victims of the coercive power of either state or church or both.

Mention must also be made of attempts to work out the implications of unfulfilled prophecy with reference to the theory of cognitive dissonance, a term introduced into social psychology more than thirty years ago (Festinger, Carroll). Cognitive dissonance deals with the stratagems by means of which a collectivity or an individual attempts to reduce the inconsistency created by the disconfirmation of well-established beliefs and convictions. Its application to unfulfilled prediction is obvious, and is well illustrated in the final verses of the book of Daniel, as also in certain New Testament passages designed to explain the delay in the second coming. Predictive prophecy, especially of the short-term kind, is a notoriously risky business because it is subject to falsification (cf. Deut. 18:21–22, which states the criterion of falsification as a means of distinguishing between the false and the true prophet). It has been observed that the effect of disconfirmation is not, as we might imagine, the collapse of the belief system that gave rise to the prediction, at least not immediately, but rather explanations, rationalizations, reinterpretations of nonfulfillment, sometimes very ingenious, rescheduling of the predicted event (e.g., the end of the world), and a more intense campaign to persuade oneself, or the group, and possibly others, of the truth of the original prediction.

Cognitive dissonance would also seem to apply more aptly to Jewish and early Christian apocalyptic than to prophecy in general. In spite of the Deuteronomic falsification criterion, it seems that an unfulfilled prediction, of the kind that a prophet might occasionally make (e.g., Amos 7:11; Micah 3:12; 2 Kings 22:18–20) did not necessarily result in the loss of prophetic credentials or lead to the rationalizations and other consequences required by the theory.

A final point is that the ethical teaching of the prophets must, whenever possible, be explained with reference to the social contexts in which the message was uttered. We will, at any rate, work on the basis of this assumption in the following chapters.

II

FROM THE BEGINNINGS
TO AMOS

5. PROPHECY IN THE NEAR EAST
AND THE PROBLEM OF ORIGINS

K. **Baltzer,** *Die Biographie der Propheten,* Neukirchen-Vluyn: Neukirchener Verlag, 1975; H. **Donner,** "Balaam Pseudopropheta," in H. Donner et al., eds., *Beiträge zur alttestamentliche Theologie,* Göttingen: Vandenhoeck & Ruprecht, 1977, 112–23; G. **Dossin,** "Sur le prophétisme à Mari," in *La Divination en Mésopotamie ancienne et dans les régions voisines,* Paris: Presses universitaires de France, 1966, 77–86; F. **Ellermeier,** *Prophetie in Mari und Israel,* Herzberg: Erwin Jungfer, 1977[2]; R. P. **Gordon,** "From Mari to Moses: Prophecy at Mari and in Ancient Israel," in H. A. McKay and D.J.A. Clines, eds., *Of Prophets' Visions and the Wisdom of Sages,* Sheffield: JSOT Press, 1993, 63–79; J. C. **Greenfield,** "The Zakir Inscription and the Danklied," *Proceedings of the Fifth World Congress of Jewish Studies,* Jerusalem: World Union of Jewish Studies, 1969, 1:175–76; A. **Guillaume,** *Prophecy and Divination among the Hebrews and Other Semites,* London: Hodder & Stoughton, 1938; J. A. **Hackett,** *The Balaam Text from Deir 'Alla,* Chico, Calif.: Scholars Press, 1984; A. **Haldar,** *Associations of Cult Prophets among the Ancient Semites,* Uppsala: Almqvist & Wiksell, 1945; J. H. **Hayes,** "Prophetism at Mari and Old Testament Parallels," *Trinity University Studies in Religion* 9, San Antonio: Trinity University Press, 1971, 31–41; S. **Herrmann,** "Prophetie in Israel und Ägypten: Recht und Grenze eines Vergleichs," *SVT* 9 (1963): 47–65; H. B. **Huffmon,** "The Origins of Prophecy," in F. M. Cross et al., eds., *Magnalia Dei,* Garden City: Doubleday, 1976, 173–86; "Prophecy (ANE)," *ABD* 5:477–82; M. **de Jong Ellis,** "Observations on Mesopotamian Oracles and Prophetic Texts: Literary and Historiographic Considerations," *JCS* 41 (1989): 127–86; J. **Lindblom,** "Zur Frage des kanaanäischen Ursprungs des altisraelitischen Prophetismus," in J. Hempel and L. Rost, eds., *Von Ugarit nach Qumran,* Berlin: Töpelmann, 1961, 89–104; *Prophecy in Ancient Israel,* Oxford: Blackwell, 1962, 29–46; A. **Malamat,** "Prophetic Revelations in New Documents from Mari and the Bible," *SVT* 15 (1966): 207–27; "Mari," *BA* 34 (1971): 2–22; *Mari and the Early Israelite Experience,* Oxford: Oxford University Press, 1989; "New Light from Mari (ARM 26) on Biblical Prophecy," in D. Garrone and F. Israel, eds., *Storia e Tradizione di Israele: Scritti in Onore di J. Alberto Soggin,* Brescia: Paideia, 1991, 186–90; W. L. **Moran,** "New Evidence from Mari on the History of Prophecy," *Bib* 50 (1969) 15–56; S. B. **Parker,** "Official Attitudes towards Prophecy at Mari and in Israel," *VT* 43 (1993): 50–68; J. R. **Porter,** "The Origins of Prophecy in Israel," in R. Coggins et al., eds., *Israel's Prophetic Tradition,* 12–31; H. **Ringgren,** "Prophecy in the Ancient Near East," in R. Coggins et al., eds., *Israel's Prophetic Tradition,* 1–11; J. F. **Ross,** "Prophecy in Hamath, Israel, and Mari," *HTR* 63 (1970): 1–28; N. **Shupak,** "Egyptian 'Prophetic' Writings and Biblical Wisdom Literature," *BN* 54 (1990): 81–102; I. **Starr,** *Queries to the Sun God: Divination and Politics in Sargonid Assyria,* Helsinki: Helsinki University Press, 1990; M. **Weippert,** "Assyrische Prophetien der Zeit Asarhaddons und Assurbanipals," in F. M. Fales, ed., *Assyrian Royal Inscriptions: New Horizons,* Rome: Biblical Institute Press, 1981, 71–113; R. R. **Wilson,** "Early Israelite Prophecy," *Int* 32 (1978): 3–16.

The Hebrew Bible itself attests that prophecy was not confined to Israel. In the early years of the reign of Zedekiah, last king of independent Judah, Jeremiah is reported to have urged rulers from the neighboring lands of Edom, Moab, Ammon, and the Phoenician cities, meeting in Jerusalem, not to heed their prophets, diviners, and other intermediaries who were backing the planned rebellion against Nebuchadrezzar (Jer. 27:1–15). This notice raises some interesting questions. Was Israelite prophecy one of several variations of a common and widespread cultural phenomenon? If writings comparable in length to those from Israel and Judah had survived from these neighboring lands, would they have documented prophetic activity similar to what we learn from the biblical texts? What were the special factors at work in Israel that dictated the direction in which prophecy developed?

Few writings of any kind have survived from the territory of the Transjordan kingdoms. The Mesha stela, found at Dibon in Jordan in 1868 and dated to the ninth century B.C.E., records a command relayed to King Mesha from the Moabite deity Kemosh to attack Nebo, an Israelite city. The command may have been passed on by an ecstatic or an oracle priest, but unfortunately we are not told.[1] An inscription roughly contemporary with Isaiah written in ink on plaster, discovered at Deir 'Alla in what was then the Ammonite Kingdom north of Moab, presents a "visionary of the gods" named Balaam who receives an ominous revelation from on high. Some connection with "the one enraptured and with eyes unveiled" of the biblical Balaam cycle (Numbers 22—24) is certain, though the homeland of the biblical Balaam is said to have been somewhere in Upper Mesopotamia (Num. 22:5; 23:7). From the city-state of

Hamath in northern Syria we have an inscription set up by its ruler Zakir (Zakkur?) dating from the eighth century B.C.E. In a moment of military duress Zakir prayed to the local Baal and received an assurance of divine assistance through seers and other inspired individuals. The message, in the divine first person, resembles oracles of salvation often recorded in the biblical literature: "Do not fear, for I made you king and I shall stand by you and deliver you."[2] Also from Syria, but about a millennium earlier, a cultic functionary of the shrine of the god Adad in or near Aleppo passed on a divine message for Zimrilim, last king of Mari, containing a conditional promise and a mildly worded threat, in some respects comparable to Nathan's dynastic oracle (2 Samuel 7).[3]

The Elijah-Elisha cycle, set in a time of close contact between Israel and the Phoenician cities, testifies to a certain type of orgiastic prophecy imported into Israel as a result of Ahab's marriage with the Tyrian princess Jezebel (1 Kings 18:19, 26–29; 2 Kings 10:19). The difference between the 450 prophets of the Phoenician Baal on Mount Carmel, who performed a limping dance, slashed themselves, and cried ecstatically to their god, and the "sons of the prophets" associated with Elijah and Elisha, was probably more one of degree than of kind. About two and one-half centuries earlier, the picaresque Egyptian tale of Wen-Amon records how this official visited Byblos (Gebal) to purchase timber and was ill-received by the prince of that city. Just when it seemed he would have to return empty-handed, a youth went into trance during a sacrificial ritual. He apparently remained in a state of transformed consciousness for a day and night, in the course of which he revealed that the visitor had been sent by the god Amon (*ANET,* 26).

The dominance of the priest and scribe classes, and of the learned traditions of which they were guardians, produced a very different situation in Egypt. A text from the Old Kingdom features a certain Neferti, priest-scribe of the goddess Bastet, who is introduced to Pharaoh Snefru of the fourth dynasty. He utters a prophecy about a coming epoch of social and political chaos that will be brought to an end by a king who will come from the south, destroy Egypt's enemies, and restore justice and order (*ANET,* 444–46). Unlike biblical messianic prophecies, this prediction of disaster brought to an end by a savior-figure is a *vaticinium ex eventu,* since it dates to the reign of Amen-em-het of the twelfth dynasty (ca. 1900–1785 B.C.E.). It was he who brought to an end the chaos of the First Intermediate Period and is the "king from the south" of Neferti's "prophecy."

The author of this prediction was neither ecstatic nor charismatic. He is introduced into the narrative as scribe and rhetorician, and in that capacity may well represent an established literary tradition of speaking about a future golden age. As late as the Ptolemaic period (third century B.C.E.), the Demotic Chronicle and the Potter's Oracle predict the destruction of foreign rulers, the coming of a savior-king, and the inauguration of a new age of well-being.[4] All this is closer to biblical apocalyptic than to prophecy as generally understood.

We conclude from these allusions scattered over space and time that such connections and comparisons with Israelite prophecy as are attested are to be sought not in Egypt but in the urban centers to the north and east, in Syria, Phoenicia, and Mesopotamia. At the same time, it appears likely that the ethical teaching contained in the numerous Egyptian instructions and admonitions that have come down to us, and which was familiar fare for the literate and educated classes in Israel, has influenced prophetic protest against social injustice during the period of Assyrian and Babylonian hegemony.[5]

Among the Hittites of Asia Minor, messages from the gods could be transmitted by many means including dreams, incubation ritual in a temple, hepatoscopy (the examination of animal livers), and oracles delivered by a priest, a "man of god" (*šiunyanza*), or a sibyl (female mantic). From the fourteenth century B.C.E. we have a prayer offered to the gods by King Mursilis II in which recourse is had to an ecstatic "man of god," in addition to omens, dreams, and incubation ritual, to discover the cause of a plague that was ravaging the kingdom (*ANET*, 394–96). In this respect as in others, the Hittites were in part dependent on religious practice in Mesopotamia where ecstasy had always been an acknowledged form of possession by and communication with the divine world.

The most impressive parallels to some types of Israelite prophecy come from the ongoing publication of the royal archives of the Amorite kingdom of Mari in Upper Mesopotamia (Tell Hariri, just inside the Syrian border with Iraq). These include letters reporting communications from several deities, principally the gods Dagan and Adad and the goddesses Annunitum and Diritum, to Zimrilim, last ruler of the city before the Babylonian conquest (ca.1730–1697 B.C.E.). In some instances the intermediary, male or female, was a private individual holding no office. Other messages were delivered through an ecstatic (*muhhûm*, fem. *muhhutûm*) or an oracle-giver (*āpilum, aplûm*, fem. *apiltûm*) employed in a temple, for example, that of Dagan in the city of Terqa near the royal capital. One of the most recently published letters also refers to a *nabû*, which may be the long-sought cognate to the Hebrew *nābî'*. In most instances the messages were delivered in the temple, often accompanied by sacrificial rites. One of the texts speaks of an oracle specialist who guarded a tent sanctuary, somewhat reminiscent of Joshua in the oracle tent in the wilderness.[6] It is not always clear whether a particular message was solicited (e.g., by incubation) or came spontaneously and unannounced.

Several communications were received in dreams, a form of revelation not unambiguously endorsed in the Hebrew Bible. Doubts about the divine origin of such nocturnal communications could be laid to rest when the dream was repeated either on the following day or after a long period of time. Others came in visions, others again to temple ecstatics in a state of trance, no doubt induced by appropriate techniques or by appropriate substances ingested or inhaled. There are indications that at Mari the official ecstatics were under the jurisdiction of the temple priesthood, as seems to have been the case in the Kingdom of Judah (see Jer. 29:26–27). The letters show evident concern to authenticate messages by seeking independent confirmation, for example, consultation of the omens. In addition, the identity of the prophetic go-between often required authentication by forwarding a lock of hair and fringe of an outer garment to the recipient.

Since the messages are generally part of reports by public officials to the palace, the actual words of commissioning by the god are not always given. We do, nevertheless, find formulae similar to those employed by Israelite prophets as, for example, "Dagan sent me," and "Thus spoke Annunitum." Less frequently, the words of the god are reported in *oratio recta,* as in the commissioning of a certain Malik-Dagan by the god Dagan: "Now go, I send you. Thus shall you speak to Zimrilim saying: 'Send me your messengers and lay your full report before me. . . .' " But the letters throw no light on the process by which a man or woman came to be recognized and acknowledged as a prophetic intermediary.

What of the content of these messages delivered to the king? Most of them have to do with military affairs—warnings about revolt and the possibility of assassination, injunctions against undertaking certain expeditions, entering into certain alliances. In some instances the warnings (e.g., about fortifying a gate or not rebuilding a house) are accompanied by threats of unpleasant consequences, though never as dire as those frequently encountered in Israelite prophecy. Others have to do with cultic matters such as holding sacrificial rites for the dead or building a temple for a deity who for some reason feels slighted by the king. There are occasional complaints and mild scoldings, as when the goddess Annunitum tells the king: "Zimrilim, even though you for your part have spurned me, I for my part shall embrace you" (*ANET*, 630). The god Adad of Aleppo, where Zimrilim had taken refuge before returning to reestablish his father's kingdom in Mari, gave him a dynastic oracle not unlike that of Nathan to David (2 Samuel 7):

Am I not Adad the lord of Kallassu who reared him between my thighs and restored him to the throne of his father's house? After restoring him to the throne of his father's house, I again gave him a dwelling-place. Now, since I restored him to the throne of his father's house, I should receive from him an hereditary property [for a temple]. If he does not give it, I am the lord of throne, territory, and city, and what I gave I will take away. If on the other hand he grants my request, I will give him throne upon throne, house upon house, territory upon territory, city upon city; even the land from east to west will I give him. (*ANET,* 625)

In general, however, the messages are supportive of the king and his political and military goals, and two, possibly three, oracles are directed against Hammurapi the Babylonian king and his allies, predicting their defeat at the hands of Zimrilim. Since it was Hammurapi who was to conquer and destroy Mari, and thus bring Zimrilim's reign to an end, we have a situation remarkably similar to that of the last days of Judah more than a millennium later when salvation prophets like Hananiah were predicting, no more successfully, the defeat of Nebuchadrezzar, king of the same city (e.g., Jer. 28:2–4).

There are sufficient indications from other sites in Syria and Mesopotamia to suggest that the situation at Mari was not untypical of the entire area. And while we are in no position to write a history of Mesopotamian prophecy, the personnel, practices, and types of oracles seem to remain fairly constant over a very long period of time. From the period of Assyrian supremacy in the eighth and seventh centuries B.C.E.—the high period of prophetic activity in Israel—we have collections of oracles delivered by "proclaimers" (*raggimū*, fem., *raggimtū*), ecstatics (*maḫḫû*, fem. *maḫḫûtu*), and others with no title, in the name of the national god Ashur, the goddess Ishtar, and other deities. The inspired persons, male and female, give directions on political and military issues (e.g., the discovery of traitors), assure the king of success in his undertakings, and indulge occasionally in mild reproof. From a collection of oracles addressed to or referring to Esarhaddon (680–669 B.C.E.), it also appears that such oracles were compiled shortly after oral delivery and arranged according to the deity from whom they originated or the inspired individual who delivered them (*ANET,* 449–50). Their survival can therefore be explained by their being deposited in the state archives.

Assyria also had its "false" prophets, that is, inspired persons who delivered oracles against the ruler and his court. Sennacherib (705–681 B.C.E.) received a letter reporting verbatim an oracle of a slave-girl from the Harran region: "This is the word of [the god] Nusku: 'The kingship is for Sasi! I will destroy the name and seed of Sennacherib!' "[7] (In fact,

Sennacherib did die by the hand of an assassin.) Since these oracles would have been destroyed, as King Jehoiakim destroyed Jeremiah's scroll (Jer. 36:20–26), or at least not preserved archivally, we cannot say how widespread opposition prophecy may have been in the Assyrian homeland.[8]

The material we have briefly surveyed does not allow us to solve the problem of the origins of Israelite prophecy. At most, it helps us pose it in a more satisfactory way and propose a working hypothesis that can be checked as we proceed with our study. It will be apparent, to begin with, that a Canaanite origin, as proposed by Hölscher, Jepsen, and others, is oversimplified. Needless to say, we know nothing about such phenomena before the Israelite settlement, and we detect no indications of Canaanite-Phoenician influence before the Omri dynasty in the ninth century B.C.E. The present state of our knowledge, or rather ignorance, about the origins of Israel also rules out the contrasting of sedentary with nomadic coordinates of prophecy once confidently proposed.[9] Max Weber, we suspect, was nearer the mark in speaking of early kinds of prophecy, especially of the communitarian kind, as precipitated by social and military crisis.[10] If this is so, the earliest $n^eb\hat{\imath}\hat{\imath}m$ would be ideologically and phenomenologically quite close to such extremist elements as Nazirites and Rechabites, with their fanatical attachment to warfare under the banner of Yahweh.

Enough has been said about the Mari reports dealing with ecstatic intermediaries to characterize what must have been a fairly standard pattern in Near Eastern urban centers with which Israel had close ties. These intermediaries were generally, but not invariably, associated with sanctuaries where they pronounced oracles often accompanied by sacrificial rituals. Their revelations were generally, but not invariably, supportive of the ruler and his political and military undertakings. One of their principal functions was to further military operations by pronouncing the curse on foreign enemies. Despite the eight centuries or so that separate Zimrilim from David and Solomon, there seems no reason to doubt that Israel was familiar with the same pattern. The important questions, however, have to do not with origins but with development, and especially the emergence of the kind of prophecy represented by Amos, Hosea, Micah, Isaiah, and those who came later.

It could be easily overlooked that, far from being a prerogative of modern critical scholarship, reflection on the origins of prophecy was going on during the biblical period. According to one view, prophecy was God's answer to the people's request for mediation made at Mount Sinai (Deut. 18:15–18; cf. Ex. 20:18–20). The "prophet like Moses" of this much-quoted Deuteronomic passage came to be interpreted eschatologically as an individual figure in Qumranic, Samaritan, and early Christian texts, but it is generally, and correctly, taken to refer to the prophetic succession as a whole.[11] It assumes that prophecy originated with, and is embodied paradigmatically in, Moses as protoprophet, and that therefore it has to do essentially with the law and the covenant. Prophecy is God's answer to Israel's request, made at Sinai, for a mediating presence throughout its history.

Another passage (Num. 11:10–30) deals with the creation, during the wandering in the wilderness, of a new office the purpose of which was to assist Moses in governing the people. He was instructed to select seventy from among the elders and officers of the community and present them at the Tent of Meeting. When he did so, Yahweh appeared, took some of the spirit that was on Moses, and put it on the seventy, with the result that they "acted like prophets" for that one time only (Num. 11:25).[12] However, two of their number, Eldad and Medad, manifested the same symptoms without having been "ordained" at the tent with the others. Speaking with the customary voice of bureaucratic authority Joshua objected, but he was overruled by Moses who refused to prevent them from engaging in whatever kind of prophetic-ecstatic activity they were engaged in. The response of Moses, often quoted, is worth bearing in mind by all those who exercise authority in the religious sphere: "would that all Yahweh's people were prophets, that Yahweh would put his spirit upon them!"

The "ordination" of the seventy elders is one of several traditions about the wilderness period dealing with aspects of the institutional life of Israel. As it stands, it cannot be interpreted as simply legitimating the Israelite presbyterate, the institution of elders, since the narrative assumes that this office was already in existence. It seems rather to aim at legitimating ecstatic prophecy by deriving it from the spirit of Moses, unquestionably of divine origin. If this is so, the two who were not "ordained" and yet who prophesied would most naturally stand for those prophets who stood outside the institutional framework, which in effect means the cult. We are reminded once again that the canonical prophets made up only a small and anomalous minority of the prophets of Israel at any point in the history.

A quite different tradition suggests that the call of Samuel at Shiloh (1 Sam. 3:1–4:1) marked the beginning, or at least a new beginning, of prophetic activity. Before that time, we are told, revelations and visions were infrequent, but the situation changed dramatically after Samuel's call (1 Sam. 3:1, 21; 4:1). At this point we are on somewhat firmer historical ground because prophecy was always intimately associated with the monarchy, beginning with Saul, and we are told that one of the principal reasons for Saul's failure was loss of prophetic support. It is also well attested that times of political crisis, such as then existed with the life-and-death struggle against the Philistines, linked perhaps with internal pressures on the settlements in the hill country, elicit the kind of prophetic activity of which we are speaking. It therefore seems safest to conclude that, in its earliest manifestations, Israelite prophecy was essentially an indigenous phenomenon with a character of its own dictated by the unique situation in which Israelites then found themselves.

6. WAR PROPHETS AND "PRIMITIVES" IN THE EARLY PERIOD

G. W. **Ahlström,** "Der Prophet Nathan und der Tempelbau," *VT* 11 (1961): 113–27; W. F. **Albright,** "Samuel and the Beginnings of the Prophetic Movement," in H. M. Orlinsky, ed., *Interpreting the Prophetic Tradition,* New York: KTAV Publishing House, 1969, 149–76; K. **Baltzer,** *Die Biographie der Propheten,* 13–105; J. **Blenkinsopp,** "The Quest of the Historical Saul," in J. W. Flanagan and A. W. Weisbrod, eds., *No Famine in the Land: Studies in Honor of John L. McKenzie,* Missoula, Mont.: Scholars Press, 1975, 75–99; N. P. **Bratsiotis,** "'îsh," *TDOT* 1 (1977): 233–35; V. **Eppstein,** "Was Saul Also among the Prophets?" *ZAW* 81 (1969): 287–304; H. **Haag,** "*ben*," *TDOT* 2 (1977): 152–53; R. **Hallevy,** "Man of God," *JNES* 17 (1958): 237–44; M. **Haran,** "From Early to Classical Prophecy: Continuity and Change," *VT* 27 (1977): 385–97; J. **Lindblom,** "The Political Background of the Shiloh Oracle," *SVT* 1 (1953): 78–87; *Prophecy in Ancient Israel,* 47–104; "Saul inter prophetas," *ASTI* 9 (1974): 30–41; P. D. **Miller, Jr.,** *The Divine Warrior in Ancient Israel,* Cambridge, Mass.: Harvard University Press, 1973; J. **Muilenburg,** "The 'Office' of the Prophet in Ancient Israel," in J. P. Hyatt, ed., *The Bible in Modern Scholarship,* Nashville: Abingdon Press, 1965, 74–97; H. M. **Orlinsky,** "The Seer in Ancient Israel," *OA* 4 (1965): 153–74; S. B. **Parker,** "Possession Trance and Prophecy in Pre-exilic Israel," *VT* 28 (1978): 271–85; L. **Perlitt,** "Mose als Prophet," *EvTh* 31 (1971): 588–608; A. **Phillips,** "The Ecstatics' Father," in P. R. Ackroyd and B. Lindars, eds., *Words and Meanings: Essays Presented to David Winton Thomas,* Cambridge: Cambridge University Press, 1968, 183–94; O. **Plöger,** *Die Prophetengeschichten der Samuel- und Königsbücher,* Greifswald: E. Panzig, 1937; J. R. **Porter,** "Bene hannebî'îm," *JTS,* n.s., 32 (1981) 423–28; R. **Smend,** *Yahweh War and Tribal Federation,* Nashville: Abingdon Press, 1970; J. **Sturdy,** "The Original Meaning of 'Is Saul Also among the Prophets?'" *VT* 20 (1970): 206–13; M. **Weber,** *Ancient Judaism,* 90–117; J. J. **Williams,** "The Prophetic 'Father': A Brief Explanation of the Term 'Sons of the Prophets,'" *JBL* 85 (1966): 344.

The point was made earlier that the prophets to whom books are attributed, and who are variously described as "canonical," "writing," or "classical" prophets—none of which terms is entirely satisfactory—correspond to a definite phase in the historical development of prophecy. The four familiar figures from the eighth century—Amos and Hosea in the north, Micah and Isaiah in the south—stand at one of the great turning points in the history of Israel and of the Near East in general. This was the century during which the overwhelming menace of Assyria threatened and eventually engulfed the Northern Kingdom and reduced the Southern Kingdom to vassalage, events that had a profound effect on specifically religious perceptions and practices. It was also a time of far-reaching political and social change within the two kingdoms precipitated by the consolidation of the state and its encroachment on a traditional agrarian way of life.

The role played by the aforementioned prophetic figures during this axial historical epoch[13] may, however, lead us to neglect or misrepresent the lines of continuity with the past. We saw that these "classical" figures are aware of a prophetic tradition already in place and refer explicitly to prophetic predecessors. The confrontation between Amos and Amaziah, priest-in-charge at Bethel (Amos 7:10–17), shows, for example, that *n*ᵉ*bî'îm* were employed in state sanctuaries under royal jurisdiction exercised through the priesthood. Another passage (Amos 2:11–12), perhaps editorial,[14] speaks of prophets and Nazirites encountering opposition even before the time of the monarchy. This bracketing of prophets with Nazirites, an order dedicated to the militant defense and propagation of the Yahweh cult, also reminds us of the close connections between prophecy and warfare in this early period as emphasized by Weber. The involvement of prophetic groups and individuals in politics, in the rise and even more so in the fall of rulers and dynasties, meant that prophecy was from the beginning a problematic and contentious phenomenon. The extraordinary behavior of these "plebeian technicians of orgiastics" (Weber) could, moreover, be interpreted with some reason as sickness or madness (e.g., 2 Kings 9:11; Hos. 9:7; Jer. 29:26), to which we may add accusations of venality (e.g., Micah 3:5–12) and of leading the people astray (e.g., Hos. 4:5; 9:7–9). Yet despite these ambiguities, Amos, Hosea, and their successors appealed to a prophetic tradition with which they could identify, one which Hosea does not hesitate to trace back to Moses himself (Hos. 12:13).

Our knowledge of prophecy during the early period depends mainly on the Deuteronomic history (Joshua through Kings), with minor contributions from the Pentateuch and the Chronicler's history. In view of the theological purposes determining the selection and presentation of events in these writings, our data will inevitably be patchy and incomplete. Abraham is described as a prophet in a passage by some attributed to the Elohist (E) source of the Pentateuch (Gen. 20:7). While this notice reflects the importance of intercessory prayer as a characteristic prophetic activity—to which let us add Abraham's pleading for the doomed city of Sodom (Gen. 18:22–33)—it cannot be used as evidence for the existence of a certain type of prophecy during the time of the ancestors. The attribution of oracles to such founding fathers as Jacob (Genesis 49) and Moses (Deuteronomy 33) has to be understood along the same lines, though the individual tribal sayings in these two passages may go back some way.

Hosea seems to have been the first to represent Moses as a prophet:

> By a prophet Yahweh brought Israel up from Egypt,
> And by a prophet he was preserved.
> (Hos. 12:13)

This characterization was taken up and developed by the Deuteronomists according to whom Moses was the prophet par excellence (Deut. 18:15–18; 34:10). But Deuteronomy and the Deuteronomic History are concerned to present prophecy according to their own understanding of the history of Israel and its institutions. This led them to stress the "Mosaic" character of prophecy, in the sense that prophecy was intended to make available throughout history a mediation along the same lines as that of Moses but of an inferior order. Eventually the entire Pentateuch came to be ascribed to Moses as a kind of prophetic legacy committed to Israel just before his death.[15] At that point Moses emerges as *the* prophet, in something of the way in which the term is applied to Muhammad in Islam.

If we were able to unravel all the traditions about Moses, tracing the different threads back to their beginnings, we might well find elements of a prophetic profile. Kaufmann and Buber argued that, together with Miriam and Aaron, Moses belonged to a family of seers whose role was comparable to that of the Arabic *kāhin*.[16] The earliest traditions about the tent of meeting (*'ōhel mô'ēd*) or oracle tent, pitched outside the camp in the wilderness, would perhaps be consistent with this hypothesis, since it was there that Moses received divine communications on behalf of the group (Ex. 33:5–11). The tent was also the scene of the ecstatic prophesying of the elders (Num. 11:16–17, 24–30) mentioned earlier, and it was there that Moses' unique status as prophet was vindicated by divine intervention (Num. 12:1–8). However, Joshua not Moses is represented, in a tradition that looks at least as ancient, as the permanent minister of the oracle-deity in the tent (Ex. 33:11), in which respect he discharged a function similar to that of Samuel in the Shiloh sanctuary.[17] But the origins of the Moses tradition are, as they say, lost in the mists of time. In fact, it is remarkable what little attention he receives in biblical texts generally deemed to be preexilic.[18]

A tradition about female prophecy that gives the impression of being ancient is represented by the figures of Miriam and Deborah, both associated with warfare. According to this tradition Miriam is a Levite, sister of Moses and Aaron, and after victory, she leads the women in celebratory and possibly ecstatic song and dance accompanied by music and percussion, in the manner of the female seer or *kāhina* of the pre-Islamic Arabs (Ex. 15:20–21). She was also involved, with Aaron, in a prophetic protest against exclusive control of mediation by Moses, resulting in punishment and temporary banishment being inflicted on her but not on Aaron (Numbers 12). The incident is no doubt paradigmatic and admonitory, reflecting a struggle for religious control at some point in the history, but the situation that precipitated it can no longer be recovered. We may suspect that it reflects hostility to female prophets of the kind expressed occasionally in the literature (e.g., Ezek. 13:17–23).

Deborah, prophet and judge, seems to have played a more central role (Judges 4—5). A married woman, she is represented as a "mother in Israel" (Judg. 5:7) engaged in settling disputes, in the course of which she received and passed on prophetic messages concerned with military activity in the manner of the female "prophets" of Mari. Unlike the latter, however, she also accompanied the tribal levy into battle, giving instruction on when and how to attack and celebrating with song and music. It seems likely that the historian has filled out the allusions to Deborah in the song (Judg. 5:7, 12, 15) with the purpose of fitting her into the series of charismatic military and judicial leaders ("judges") with which this part of the history is concerned.

The Deuteronomic History (Dtr) was apparently written to explain the disasters that overcame both kingdoms as the result of failure to heed prophetic warnings. The fact that, with the exception of Deborah, there are no named prophets in the narrative covering the period preceding the monarchy (i.e., in Joshua and Judges) is to be explained by the author's clearly structured ideas about charismatic succession.[19] Joshua was appointed as first successor to Moses and charismatic mediator for the period of the conquest (Num. 27:15–23; Deut. 34:9; Josh. 1:1–9), and after his death we are told that judges—leaders combining military and judicial functions—were "raised up," the last of whom was Samuel (Judg. 2:16–23; 1 Sam. 12:11). Dtr attests to close links between prophets and rulers. From the death of Solomon to the fall of Jerusalem prophets make frequent appearances to predict the fall of kings and dynasties for failure to observe the Mosaic law. Hence the pattern of prophecy-fulfillment is structurally decisive, providing the key to interpreting the history and leaving no doubt as to who was responsible for the disasters that the historian's surviving contemporaries had experienced.

In the Deuteronomic scheme of things, prophecy in the strict sense begins with Samuel. Before his call the word of Yahweh was rare; after it, divine revelations were frequent (1 Sam. 3:1; 3:19–4:1). The call itself, which took place in the Shiloh sanctuary during an incubation ritual (3:2–18), resulted not in a commission to speak or act (cf. Isaiah 6) but in the authentication of Samuel as prophet to all Israel and the acknowledgment by the people of his new status (1 Sam. 3:20). We note, too, in this episode, the intimate connection between prophecy and cult. The historian introduces an anonymous "man of God" who condemns the corruption of cult at Shiloh and the Eli priesthood responsible for it (2:27–36). The same message is delivered to Samuel (3:11–14), in spite of which Shiloh remained the designated place for divine communications (3:21). Samuel, correspondingly, is a cultic prophet in the sense that he ministered in the sanctuary and received divine revelations there; which, however, neither prevented him from condemning the cult and its personnel nor from operating outside the sanctuary. The Shiloh narrative, then, clearly reflects ideas about prophecy current at different times throughout the history, and especially the process by which the prophet was commissioned and subsequently acknowledged as such by his public, and the relation between the prophet and the cultic institutions of Israel, especially the sacrificial ritual.

The Samuel narratives are so overlaid with theological interpretation that it is now impossible to say anything certain about Samuel as a historical figure. He is represented as judge, in both the military (1 Sam. 11:11) and judicial sense (7:15–17), as seer (9:11, 19), sacrificing priest (7:10; 13:8–15), man of God (9:3–10), and paradigm of prophetic opposition to kingship (13:8–15; 15:1–31). In this last capacity he pronounces a message indistinguishable from that of later prophets (1 Sam. 15:22–23; cf. Hos. 6:6). A further complication is that the birth story in 1 Samuel 1—3 clearly implies that he is to be a Nazirite, an implication supported by one of the Samuel fragments from Qumran (4QSam^a): "I will give him as a Nazirite for ever, all the days of his life," corresponding to 1 Sam. 1:22. But the Hebrew reader will at once notice that the name etymology refers to Saul and not to Samuel (1:20, 28). It is Saul moreover, and not Samuel, who acts the part of the Nazirite by his violent and spirit-driven participation in Israel's holy war. We therefore conclude that a birth and conception story of a familiar type, referring originally to Saul, has been transferred to Samuel and conflated with a prophetic commissioning narrative which, for the

Deuteronomic historian, marked the beginning of the history of prophecy under the monarchy.

One pericope in 1 Samuel featuring both Saul and Samuel provides something of a clue to the latter's identity. Pursued by Saul, David took refuge in an ecstatic coenobium directed by Samuel in Ramah (1 Sam. 19:18–24). After the troops sent ahead by Saul to arrest David were caught up in the communal ecstasy, Saul himself arrived, was similarly affected, and ended up tearing off his clothes and lying naked on the ground in a catatonic state for an entire day and night. According to this tradition, then, Samuel was the leader or "father" of an ecstatic brotherhood, not unlike the sheik presiding at a later day over the Sufi dervish community. Another tradition, recording Saul's appointment as military overlord by Samuel (1 Sam. 9:1–10:16), tells how Saul was caught up in the prophetic frenzy, stimulated by music and percussion, of a group of ecstatics encountered on the way. Since the ecstatic brotherhoods were active in warfare, and since *nᵉbî'îm* are recorded as designating or anointing leaders and kings (Judg. 4:6–9; 1 Kings 11:29–40; 16:2; 2 Kings 9:4–10), these two traditions need not be mutually exclusive. Yet a careful reading of the story of the straying donkeys in 1 Samuel 9—10 suggests that it dealt originally with an anonymous "man of God" or clairvoyant who only at a later stage of editing was identified with Samuel the kingmaker.[20] Seers of this kind should be distinguished from the ecstatic dervishes over whom Samuel presided, and it does not seem likely that Samuel filled both roles.

The condition of trance or mental dissociation so often attested in this early period is presumed to derive from the spirit of Yahweh (e.g., 1 Sam. 10:6, 10; 19:20, 23; 1 Kings 22:21–23). Whatever the archaic, magical connotations of *rûaḥ* (spirit, wind, breath), in these narratives, it is understood as a force deriving from Yahweh and driving the inspired one to a certain course of action. The case of Saul, whose association with the ecstatic brotherhoods is mentioned more than once (1 Sam. 10:11; 18:10; 19:24), serves to illustrate one of the ambiguities from which prophecy is rarely free. For here was a man who appears to have been psychologically predisposed to "stand outside himself," as may be seen in the way he called the tribes to war (1 Sam. 11:6–7), and in the tendency to throw spears at people he didn't like (18:10–11; 19:9–10). We saw that, on his way to his designation as tribal leader, he fell in with a prophetic band and at once, in the telling phrase used at that point, "became another man" (1 Sam. 10:5–6). Violent behavior of this kind would in our culture result in a diagnosis of manic depression or dementia praecox, and even in ancient Israel it could be interpreted as a form of sickness or madness (see, e.g., 2 Kings 9:11; Hos. 9:7; Jer. 29:26). In other words, extraordinary behavior of this kind was susceptible of more than one interpretation. Since prophecy could not function without a degree of social acceptance, there had to be a "discerning of spirits" by the society or that segment of it addressed by the prophet.

In spite of the obscurity and dubiety surrounding Israelite origins, it would be agreed that Israel was forged as a nation in the crucible of warfare. As Wellhausen put it, war was the cradle of the nation. Samuel and the prophetic conventicles with which he was closely associated were involved in the sporadic war with the Philistines. Saul's connections with ecstatic prophets have already been noted, and it is particularly significant that his career as charismatic warlord followed the spectacular encounter with an ecstatic troupe (*ḥebel nᵉbî'îm*) near a town occupied by a Philistine garrison.[21] It is also clear from the subsequent narrative that his political failure was due in good measure to loss of prophetic support (1 Sam. 13:8–15; 15:1–35; 28:6).

With David's establishment of a Judean dynasty, creation of a professional army in place of the tribal levy, and subjugation of the tribal structures to a complex state system,[22] these older forms of prophecy were bound to undergo change. The secession of the northern and central tribes after the death of Solomon, though judged negatively in the dominant Judean tradition, was in reality a protest against these innovations and a reaffirmation of an archaic pattern. It is for this reason that ecstatic war prophecy continued to thrive in the Northern Kingdom and is unattested in Judah, at least until the resurgence of Assyria posed a direct threat to its existence in the eighth century.

Under the United Monarchy in Judah we find, nevertheless, a type of court prophecy similar in some respects to that of the Mari "prophets" discussed earlier. Wishing to build a temple to Yahweh in Jerusalem, we are told that David consulted with Nathan, his court seer, who at first gave a favorable reply but then, after a night vision, discouraged him from doing so (2 Sam 7:4–17). In keeping with a conservative aversion to Canaanite cult places, the original form of this oracle opposed the building of a temple without qualification. In the following reign, however, an editor added a qualification—"he (i.e., Solomon) shall build a house for my name" (v. 13)—obviously in acknowledgment of the fact that the temple actually was built. The point is made by a play on the word *bayit* (house), which can signify "temple" or "dynasty": David will not build me a house (temple); I will build him a house (dynasty). Appropriately, therefore, it was Nathan who named David's heir by Bathsheba (2 Sam. 12:25), and we find him active at her side in the palace intrigues leading to the ousting of the pretender Adonijah (1 Kings 1). Another court seer, Gad, was associated with David even before his accession (1 Sam. 22:3–5) and continued to play an important part thereafter, guiding him in such crucial decisions as choosing the site of the future sanctuary (2 Sam. 24:18–19; 1 Chron. 22:1). Other prophetic oracles predicting the permanence of the dynasty and expansion of the kingdom (2 Sam. 3:9–10; 5:2; Gen. 49:8–12; Num. 24:15–19) may also have emanated from the circle of court prophets with which early Judean kings surrounded themselves.

7. PROPHECY IN THE NORTHERN KINGDOM: ELIJAH AND ELISHA

E. **Ben Zvi**, "Prophets and Prophecy in the Compositional and Redactional Notes in 1 and 2 Kings," *ZAW* 105 (1993): 331–51; R. A. **Carlson**, "Elie à l'Horeb," *VT* 19 (1969): 416–39; R. P. **Carroll**, "The Elijah-Elisha Sagas," *VT* 19 (1969): 400–15; R. B. **Coote**, ed., *Elijah and Elisha in Socioliterary Perspective*, Atlanta: Scholars Press, 1992; F. M. **Cross**, *Canaanite Myth and Hebrew Epic*, Cambridge, Mass.: Harvard University Press, 1973, 223–29; W. **Dietrich**, *David, Saul und die Propheten*, Stuttgart: Kohlhammer, 1992; G. **Fohrer**, *Elia*, Zurich: Zwingli Verlag, 1968[2]; F. S. **Frick**, "Rechabites," *IDBS*, 726–28; A. J. **Hauser** and R. **Gregory**, *From Carmel to Horeb: Elijah in Crisis*, Sheffield: Almond Press, 1990; J. H. **Hayes** and J. **Maxwell Miller**, eds., *Israelite and Judaean History*, 381–414; A. **Jepsen**, "Elia und das Gottesurteil," in H. Goedicke, ed., *Near Eastern Studies in Honor of W. F. Albright*, Baltimore: Johns Hopkins University Press, 1971, 291–306; B. O. **Long**, "2 Kings 3 and Genres of Prophetic Narrative," *VT* 23 (1973): 337–48; S. L. **McKenzie**, "The Prophetic History and the Redaction of Kings," *HAR* 9 (1985): 203–20; J. M. **Miller**, "The Elisha Cycle and the Accounts of the Omride Wars," *JBL* 85 (1966): 441–54; "The Fall of the House of Ahab," *VT* 17 (1967): 307–24; M. **Pope**, "Rechabites," *IDB* 4, (1962): 14–16; A. **Rofé**, *The Prophetical Stories*, Jerusalem: Magnes Press, 1988; H. H. **Rowley**, "Elijah on Mount Carmel," *BJRL* 43 (1960–61): 190–219 (= *Men of God*, London: Thomas Nelson & Sons, 1963, 37–65); H.-C. **Schmitt**, *Elisa*, Gütersloh: Gerd Mohn, 1972; "Prophetie und Tradition: Beobachtungen zur Frühgeschichte des israelitischen Nabitums," *ZTK* 74 (1977) 255–72; H. **Seebass**, "Elia und Ahab auf dem Karmel," *ZTK* 70 (1973): 121–36; "Der Fall Naboth in 1 Reg 21," *VT* 24 (1974): 474–88; "Tradition und Interpretation bei Jehu ben Chanania und Ahia von Silo," *VT* 25 (1975): 175–90; R. **Smend**, "Das Wort Jahwes an Elia," *VT* 25 (1975): 525–43; O. H. **Steck**, *Uberlieferung und Zeitgeschichte in den Elia-Erzählungen*, Neukirchen-Vluyn: Neukirchener Verlag, 1968; R. **de Vaux**, "The Prophets of Baal on Mount Carmel," *The Bible and the Ancient Near East*, Garden City: Doubleday, 1971, 238–51; S. J. **De Vries**, *Prophet against Prophet*, Grand Rapids: Eerdmans, 1978; R. R. **Wilson**, "Early Israelite Prophecy," *Int* 32 (1978): 3–16; E. **Würthwein**, "Zur Komposition von 1 Reg 22:1–38," *Das Ferne und Nahe Wort*, Berlin: Töpelmann, 1967, 245–54; "Elijah at Horeb: Reflections on 1 Kings 19:9–18," in J. Durham and J. R. Porter, eds.,

Proclamation and Presence: Old Testament Essays in Honour of Gwynne Henton Davies,
London: SCM Press, 1970, 152–66; "Die Erzählung vom Gottesmann aus Juda in
Bethel," in H. Gese and H. P. Rüger, eds., *Wort und Geschichte: Festschrift für Karl
Elliger zum 70. Geburtstag,* Kevelaer: Batzon & Bercker, 1973.

During the two centuries from the death of Solomon to the fall of
Samaria to the Assyrians the references in the history to prophets and
prophecy are restricted entirely to the Northern Kingdom. One explanation would be that the historian wished to apply the lesson of
Samaria's fate to Judah: If you ignore your prophets as they did theirs,
the same will happen to you (2 Kings 17:7–18). But another explanation
is that the ideal of charismatic leadership remained alive in the territory
of the Northern Kingdom, acting as a counterforce to hereditary kingship, and leaving more space for the involvement of prophets in public
affairs. Therefore, it is not surprising to find them playing an important
role in the making and unmaking of rulers and dynasties throughout
these two centuries.

It may be useful, first, to sketch briefly the political situation at that
time. The rather precarious tribal and territorial unity brought about by
David lasted only through the lifetime of Solomon, his successor. The basis for David's rule as chieftain of the tribal groupings of the central and
northern regions was an agreement or covenant between himself and
their elders (2 Sam. 5:1–3). Despite opposition and sporadic attempts to
repudiate this agreement, for example, by the Benjaminite Sheba ben-
Bikri (2 Samuel 20), the covenant survived throughout his reign and
must have been renewed at the accession of Solomon. After the latter's
death his successor Rehoboam duly betook himself to Shechem, sanctuary of the Joseph tribes, to seek renewal of the agreement. This time,
however, the tribal leaders were no longer content to go through with a
purely formal ratification but laid down conditions that Rehoboam un-
wisely rejected out of hand (1 Kings 12:1–15). The outcome was the accession of Jeroboam, one of Solomon's officials, as ruler of a separate
kingdom. The revolt against Solomon was, in effect, a reaffirmation of
the traditional pattern of tribal separatism as against the innovation of
hereditary and dynastic kingship. The result was that, while the Davidic
dynasty lasted, with only one brief interruption, for well over three centuries in Judah, the Northern Kingdom witnessed the rapid rise and fall
of petty dynasts (belonging to nine different families) with the army playing a dominant role as in some Latin American countries in recent times.
In this situation the old war prophecy continued to flourish, while in
Judah it was, in effect, "demilitarized" and forced into different forms
and directions.

In describing the rise to power of the Ephraimite Jeroboam ben-Nebat, the historian assigns a role of the greatest importance to a Shiloh prophet named Ahijah who, following the example of Samuel, designated Jeroboam king of the ten tribes (1 Kings 11:29–39). After enjoying prophetic support, possibly also from Judah (12:22–24), Jeroboam was condemned by Ahijah, who also predicted the death of the king's son who was sick (14:1–18), and in due course the fulfillment of the prediction is noted (15:29). After the intervention of a "man of God" called Shemaiah (12:22–24), the pattern recurs with the prophet Jehu ben-Hanani, who first supported and then condemned the equally short-lived dynasty of Baasha (16:1–4, 7, 12–13), the coming to pass of this prophetic word also being duly noted (16:12). Elijah, Elisha, and Micaiah (1 Kings 22) were, in different ways and to different degrees, in conflict with the Omrids. They predicted the collapse of the Omri dynasty and helped to bring it about by their involvement in the coup that brought Jehu to the throne (1 Kings 20:33–43; 21:19, 21–24; 22:28; 2 Kings 1:6; 9:1–10). Prophetic involvement in politics is carried forward by Amos and Hosea who condemned the dynasty of Jehu and predicted its collapse (Amos 7:9, 11; Hos. 1:4–5). While there are clear indications that the Deuteronomic historian has substantially edited these reports—for example, by extending prophetic predictions to cover the fall of the Northern Kingdom and by highlighting prophetic opposition to the cult of Bethel and Dan—it does seem that prophetic circles played a significant if ambiguous role as brokers of political power in the Northern Kingdom.

With the successful coup of the army commander Omri (ca. 876) an era of relative stability was inaugurated for the first time in half a century. One of Omri's first moves was to found a new capital city on the virgin site of Samaria, though the city of Jezreel at the foot of Mount Gilboa continued to serve as a royal residence. Peaceful relations with Judah allowed the Omrids to pursue a vigorous policy of expansion to the north and east, a policy that included commercial alliances with the prosperous Phoenician cities. To further these ends Omri arranged a marriage between his son Ahab and Jezebel (Izebul), daughter of the Tyrian king Ittobaal. A typical *mariage de convenance* of this kind would hardly have merited comment had she not turned out to be a zealous devotee of the Tyrian Baal. Using her position to advantage, she actively promoted the Baal cult during the reign of her husband and their two children, Ahaziah and Jehoram, who succeeded him. Her influence even spread to Judah, where her daughter Athaliah engineered a palace coup and spent the five years of her reign attempting to impose a new political and religious direction on Judah, an attempt that was thwarted by the priesthood of the Jerusalem temple.

The partisan point of view of the historian makes it difficult for us to get a correct picture of the religious situation in Israel during the reign of Ahab (ca. 869–850). He gave his children Yahwistic names, allegedly supported Yahwistic prophets (1 Kings 22:5–12) and, at least initially, showed respect for native Israelite custom (21:1–4). Yet we are told that he built sanctuaries in Samaria for the Tyrian Baal and his consort Asherah that were staffed by hordes of male and female cult ecstatics. His wife seems to have had a free hand because the historian reports, no doubt with some exaggeration, the persecution of prophets and demolition of Yahweh altars (1 Kings 18:4, 22, 30; 19:10, 14). Even the majordomo of the court had to act secretly in rescuing prophets of Yahweh from death (18:3–4).

The historian (Dtr) also represents the "golden (or gilded) calves" set up at Bethel and Dan as genuine cult objects whose worship implied rejection of the Yahweh cult (1 Kings 12:28–30; cf. Ex. 32:1–6); but it seems more likely that the bull icon either represented Yahweh or served as his pedestal. By the time of Ahab much of the population of the kingdom had accommodated the cult of Yahweh to that of the old Canaanite-Phoenician deities. Of the personal names on ostraca discovered on the site of Samaria, from the late ninth or early eighth century, eleven contain the element YW (an abbreviated form of Yahweh) and eight are formed with Baal.[23] From about the same time an inscription on a storage jar at Kuntillet 'Ajrud in the Negev reads "I bless you by Yahweh of Samaria and his Asherah," the last word referring either to the goddess herself or her cult object.[24] These and similar data would seem to indicate practices and beliefs that were uncontentiously held by the majority of the population at that time in the kingdom of Samaria. But the arrival of Jezebel, clearly a quite exceptional individual, seems to have precipitated a violent struggle between conservative Baalist and Yahwist elements at each end of the spectrum. It is in this context that the narratives about Elijah have to be read and understood.

The abrupt introduction of Elijah into the chronicles of the kingdoms (1 Kings 17:1) suggests that the historian has excerpted stories and legends about this powerful figure from a deposit of hagiographical material in circulation. The chance reference to "Beersheba which belongs to Judah" (19:3) also suggests that much of this material could have been written down before the fall of Samaria. The historian has limited himself to adding comments here and there to bring the prophetic legends into line with his own point of view and purposes.[25] Elijah's role as covenant mediator is therefore stressed, and the Baalist prophets are put to death on Mount Carmel in keeping with the Deuteronomic law about false prophecy (Deut. 18:20).

Like the *Legenda Sanctorum,* much of the Elijah material belongs to the genre of hagiography, and therefore it can be compared with, among other things, the Life of Anthony the Hermit by Athanasius, the rabbinic traditions about Hanina ben Dosa the Galilean wonder-worker, or the biographical memoir of the Pythagorian sage Apollonius of Tyana written by Philostratus. Certain motifs tend to recur: the saint is fed miraculously by birds (1 Kings 17:2–7) or by angels (19:5–8), he controls the weather (17:1), multiplies food (17:8–16), raises the dead to life (17:17–24), levitates (18:12; 2 Kings 2:1–12, 16), and performs preternatural feats of endurance (2 Kings 18:46; 19:8). This is in the nature of legends, but from these legends there still comes to us from that remote time in the past an impression of enormous and dangerous spiritual power and energy.

The narrative opens with Elijah bringing drought on the land through the curse and then taking refuge outside Ahab's jurisdiction. While his act was designed to emphasize a central religious issue, namely, control of rainfall and therefore of physical and economic survival, it also would have precipitated a political crisis, since a disaster of this magnitude would tend to raise questions about the legitimacy of the dynasty (cf. the three-year drought at the beginning of David's reign, 2 Sam. 21:1–14). The denouement, with the confrontation on Carmel (1 Kings 18:20–40), has undergone considerable editing. The site, a prominent cult center from at least the second millennium, may have changed hands following treaties between Israel and the Phoenician cities. At any rate, the demolition and rebuilding of the altar to Yahweh (1 Kings 18:30) suggest a dispute over ownership of this piece of real estate, since the erection of an altar was a conventional way of staking a claim to disputed territory. The Deuteronomic historian has expanded the episode into a pan-Israelite convocation around an altar built of twelve stones. The occasion also was taken for a little satire at the expense of the Phoenician deity, and the sober prayer of Elijah is contrasted with the orgiastic delirium of the Baalist prophets with their limping dance and self-laceration.[26] The episode ends grimly with more bloodletting and, in due course, the first rain in three years.

In view of Elijah's complete triumph we are surprised to find that subsequently he had to flee for his life into the Negev, whence he made a forty-day pilgrimage to Horeb (1 Kings 19:1–18). This unexpected sequel may be due to the way originally independent narratives have been arranged, or it may suggest that Elijah's triumph was less complete than the historian gives us to believe. Baalist prophets, in fact, continued to flourish (2 Kings 10:19), and it was left to Jehu to exterminate the Baal cult, for the time being at any rate, in an unprecedented bloodbath shortly after his seizure of power (ca. 845 B.C.E.). It is also possible that the visit to Horeb served originally as the call and commissioning of Elijah, and that the account of the drought and its termination came from a quite different source and was placed first for dramatic effect.

Editorial accretions to the Horeb episode (1 Kings 19:9–18), which cannot be discussed here, have created severe problems for the interpreter. How, for example, reconcile the "still, small voice" (NRSV: "a sound of sheer silence"; NEB: "a low murmuring sound") with the giving of commissions leading to bloodshed and destruction, including the commissioning of Elisha as a licensed killer? Some refer the *qôl d^emāmâ daqqâ* (19:12: still small voice or sound?) to lethargic trance as opposed to orgiastic ecstasy.[27] Others take the theophany (1 Kings 19:11–13a) to be an insertion the purpose of which is to contrast the primordial theophany at Sinai (Ex. 19:16–19) with indirect revelation addressed to the prophet's inner ear.[28] If this passage is interpolated, and if we bracket it, we are left with Elijah describing a situation of almost total apostasy and Yahweh, in response, commanding the destruction of unfaithful Israel through Hazael king of Damascus, Jehu the fanatical army commander, and Elisha, all three to be anointed by Elijah. Only a remnant of seven thousand will survive as the nucleus of a new and faithful community. We have here already, in essence, the message of the great prophets of the eighth and seventh centuries.

Other somewhat different traditions about Elijah set him in opposition to the Omrid dynasty in the manner of Samuel's opposition to Saul. Ahab's attempt to push through a forced sale of a vineyard next to the royal palace at Jezreel was thwarted by the owner's appeal to ancient Israelite legal custom forbidding alienation of family property (1 Kings 21:1–19). Though obviously displeased, Ahab did not, to his credit, insist. Jezebel, however, suborned two ruffians to bring capital charges against Naboth the owner, as a result of which he was executed and his property confiscated by the crown. Typically, Elijah's condemnation of Ahab has been expanded to take in the fall of the dynasty, the fulfillment of which is duly noted at the appropriate point (2 Kings 10:10, 17). Ahab's son and successor, Ahaziah, also fell foul of Elijah, being condemned for recourse to foreign gods after suffering an accident at the palace. His death also was interpreted as resulting from the prophet's curse (2 Kings 1:2–17).

These traditions, of varying historical, religious, and ethical value, tend to give the impression of a figure who emerges abruptly from nowhere in particular and, after a stormy career, disappears in a flaming chariot into the sky. We have the impression, above all, of a *solitary* figure. The impression may, however, be misleading. Both he and his disciple Elisha are addressed as "father" (2 Kings 2:12; 13:14), the title implying leadership of the prophetic coenobia that Elijah visited for the last time shortly before his mysterious disappearance from the scene (2 Kings 2:2–12). In this respect, therefore, he resembles Samuel presiding over an ecstatic group in Ramah (1 Sam. 19:18–24), a function that did not preclude operations outside the group context, including interventions in political and military affairs.

We would like to know more about the way of life of these small prophetic communities known as "sons of the prophets" or simply "prophets" (*nᵉbî'îm*). We have seen that they were of low socioeconomic status. Like certain peripheral groups in our day, they expressed their rejection of the dominant urban culture by a distinctive attire (cf. 2 Kings 1:8), simple diet, and physical segregation from the amenities of city life. In these respects they were comparable to, and perhaps in some ways associated with, both Nazirites and Rechabites, especially in their fanatical dedication to religious warfare. Nazirites abstained from alcohol and let their hair grow long (Judges 13—16).[29] Rechabites, led by Jonadab, supporter of Jehu's coup and subsequent purge, lived in tents, avoided agriculture, and also eschewed intoxicants.[30] These "primitives" remind us that prophecy can consist not just in a commission to speak but in the adoption of a certain style of living that dramatizes the rejection of what passes for reality in the society as a whole.[31]

A prominent feature of prophecy during this period is its association with warfare and religious crusades. At a certain point in the Syrian wars Elisha saw, and caused his disciple to see, the mountain full of horses and fiery chariots (2 Kings 6:17). As he lay dying, the same prophet was visited by King Joash who called out, "My father, my father! The chariots of Israel and its horsemen!" (13:14), recalling the vision seen by Elisha when his master was taken up (2:11–12). An ancient poem describes Yahweh as "charioteer on the clouds" (Ps. 68:5, *rōkēb bā'ᵃrāpôt*, emended text), a title attributed to Baal in the Ugaritic texts. The connotation is that of heavenly warrior, lord of chariotry (cf. Ps. 68:18), consonant with the title "Yahweh of the hosts" (i.e., the heavenly army), which first appeared during the Philistine wars. Since the term *Rechabite* is in some way related to chariots and charioteers, and it may be understood in the sense of "devotee of the chariot god" (cf. the Syrian deity Rakkab-el or Rakkub-el), Rechabites may have been more closely associated with Elijah and Elisha than appears. Jonadab, the Rechabite leader, was known as "father" (Jer. 35:6), and all three were fanatical Yahwists committed to the destruction of the Baal cult.

The *res gestae* of other prophetic figures of the ninth century may have been in circulation, but the only one (apart from Elijah and Elisha)

known to us by name is Micaiah ben-Imlah. His confrontation with the
mantics employed by an unnamed king of Israel (1 Kings 22:1–36) is a
classic example of interprophetic conflict. The rulers of the two kingdoms agreed on a little campaign of conquest, but in such cases it was
considered *de rigueur* to obtain prophetic support. Given the Judean
redaction of the narrative, it is not surprising that it was the king of Judah who suggested inquiring of Yahweh and then expressed dissatisfac-
tion with the enthusiastic approval of the operation by the Samarian
court prophets. Under the direction of Zedekiah, the court prophets put
on an ecstatic performance—the analogy of a pep rally comes to mind—
before the two kings in the plaza by the city gate. Zedekiah himself acted
out the promised victory proleptically by putting on iron horns and ut-
tering an oracle of assurance introduced by the standard formula "thus
says Yahweh." Micaiah also foresaw success in the campaign but went on
to relate two visions. In the first he saw the people leaderless on the hills,
and in the second he was admitted to the heavenly court with Yahweh on
his throne and the hosts around him. At Yahweh's request one of his attendants, called simply "the Spirit," offered to deceive the king of Israel
into making the wrong decision by becoming a lying spirit in the mouth
of his prophets; and so it happened.

This incident is particularly significant for understanding how the
problematic aspects of prophecy were handled at a much later time. The
crucial question was that of resolving conflicting claims to revelation.
How to distinguish between true and false prophetic claims? This test
case juxtaposes two quite different types of prophecy. Theologically, only
the prophet who has been admitted to the divine presence can claim a
hearing. But since this claim is unverifiable other criteria are needed. It
is not enough to speak in the name of Yahweh, using familiar forms of
address, for Zedekiah also did that. It is implied, though not stated, that
visions and rational discourse are more authentic expressions than the
ecstatic behavior and sympathetic magic of the court prophets. Predictions are also important diagnostically, especially when they can be verified or falsified (i.e., proved true or false) shortly after they have been uttered. But there is also the sense that the onus of proof falls on the
prophet who reassures rather than the one whose message contradicts
the expectations of the hearers. We shall see later on how this problem
of discrimination, the Achilles' heel of prophecy, came to a head during
the last days of the monarchy.

The metaphor of fatherhood and sonship current in prophetic
groups lies behind the conferring of a double share of Elijah's spirit on
Elisha (2 Kings 2:9–10) since, according to law, the first son received a
double share of the estate by virtue of primogeniture (Deut. 21:17). Fol-

lowing on his call to discipleship (1 Kings 19:19–21), Elisha was appointed to succeed Elijah as head of the prophetic communities, a position that was authenticated in their presence by miracles (2 Kings 2:13–14, etc.). The call of Elisha was to become a paradigm of charismatic succession, since it appears to lie behind the commissioning of the seventy elders (Numbers 11) and the succession of Joshua to Moses (Num. 27:15–23; Deut. 34:9). It also served as a model for discipleship in early Christianity.[32]

The narrative tradition about Elisha has had a long and complex history, its interaction with the Elijah tradition being particularly problematic. It is possible, for example, that some of the miracles of Elisha have been attributed to Elijah and that the revolutions fomented by Elisha in Samaria and Damascus (2 Kings 8:7–15; 9:1–13) were given firmer legitimation by reference back to the more prestigious figure (1 Kings 19:15–16). Elisha, from Abel-meholah in the Jordan Valley, is associated more explicitly with the ecstatic communities than Elijah. He is, in all respects, a more "primitive" figure, embodying the more destructive forces that could be concentrated in that kind of personality. It was he who, through a prophetic deputy, set in motion the revolution of Jehu with the massacres, unparalleled in Israelite history, that went with it—the same revolution that would later be condemned by Amos and Hosea. Not untypically, he ended his life urging the king to another campaign against Syria and venting his anger at what he considered a less than total dedication to seeing it through (2 Kings 13:14–19).

Apart from Elisha's active involvement in the Syrian wars, the Elisha tradition has concentrated on his role as charismatic wonder-worker. The core of the narrative is a chain of miracles that exhibit the power transferred to him in his calling. Some are works of healing and resuscitation (2 Kings 4:8–37; 5:1–19), one of them posthumous (13:20–21). Others demonstrate control over the forces of nature (2:14, 19–22; 4:38–41; 6:1–7), including the multiplication of food (4:1–7, 42–44). Others again would be classified today as examples of clairvoyance and extrasensory perception (6:8–10, 12, 17). There are, finally, what we might call punitive miracles of the kind encountered in the apocryphal gospels (2:23–25; 6:18). Comparison with miracles attributed to other saints, including the miracles of Jesus, would reveal common structural features of the genre and thus provide clues to its function and intent. But to pursue these suggestions further would take us away from our main line of inquiry.

Elisha died in the early years of the eighth century, during the reign of Joash (ca. 801–786 B.C.E.). Jeroboam II, son of Joash, succeeded him and led Israel to a high point of political success and economic prosperity. Amos, who was most probably born while Elisha was still alive, was to pass judgment on Jeroboam, second-last representative of the dynasty set up with Elisha's backing, and to usher in a decisive new phase in the history of the prophetic movement. At this point, however, we must break off the story to take it up again in the following part.

III

THE PERIOD
OF ASSYRIAN EXPANSION

8. THE INTERNATIONAL SITUATION

P. R. **Ackroyd,** "The Biblical Interpretation of the Reigns of Ahaz and Hezekiah," in W. Boyd Barrick and J. R. Spencer, eds., *In the Shelter of Elyon: Essays on Ancient Palestinian Life and Literature in Honor of G. W. Ahlström*, Sheffield: JSOT Press, 1984, 247–59; R. **Albertz,** *A History of Israelite Religion in the Old Testament Period*, vol. 1, Louisville: Westminster/John Knox, 1994, 156–86; B. **Albrektson,** "Prophecy and Politics in the Old Testament," in H. Biezais, ed., *The Myth of the State*, Stockholm: Almqvist & Wiksell, 1972, 45–56; *ANET*, 282–301 (Assyrian royal annals); 532–41 (Assyrian vassal treaties); B. S. **Childs,** *Isaiah and the Assyrian Crisis*, Naperville, Ill.: Alec R. Allenson, 1967; R. E. **Clements,** *Isaiah and the Deliverance of Jerusalem*, Sheffield: JSOT Press, 1980; M. **Cogan,** *Imperialism and Religion: Assyria, Judah and Israel in the Eighth and Seventh Centuries B.C.E.*, Missoula, Mont.: Scholars Press, 1974; J. A. **Dearman,** *Religion and Culture in Ancient Israel*, Peabody, Mass.: Hendrickson, 1992, 51–99; H. **Donner,** "The Beginning of the Assyrian Period of the History of Israel and Judah," in J. H. Hayes and J. M. Miller, eds., *Israelite and Judaean History*, 415–34; N. K. **Gottwald,** *All the Kingdoms of the Earth*, New York: Harper & Row, 1964, 93–217; S. **Herrmann,** *A History of Israel in Old Testament Times*, Philadelphia: Fortress Press, 1975, 243–62; D. W. **Jamieson-Drake,** *Scribes and Schools in Monarchic Judah: A Socio-anthropological Approach*, Sheffield: Almond Press, 1991; A. **Mazar,** *Archaeology of the Land of the Bible 10,000–586 B.C.E.*, New York & London: Doubleday, 1990, 403–62; W. **McKane,** "Prophet and Institution," *ZAW* 94 (1962): 251–66; J. W. **McKay,** *Religion in Judah under the Assyrians*, Naperville, Ill.: Alec R. Allenson, 1973; J. Maxwell **Miller** and J. H. **Hayes,** *A History of Ancient Israel and Judah*, Philadelphia: Westminster, 1986, 250–415; S. **Parpola** and K. **Watanabe,** *Neo-Assyrian Treaties and Loyalty Oaths*, Helsinki: Helsinki University Press, 1988; H. **Spieckermann,** *Juda unter Assur in der Sargonidenzeit*, Göttingen: Vandenhoeck & Ruprecht, 1982.

During the period covered in the previous chapter, the ninth century B.C.E., the international context of events in the kingdoms of Israel and Judah was, for the most part, restricted to the other states of comparable size in the Syro-Palestinian corridor, the most powerful of which was Damascus. The Assyrians had begun to impinge on the area under Ashurnasirpal II (884–859) and Shalmaneser III (858–824), but their forward movement had been halted by a rare coalition of these Aramean states, including Israel, at the battle of Karkar on the Orontes (853). With the accession of the usurper Tiglath-pileser III to the Assyrian throne in 745, however, a century of sustained imperial expansion by the Assyrians resulted in the subjugation of these western states and even, for a time, the occupation of Egypt. This phase of Assyrian imperial expansion created an entirely new situation for the kingdoms of Israel and Judah, one which was bound to leave its mark on traditional religious beliefs and practices. It signaled the beginning of the great world empires (Assyria, Babylon, Persia, Macedon, Rome) on whose policies the fortunes of the Jewish people were to depend, and whose rise and fall would be depicted in impressive symbolism by the writers of apocalyptic.[1]

The period into which we now enter begins a few decades before the accession of Tiglath-pileser and ends with the death of Ashurbanipal about 627 B.C.E., after which point the Assyrian empire rapidly came to an end. As far as the two kingdoms are concerned, it corresponds to the period from the last years of the dynasty of Jehu in the Kingdom of Samaria to the religious reforms of Josiah (640–609) in Judah. If we speak of it as the age of "classical" prophecy, we must bear in mind the lines of continuity with the past alluded to earlier. So, for example, the first of the oracles against foreign nations in Amos concerns Damascus and its king Hazael (Amos 1:3–5) designated by Elisha (2 Kings 8:7–15), and it condemns Damascus for its barbarous treatment of Gilead, no doubt during the campaigns recorded in 2 Kings 10:32–33.

The conventional distinction between "primitive" and "classical" prophecy can therefore be seriously misleading. The most obvious difference is, of course, at the literary level: we have a book of Amos but no book of Elijah and, correspondingly, we have more emphasis on sayings and less on prophetic biography or hagiography. Presumably this was due in some way to the Assyrian threat, foreseen and soon to be experienced, which gave rise to more concentrated and urgent reflection on the religious condition of the two kingdoms and provided motivation to preserve the comminations and predictions of these inspired individuals, especially when they were in the course of time verified. The compiling of oracular utterances in contemporary Assyria (admittedly of a rather different kind) also may have influenced practice in Israel and Judah.

If Weber was correct in asserting that the primary concern of Israel's prophets was with foreign politics, our first task should be to familiarize ourselves with at least those events and movements in the Near East that impinged more or less directly on the kingdoms of Israel and Judah at that time. Our brief survey begins, then, in the early years of the eighth century B.C.E. and continues down to the end of national independence with the fall of Jerusalem to the Babylonians in 587/586 B.C.E.

After a brief surge forward in the ninth century, the Assyrians experienced a period of decline during which the Syro-Palestinian states were able to pursue their own policies unmolested. The dynasty founded by Jehu in 841 B.C.E., apparently with Assyrian backing, was therefore able to consolidate itself, reaching a high-water mark of political success and economic expansion under Jeroboam II (786–746). In Judah much the same situation prevailed during the long reign of Uzziah (783–742).[2] The assassination of Jeroboam's son and successor Zechariah after less than a year's reign coincided with the accession of Tiglath-pileser and may not have been unconnected with it. The Jehu dynasty therefore, after lasting a century, came to a violent end and was followed in the Northern Kingdom by a period of chaos (745–722) during which five kings ascended the throne, of whom three were assassinated and another, the last, was either executed or deported by the Assyrians.

The accession of Tiglath-pileser III marked the beginning of a century of imperial expansion following what was clearly a deliberate plan of empire building. Assyrian success was built on a highly organized standing army which, unlike the forces put into the field by the smaller powers, did not have to return home at intervals to bring in the crops. The Assyrians are not especially noted for their contribution to literature and the arts. As one scholar has put it, with some exaggeration, they have left behind texts remarkable for their linguistic difficulty and intellectual poverty.[3] But in warfare, and especially siege warfare, they were technologically far in advance of potential opponents. They also appear to have used atrocities against civilian populations and mass deportations as deliberate instruments of policy. Perhaps for the first time in history, Tiglath-pileser also set up an imperial administration comprising provinces governed by Assyrian officials and, especially at the periphery, vassal states bound by treaties some of which are extant (*ANET*, 532–41; Parpola). By these means Assyria managed during the following century to extend its rule from the Caucasus to the Persian Gulf and from the Tigris to the Mediterranean.

The "king of the world," as Tiglath-pileser modestly called himself, began to campaign in North Syria in 738, occupying Hamath and reducing Damascus and Israel to vassalage. Assyrian annals record that the kings of these two states, Rasunnu (Rezin, Isa. 7:1) and Menahem respectively, were obliged to pay tribute (cf. 2 Kings 15:19–20). Four years later Tiglath-pileser campaigned against the Philistine cities, occupied Gaza whose king Hanno fled to Egypt, and reached as far as the Wadi el-'Arish, the traditional boundary with Egypt. During or shortly after this campaign, probably in the summer of 734, Damascus and Israel, the latter now ruled by the usurper Pekah (737–732), tried to force Ahaz of Judah into an anti-Assyrian alliance. When the latter sensibly demurred, the Syria-Israel axis invaded Judah, intending to replace Ahaz with a puppet of their own (2 Kings 16:5; Isa. 7:1–8:15; 17:1–6; Hos. 5:8–14; 8:7–10). Against prophetic advice Ahaz appealed to the Assyrians for help, a fateful move that was to inaugurate a long period of vassalage involving both kingdoms. In the following year Tiglath-pileser annexed Galilee and the upper Transjordan region, carving out of these regions the provinces of Megiddo and Gilead, respectively. After the customary deportations, all that was left was the rump state in and around the city of Samaria. Pekah was assassinated and Hoshea, last king of Israel, came to power as an Assyrian vassal, by which time Damascus had been incorporated into the Assyrian imperial system.

Some time after the accession of Shalmaneser V, Hoshea broke his oath of allegiance by conspiring against Assyria together with one of two rival dynasts in Egypt at that time. The predictable outcome was the siege and capture of Samaria, the deportation of 27,290 of its inhabitants (according to the display inscriptions of Sargon II), and the creation of the Assyrian province of Samerina (722 B.C.E.). Foreigners were moved in, at that time and later (Ezra 4:2, 10; Isa. 7:8), and for all practical purposes, the ten tribes disappeared from history.

The outcome of Ahaz' appeal to Tiglath-pileser was that for more than a century Judah remained both de jure and de facto an Assyrian vassal. This political status would not have left Judean religious life unaffected. Assyrian chronicles and vassal treaties assign pride of place to Ashur, principal deity of the imperial pantheon, in whose name the vast conquests around the Middle East were undertaken. He was "lord of all lands," vassal treaties such as bound Judah to the imperial court were signed and sworn to in his name, and the vassal assumed "the yoke of Ashur." With respect to local cults Assyrian policy was not entirely consistent. Some were dismantled, others, more rarely, restored. Dtr records that after the fall of Samaria the imperial administrators of the city imported an Israelite priest to teach the settlers the traditional law (2 Kings 17:24–28), in much the same way as when the Persian court sent Ezra to teach the "law of the God of heaven" in the Trans-Euphrates satrapy (Ezra 7). There were also occasions when Assyrian cults were imposed, though this does not seem to have been the regular practice. All vassals, however, supported the imperial cult by way of annual tribute.

It must have seemed to many of the survivors in Israel that Yahweh had been defeated by Ashur, or alternatively that the disaster was the result of abandoning the old Canaanite cults, especially that of Asherah, queen of heaven. We hear this alternative account of national disaster being presented years later, after the destruction of Jerusalem (Jer. 44:15–19). At the least, vassalage would have strengthened syncretic tendencies. On the other hand, the frequent attempts at political emancipation were invariably associated with movements of religious repristination and reform.

Shalmaneser V died soon after the fall of Samaria, but his successor Sargon II (722–705) followed the same expansionist policy. Shortly after his accession he had to put down a rebellion in Gaza supported by Egypt, and eight years later it was the turn of Ashdod, another Philistine city. His annals inform us that Judah under Hezekiah (715–687) took part in this revolt, but we are not told what came of it. We also learn that Hezekiah was involved in rebellion together with the Babylonian king Marduk-apla-iddin (Merodach-baladan, 2 Kings 20:12–19), with Elamites and Arabs in a supporting role.

The disputed accession of Sennacherib in 705 was the signal for further unrest throughout the empire. Hezekiah's religious reforms (2 Kings 18:1–4; 2 Chron. 30:14; 31:1), as well as his fortification of the city and securing of its water supply (2 Kings 20:20; 2 Chron. 32:5, 30; Isa. 22:9–11),[4] were no doubt carried out with a view to profiting by this situation. Sennacherib, however, came out on top, and by 701 had reasserted his hold on the Phoenician and Philistine cities, devastated Judah, and invested Jerusalem.

At this point the Assyrian annals (represented by the Oriental Institute Prism) are quite clear: shut up in Jerusalem like a bird in a cage, with the rest of his country ravaged, Hezekiah had to submit and pay heavy tribute. The biblical record, however, seems to have conflated two accounts of what happened. One of these (2 Kings 18:13–16) is in essential agreement with the Assyrian version, while the other (memorialized in Byron's poem about the Assyrian coming down like a wolf on the fold) concludes on an upbeat note with the mysterious annihilation of the besieging army followed soon after with the death of the tyrant (19:35–37). Whatever happened, Judah was not incorporated into the Assyrian empire, though it continued in vassalage to Assyria. The survival of Jerusalem at that crucial juncture must have greatly reinforced the assurance of divine protection and inviolability that finds expression in the psalms of Zion and that was to be so cruelly disconfirmed a little over a century later.

Sennacherib lost his life in a palace revolt, not immediately after the campaign of 701, as the biblical record insinuates (2 Kings 19:37), but some twenty years later. His successor was Esarhaddon (680–669) who not only held on to the strategically vital Syro-Palestinian corridor but succeeded in occupying Egypt in 671. Little is known of Judean affairs between 701 and the accession of Josiah in 640. The annals of Esarhaddon mention Manasseh (Menasii), Hezekiah's son and successor (689–642), as one of a number of loyal western vassals. The biblical historian, on the other hand, has nothing good to say about him. He undid the work of his predecessor, reintroduced "pagan" cults including those of Assyria, and was even held responsible for the deportations and exile Judah was to suffer about half a century after his death (2 Kings 21:1–18). Reading between the lines, however, we may suspect that Manasseh preserved a degree of autonomy for Judah by prudently avoiding open confrontation with the Assyrian superpower. The Chronicler, not generally considered a reliable historical source, reports that Manasseh was deported to Babylon, made his submission, and was duly reinstated (2 Chron. 33:10–13), whereupon he strengthened the defenses of Jerusalem and carried out a reform of the cult (33:14–17). This notice is often interpreted as the Chronicler's way of explaining why Manasseh had such a long reign, in apparent defiance of divine retributive justice, while Josiah, a transparently good king, came to an untimely and violent end. This may be so, but the notice about the fortification of the city does not look like a fabrication, and it is possible that Manasseh did rebel, perhaps in support of Shamash-shum-ukin, brother of Ashurbanipal (669–627), who claimed the throne of Babylon in 652.

Of Manasseh's son Amon, who reigned for two years or less (642–640), we know only that he was assassinated following a palace conspiracy and that his assassins were in their turn eliminated by a group known as "the people of the land" (*'am hā'āreṣ*) who put Amon's eight-year-old son Josiah on the throne (2 Kings 21:19–26). These disturbances were no doubt part of the larger conflict between those in favor of acquiescing in the political status quo and the party at court in favor of rebellion. Assyrian success in repressing revolts in Babylon and in conquering Elam two years later (646) suggests that the prudent course was that of acquiescence. A favorable opportunity for emancipation would present itself only with the death of Ashurbanipal and the rapid decline of Assyrian fortunes some years into the reign of Josiah.

As chance or providence would have it, Assyria began to present an overwhelming threat to the existence of the Israelite and Judean kingdoms at a time (the second half of the eighth century B.C.E.) when the ruling elites of these kingdoms were beginning to consolidate and extend their power. Both the biblical record and archaeological data, scant and often uncertain of interpretation as both are, indicate that this was an epoch of urban development, expanding trade, and increased availability of luxury items. The size and population of Jerusalem expanded significantly at this time, and excavations testify to similar development at such major centers as Lachish (strata IV and III), Megiddo (IVa), Hazor (VIII), and Dan (III, II).

The ivory objects discovered in the royal enclave in Samaria, the new capital founded by Omri in the previous century (1 Kings 16:24), typify the contrast between the wealth and affluence of the ruling class and the subsistence-level existence of most of the population living off the land. Of greater diagnostic value are the sixty-five inscribed potsherds (ostraca), found at the same location, that record shipments of wine and oil from various sites in the kingdom destined for palace personnel including the royal family. We can take this item as typical of the upward redistribution of resources going on at that time. Some of the places of origin are tribal settlements known from biblical lists (e.g., Shechem), while others are probably villages or farms in the vicinity of the capital city.[5] This combination provides one of several indications of the emerging and consolidating state system in the process of bearing down on and assimilating existing traditional social arrangements. These were based on the kinship network (household, clan, tribe), with its own customary mores and rituals, and the (theoretically inalienable) possession of a plot of land by each household. The extension into every sphere of existence of the coercive power of the state—including taxation, military service, the corvée, and the expropriation of patrimonial domain—created a situation of social disorientation, a starker contrast between rich and poor and, in general, increased hardship for the great mass of the population.

The situation of internal disequilibrium was linked in the prophetic interpretation of events with the external—and in the event terminal—threat posed by the Assyrian superpower. Before dealing sequentially with the four great figures from the eighth century (Amos, Hosea, Micah, Isaiah), a few preliminary observations are in order. First: while all four "books" have been subjected to much editorializing and are, in their present form, the product of a much later age, we assume it is possible to identify, with a fair degree of probability, a nucleus of sayings going back to the individual named in the superscription. Second: none of the four is identified as a *nābî'* in the superscriptions to the books, added at a later date, and we have seen good reasons to believe that none of them would have wanted to be known as a *nābî'*. Both the form and content of their sayings oblige us to think of them as of a relatively high social, cultural, and educational level. Weber described them as demagogues and pamphleteers, others have found the designation of poet, orator, or dissident intellectual more appropriate.[6] After working through the texts, the reader can decide for himself or herself which, if any, of these designations is appropriate. Third: although the four in question come from different environments, are very different in other respects, and never refer explicitly to one another, their public pronouncements coalesce in a single but multiform tradition that will have a powerful effect throughout the remaining two centuries of the monarchy and far beyond.

9. AMOS

F. I. **Andersen** and D. N. **Freedman,** *Amos: A New Translation with Introduction and Commentary*, New York and London: Doubleday, 1989; H. M. **Barstad,** *The Religious Polemics of Amos*, Leiden: Brill, 1984; K. **Budde,** "Zur Text und Auslegung des Buches Amos," *JBL* 43 (1924): 46–131; J. F. **Craghan,** "Amos in Recent Literature," *BTB* 2 (1972): 242–61; G. **Farr,** "The Language of Amos, Popular or Cultic?" *VT* 16 (1966): 312–24; F. C. **Fensham,** "Common Trends in Curses of the Near Eastern Treaties and Kudurru-Inscriptions Compared with the Maledictions of Amos and Isaiah," *ZAW* 75 (1963): 155–75; R. **Gordis,** "The Composition and Structure of Amos," *HTR* 33 (1940): 239–51; W. R. **Harper,** *A Critical and Exegetical Commentary on Amos and Hosea*, Edinburgh: T. & T. Clark, 1905; Y. **Hoffman,** "Did Amos regard himself as a *Nābî* ?" *VT* 27 (1977): 209–12; A. S. **Kapelrud,** *Central Ideas in Amos*, Oslo: Oslo University Press, 1961[2]; P. J. **King,** *Amos, Hosea, Micah—An Archaeological Commentary*, Philadelphia: Westminster, 1988; K. **Koch,** *The Prophets*, vol. 1, *The Assyrian Period*, London: SCM Press, 1982, 36–75; J. L. **Mays,** *Amos: A Commentary*, Philadelphia: Westminster, 1969; S. M. **Paul,** *Amos*, Minneapolis: Fortress Press, 1991; M. E. **Polley,** *Amos and the Davidic Empire: A Socio-Historical Approach*, New York: Oxford University Press, 1989; H. **Reventlow,** *Das Amt des Propheten bei Amos*, Göttingen: Vandenhoeck & Ruprecht, 1962; S. N. **Rosenbaum,** *Amos of Israel: A New Interpretation*, Macon, Ga.: Mercer Press, 1990; W. H. **Schmidt,** "Die deuteronomistische Redaktion des Amosbuches," *ZAW* 77 (1965): 168–93; L. A. **Sinclair,** "The Courtroom Motif in the Book of Amos," *JBL* 85 (1966): 351–53; J. A. **Soggin,** *The Prophet Amos*, London: SCM Press, 1987; S. L. **Terrien,** "Amos and Wisdom," in B. W. Anderson and W. Harrelson, eds., *Israel's Prophetic Heritage*, New York: Harper & Row, 1962, 106–14; J. M. **Ward,** *Amos and Isaiah: Prophets of the Word of God*, Nashville: Abingdon Press, 1969; J.D.W. **Watts,** *Vision and Prophecy in Amos*, Leiden: Brill, 1958; B. E. **Willoughby,** "Amos, Book of," *ABD*, 1:203–12; H. W. **Wolff,** *Amos the Prophet: The Man and His Background*, Philadelphia: Fortress Press, 1973; *Joel and Amos*, Philadelphia: Fortress Press, 1977; E. **Würthwein,** "Amos-Studien," *ZAW* 62 (1949–1950): 10–52.

It has become part of the conventional wisdom to date the beginnings of "classical" prophecy to Amos in the middle decades of the eighth century. Periodizations of this kind seem to be inevitable, but they may lead us to overlook lines of continuity with the past and mislead us into accepting without question certain implied generalizations about prophecy. One of these is that paranormal psychic states were characteristic of the "primitives" in contrast to the "classical" prophets, whose authority rested on the spoken word rather than on extraordinary manifestations of the spirit. But this assumption, characteristic of nineteenth-century liberal Protestant scholarship, overlooks evidence for ecstatic experiences among the prophets of the eighth to the sixth century, not to mention the frequency with which verbal communications are described as rooted in extraordinary inner experience; witness the opening lines of several of the prophetic books, for example, "the sayings of Amos . . . which he *saw in vision*" (Amos 1:1; cf. the opening verses in Isaiah, Micah, and Habakkuk).

To repeat a point made earlier: The impression of discontinuity in the mid–eighth century has much to do with the compilation of prophetic sayings in which the biographical element, where present, is minor and incidental. In the Elijah narrative, sayings are introduced with the formula "the word of Yahweh came to him" (e.g., 1 Kings 17:2), which in the prophetic books is transposed into the first person (e.g., Hos. 1:1). When Elijah passes on such sayings to others, he uses the standard incipit "thus says Yahweh" (e.g., 1 Kings 17:14) or the somewhat less common "as Yahweh the God of Israel lives" (e.g., 1 Kings 17:1). Yet his sayings were not collected to make a Book of Elijah. On the other hand, biographical *legenda* occur in the prophetic books (Isaiah 36—39; Jeremiah 52); we also have what appear to be parallel versions of the same event, one in the third, the other in the first person (e.g., Hos. 1:2–2:1; 3:1–5; Jer. 7:1–20; 26:1–6). The account of Amos' confrontation with the priest of Bethel (7:10–17) is the only biographical passage about this individual, one which stands in some relationship to Dtr's account of the reign of Jeroboam II (2 Kings 14:23–29), the prediction of whose violent end by Amos was the occasion for the confrontation in the first place.

The greater importance attached, from the eighth century on, to what the prophet said rather than what the prophet did, may be further explained by the fact that the sayings are now addressed for the most part to the entire people rather than to an individual, generally the ruler. This relatively novel feature may in its turn be explained by the new situation, one of absolute threat, facing the nation on the international scene.[7] Once events had run their course and the two kingdoms had been swallowed up by the great empires, attention would focus once again on the person and work of the prophet, a situation that can be observed with respect to Jeremiah, the Isaian Servant, and the Deuteronomic portrait of Moses.[8]

Amos is third (second in the LXX) in the Book of the Twelve or Dodekapropheton, a collection that was already in existence by the time of Ben Sira in the early second century B.C.E. (Sir. 49:10). The principle according to which the Twelve are arranged appears to be chronological, though critical scholarship has found it necessary to revise it in some respects. The juxtaposition of Joel with Amos may be due to the many themes that the two books have in common: a plague of locusts, drought represented as fire, ritual lamentation, the Day of Yahweh, cosmic disturbances, the promise of miraculous fertility. The motto at the beginning of Amos (1:2) also occurs, in a slightly different form, toward the end of Joel (3:16 [MT 4:16]), and it appears that the books have been linked intentionally by the theme of Yahweh's presence in the temple. These and other indications suggest a Jerusalemite recension of the prophetic books sometime during the period of the Second Temple. And this brings us to the crucial issue of the editorial history of Amos.

The book falls fairly easily into three parts: (1) after the superscription (Amos 1:1) and the motto (1:2) there are eight sayings against various nations, the last being Israel, condemning them for different atrocities and crimes (1:3–2:16); (2) the central part of the book contains a collection of mostly short sayings attributed to Amos (3—6); (3) the last section (7—9) consists of five vision reports (7:1–3, 4–6, 7–9; 8:1–3; 9:1–4) with expansions and interpolations. We shall deal with these three sections briefly in order.

1. The syntax of the first verse, with its double relative clause, suggests that the phrase "who was among the shepherds of Tekoa" has been inserted into a title that read "words of Amos which he saw in vision concerning [or: against] Israel in the days of Uzziah king of Judah and in the days of Jeroboam the son of Joash, king of Israel." This type of introduction, which prefaces other prophetic books (Isaiah, Jeremiah, Hosea, Micah, Zephaniah), is reminiscent of Dtr's practice of synchronizing reigns in the two kingdoms (cf. Hos. 1:1). It has therefore given rise to the suggestion that the Deuteronomic school put out a collection of prophetic books, perhaps restricted to those listed above, which have this characteristic title.[9]

The motto following the superscription (1:2) derives the judgments pronounced by Amos from the Jerusalem temple as their ultimate source—the first of several indications that the sayings underwent a Judean redaction after 722 B.C.E. There follow oracles against a series of neighboring states, which is to say enemies, in a counterclockwise direction from north to east (1:3–2:5).[10] Rooted in age-old ritual practice connected with warfare, this kind of saying could be readily recycled to fit the changing international situation; and, in fact, it is generally agreed that at least the sayings against Tyre, Edom, and Judah are later than Amos. If so, we are left with a series of five (the first of several pentads in the book[11]) ending, in crushing paradox, with Israel itself. The Judah saying (2:4–5) is couched in typical Deuteronomic language, while the other two (Tyre and Edom) could have been added, or updated, anytime during the exilic or early Second Temple period (cf. Joel 3:4–8 [MT 4:4–8]). It also seems likely that the historical reproach against Israel (2:9–12), again reminiscent of well-known Deuteronomic themes, has been inserted between the indictment (2:6–8) and the verdict (2:13–16), which usually come together in Amos.[12]

2. The opening apostrophe of the sayings source (3:1–2), of Deuteronomic character, applies the prophet's message to all Israel, not just the kingdom of Samaria, and therefore reinforces the point made by the insertion of the anti-Judah saying. The poem about prophetic inspiration (3:3–8), often taken as evidence of sapiential influence on Amos,[13] has been annotated with a very telling Deuteronomic gloss at v. 7:

> Surely Yahweh God does nothing
> without revealing his secret
> to his servants the prophets.

The preceding verse,

> Does evil befall a city
> unless Yahweh has done it?

could easily have been read as an indictment of Israel's God for actually willing the destruction of Samaria, and indeed also of Jerusalem. The interpolation, therefore, served as an apologia, in keeping with one of the dominant Dtr themes, that is, that Yahweh cannot be held responsible for the disasters that had overtaken the kingdoms because he had warned the people through "his servants the prophets," definitely a Deuteronomic expression.[14] This is the first of several hints in the book of disquietude at certain aspects of the message of Amos; others will be noted as we read further.

It also seems likely that at least some of the references to Bethel (3:14 and especially the gloss "concerning Bethel" at 5:6) reflect the extension of Josiah's reforms into the territory of the Northern Kingdom absorbed a century earlier into the Assyria empire (see 2 Kings 23:15–20). Dtr never tires of condemning the setting up of the Bethel cult by Jeroboam, and includes in the history a prophetic legend about a man of God who came from Judah during the reign of Jeroboam I to predict the ignominious end of the Bethel sanctuary and cult (1 Kings 13).[15]

The origin of the hymn stanzas or "doxologies" (4:13; 5:8–9; 9:5–6) has long been discussed, with most scholars denying them to Amos. The hymnic motif of divine power on a cosmic scale nevertheless serves to reinforce one of the major themes of the book, that is, that Israel's warrior god, the god of the ecstatic prophets of the earlier period, has now declared war against his own people. The first of the three in particular (4:13), coming directly after the threatening "prepare to meet your God, O Israel," appropriately closes out the preceding five reproaches (4:6–11).[16]

The series of three exhortations to seek Yahweh rather than the provincial sanctuaries or, alternatively, to seek good rather than evil (5:4–5, 6, 14–15), poses a special problem. These sayings appear to substitute a "perhaps" (5:15) for the unconditional "no" with which Amos elsewhere confronts the kingdom of Israel. Furthermore, the exhortatory and homiletic mode is characteristic of the Deuteronomic style more than it is of Amos. The Deuteronomists enjoin the "seeking" (verbal form *drš*) of Yahweh, especially in connection with the cult at the one legitimate sanctuary (Deut. 4:27–31; 12:2–7), often adding the motivational clause "that you may live . . ." (e.g., Deut. 4:1; cf. Amos 5:4, 6, 14). It can therefore be plausibly suggested that here too sayings have been added to the book in response to the new hope for the irredentist northern territories awakened by the religious revival during Josiah's reign.[17]

3. The nucleus of the third part of the book is the series of five vision reports in the first person. The first two (7:1–3, 4–6), threatening locusts and drought, respectively, are constructed in the same way and record the successful intercession of the prophet. The third, the vision of the plumb line (7:7–9),[18] threatens earthquake, the destruction of the high places, and the violent end of the dynasty. At this point the time for intercession has passed, and the last two visions (8:1–3; 9:1–4) make it clear that judgment on Israel is now final and irreversible. Possibly the visions formed a separate collection originating with the prophet himself and transmitted by a disciple. If so, they have been expanded here and there,[19] a particularly important case being the prediction of the violent end of the Jehu dynasty, added after the coup of Shallum in 745 B.C.E., and with the additional intent of correcting Amos' unverified prediction of the violent end of Jeroboam II (7:9; cf. 7:11).

The only biographical narrative in the book (7:10–17) was inserted between the third and the fourth vision. It records how Amaziah, priest-in-charge at Bethel, forwarded to the king an accusation against Amos of conspiracy, based on the prophet's public prediction that Jeroboam would die by the sword and the people would go into exile. Amaziah ordered Amos to leave the state sanctuary and find employment in Judah, a surprisingly mild sentence, perhaps testifying to the fear that such individuals were capable of generating. In replying, Amos denied that he was a *nābî'* or a member of a prophetic conventicle (a *ben-nābî'*), asserted that he had his own occupation that provided the needed support, and informed Amaziah that he had nevertheless been called by Yahweh to carry out an ad hoc commission to prophesy to the people of Israel.[20] Not content with this, he went on to predict an atrocious fate for Amaziah and his family, assuring him that both he and the whole people were destined to end up in exile.

This passage, of different provenance from that of the sayings and the visions, has been inserted at this point because of the immediately preceding reference to the impending fate of the dynasty (7:9). It has the appearance of having been excerpted from a longer narrative, and it may have begun its career as an alternative account, less favorable than 2 Kings 14:23–29, of the reign of Jeroboam.[21] As was pointed out earlier, in the latter passage Dtr goes to the trouble of denying that Yahweh had passed final and complete judgment on Israel (2 Kings 14:27), which leaves one wondering whether he had Amos in mind, especially considering that he passes over Amos's activity in silence. If the tradition represented by Amos 7:10–17 was known to Dtr, it is understandable that he would have favored a different and more benign judgment on this king. Also, not unimportant in view of the Deuteronomic criteria for true prophecy (Deut. 18:21–22), Amos's prediction of the violent end of Jeroboam apparently did not come true. In the context of the book as a whole, the episode functions not only to legitimate Amos's mission but to show what happens when the prophetic message is disregarded.[22]

The fourth and fifth visions have been separated by a supplementary collection of sayings (Amos 8:4–14; 9:7–10) including several variants of utterances in the main corpus.[23] The strong saying putting Israelites on the same level in the eyes of God as Nubians and Philistines (9:7–8) has been quite radically modified by a later editor who, like the historian (2 Kings 14:27), was not prepared to accept the verdict of unconditional and total destruction ("except that I will not utterly destroy the house of Jacob," v. 8b). The eschatological finale, promising the restoration of the Davidic dynasty, the reintegration of dispersed Israel, and a golden age in which ancient curses would be turned into blessings (9:11–15), matches the hopes entertained by different circles during the exilic and early Second Temple period and could not have been part of the book before that time.

We can now present a tentative summary of the editorial history of the book. We are not told that Amos had disciples, but he must have had a support group of some kind in which his sayings and some account of his activities were preserved. The initial impetus to their preservation may have been the great earthquake (1:1) that Amos was perhaps thought to have predicted, to judge by frequent allusions in the book as well as the chronological indication (two years before the earthquake) in the title.[24] Some additions and modifications (e.g., 7:9) may have been made following the coup of Shallum in 745 that brought the Jehu dynasty to an end. The message of Amos would inevitably have been applied to Judah after the fall of the Northern Kingdom in 722 B.C.E., and this too has left some traces in the book (6:1, 5), as also here and there in Isaiah (e.g., the [prophetic] word sent against Jacob/Israel, Isa. 9:8). Somewhat later, Josiah's attempt to reincorporate the territory of the Northern Kingdom, together with his destruction of the Bethel sanctuary, may lie behind those editorial editions that bear the hallmark of the Deuteronomic school that, as noted earlier, brought out a collection of prophetic material as a supplement to the history some time in the sixth century B.C.E. At this stage the title was expanded into the typically Deuteronomic form, the oracle against Judah added (Amos 2:4–5), the diatribe against the cult expanded (and its meaning rather radically modified, 5:25–27), and other additions introduced to make the book serviceable for the needs of that age. Later still, the eschatological finale (9:11–15) transformed the grim harbinger of doom into a messenger of hope and herald of a new age dawning. Judgment and death do not, after all, have the last word.

Since we are concerned with historical and social realities, we must now ask what we can learn from this book, so long in the making, about the person whose name is on the title page. The superscription dates his activity to the reigns of Uzziah in Judah (783–742) and Jeroboam (second of that name) in Israel (786–746). The additional information that his revelation came to him two years before the earthquake would be helpful if we knew when this earthquake took place. Since an earthquake during Uzziah's reign was still being talked about centuries later (Zech. 14:5) it must have been high on the Richter scale, and it may be the same one that left its mark on stratum VI at Hazor, dated by pottery finds to the eighth century, more probably the first half of the century.[25] Allusions to historical events in the sayings, especially the invitation to inspect Calneh and Hamath Rabbah (Amos 6:2), Syrian city-states taken by Tiglath-pileser III in 738, have led some scholars to date his activity after the westward drive of Tiglath-pileser had begun, and therefore after the death of Jeroboam II. But we are then left with the problem that the book, and this passage in particular (Amos 6:1–8), in no way reflect the dangerous and stressful situation in the kingdom of Samaria in and after the year 738. We therefore prefer to date Amos' activity in the north, which may have been of quite brief duration, to about the middle of the eighth century B.C.E.

The expanded form of the superscription describes Amos[26] as one of the sheep breeders (*nōqᵉdîm*) of Tekoa, a settlement about eight miles south of Jerusalem in the Judean wilderness. It does not say that Amos was *from* Tekoa, which in any case is the wrong location for sycamores, so that we may entertain the alternative hypothesis that he began his career as an official of some kind in the kingdom of Samaria.[27] In the account of his arrest at Bethel he himself describes his profession as tending herds and dressing sycamore fig trees (7:14), which, whatever we make of it, does not warrant the image of an uneducated rustic visionary.[28] Any interpretation must allow for the knowledge of international affairs, acquaintance with sacred tradition, and poetic skill attested by the sayings deemed to be authentic. On the other hand Amos was not, on his own admission, and at least at the time of his confrontation with Amaziah, a "professional" *nābî'* (7:14), and the same can be said of Hosea, Micah, and Isaiah, all more or less contemporary with him. No label covering the role and activity of these individuals will be entirely satisfactory, but perhaps the designation, suggested earlier, of "dissident intellectual" will not be entirely inappropriate.

The biographical memoir (7:10–17) records Amos' arrest in the state sanctuary at Bethel on a charge of sedition. If Jeroboam's expansionist policy involved him in warfare with Judah, as was the case during the previous reign (2 Kings 14:11–15), it would have been natural to interpret the activity of Amos, whatever his origin, as an attempt by the agent of a hostile power to undermine morale.[29] The command to "prophesy to my people Israel" (Amos 7:15) probably came to him accompanied by the visions recorded in the third part of the book, though we don't know whether the five visions were thought to have been spread over a period of time or as occurring in rapid succession, as with Zechariah in the late sixth century (Zech. 1:7–6:15). The first two (7:1–3, 4–6) threaten disasters that were averted by prophetic intercession. The third, the vision of the plumb line (?) (7:7–9), appears to predict an earthquake, while in the last two Amos could only look on helplessly as the panorama of destruction by earthquake and military action, the piles of corpses and the deadly harvesting, unfolded before his eyes. The visions of Amos, as described here, successfully convey an impression of one who has seen it happen; one who, as has been said, walks among people condemned to death who do not know it.

While the original nucleus of the sayings reveals a remarkable variety of forms, a constant structural feature, already apparent in the sayings against foreign nations, is the sequence indictment-verdict, the latter element generally introduced by the particles "therefore" (*lākēn*) or "behold" (*hinnēh*).[30] Though exact parallels are lacking, there are grounds for believing that this indictment-verdict pattern is taken over from the language of international relations, especially those between imperial overlord and vassal. The different forms taken by the verdict correspond quite closely to curses incorporated into treaties, with special reference to the threat of exile in Assyrian vassal treaties (*ANET*, 532–41; Parpola and Watanabe).[31] The theme of calamitous military defeat, occupation by a foreign power, and eventual exile is taken up in the traditional language of the holy war, with the difference that Yahweh is now warring against his own people (see especially Amos 4:12). In keeping with this reversal, the traditional theme of the Day of Yahweh is turned upside down: It will not bring salvation but destruction, not light but darkness.[32]

One of the most remarkable features of Amos's diatribe is this systematic reversal of the traditional symbols and images that sustained the common life of the state and came to expression in the national cult. It is apparent from the beginning of the book with the inclusion of Israel among the nations falling under the curse, a device that not only distorts the sense of a traditional oracle of salvation but, in effect, turns the rest of the book into a condemnation of Israel as one nation among many. The point is made clearly near the end:

> "Are you not like the Ethiopians to me,
>   O people of Israel?" says Yahweh.
> "Did I not bring up Israel from the land of Egypt,
>   and the Philistines from Caphtor and the Syrians from Kir?
> Behold, the eyes of Yahweh God are upon the sinful kingdom,
>   and I will destroy it from the surface of the ground."
>
>   (9:7–8a)

Amos applied the same reversal of expectations to the cult, especially the great autumn festival of the ingathering, a joyful occasion, with the prospect of disaster taking the place of salvation and mourning that of joy.[33] One of the more remarkable aspects of the book is the presentation of worship as the expression of a radically sinful way of life (Amos 4:4–5). The entire apparatus of festivals, sacrifice, religious music, and tithing is rejected as hateful to Yahweh (5:21–24), a rejection repeated often in prophetic books (e.g., Hos. 6:6; 8:13; Isa. 1:10–17; Jer. 6:20). Much of the critical discussion of these passages has been clouded by denominational assumptions about what are thought to be appropriate or inappropriate forms of *Christian* worship. The idea of anyone in eighth century B.C.E. Israel rejecting worship as such in favor of a purely spiritual and ethical religion is, however, quite implausible. Rather, the point seems to be that worship was (as it still is) a very powerful way of legitimating the current political and social status quo. Quite simply, Amos was not taken in by the religiosity of his contemporaries.

A further and more specific point is that state cults were wealthy and complex operations, owning land, employing slaves, and supported by contributions, not all voluntary, from the population at large. Cultic personnel were, in addition, tax exempt,[34] and the sacrificial system must have represented a significant drain on commodities and livestock; all of which will help to explain the frequent denunciations of priests and the sacrificial cult in the prophetic literature.

Any attempt to elaborate a prophetic ethic will have to start with the indictments on the basis of which the prophet passed judgment on and predicted disaster for contemporary society.[35] Since the basic situation that Amos is addressing is the encroachment of the state system on a traditional way of life, it is understandable that his animus is directed in the first place against the ruling elite in Samaria, the capital (3:15; 4:1–3; 6:1–7). The drive toward centralization, the need to subsidize a royal court and an elaborate cult, heavy taxation ("exactions of wheat," 5:11), frequent confiscation of patrimonial domain following on insolvency, military service, and forced labor were the major factors undermining the old order and leading to a kind of rent capitalism. The great expansion of trade, especially with the Phoenician cities, and the wealth confiscated during successful military campaigns brought about a new prosperity that, however, did not trickle down to the lower social levels. In this situation Amos, like Hesiod a little over half a century later, took up the cause of the dispossessed and marginalized, and did so in the name of traditional values.

For the eighth century prophets the sphere of morality is the social and political domain, and therefore includes what for us falls under international law, social justice, and civil rights. Amos is much less concerned than Hosea with forms of worship and much more concerned to excoriate what he takes to be an oppressive and exploitative sociopolitical set up. In doing so he itemizes: selling into slavery for trivial debts (2:6; 8:6), excessive fines (2:8), falsifying weights and measures (8:5), dishonest trade practices (8:6), corrupting the legal process (2:7; 5:10, 12), and so on. These accusations are not random nor are they based simply on his own ethical perceptions. In most cases his indictments draw on a traditional, consensual ethic that finds partial expression in Israel's aphoristic and instructional literature and in formulations of apodictic and casuistic law (especially the so-called Covenant Code in

Ex. 20:23–23:19). One example will suffice. The refusal to return a pawned cloak to a poor man by evening (Amos 2:8) violates a stipulation of law in the above-mentioned code designed to protect the disadvantaged:

> If ever you take your neighbor's garment in pledge, you shall restore it to him before the sun goes down; for that is his only covering, it is his mantle for his body; in what else shall he sleep? And if he cries to me, I will hear, for I am compassionate. (Ex. 22:26–27)

What appears to be a parallel to this situation came to light with the discovery of the Yavneh-Yam ostracon (from Meṣad Ḥashavyahu south of Tel Aviv), from about a century after Amos, in which a farm laborer petitions the local governor for the return of his cloak, confiscated probably for failure to repay a loan.[36] Neither Amos nor the anonymous petitioner refers to the stipulation of law quoted above, so it is possible that all three draw on a traditional, humanitarian community practice, one facet of a consensual ethic in danger of disappearing under pressure from the coercive power of the state.

A further and final point: By linking indictment and verdict as cause and effect, and by affirming that the verdict is to be carried out by means of natural events (locusts, drought, earthquake), but even more through political events, and specifically the Assyrian campaigns in the west,[37] Amos laid the basis for a certain understanding of divine action in history that would be immensely influential but also very problematic. His is only one prophetic voice, and some of the limitations of his vision were already apparent to those who preserved and transmitted his words. It is arguable, nonetheless, that his career marks a major turning point in the religious history of Israel, indeed of the ancient world in general.

10. HOSEA

P. R. **Ackroyd,** "Hosea and Jacob," *VT* 13 (1963): 245–59; F. I. **Andersen** and D. N. **Freedman,** *Hosea: A New Translation with Introduction and Commentary,* Garden City: Doubleday & Co., 1980; E. **Baumann,** "'Wissen um Gott' bei Hosea als Urform von Theologie?" *EvTh* 15 (1955): 416–25; M. J. **Buss,** *The Prophetic Word of Hosea,* Berlin: Walter de Gruyter, 1969; J. F. **Craghan,** "The Book of Hosea: A Survey of Recent Literature," *BTB* 1 (1971): 81–100, 145–70; G. I. **Davies,** *Hosea,* Sheffield: JSOT Press, 1993; G. I. **Emmerson,** *Hosea: An Israelite Prophet in Judean Perspective,* Sheffield: JSOT Press, 1984; G. **Fohrer,** *Die symbolischen Handlungen der Propheten,* Zurich: Zwingli Verlag, 1968²; A. **Gelston,** "Kingship in the Book of Hosea," *OTS* 19 (1974): 71–85; W. R. **Harper,** *A Critical and Exegetical Commentary on Amos and Hosea,* Edinburgh: T. & T. Clark, 1905; E. **Jacob,** "L'Héritage cananéen dans le livre du prophète Osée," *RHPR* 43 (1963): 250–59; A. W. **Jenks,**

The Elohist and North Israelite Traditions, Missoula, Mont.: Scholars Press, 1977, especially 112–17; P. J. **King,** *Amos, Hosea, Micah—An Archaeological Commentary,* Philadelphia: Westminster Press, 1988; K. **Koch,** *The Prophets,* vol. 1, *The Assyrian Period,* 76–93; M. **Köckert,** "Prophetie und Geschichte im Hoseabuch," *ZTK* 85 (1987): 3–30; N. P. **Lemche,** "The God of Hosea," in E. Ulrich et al., eds., *Priests, Prophets and Scribes,* Sheffield: JSOT Press, 1992, 241–57; H. G. **May,** "The Fertility Cult in Hosea," *AJSL* 48 (1932): 73–98; J. L. **Mays,** *Hosea: A Commentary,* Philadelphia: Westminster, 1969; H. S. **Nyberg,** *Studien zum Hoseabuch,* Uppsala: Almqvist & Wiksell, 1935; H. H. **Rowley,** "The Marriage of Hosea," *BJRL* 39 (1956): 200–23 (= *Men of God,* London: Thomas Nelson & Sons, 1963, 66–97); W. **Rudolph,** *Hosea,* Gütersloh: Gütersloher Verlagshaus Gerd Mohn, 1966; M. **Scott,** *The Message of Hosea,* London: S.P.C.K., 1921; C. L. **Seow,** "Hosea, Book of," *ABD* 3:291–97; J. A. **Soggin,** "Hosea und die Aussenpolitik Israels," in J. A. Emerton, ed., *Prophecy,* 131–36; J. M. **Ward,** *Hosea: A Theological Commentary,* New York: Harper & Row, 1966; "The Message of the Prophet Hosea," *Int* 23 (1969): 387–407; H. W. **Wolff,** " 'Wissen um Gott' bei Hosea als Urform der Theologie," *EvTh* 12 (1952–53): 533–54; "Hoseas geistige Heimat," *TLZ* 91 (1956): 83–94; *Hosea,* Philadelphia: Fortress Press, 1974; T. **Worden,** "The Literary Influence of the Ugaritic Fertility Myth on the Old Testament," *VT* 3 (1953): 273–97.

The title of Hosea is similar to that of Amos, naming Jeroboam (second of that name) as ruler of Samaria but adding the three Judean kings who followed Uzziah, namely, Jotham, Ahaz, and Hezekiah (Hos. 1:1). This notice, possibly of Deuteronomic origin, is not very helpful, however, since Jeroboam's reign ended in 746 and Hezekiah came to the throne in 715, therefore *after* the fall of Samaria in 722.[38] It is generally assumed, nevertheless, that the prophet's career spanned a period of more than thirty years, but it came to an end before 722. This conclusion would be consistent with the absence of allusion to the fall of Samaria in the book, though a passage toward the end implies that the monarchy has come to an end (13:9–11), presumably with reference to the fate of Hoshea last ruler of the Northern Kingdom and the prophet's namesake. We take it, then, that Hosea was a contemporary of Amos but that his prophetic activity lasted longer.

The historical allusions in the book support, or at least are not inconsistent with, a career covering the last two decades of the kingdom of Samaria. The early chapters (Hosea 1—3) presuppose a period of political stability, and the condemnation of the Jehu dynasty (the reference to Jezreel in 1:4–5) would most naturally be understood as preceding the coup of Shallum in 745 B.C.E. The frequent denunciations of the monarchy and of those who "devour their rulers" (7:7) in the rest of the book fit the last quarter century of the Northern Kingdom during which four out of six kings were assassinated. The allusion to Ephraim's going to

Assyria (5:13) may refer to the submission of Menahem (2 Kings 15:19–20), or possibly that of Hoshea (2 Kings 17:3), and there is also a reference to overtures in the direction of Egypt (Hos. 7:11; cf. 9:3; 11:5; 12:1 [MT 12:2]), a standard response to danger from the opposite direction. It seems likely that the long passage 5:8–6:6 reflects the fateful events of 734–733 B.C.E., the so-called Syro-Ephraimite war, when Israel and Damascus attempted to force Judah into an anti-Assyrian coalition. The result was that Ahaz of Judah called in the Assyrians, which led to the extension of Tiglath-pileser's empire into Damascus and the northern and eastern regions of the kingdom of Samaria.[39] The last of such historical or history-like references is to the deposition of Hoshea and the end of the monarchy (13:9–11) two or three years before the fall of Samaria, followed by the incorporation of the entire kingdom into the Assyrian empire. What happened to Hosea thereafter we have no way of knowing.

That Hosea stands in a prophetic tradition of opposition to monarchy in the Northern Kingdom, a tradition represented by Ahijah of Shiloh, Elijah, and others mentioned earlier, will be obvious at once. His description of the prophets as the instruments by which the divine decree of judgment is carried out (Hos. 6:5) may be taken to refer to these predecessors; and since it follows a passage referring to the disastrous effects of the Syro-Ephraimite war (cf. 2 Kings 16–17; Isaiah 7) it also could include Amos whose predictions of disaster were proving only too correct.[40] Elsewhere Hosea quotes an opinion, no doubt widely shared, that "the *nābî* is a fool, the man of the spirit (*'îš harûah*) is mad" (Hos. 9:7), and goes on to state that, nevertheless, the prophet is the watchman (*ṣōpeh*) of Ephraim (9:8).[41] Here too Hosea places himself within a tradition reaching back into the past:

> I spoke to the prophets;
>   it was I who multiplied visions,
>   and through the prophets give parables.
>   (Hos. 12:10 [MT 12:11])[42]

Recent attempts to describe that tradition more precisely have focused on the thesis of Hans Walter Wolff that Hosea was associated with Levites in the Northern Kingdom who not only formed part of Hosea's support group but took a leading role in transmitting his sayings.[43] Wolff claimed that this association provides the best explanation of several features of the book that have long been acknowledged: Hosea's concern for the cult and the sacred traditions of the old tribal federation, his opposition to the state priesthood (Hos. 4:4–10), his identification of Moses the Levite as prophet (12:13 [MT 12:14]) and fountainhead of "amphictyonic" prophecy, and the close linguistic and thematic links between his reported sayings and Deuteronomy. Wolff does not say that Hosea himself was a Levite but, given his arguments, it is difficult to see how that possibility could be excluded.

While it has the advantage of highlighting several dominant themes in Hosea, the hypothesis is weakened by the obscurity shrouding the early history of the priesthood in Israel. Certain underlying assumptions about early Israel in general, and its putative amphictyonic organization in particular, also call for revision. However, Dtr blames Jeroboam for appointing some priests to the state sanctuary of Bethel (and presumably also to Dan) who were not of Levitical descent (1 Kings 12:31), and it is possible that the Levitical clergy excluded from employment joined the ranks of the opposition, as Wolff suggests, or emigrated to Judah, as 2 Chron. 11:14 states. Hosea's opposition to the state cults could, therefore, give some plausibility to the hypothesis, though Levites are never mentioned in Hosea and those features of the book to which Wolff alludes do not absolutely require this explanation.[44]

Like Amos, Hosea contains both biographical and autobiographical passages and ends with the prospect of eventual well-being. The biographical passage with which the book opens (1:2–2:1 [MT 1:2–2:3]) has its own title, "the beginning of Yahweh's speaking with Hosea," which suggests a rather lengthy prophetic activity. The passage has been expanded by a statement exempting Judah from the same fate as Israel (1:7) and a final note promising reunification of north and south under a Davidic ruler (1:10–2:1 [MT 2:1–3]). The brief autobiographical passage dealing with the treatment of an unfaithful wife (3:1–5) has also been expanded, at least by the addition of the phrase "and David their king" (v. 5), more likely by the addition of the entire passage dealing with political reunion under a Davidic ruler (vv. 4–5). Like certain editorial expansions in Amos and Isaiah, these retouchings probably reflect the extension of Josiah's activity into the northern territories in the last decades of the Assyrian empire. Judean editing is apparent also at several points later in the book (4:15; 5:5; 6:11; 8:14).

The first three chapters comprise a distinct unit with its own logic. The problems it creates for the reader are well known: Is it a real account of Hosea's marital vicissitudes or purely fictional? In either case, Were two women involved or one only? If one, was this "wife of whoredom" (NRSV; *'ēšet z^enûnîm*) sexually promiscuous before Hosea had relations with her or did she become so afterward? If she was not a woman of easy morals whom Hosea was told to "make respectable," was she perhaps, or did she subsequently become, a cult prostitute? Or finally, since one cannot go on indefinitely, was she just one of the many Israelite women who, following an alleged local custom, played the role of the hierodule once only before marriage to ensure fertility?[45]

One plausible solution to one of these issues is that the first-person narrative in chapter 3 is an alternative version of the biographical passage in chapter 1, but that it has been subsequently reinterpreted as a sequel to it by the simple expedient of adding the adverb "again": "Go *again,* love a woman . . ." (3:1).[46] The effect of this rereading of the text is to bring the prophet's marital vicissitudes, real or fictional, more into line with a historical perspective on Yahweh's dealings with Israel, which include the possibility of a reestablished relationship, a possibility that Hosea leaves open.

If this reading of the two passages is correct, the allusion to the "children of Israel" (*bᵉnē yiśrāʾēl,* Hos. 3:1) has probably suggested the extension of the marital metaphor in the first chapter to include the three named offspring of Hosea's union with Gomer daughter of Diblaim.[47] These children are given names of progressively sinister connotation. Jezreel, punningly close to Israel, refers back to the bloody coup of Jehu in the city of that name (2 Kings 9—10) and forward to the extermination of the dynasty (2 Kings 15:10). The name of the second, a daughter Lo-Ruhama (Not-Pitied), meant that the time for mercy and forgiveness, and therefore for prophetic intercession, had run out. We are reminded of the point between the second and third vision of Amos when the intercessory voice falls silent:

> I will no longer pass by them.
> (Amos 7:8)

> I will no longer have pity on the house of Israel.
> (Hos. 1:6)

The third child's name, Lo Ammi (Not-My-People), marks the end of the special relationship established, as the tradition tells it, long ago in the wilderness: "You are not my people, and I am not your I AM" (Hos. 1:9; cf. Ex. 3:14).[48] Here, too, we are reminded of the verdict pronounced by Amos after the fifth and last vision that negates the special relationship based not on the theophany of the burning thornbush, as in Hosea, but on the exodus (Amos 9:7–8).

The central panel of this triptych (2: 2–23 [MT 2:4–25]), consisting in a legal indictment of the land of Israel (*ʾereṣ,* a feminine noun) represented as an unfaithful wife, is intended as a key to decrypt the marriage symbolism. The forensic metaphor (sons bringing legal action against their mother) was suggested by the political situation of that time when, as the book attests at several points, confederate and vassal treaties were being made and unmade and oaths sworn and foresworn (cf. 6:7; 8:1; 10:4; 12:2 [MT 12:3]). The sustained homiletic style of this and subsequent discourses, quite different from the Amos sayings, has contributed notably to the high cadence of the Deuteronomic school, which also developed Hosea's theme of the broken covenant.[49] At the end of this section there are two editorial expansions, both introduced by the phrase "in that day" (*bayyôm hahû'*), which promise the end of idolatry, freedom from the ravages of wild beasts, fertility, and a secure and permanent relationship between Israel and its God (Hos. 2:16–20, 21–23 [MT 2:18–22, 23–25]). The same reversal from curse to blessing has been noted in Amos and will be seen to be a regular feature of preexilic prophetic books.

From the remainder of the book (Hosea 4—14) it is clear that the process of transmission followed different lines from that of Amos, perhaps because of the much longer time span of Hosea's activity. These chapters appear to fall into two sections (Hos. 4:1–12:1 [MT 12:2]; 12:2–14:9), both presented as legal indictments of an unfaithful people. The individual units are not always easy to distinguish because there are few lead-in formulae of the kind frequently encountered in Amos. They appear to be transcriptions or reconstructions of discourses delivered on different occasions over a period of at least two decades. We have the distinct impression that the editors aimed at a rough chronological order, ending with the deposition of Hoshea and the prospect of military occupation (Hos. 13:9–16 [MT 13:9–14:1]). In addition, some of the discourses are organized around dominant metaphors such as harlotry (4:11–19) or a heated oven (7:4, 7).

The style is remarkably homogeneous with relatively few indications of editorial reworking. Apart from the passage referring to the Syro-Ephraimite war (Hos. 5:8–6:6) allusions to Judah are cautionary, if not condemnatory (4:15; 5:5; 6:11; 8:14); understandably so if Judah was to learn from the fate of its northern neighbor. These editorial adjustments may be from disciples of Hosea who went south after the fall of Samaria. It is even possible that they came to the attention of Hezekiah, who was inclined to listen to prophets (2 Kings 19:2–7, 20–34; 20:1–19) and whose reforms aimed at preventing Judah from suffering the same fate as Israel. The Judean strand in the book would, at any rate, help to explain the connections that many scholars claim to detect between Hosea and the Deuteronomic reform movement in the kingdom of Judah.[50]

Needless to say, there is no consensus on how the books of Amos and Hosea reached the form in which we have them, but a conservative reconstruction of the process would run somewhat as follows. The first small collections of sayings were put together during the careers of the prophets or shortly thereafter. Oral composition and transmission played a limited role at this stage, and the sayings may have been transcribed in some cases shortly after they were delivered. The generally bad state of the text of Hosea may, in fact, be due in part to the difficulty of transcribing relatively long discourses delivered over several decades and probably not under ideal conditions. Indictments pronounced in the kingdom of Samaria would inevitably have been applied, with the necessary modifications, to Judah after the disaster of 722 B.C.E., perhaps even earlier. We assume that this process was furthered by Hezekiah who carried out extensive reforms (2 Kings 18:4, 22; 2 Chron. 29:3–31:21) and sponsored considerable literary activity (Prov. 25:1). The short-lived hope of reunification inspired by Josiah's activity, about a century later (2 Kings 23:15–20), marked a further and particularly important stage in the editorial history of eighth century prophecy. The publication of a Deuteronom(ist)ic edition during or shortly after the Babylonian exile did not prevent further expansions and glosses during the period of the Second Temple, though these are much less in evidence in Amos and Hosea than in Isaiah and other prophetic collections of originally Judean origin. We see that during this entire period there were those who felt authorized not only to reinterpret prophetic sayings in the light of new situations but to incorporate their commentary in the text itself.

The symbolic marriage narrative in the first three chapters leads into the question of Hosea's appropriation of historical traditions as they circulated at that time. As we read on in the book, it becomes apparent that for Hosea the first encounter between Yahweh and his people took place in the wilderness (Hos. 9:10a; also 2:14 [MT 2:16]; 11:3–4; 12:9 [MT 12:10]; 13:5–6) and that, after entry into the land, Israel abandoned Yahweh for another partner (Hos. 9:10b). For the symbolism to work, therefore, it would be necessary for Hosea to marry a woman who only subsequently "went wrong" rather than one who was transgressive before the marriage. The allegory of the unfaithful spouse in Ezekiel 16, certainly based on Hosea 1—3, confirms this reading, since it presents Yahweh's betrothal to a young girl who only later became a prostitute. It would also be consonant with denunciations of the Baal cult in the book to suppose that the prostitution in question was of the cultic variety (Hos. 4:12–14). Whatever the state of mind of the patrons of these "holy ones" (*qᵉdēšôt*, 4:14), on which it is hardly necessary to speculate, the practice was intended to reenact the marriage between the fertility deity and his consort and thus ensure the fertility of the fields, the cattle, and the womenfolk.[51] The woman, therefore, whether she existed only as a literary figure or as the prophet's partner, corresponds to Israel in the phase of its existence that began with the settlement on the land.

Following the lead of Elijah, the ecstatic conventicles, Rechabites, and other groups that rejected any form of cultural accommodation, Hosea presented the religious situation in terms that are starkly contrasted—Baal against Yahweh—and also greatly (and perhaps inevitably) oversimplified. The depiction of pagan priests (*k*ᵉ*mārîm*, Hos. 10:5) servicing the state sanctuary, worshipers kissing calves (13:2), and so on, is clearly tendentious, and must be balanced by a close reading of other biblical and nonbiblical (especially Ugaritic) texts together with the archaeological record.[52] These suggest a somewhat more nuanced conclusion. The dominant religion, not only in Israel but in Judah, and not only then but throughout almost all of history, was a syncretic blend of the Yahweh cult with other cults of the region, especially those directed to the Canaanite pantheon (especially El, Asherah, Baal, Anath). The basic motivation behind this option was not a characteristically Canaanite addiction to sexual excess—in keeping with a routine way of discrediting the opposition—but the desire to survive and perhaps even flourish in the kind of subsistence agrarian economy characteristic of the entire Mediterranean rim.

Having made this point, we would have to add that for Hosea false worship, "turning to other gods" (Hos. 3:1), is at the root of both moral failure and social disintegration. False worship is, however, conceivable only when a community abandons its traditions, that for Hosea happened when Israel settled in the land (9:10) and passed over to monarchy (8:4; 9:15). Hence any prospect of reformation depended on recovering and reappropriating the traditions that conferred on Israel its specific character and identity.[53]

In Hosea, for the first time, we find an outline of the Hexateuchal narrative, if in fragmentary and rudimentary form and with many gaps. He is familiar with one version of the fate of the twin cities by the Dead Sea (Hos. 11:8; cf. Gen. 19:24–29; Deut. 29:23) and the Jacob story (Hos. 12:3–4,12 [MT 12:4–5,13]), though not quite as it is presented in Genesis 25—35.[54] The liberation from Egypt under prophetic leadership (Hos. 2:15 [MT 2:17]; 11:1; 12:13 [MT 12:14]) is for him of unique significance because it places the God of Israel in the context of history rather than nature (cf. "your God from the land of Egypt," 12:9 [MT 12:10]; 13:4). In spite of the "murmurings" (13:5–6), the wilderness period was the time of Israel's innocence and intimacy with its God (2:14 [MT 2:16]; 9:10; 11:3–4; 12:9 [MT 12:10]), and it was there that Yahweh revealed himself as EHYEH, the "I AM" of the burning thornbush, the one who is with his people (1:9). Appeal to these normative events and disclosures implied for Hosea a drastic relativizing of contemporary sociopolitical and religious structures. In refusing to acquiesce in them or to take them seriously, Hosea demonstrated the revolutionary strength of the prophetic movement of the eighth century B.C.E. In his inability to propose an alternative, other than condemnation or the utopian and unrealistic option of a return to some kind of nomadic existence, he demonstrated one of the fundamental weaknesses of Israelite prophecy in general. In the Deuteronomic school, in some but by no means all respects the heir of Hosea, we find something of the same utopianism, but blended with a more solid sense of the realities of life in society.

Hosea concentrates so much on false worship ("harlotry," "whoredom," and the like) that, unlike Amos, he has relatively little to say about social justice and the civil rights of the disadvantaged. If justice and righteousness (*mišpāṭ, ṣᵉdāqâ*) are key words for Amos (5:24), Hosea prefers to speak of fidelity (*ḥesed*) and the knowledge of God (*daʿat ᵉlohîm*), the latter term implying fidelity to the traditions with all that that implied, including what we might call an emerging consensual ethic. In the indictment with which the second section of the book begins there is what appears to be an earlier form of the Decalogue—swearing, lying, murder, stealing, adultery, with the perhaps significant omission of the sabbath precept (Hos. 4:2; cf. Jer. 7:9). This does not necessarily imply that the Decalogue was already there to be quoted, since it is equally possible, even likely, that the prophets contributed to its mature formulation in Deuteronomy (5:6–21).

The eighth century prophets are also thought to have contributed to the language of covenant-making and covenant-breaking as we find it in the Deuteronomic corpus. Covenant language is not, however, used in connection with Hosea's marriage, the covenant with the animal world (2:18) is ecologically interesting but of a quite different kind, and the reference to breaking the covenant and trangressing the law (8:1) may be one of the few examples in the book of Deuteronomic editing. In fact, covenant language in the eighth century prophets is more conspicuous by its absence than by its presence. In view of the frequent making and breaking of treaties at that time (cf. Hos. 10:4 and 12:1 [MT 12:2]), and the parallels with Assyrian vassal treaties noted earlier, it would nevertheless not be surprising if the language of international relations began to find its place in prophetic teaching during that crucial passage of history. And even if marriage was not yet being expressed in covenantal terms, the metaphor of sexual union in the opening chapters of the book represented a rare breakthrough in the use of language, opening up new and rich veins of meaning.

11. MICAH

M. **Collin,** "Recherches sur l'histoire textuelle du prophète Michée," *VT* 21 (1971): 281–97; O. **Eissfeldt,** *The Old Testament: An Introduction,* 406–13; H. **Gunkel,** "The Close of Micah: A Prophetic Liturgy," in *What Remains of the Old Testament,* London and New York: Griffin, 1928, 115–49; D. G. **Hagstrom,** *The Coherence of the Book of Micah: A Literary Analysis,* Atlanta: Scholars Press, 1988; D. R. **Hillers,** *Micah,* Philadelphia: Fortress Press, 1984; *ABD,* 4:806–10; K. **Jeppesen,** "New Aspects of Micah Research," *JSOT* 8 (1978): 3–32; J. **Jeremias,** "Die Bedeutung der Gerichtsworte Michas in der Exilzeit," *ZAW* 83 (1971): 330–53; K. **Koch,** *The Prophets,* vol. 1, *The Assyrian Period,* 94–104; J. L. **Mays,** *Micah: A Commentary,* Philadelphia: Westminster Press, 1976; G. B. **Pixley,** "Micah—A Revolutionary," in D. Jobling et al., eds., *The Bible and the Politics of Exegesis: Essays in Honor of Norman K. Gottwald on His Sixty-fifth Birthday,* Cleveland: Pilgrim Press, 1991, 53–60; B. **Renaud,** *La Formation du Livre de Michée,* Paris: J. Gabalda, 1977; W. **Rudolph,** *Micha-Nahum-Habakkuk-Zephanja,* Gütersloh: Gütersloher Verlagshaus Gerd Mohn, 1975; C. S. **Shaw,** *The Speeches of Micah: A Rhetorical-Historical Analysis,* Sheffield: JSOT Press, 1993; J. M. **Ward,** "Micah," *IDBS,* 592–93; J. T. **Willis,** "The Structure of the Book of Micah," *SEÅ* 34 (1969): 5–42; H. W. **Wolff,** "Wie verstand Micha von Moreschet sein prophetisches Amt?" *SVT* 29 (1978): 403–17; *Micah: A Commentary,* Minneapolis: Augsburg Press, 1990; A. S. van der **Woude,** "Micah in Dispute with the Pseudo-prophets," *VT* 19 (1969): 244–60; "Deutero-Micha: ein Prophet aus Nord-Israel?" *NTT* 25 (1971): 365–78.

The book of Micah presents the reader with a degree of difficulty disproportionate to its length, beginning with a text as badly preserved as that of Hosea. Some help is at hand in the ancient versions and fragments of text and commentary from the Judean desert (1QpMi; 4QpMi; Muraba'at 88), but much remains obscure, especially the poem listing Judean towns in 1:10–16.

The Deuteronomic title to Micah puts him within much the same time span as Isaiah, that is, the second half of the eighth century B.C.E. At the end of the following century it was known that he predicted the destruction of Jerusalem under Hezekiah (Jer. 26:18), which again makes him a contemporary of Isaiah. The book itself offers few clues to the date of his activity. The title states that he spoke against Samaria (Micah 1:1), and his prediction of the destruction of that city (1:5–7) would very likely be earlier than 722 B.C.E. The aforementioned poem listing towns in the Shephelah (1:10–16) assumes either the reality or the prospect of military conquest. It is generally taken to refer to Sennacherib's campaign in 701, during which Isaiah played a leading role in Jerusalem, but this is not the only possibility. One might consider as an alternative Sargon II's campaign against the Philistine cities in 712/711 during which Isaiah walked naked, or nearly naked, through Jerusalem (Isa. 20:1–6; cf. Micah 1:8 "for this I will lament and wail; I will go stripped and naked"). Gath, a Philistine town and the first in Micah's list, about six miles as the crow flies from Moresheth-gath, was occupied by the Assyrians during the campaign (*ANET*, 286), which must have made a deep impression in Jerusalem (Isa. 20:1–6; 22:1–14). Sayings directed against Judah in chapters 1—3 would fit quite well the early years of Hezekiah's reign, though some may date from the previous reign, that of Ahaz.

As noted a moment ago, Micah's prediction of the destruction of Jerusalem is quoted during Jeremiah's trial for sedition in 609 B.C.E. The context in which the quotation is presented by rural elders (Jer. 26:17–19) suggests the possibility that there existed a Micah *legendum* familiar to the speakers, or a prophetic history of some kind dealing with Micah, Uriah (Jer. 26:20–23), and others on which the elders and others could draw. If so, it is unfortunately no longer extant. Somewhat more speculative is the suggestion that the Micaiah ben Imlah narrative recorded in Dtr (1 Kings 22) has been written or rewritten with Micah of Moresheth in mind. The names are virtually identical, Micaiah quotes verbatim a line from Micah (1 Kings 22:28b; cf. Micah 1:2), the issue of prophetic conflict is dominant in both, and both associate prophecy explicitly with the spirit, a by no means common association in preexilic prophetic material.[55]

These difficulties are compounded by the obscure editorial history of the book. There is broad agreement that the eight or nine sayings in Micah 1—3 go back to Micah himself with the exception of 2:12–13 predicting national restoration under the native dynasty and one or two minor editorial adjustments.[56] The second section (chapters 4—5) deals with a cluster of themes encountered in the literature of the exilic and restoration periods: the ascendancy of Jerusalem and divine rule in the city (4:1–8), exile in Babylon and return (4:9–10), the eschatological battle at the gates of Jerusalem (4:11–13), the Davidic ruler (5:2–4 [MT 5:1–3]), and the destruction of idolatry (5:10–15 [MT 5:9–14]).[57] While sayings transmitted from Micah and his disciples may have provided the impetus to this collection (e.g., 5:5–6 [MT 5:4–5], the defeat of Assyria by a coalition of princes), indications of a later date are not lacking. The occurrence of Micah 4:1–4 in Isa. 2:2–4 is only the most obvious of the indications that Micah and Isaiah at some point passed through the hands of the same tradents. There are, finally, explicit allusions to exile and eventual return (4:9–11).

The provenance and literary form of the last section (chapters 6—7) have proved much more elusive. The opening indictment and reproach

(6:1–5), strongly reminiscent of Amos and Hosea, may well be from Micah himself or his immediate discipleship. The criticism of animal sacrifice divorced from ethical concern (6:6–8) reflects the same prophetic tradition (cf. Amos 5:21–24; Isa. 1:12–17) and should also be attributed to him. The difficulty with the last part of the chapter (6:9–16) has always been the allusion to the statutes of Omri and the deeds of Ahab's house (v. 16), leading some scholars to assign it to a prophet from the kingdom of Samaria, perhaps even earlier than Micah.[58] Dtr, however, accuses two Judean kings, Jehoram and Ahaziah, of going the same way as the house of Ahab (2 Kings 8:18, 27). Manasseh also is condemned for following Ahab's example in making an Asherah (2 Kings 21:3). There is therefore no reason why such a reproach could not be addressed to a Judean king, and it is perhaps along these lines that we are to explain Micah's indictment of Lachish for leading Jerusalem into sin by imitating "the transgressions of Israel" (Micah 1:13).[59] The city addressed in this passage is therefore undoubtedly Jerusalem (6:9), and while the form of the accusation is consonant with Deuteronomic rhetoric, it could as well be an example of Deuteronomic dependence on Micah or his disciples as the reverse.

The last chapter is quite different in character and has a distinctly liturgical flavor that has long been recognized. It consists of a lament in the first-person singular (7:1–10) with a response in the form of prophecies of well-being (vv. 11–17). This structure, identified in several of the so-called prophetic psalms (e.g., Pss. 60 and 108), reflects the role of the cult prophet in certain acts of worship.[60] The character of this kind of material makes it almost impossible to date, but it is highly unlikely that it was written before the Persian period and may even be later.

The only biographical information provided by the book is the name, which is quite common, and the place of origin, Moresheth (1:1), probably identical with Moresheth-gath (1:14), and perhaps at or near Tell el-Judeideh about twenty-five miles southwest of Jerusalem, therefore in the region of Lachish (Tell ed-Duweir), second city of Judah. We may then assume that he was a provincial, which may help to explain his sharp criticism of the capital (1:5, 9; 3:9–12). Micah is a fierce defender of the rights of the small farmers whose ancestors in many cases had been working the same plot of land, guaranteed by ancient custom (2:5), for centuries. His indictment is directed therefore against the ruling classes in the capital who, in his view, were breaking up the old order and driving the independent farmer off his land. The ways of doing this are depressingly familiar: enclosure of fields (2:2, 4); foreclosure following on insolvency (2:2, 9)—literally stripping the clothes off their backs (2:8; cf. Amos 2:8); forced labor (3:10); the falsification of weights and measures

(6:11); bribery and corruption of the judicial system (3:11), and so on. It must also be borne in mind that the strain of resentment expressed by Micah and others against the endless round of animal sacrifice (6:6) probably had less to do with liberal religious convictions, as assumed by so many scholars during the nineteenth and early twentieth century, than with the economic burden that the sacrificial system represented for the agrarian class. No one, in short, not even Amos, equals Micah in protesting the exploitation of the powerless:

> You who hate good and love evil,
> who tear the skin from off my people,
>   and their flesh from off their bones
> who eat the flesh of my people,
>   and flay their skin off them,
> break their bones to pieces,
>   chop them up like meat in a kettle,
>   like flesh in a cauldron . . .
>   (Micah 3:2–3)

The more perceptive among the commentators have noted the element of deep personal involvement in his attack on the perpetrators of social injustice, depicted in the passage just quoted as cannibals. Several have suggested that Micah himself belonged to the class of free farmers whose way of life was threatened by the encroaching state system in Judah, aggravated by the greed of the bureaucrats who ran it. Perhaps we can be more specific and suggest that he may have belonged to the social class known during the monarchy as "the people of the land" (*'am hā'āreṣ*), that is, independent landowners who actually worked the land rather than just living off it and, typical of this stratum everywhere, were socially and politically conservative, suspicious of civil and religious bureaucracies, and attached to the native dynasty. In the ninth century these people had played a leading role in the overthrow of the Baalist queen Athaliah and the subsequent accession of the Davidite Jehoash (2 Kings 11:18–20). About a half century later it was again "the people of the land" who secured the accession of Uzziah after his predecessor had been assassinated in Lachish, whither he had no doubt fled in the hope of finding protection and support (2 Kings 14:21). And once again, in 640, they were to play a leading part in punishing the assassins of Amon and putting the child Josiah on the throne (2 Kings 21:24). It was, finally, "the elders of the land" who, we are told, were able to remember and quote a saying of Micah (Jer. 26:17–19).[61]

The suggestion will be advanced in due course that the preaching of Micah contributed either directly or indirectly to the Deuteronomic reform movement in Judah, and that the connection is apparent especially in the Deuteronomic agrarian legislation and the conservative attitude to institutions. The fact that, unlike other prophets, Micah does not attack the monarchy may be explained by the attachment of the *'am hā'āreṣ* to the dynasty, and it fits the Deuteronomic ideal of a constitutional monarchy (Deut. 17:14–20). The use of such traditional terms as "heads" (*rā'šîm*) and "rulers" (*qᵉṣînîm*) (3:1, 9, 11), together with insistence on their responsibility to promote justice (3:1), is only one example of the strong conservatism that fed the Deuteronomic reform movement.

We can learn something about Micah's perception of his role from the criticism that he levels at the professional prophets who supported state policies and were employed in the Jerusalem temple. Like Amos (Amos 7:12–13, 16; cf. 2:12), he was commanded not to preach that disaster will overtake the kingdom, or that Yahweh's patience has come to an end, or that he (Yahweh) is responsible for such evils as are threatened (Micah 2:6–7).[62] The message of the *nᵉbî'îm* is quite different. It is one of well-being (*šālôm*, 3:5), meaning that "disgrace will not overtake us" (2:6), and "no evil shall come upon us" (3:11), the reason being that Yahweh is in our midst (3:11). Thus the *nᵉbî'îm* expounded the official theology of church and state based on the doctrine of the divine election of people, dynasty, and city, a theology underlying the temple cult and generated a high level of confidence and morale.

We can discount Micah's accusations of venality (3:5, 11), a standard polemical topos, and his linking prophecy with divination (3:6, 7, 11). The main point was that contemporary prophets were deceiving the public by feeding their need for reassurance and telling them what they wanted to hear (2:11; 3:5). It is clear that Micah wanted nothing to do with this kind of prophecy, and it is tolerably clear that he would not have wished to be known as a *nābî'*.

What is particularly interesting about Micah's role is that he defines it *over against* the prophetic office. After denouncing the professional prophets for leading people astray and prophesying for profit, he makes a statement about himself of a kind rare in the history of prophecy: "but as for me, I am filled with power and justice and strength, to declare to Jacob his transgression and to Israel his sin" (3:8).[63] The contrast is somewhat parallel to, but more clearly expressed than, the statement of Amos when he was silenced by the "religious establishment": "I am no prophet nor a prophet's son; but I am a herdsman . . . and Yahweh took me from following the flock, and Yahweh said to me, 'Go, prophesy to my people Israel'" (Amos 7:14–15). In both cases association with the institution of prophecy is disavowed, yet full authorization is claimed for a personal mission.

Starting out from this avowal, Hans Walter Wolff has argued that Micah was one of the elders of Moresheth who took up the cause of his own constituency, that is, the people who worked the land, with the authorities in Jerusalem on those occasions when the elders of the country towns were summoned to the capital. Acting in such a capacity, he does not fit the prophetic profile, has left no account of a calling, hardly ever uses the "standard" messenger form ("thus says Yahweh"), and almost always speaks in his own name rather than that of Yahweh. It is particularly significant, continues Wolff, that when he speaks of "my people," he is not speaking for God, as is almost always the case elsewhere in prophetic writings, but really means his own constituency, the people back home on the land around Moresheth (Micah 2:4, 8, 9; 3:2, 3). It is therefore no surprise that, in contrasting himself with the prophets, he speaks of being "filled with justice," that is, equipped to fight for justice on behalf of the oppressed who have no voice.[64]

Wolff, who has a reputation for probing beneath the anonymity of individual prophetic figures, has made a particularly valuable contribution, in his essays and commentary, to our understanding of Micah and of the canonical prophets in general. If, as he argues, both Micah and Amos held the office of elder, it would be easier to explain several aspects of their teaching, for example, their traditionalism, their use of language and themes related to the consensual ethic developed within the kinship network, and their opposition to highly developed state cults and the personnel who operated them. But one aspect that this hypothesis would not explain so well would be the range of interest manifested in these books, especially Amos, which led to the designation "dissident intellectual" proposed earlier in our study. Both prophets condemn Samaria, and Amos ranges much farther afield into the world of international politics.[65] Also, we would want to ask whether what Wolff says about Micah is not the case, mutatis mutandis, with all the canonical prophets who define their identity and mission over against the contemporary phenomenon of prophecy.

Micah, or one of his disciples, formulates for his contemporaries the fundamental religious question in order to show how the prophetic word provides the answer (6:6–8). Typically, the question is not concerned with theological or philosophical understanding and inquiry but with behavior, the conduct of life: What must I do in order to approach God? For the normative, state religion of Israel the answer is clear. God can only be approached, meaning in effect, sin can only be removed, through the sacrificial system: "Without the shedding of blood there is no forgiveness of sins" (Heb. 9:22). Hence the rhetorical questions in the Micah texts in ascending hyperbole: Shall I offer burnt offerings, thousands of rams, rivers of oil, even my own son in order to bridge the gap between the sinner and the sinless God? The answer is communicated through the prophetic message. These are things that you choose to do. What God demands of you is to fulfill the requirements of justice, be faithful to commitments, and live your life in humble and attentive openness to God. This sentence has rightly been prized as one of the best summaries of the teaching of the great eighth century prophets. And in no way does it detract from its value that, in its very formulation, it raises but does not solve the crucial issue of the relation between prophecy and institution.

12. ISAIAH OF JERUSALEM

P. R. **Ackroyd,** "Isaiah 1—12: Presentation of a Prophet," *SVT* 29 (1977): 16–48; "Isaiah 36—39: Structure and Function," W. C. Delsman et al., eds., *Von Kanaan bis Kerala: Festschrift für J.P.M. van der Ploeg, O.P.*, Neukirchen-Vluyn: Neukirchener Verlag, 1982, 3–21; A. G. **Auld,** "Poetry, Prophecy, Hermeneutic: Recent Studies in Isaiah," *SJT* 33 (1980): 567–81; P. **Auvray,** *Isaïe 1–39*, Paris: J. Gabalda, 1972; H. **Barth,** *Die Jesajaworte in der Josiazeit: Israel und Assur als Thema einer produktiven Neuinterpretation der Jesajaüberlieferung*, Neukirchen-Vluyn: Neukirchener Verlag, 1977; W. H. **Brownlee,** *The Meaning of the Qumran Scrolls for the Bible with Special Attention to the Book of Isaiah,* New York: Oxford University Press, 1964; W. **Brueggemann,** "Unity and Dynamic in the Isaiah Tradition," *JSOT* 29 (1984): 89–107; B. S. **Childs,** *Isaiah and the Assyrian Crisis*, Naperville, Ill.: Alec R. Allenson, 1967; *Introduction to the Old Testament as Scripture*, 216–25, 325–34; R. E. **Clements,** *Isaiah and the Deliverance of Jerusalem: A Study of the Interpretation of Prophecy in the Old Testament,* Sheffield: JSOT Press, 1980; "The Unity of the Book of Isaiah," *Int* 36 (1982): 117–29; W. **Dietrich,** *Jesaja und die Politik,* Munich: Chr. Kaiser Verlag, 1976; G. R. **Driver,** "Linguistic and Textual Problems: Isaiah 1–39," *JTS* 38 (1937): 36–50; "Notes on Isaiah," BZAW 77 (1958): 42–48; B. **Duhm,** *Das Buch Jesaia,* Göttingen: Vandenhoeck & Ruprecht, 1968[5] (first published 1892); J. H. **Eaton,** "The Origin of the Book of Isaiah," *VT* 9 (1959): 138–57; C. A. **Evans,** "On the Unity and Parallel Structure of Isaiah," *VT* 38 (1988): 129–47; J. **Fichtner,** "Jesaja unter den Weisen," *TLZ* 74 (1949): 75–80; G. **Fohrer,** "The Origin, Composition and Tradition of Isaiah 1–39," *ALUOS* 3 (1961–62): 29–32; *Das Buch Jesaja,* Zurich: Zwingli Verlag, 1966–72; G. B. **Gray,** *The Book of Isaiah,* Edinburgh: T. & T. Clark, 1912 (reprint 1947); J. H. **Hayes,** "The Tradition of Zion's Inviolability," *JBL* 82 (1963): 419–26; J. H. **Hayes** and S. A. **Irvine,** *Isaiah the Eighth-Century Prophet: His Times and His Preaching,* Nashville: Abingdon Press, 1987; W. L. **Holladay,** *Isaiah: Scroll of a Prophetic Heritage,* Grand Rapids: Eerdmans, 1978; J. **Jensen,** *The Use of Tôrâ by Isaiah: His Debate with the Wisdom Tradition,* Washington, D.C.: Catholic Biblical Association of America, 1973;

ne Traditio of the Oracles of Isaiah of Jerusalem," *ZAW* 67 (1955): O. **Kaiser,** *Isaiah 1—12: A Commentary,* Philadelphia: Westminster Press, ; *Isaiah 13—39: A Commentary,* Philadelphia: Westminster Press, 1974; K. **Koch,** *The Prophets.* vol. I, *The Assyrian Period,* 105–56; L. J. **Liebreich,** "The Compilation of the Book of Isaiah," *JQR* 46 (1955–56): 259–77; 47 (1956–57): 114–38; S. **Mowinckel,** "Die Komposition des Jesaiabuches Kap. 1–39," *AcOr* 11 (1933): 267–92; G. von **Rad,** *Old Testament Theology,* vol. 2, 147–75; R. **Rendtorff,** "Zur Komposition des Buches Jesaja," *VT* 34 (1984): 295–320; *Canon and Theology: Overtures to an Old Testament Theology,* Minneapolis: Fortress Press, 1993, 146–89; R.B.Y. **Scott,** "The Literary Structure of Isaiah's Oracles," in H. H. Rowley, ed., *Studies in Old Testament Prophecy presented to T. H. Robinson,* Edinburgh: T. & T. Clark, 1950, 175–86; I. L. **Seeligmann,** *The Septuagint Version of Isaiah,* Leiden: E. J. Brill, 1948; C. R. **Seitz,** *Zion's Final Destiny: The Development of the Book of Isaiah; A Reassessment of Isaiah 36—39,* Minneapolis: Fortress Press, 1991; *Isaiah 1—39,* Louisville: John Knox Press, 1993; "Isaiah, Book of," *ABD,* 3:472–88; G. T. **Sheppard,** "The Anti-Assyrian Redaction and the Canonical Context of Isaiah 1—39," *JBL* 104 (1985): 193–216; P. W. **Skehan,** "Some Textual Problems in Isaiah," *CBQ* 22 (1960) 47–55; J. **Skinner,** *Book of the Prophet Isaiah,* Cambridge: Cambridge University Press, 1925²; M. A. **Sweeney,** *Isaiah 1—4 and the Post-Exilic Understanding of the Isaianic Tradition,* Berlin: W. de Gruyter, 1988; C. C. **Torrey,** "Some Important Editorial Operations in the Book of Isaiah," *JBL* 57 (1938): 109–39; J. **Vermeylen,** *Du Prophète Isaïe à l'apocalyptique,* 2 vols., Paris: J. Gabalda, 1977–78; ed., *The Book of Isaiah—Le Livre d'Isaïe,* Louvain: Louvain University Press, 1989; J. M. **Ward,** *Amos and Isaiah,* Nashville: Abingdon Press, 1969; J. W. **Whedbee,** *Isaiah and Wisdom,* Nashville: Abingdon Press, 1971; H. **Wildberger,** *Jesaja,* Neukirchen-Vluyn: Neukirchener Verlag, 1972, 1978, 1982.

The book of Isaiah, one of the longer units in the Hebrew Bible, comprises prophetic material in verse and prose collected over a period of at least half a millennium. From the late eighteenth century critical scholarship has followed Gesenius, whose commentary on Isaiah was published in 1821, in treating chapters 40—66 as a distinct unit that cannot be dated earlier than the Babylonian exile, and therefore two centuries after the putative author of chapters 1—39 (or 1—35).[66] Following Bernhard Duhm (1892), most scholars have also accepted that chapters 56—66 form a distinct unit within 40—66 that, even if it includes earlier sayings, must be dated later still. But historical-critical analysis also led to the conclusion that the first section, chapters 1—39, is an aggregate of different compilations, not all the same age and provenance, and each having its own editorial history prior to its incorporation into the book. This kind of analysis by itself cannot do more than propose a hypothetical reconstruction of the stages by which the book, or part of it, reached its present form, hence the bewildering range of opinion on the subject. But if we are to say anything, however tentatively, about a prophetic figure from the eighth century B.C.E. named Isaiah, we have no other access to him and the world in which he lived. The least we can say is that, while much is uncertain, some conclusions are less uncertain than others.

It should be added that the tendency in Isaiah studies today is to move beyond the tripartite division, standard since Duhm published his commentary, in search of structural, thematic and lexical clues to an underlying unity of the entire book at the redactional level (Ackroyd, Clements, Rendtorff, et al.). The accumulated effect of these studies will inevitably call into question the practice of writing distinct commentaries on First, Second, and Third Isaiah, a practice in vogue since the early nineteenth century. But since our present concern is directly historical and only indirectly literary, our purpose will best be served by retaining the conventional divisions in the interests of orderly presentation of the relevant material.

The discovery of the Qumran Isaiah scroll (lQIsa^a), dated on epigraphic grounds to the second century B.C.E., together with the Old Greek translation, of unknown date but probably made about the same time, provide a terminus ad quem for the editorial history of the book, implying that exegetical activity was, up to that time, incorporated in the book itself. Writing in the early second century B.C.E., Jesus ben-Sira shows familiarity with at least the biographical legends in Isaiah 36—39 and all or part of Isaiah 40—55 (Sir. 48:22–25). The biographical or hagiographical tradition about Isaiah, which goes back to these legends incorporated in the book and in Dtr (2 Kings 18—20), was taken up and amplified by the Chronicler (2 Chronicles 32), Ben Sira, Josephus (*Ant*, 10:11–35), and the Martyrdom of Isaiah. It made its contribution to the pattern of prophetic biography, well developed by the Greco-Roman period, and left its mark on the Gospel portrait of Jesus, especially in Luke's Gospel.

This biographical material makes up the last of several distinct compilations in Isaiah 1—39. The first (chapters 1—12) consists of biographical and autobiographical prose together with sayings, discourses, and poems from different periods, rounded off with a short hymn. There follow sayings directed against several hostile foreign nations, primarily Assyria and Babylon, covering a period of several centuries (chapters 13—23). These lead into a section (chapters 24—27), known since Duhm as "the Isaian apocalypse," which includes songs or psalms celebrating the downfall of an unnamed city, but also much nonapocalyptic material. There follow sayings pronouncing judgment on Israel and Judah, many of them in the form of woe oracles, but concluding with predictions of disaster for Assyria and Egypt (chapters 28—31). The final section consists of miscellaneous poems and prayers dealing with the coming age of judgment and redemption (chapters 32—35), the last section of which leads directly into chapters 40—55, the so-called Second Isaiah of the exilic period. The connection was broken by the insertion of the historical appendix of chapters 36—39, which however creates its own linkage by concluding with a prediction of the Babylonian exile (39:5-8).

The biographical *legendum* about Isaiah in chapters 36—39 deals with three incidents: his intervention in favor of King Hezekiah and the beleaguered city during the campaign of Sennacherib in 701 B.C.E. (chapters 36—37), Hezekiah's sickness and Isaiah's intervention on his behalf (chapter 38), and Isaiah's prediction of exile in Babylon delivered during the embassy from Merodach-baladan, ruler of Babylon (chapter 39). With the exception of a poetic lament of Hezekiah composed during his sickness (Isa. 38:9-20), the same narrative material is found in 2 Kings 18:13—20:21. Its origin is uncertain. Dtr and the Isaian editor could have drawn on a common source, perhaps composed at the court of Hezekiah, adding their own modifications and adaptations, but it is also possible that these narratives were introduced into Isaiah from Dtr at a relatively late date. At least the arguments against this possibility, in particular the chronological disorder in both, do not exclude it. As was noted earlier, while the historical narrative in chapters 36—39 cuts chapter 35 off from chapters 40 and the following with which it belongs, the prediction of exile in Babylon (39:5-7) contrasts well with the promise of return from captivity with which Second Isaiah begins.

Whatever the origin of chapters 36—39, they represent a tradition remarkably different from that of the sayings in other sections of the book. Only here is Isaiah called a *nābî'* (37:2; 38:1; 39:3) and presented as a miracle worker, rather like a kinder and gentler version of Elisha (38:7-8, 21). What is even more significant, he is presented here essentially as an optimistic prophet working closely in tandem with the ruler. It is probably for this reason that Dtr wove this material into his account of Hezekiah's reign while passing over in silence the quite different Isaiah of the sayings collections.

Isaiah's intervention in the Assyrian campaign brought on by Hezekiah's revolt (Isaiah 36—37), which must have happened toward the end of his career, has come down to us in more or less parallel versions that have been conflated. One of these describes an Assyrian official's boastful challenge to the king and his ministers, following which Hezekiah went to the temple and sent a delegation to request Isaiah's intercession. This resulted in the prophet's giving an oracle of assurance ("Do not fear," 37:6) that predicted the retreat and death of Sennacherib

(36:1–37:7). The other version has the Assyrian king himself challenging Hezekiah, who then went to the temple, prayed, and received assurance from Isaiah that his prayer had been heard. This version too ends with an assurance of Assyrian failure backed up with a confirmatory sign that, in the present state of the text, precedes the oracle (37:9–35). This second version gives more prominence to the king, whose prayer averts disaster, and presents the oracle (37:33–35; cf. 37:6–7), or at least its conclusion, in Deuteronomic language (". . . for my own sake and for the sake of my servant David," v. 35). It may represent an exilic expansion of a short narrative in which Isaiah played a sustaining role vis-à-vis Hezekiah comparable to the Mari ecstatics vis-à-vis Zimrilim.

Comparable in some respects is the chronistic account of Isaiah's intervention in the Syro-Ephraimite war thirty-three years earlier (Isa. 7:1–17). Here, too, the narrative has affinities with Dtr (2 Kings 16:5, 7–9; cf. Hos. 5:8–14). The situation described in this passage is the crisis that faced Ahaz, father of Hezekiah, in 734 B.C.E. with the prospect of invasion by the armies of Damascus and Israel after he refused to join them in an anti-Assyrian alliance. As in the Hezekiah narrative, Isaiah's intervention takes the form of an oracle of assurance ("Do not fear," Isa. 7:4) and a sign that the crisis will be resolved within a relatively short period of time (7:10–16; cf. 37:30–32).[67]

There are, however, some distinctive features. One is that the fulfillment of the oracle is contingent on Ahaz's trusting that it will be fulfilled ("If you do not stand firm in faith, you shall not stand at all," 7:9). The other is the role of his child to whom, following the example of Hosea, he gave a symbolic name, Shear-Yashub ("A remnant will return"). Accompanied by this child, he met the king at the precise place where, thirty-three years later, the Assyrian commander would call for the surrender of the city (7:3; cf. 2 Kings 18:17). The sign that would assure Ahaz that the prophetic oracle could be trusted was to be the birth of a child called Immanuel (God with us) of a mother cryptically alluded to as The Young Woman (Isa. 7:14). While the symbolic structure would best be satisfied if this child of good omen, like the other two, were Isaiah's (cf. the three children of Hosea), the earliest interpretation appears to have a ruler in mind who would then very likely be none other than Hezekiah, son and heir to Ahaz (8:8), an identification that has been widely accepted.[68] The third child, with the improbable name Maher-shalal-hash-baz (Speed spoil, hasten plunder), presages the devastation of Damascus and Israel by the Assyrians (8:1–4), which was precisely what happened during the campaigns of 734–733 B.C.E.

The decisive political fact was that Ahaz, against Isaiah's advice, invited in the Assyrians to stave off the threat from the Damascus-Samaria

axis at the cost of accepting vassal status. This situation remained unchanged until well into the reign of Josiah (640–609), when the weakened condition of the Assyrian empire under Ashurbanipal held out re-
alistic hope for emancipation.

Like Isaiah 36—37, therefore, the report in Isa. 7:1–17 deals with ruler
and prophet at a fateful moment of the nation's history, the beginning
of vassalage to Assyria. There have been appended to it four brief expansions beginning "on that day" (*bayyôm hahû'*), the ambiguity of which
is perhaps due to their reflecting the changing fortunes of Judah under
Assyrian vassalage in the century following the Syro-Ephraimite war
(7:18–19, 20, 21–22, 23–25). The thesis of an anti-Assyrian redaction and
relecture of existing oracles during the reign of Josiah is entirely plausible,
and should be borne in mind in reading Isaiah 1—35, though attempts
to precisely identify Josian passages should be treated with caution.[69] In
a further extension of the same process, Assyria and Egypt will, much
later, be identified with the Seleucids and Ptolemies respectively (Isa.
19:18–25), at which point we have just about reached the final stage in
the formation of the book.

The Syro-Ephraimite war record and its appendices (7:1–25) have
been sandwiched between two first-person narratives (6:1–13; 8:1–9:1a
[MT 8:1–23a]) in what looks like a deliberate and meaningful arrangement. The first is dated to the death of Uzziah, which took place sometime between 742 and 735. It describes in exalted language how Isaiah
received a commission in a vision to speak to an unresponsive audience.
The structure of the vision-report is almost exactly parallel to that of Micaiah ben-Imlah noted earlier (1 Kings 22:19–23). Yahweh is seated on
his throne surrounded by his attendants, the seraphs or "burning ones"
(cf. "all the host of heaven," 1 Kings 22:19). After the chant of the hosts
and the purging of guilt (not attested in Micaiah's vision), Yahweh calls
for a volunteer to perform a mission, in the one case to deceive Ahab, in
the other to harden the hearts and obfuscate the senses of the people.[70]
In the earlier narrative the response comes from one of the attendants,
called simply "the spirit" (*hārûah*), who will make use of false prophets
to achieve his end, while in Isaiah 6 the prophet himself volunteers and
is commissioned. Isaiah's vision, which lives on in the liturgical forms of
Kedushah, Trisagion, and Sanctus, has become a classical locus for the
study of religious experience (e.g., in Rudolf Otto's *The Idea of the Holy*,
at one time very influential). But if we give due importance to its structural role in the section (the first person/third person/first person unit,
Isa. 6:1–9:1a) we would think that it refers to the rejection of the
prophet's message by Ahaz and those who supported his pro-Assyrian
policy.[71]

In the last section of the same unit (8:1–9:1a) Isaiah describes the symbolic act of writing and notarizing a deed handing over the territory of Damascus and Samaria to the Assyrians, followed by his cohabiting with "the prophetess"[72] and, in due time, the birth of the child with the ominous name suggestive of defeat and pillage. The force of the act and the name corresponds to that of the Immanuel sign (7:14–16), namely, that the enemies threatening invasion from the north will be discomfited without the need for Judah to bring in the Assyrians. The sequel, however, reflects the actual course of events: subjection to the Assyrians (8:5–8, perhaps from the time of Hezekiah), accusations of sedition and conspiracy leveled at the anti-Assyrian party with which Isaiah was identified (8:11–15), and the retirement of Isaiah and his group into the wings, taking with them a copy of the prophet's sayings against the day of their fulfillment and vindication (8:16–9:1a [MT 8:16–23a]).[73]

This central section, dealing with the events of the critical year 734–733, forms the centerpiece of the first collection in the book (Isaiah 1—12), rounded off with a psalm of thanksgiving for salvation ($y^e\check{s}\hat{u}'\hat{a}$) allowing for play on the name Isaiah ($y^e\check{s}a'y\bar{a}h\hat{u}$, Yahweh is salvation), thereby also recalling the three children with the names of good omen (12:1–2, 4–6).[74] But since the centerpiece interrupts a poem on the divine anger (5:24–25; 9:8–10:4) and a series of sayings about Assyria (5:26–30; 10:5–19, 27b–34), it appears to have been spliced into a compilation already in existence.

The book as a whole bears the title A Vision ($h\bar{a}z\hat{o}n$), the same term used by the Chronicler for Isaiah (2 Chron. 32:32) and apparently standard in Jerusalemite cultic circles (cf. Obadiah and Nahum). This descriptive label has been combined with the standard Deuteronomic superscription listing the reigns during which Isaiah was active and thus indicating a career of between thirty and forty years. The presence of a second title at the beginning of Isaiah 2 directs us to read the first chapter as a separate collection of sayings. For the most part they describe a situation of devastation in Judah overrun by foreign armies with only Jerusalem intact. Several attempts have been made to match these sayings with what little we know of the history of the kingdom during Isaiah's career. It seems, on the whole, more likely that they describe conditions during the short war with Damascus and Israel in 734–733 than the Assyrian crisis about three decades later under Hezekiah. Denunciation of the "rulers of Sodom" (Isa. 1:10), that is, Jerusalem, is difficult to reconcile with Isaiah's attitude to Hezekiah in the biographical material (chapters 36—39), and the rejection of the cult in 1:10–17 would be hard to understand after the religious reforms sponsored by Hezekiah according to Dtr (2 Kings 18:3–6) and Chronicles (2 Chronicles 29—31).

We also catch echoes of Amos here and there, not least in the contrast between the sacrificial cult and the demands of social justice (1:12–17), which would fit better the early stages of Isaiah's career.

At the same time indications are not lacking, especially in the latter part of the chapter (vv. 24–31), that this first series has been "recycled" at different points of the traditioning process. It may even have been placed at the beginning as a summary and preview of the book as a whole in which the themes of judgment, repentance, and restoration feature prominently. The thematic and linguistic links between these sayings and the concluding passage in the book (Isa. 66:15–24), which are easily verified, provide additional confirmation of the broader function that this first chapter was intended to serve.[75]

The next section (Isaiah 2—4) is also reminiscent of Amos in its condemnation of the ruling classes who "grind the face of the poor" (3:15) and of the society women of Jerusalem whose lifestyle reflects a lack of concern for traditional moral values (3:16–17, 24–26; cf. Amos 4:1–3). The poem on divine judgment (Isa. 2:6–22) restates for the benefit of Judah the central message of Amos: that the God of Israel has now abandoned his people and left them at the mercy of history. The importance of this poem can be gauged by the amount of exegetical activity it has occasioned (especially vv. 9–11, 17–22), including expansions and comments of an apocalyptic character.[76] But the last word is not one of judgment, for the circles that preserved Isaiah's sayings also have prefaced the poem with a promise of renewal after judgment (2:2–5). The theme of Jerusalem as center of pilgrimage for the nations, also found with slight variations at Micah 4:1–5,[77] is matched with a final word of promise at the end of the section predicting the restoration of the devastated city (4:2–6).

That Isaiah was familiar with Hosea as well as with Amos is suggested by echoes and allusions here and there (e.g., Isa. 9:18; cf. Hos. 7:6), and it was perhaps Hosea who suggested the theme of the faithless children (Isa. 1:2–3) and the harlot city (1:21–26). The love song of the vineyard, with its undertones of the fertility cult and vintage festivals (5:1–7), may also have been inspired by Hosea (Hos. 10: 1). The series of woes in Isa. 5:8–23 appears to be modeled on those of Amos (Amos 5:7, 18; 6:1, 4) and indicts the economic and political elite for the same attitude of social irresponsibility as is castigated by Amos, occasionally even using the same language. The gravamens are identical: enclosure of fields, distraining the property of the insolvent, bribery, denying the poor their rights, drinking, reveling, and so on. The poem on the divine anger (Isa. 5:24–25; 9:8 [MT 9:7] through 10:4), each of the five stanzas of which ends with the refrain,

for all that his anger is not turned away,
and his hand is stretched out still

is directed against the kingdom of Samaria and opens with what is very probably an indirect allusion to Amos:

Yahweh has sent a word against Jacob,
and it will light upon Israel.

(Isa. 9:8)

The refrain itself, reminiscent of Amos 1:3,[78] the use of quotations (Isa. 9:9–10; cf. Amos 6:13), the condemnation of social oppression and judicial corruption (Isa. 10:1–2), even what appears to be an allusion to the earthquake mentioned in the title of the book of Amos (5:25), suggest that Isaiah was taking up where Amos left off and that his intent was to apply the message of his older contemporary to Judah. Other denunciations of the Northern Kingdom reproduce themes found in the earlier prophet (17:1–6; 28:1–4), and the same criteria by which Israel is judged and found wanting are applied to Judah. This will serve to show once again that prophecy is not explicable purely in terms of personal experience, but it requires that we take account of an emerging tradition within which events are interpreted and through which the personal experience is mediated.

Isaiah is more explicit than Amos in his reference to the Assyrians and the role they were destined to play in Israel's future (Isa. 5:26–30; 10:5–34). It was common practice in antiquity to explain or justify conquest with reference to the anger of native deities at their negligent or impious devotees. According to our historian (Dtr) Sennacherib used this argument to justify his campaign against Judah, even claiming to have received an oracle from Yahweh commanding him to destroy that kingdom (2 Kings 18:22, 25). Isaiah, for his part, described the Assyrians as an instrument of judgment—an ax, a saw, an overseer's rod—in the hands of the national deity (Isa. 10:5–19). Adopting a familiar metaphor, he depicted the irresistible Assyrian army descending from the north as a swarm of locusts (5:26–29; 10:27–34). But with the passing of time, perhaps during the career of Isaiah himself, perhaps during the movement for national independence during Josiah's reign, the attitude to the Assyrians expressed throughout these chapters hardens (10:7–11, 13–19; 14:24–27; 37:6–7, 22–35). We are reminded that one of the most durable legacies of Israelite prophecy and apocalyptic is their critique of imperial ideology, a critique that reaches a high point in the imagery of beasts and horns in Daniel, together with its counterpart or mirror-image in the coming of the kingdom of God.

Assuming a nucleus of material that can be traced back to Isaiah and his immediate following, what information of a biographical nature can we extract from Isaiah 1—35? Given the nature of the material contained in these chapters and the uncertainty besetting the editorial history of the book, our expectations cannot be set very high. We know his name and that of his father. He was married, perhaps to a female prophet but we have seen that that is uncertain, with at least two children. We have no indication of his profession prior to his prophetic commission, nor of what he did for a living. Occasional use of scribal conventions does not make him a scribe any more than the vision in the temple (if that is where it took place) makes him a member of the temple staff.[79] It is even less likely that he was the official historian of that time as the Chronicler (2 Chron. 26:22; 32:32) appears to suggest. He was certainly a well-known public figure with access to leading members of the court (22:15–25; cf. 2 Kings 18:18; 19:2–7) and to the king, at least in times of national crisis. While obviously a well-educated person and a gifted poet, he and his followers, probably a very small group, were actively engaged in political life over a period of at least three decades. After Sennacherib's campaign in Judah, on which the historian has focused attention, we hear no more of him. He must have died later in Hezekiah's reign or in the early years of Manasseh his successor. The story of his martyrdom, presented with suitably gruesome details, is of course a later elaboration.

Isaiah was clearly not an intellectual elaborating a political theory or a theology of history, but he was actively engaged in politics, taking sides and giving advice that was presumably meant to be translated into political action. He would have been identified with the anti-Assyrian party during his early career, and we know that this party continued to oppose the official policy of the court after Ahaz made his fateful decision to call in the Assyrians. We hear accusations of conspiracy directed at him (8:11–15), sarcastic allusions to the plan of Yahweh (as expounded by Isaiah, 5:19), and prophetic voices in support of both positions (29:10; 30:10). The replacement of Shebna by Eliakim as majordomo of the palace (22:15–24; cf. 2 Kings 18:18) may also have come about as a result of differences of opinion or policy shifts on the Assyrian issue. For the balance of the reign of Ahaz, at any rate, Isaiah was no longer *persona grata* at the court, even if he did not, as is often alleged, retire from public life (8:1–22).

Ahaz died ca. 715 B.C.E. and an oracle against the Philistines is dated to that year (Isa. 14:28–32) presaging the campaigns against the cities of the Philistine Pentapolis waged by Hezekiah (2 Kings 18:8).[80] The first years of Hezekiah's reign saw much plotting and scheming between the Philistine cities and Egypt, whose ambitions in Asia were reviving under Shabaka (716–701) of the twenty-fifth or Ethiopian dynasty (see Isa.

18:1–19:15). The chronological sequence of events for the first decade of Hezekiah's reign is not well known. In spite of the fact that the Assyrian empire now reached to within a few miles of Jerusalem, Hezekiah conducted an aggressive policy of expansion, attacking Edomites to the south (Isa. 21:11–17) and Philistines to the west. In pursuing this new, expansive nationalism, inspired by the example of a resurgent Egypt and abetted by a vigorous lobby of counselors and prophets at the court (Isa. 29:9–10, 14; 30:10), Hezekiah was evidently courting disaster. The sayings that can be plausibly dated to this period (22:1–8, 12–14; 30:8–17) suggest that Isaiah's main concern was to dissuade the young king from being drawn into an anti-Assyrian alliance that had little prospect of success. In the year 712 Sargon II conducted a successful campaign against the Philistine city of Ashdod (*ANET*, 286) during which the promised help from Egypt did not materialize. Isaiah took the occasion, which certainly had repercussions in Jerusalem, to walk naked, or nearly so, through the capital (perhaps accompanied by his followers) to simulate the fate of the Egyptians, and those foolish enough to rely on them, as prisoners of war being led off into captivity (20:1–6). This kind of protest, characteristic of marginal groups, confirms the impression that during the fairly long period from the beginning of vassal status under Ahaz to the revolt of Hezekiah, Isaiah and his disciples (see Isa. 8:16) were deprived of power and opposed to official policies. This marginalized situation would explain not only the vehemence of his invective (e.g., 28:7–8 directed against priests and prophets), and the counterinvective of those whom he attacked (e.g., 28:9–10), but also the remarkably contrasting tone of the biographical narrative in chapters 37—39.

While the primary nucleus of sayings provides few clues on Isaiah's own perception of his prophetic role, we can conclude that he saw himself as part of a tradition of social criticism and diatribe. In the early phase of his career, he borrowed extensively from Amos and, to a lesser extent, from Hosea, applying their message to the contemporary situation in the kingdom of Judah. He was familiar with the tradition of the true prophet silenced and ignored (Isa. 30:10–11; cf. Amos 2:12) and saw it still at work in his own career. There are few if any indications in this material of a specifically Judean, as opposed to Ephraimite, understanding of the prophetic function. Judean intermediaries are called either prophets ($n^e b\hat{\imath}\,\hat{\imath}m$) or seers ($h\bar{o}z\hat{\imath}m$) (Isa. 29:10; 30:9–10); they are bracketed with priests (28:7; cf. Hos. 4:4–5); they receive their call in the same way, that is, through vision; and they deal in the spoken word (5:24; cf. 9:8 [MT 9:7]). The prophet who stands in this tradition tends to align optimistic prophets (the speakers of "smooth things," 30:10) with the practitioners of questionable forms of mediation such as divining, soothsaying, and necromancy (2:6; 3:2–3; 8:19), deemed to be more characteristic of foreign lands such as Egypt, 19:3. Perhaps the only distinctive mark of Judean prophecy is the identification of the prophet's message as a form of teaching (*tôrâ*, 5:24; 30:9). It also seems to have been seen in that way by his opponents who satirized him as a pedantic schoolmaster repeating the same lesson over and over (28:9–10). Isaiah replied in kind: Since you are unwilling to learn your lesson from me you will have to learn it from the Assyrians who don't even speak your language (vv. 11–13).

Since Isaiah is presumed to have been a native of Jerusalem (though we are never told this), it has often been concluded that he inherited a religious tradition different in important respects from that of Ephraimite prophets. The latter drew freely on the memory of founding events, events memorialized in the religious tribal shrines of the central hill country, while in Judah and Jerusalem it was the dynastic promise to the Davidites (2 Samuel 7) and Yahweh's choice of Jerusalem as his dwelling place (2 Samuel 6, etc.) which were of decisive importance. But for much of his career Isaiah was in opposition to official policies that the state cult existed to legitimate and sustain. The Zion theology of the book, if we may call it that, differs therefore in some basic respects from the official "state church" ideology. It is therefore understandable that Isaiah should have drawn on patterns of prophetic opposition originating in the Northern Kingdom. Interest in the fate of the northern neighbor, indeed of Israel in the inclusive sense, is a noteworthy feature of the book, and it is reflected in the appellative "house of Jacob" (Isa. 2:5, 6; 8:17; 9:8 [MT 9:7]; 10:20, 21) and the divine title "the Holy One of Jacob" (29:23).

The use of divine titles in Isaiah is only one indication of the need for caution in making clear distinctions between Judean and Ephraimite traditions. By far the most common one is "Yahweh of the hosts" (*YHWH ṣᵉbā'ôt*), which seems to have originated at Shiloh and is first attested during the Philistine wars. While it was probably established in cultic usage in Jerusalem before Isaiah, it also serves to link both Isaiah and Amos with the old war prophecy that flourished in the central and northern regions. The title "the Holy One of Israel" (*qādôš yiśrā'ēl*), also favored by Isaiah,[81] occurs previously only in the Ephraimite prophet Hosea (Hos. 11:9; perhaps also 11:12 [MT 12:1]), while "the Mighty One (*'abîr*) of Israel" (Isa. 1:24) and "the Rock of Israel" (30:29) are found in practically the same form in the tribal oracles in Gen. 49:24 (the one on Joseph). Too much should not be made of these observations, but they at least suggest that the liturgical usage on which Isaiah drew was not as highly distinctive as it is generally represented to be.

The mythic language about Jerusalem as the city of the divine presence, center of world pilgrimage, exalted and inviolable female, and the like, is not a creation of either Isaiah himself or his disciples (Isa. 2:2–4; 4:2–6). He would of course have been aware of these ideas and their cultic expression, but where we encounter such language throughout the book—and not just in the "authentic" sections—it more often than not refers to an ideal construct over against the empirical reality. Isaiah himself does not hesitate to compare this real Jerusalem with Sodom (1:10), denounce it as a harlot city (1:21), and hold out the prospect of ruin and destruction (8:5–8, etc.). Only in one saying, probably from the time of Hezekiah's rebellion (31:4–5), does he speak of Yahweh fighting for and protecting his city, though even in this instance there are conflicting interpretations.[82]

To the extent that we can reconstruct it, Isaiah's attitude to the Davidic dynasty was generally positive though tempered with political realism. At least he never condemns the institution of monarchy, as did Hosea during the last decades of the Northern Kingdom. The major difficulty here is the interpretation of the "royal poems." The first (9:2–7 [MT 9:1–6]) celebrates the birth of an heir to the throne or the accession of a king as the inauguration of a new era of well-being and peace. The language, similar to that of certain psalms with a similar theme (Pss. 2; 72; 110), embodies an ancient royal titulary and ideology probably of Egyptian origin. Attempts to identify the royal heir and ruler designate have been inconclusive. If the poem was composed around the time of the Syro-Ephraimite war, one would be inclined to think of Hezekiah whose accession Isaiah may well have greeted, prematurely as it happened, as the beginning of a more hopeful era. Since, however, the context in which the poem is embedded speaks of the destiny of the northern territories, we would be more inclined to assign it to the time of Josiah when hopes for reunification were running high.[83]

The dating of the second poem (11:1–9) is equally problematic. Its thematic affinity with the first of the misnamed "servant songs" (Isa. 42:1–4), and with those passages that speak of the Davidic scion as "the branch" (*ṣemaḥ*), create a strong presumption in favor of an exilic or early postexilic origin.

What, in the last analysis, is most characteristic of Isaiah and perhaps most difficult for us to comprehend, is his overwhelming sense of divine reality. The attribution of holiness to God (the Holy One of Israel, the Holy God) implies not so much the ethical character of Yahweh, which is not a major concern for Isaiah, as absolute, transcendent otherness. The reaction of Isaiah in the temple vision (chapter 6) illustrates how,

ɔf reality, sin is understood not so much in the act of ethical
, rather in the awareness of the reality of this Other breaking
o consciousness; "Woe is me! For I am lost; for I am a man of
ıs, and I dwell in the midst of a people of unclean lips" (Isa.
6:5).

The power of divine reality at work in the world follows from this intuition of divine essence, and so Isaiah is able to communicate with remarkable immediacy the sense of this power acting on the world, and therefore also the reality of judgment. Yahweh has a plan, a purpose, which does not necessarily conform to political feasibility (14:24–27; 28:23–29; 37:26). Isaiah does not believe in realpolitik, and therefore he does not take with ultimate seriousness those who appear to be the movers and shakers in national or international affairs—"the Egyptians are men and not God" (31:3). The reason is not that he keeps his private world of religious experience to himself as the only convincing reality. On the contrary, it is that experience that must take over and transform political and social life.

Isaiah makes it clear that the appropriate response to this perception of reality is an attitude of positive and active acceptance or, in other words, faith. He does not try to prove that this will work out well in the life of the individual or the community, but he simply states that it is so:

> If you are willing and obedient,
> you shall eat the good of the land.
> (1:19)

> If you do not stand firm in faith (*ta'ᵃmînû*),
> you shall not stand at all (*tēʾāmēnû*).
> (7:9)

> In quietness and in trust shall be your strength.
> (30:15)

IV

THE END OF NATIONAL
INDEPENDENCE

13. THE LAST ATTEMPT
AT EMANCIPATION AND REFORM

G. W. **Anderson,** "The Idea of the Remnant in the Book of Zephaniah," *ASTI* 11 (1978): 11–14; A. **Berlin,** *Zephaniah: A New Translation with Introduction and Commentary,* New York & London: Doubleday, 1994; H. **Cazelles,** "Sophonie, Jérémie et les Scythes en Palestine," *RB* 74 (1964): 24–44 [= "Zephaniah, Jeremiah, and the Scythians in Palestine," in L. Perdue and B. W. Kovacs, eds., *A Prophet to the Nations: Essays in Jeremiah Studies,* Winona Lake: Eisenbrauns, 1984, 129–49]; J. H. **Eaton,** *Obadiah, Nahum, Habakkuk and Zephaniah,* London: SCM Press, 1961, 119–59; F. C. **Fensham,** "Zephaniah, Book of," *IDBS,* 983–84; G. **Gerleman,** *Zephaniah textkritisch und literarisch untersucht,* Lund: S.W.K. Gleerup, 1942; J. **Gray,** *1 & 2 Kings: A Commentary,* Philadelphia: Westminster Press, 1970², 713–48; J. P. **Hyatt,** "The Date and Background of Zephaniah," *JNES* 7 (1948): 156–73; A. S. **Kapelrud,** *The Message of the Prophet Zephaniah: Morphology and Ideas,* Oslo: Universitetsforlaget, 1975; G. **Langohr,** "Rédaction et composition du livre de Sophonie," *Le Muséon* 89 (1976): 51–73; A.D.H. **Mayes,** *Deuteronomy,* London: Oliphants, 1979; E. W. **Nicholson,** *Deuteronomy and Tradition,* Oxford: Basil Blackwell, 1967; G. **von Rad,** *Studies in Deuteronomy,* Naperville, Ill.: Alec R. Allenson, 1944; *Deuteronomy: A Commentary,* Philadelphia: Westminster Press, 1966; J.J.M. **Roberts,** *Nahum, Habakkuk and Zephaniah,* Louisville: Westminster/John Knox Press, 1991, 161–223; W. **Rudolph,** *Micha-Nahum-Habakuk-Zephanja,* Gütersloh: Gütersloher Verlagshaus Gerd Mohn, 1975; L. P. **Smith** and E. L. **Lacheman,** "The Authorship of the Book of Zephaniah," *JNES* 9 (1950): 137–42; J.M.P. **Smith,** *Michah, Zephaniah, Nahum, Habakkuk, Obadiah amd Joel,* Edinburgh: T. & T. Clark, 1912, 159–263; R. L. **Smith,** *Micah-Malachi,* Waco, Tex.: Word Books, 1984, 120–44; D. L. **Williams,** "The Date of Zephaniah," *JBL* 82 (1963): 77–88.

Under Ashurbanipal, who died in either 629 or 627 B.C.E., the Assyrian empire, after reaching its greatest extent with the conquest of Egypt by Esarhaddon, began to disintegrate. The central government was finding it increasingly difficult to hold down the subject provinces, and its difficulties were compounded by pressure from new enemies, including Elamites from the Iranian highlands, who revolted in 641, and Scythians from the Caucasus region. A few years into the reign Egypt regained its independence under the twenty-sixth Saitic dynasty, and in 650 the king's brother Shamash-shum-ukin, viceroy of Babylon, raised the standard of revolt in that city in concert with other vassals, including perhaps the Judean king Manasseh. Ashurbanipal managed to hold on, but the empire was fatally weakened, and after his death events moved rapidly to their conclusion.

The kingdom of Babylon, founded by Nabopolassar in 625, pressed home its attack in alliance with Medes to the east and Scythians to the north. The Babylonian Chronicle, supported by the archaeological record, documents the capture and destruction of the major Assyrian cities, including Ashur, the ancient capital, Kalah and Dur-Sharrukin, and in 612 it was the turn of Nineveh. Ashur-uballit, last of a long line of Assyrian kings, held out for a short time in the Haran region in northern Mesopotamia where the Egyptians, now alarmed at the rapid shift in the balance of power, tried unsuccessfully to come to his assistance. With the decisive defeat of the Egyptian army at Carchemish in 605, the fate of Assyria was finally sealed and the country reverted to a condition almost as primitive as in the hyperbolic fantasies of Nahum and other anti-Assyrian seers.

The decline and fall of Assyria, and the subsequent struggle between Babylon and Egypt to fill the vacuum, bore decisively on the vassal provinces and states of the Syro-Palestinian corridor obliging them to make decisions which, in view of the uncertain outcome, could not have been free of danger. During his long reign (687–642), Manasseh seems to have stayed for most of the time in the good graces of the Assyrian overlord, for which he is accorded no credit at all by Dtr (2 Kings 21:1–16). The same policies were pursued by his son who succeeded him (2 Kings 21:19–22), leading to his assassination after about two years by the anti-Assyrian faction (2 Kings 21:23). Perhaps fearful of Assyrian retribution following on the suppression of revolts in 641–640, the group described as "the people of the land" avenged the death of Amon and put his eight-year old son Josiah on the throne, an act that must have put them in a commanding position during the king's minority.

It seems that the *'am hā'āreṣ* maintained this position down to the end of the kingdom of Judah, at which time the enmity of Jeremiah, who belonged to the appeasement faction, and the eventual execution of several of them by the Babylonians, indicate their continued commitment to opposing foreign rule (Jer. 1:18; 37:2; 2 Kings 25:19). But at that time, 640 B.C.E., it was still too early to make a clear bid for independence by denying the annual tribute, which weighed most heavily on the agrarian class represented by the "people of the land." According to the Chronicler (2 Chron. 34:3), not generally the most reliable of sources, a thoroughgoing religious reform was launched in the twelfth year of Josiah's reign. While we do not have the means to fine-tune our chronology of the period enough to answer the question, the date is close enough to Ashurbanipal's death to suggest the possibility that the reform was in part motivated by the anticipated change of ruler in Nineveh. Dtr, however, dates the reform six years later, after the discovery of a lawbook during repairs on the temple fabric (2 Kings 22:3–8). But since it is marginally easier to explain why the historian would want to suggest that the reform was inspired by this discovery than to suppose that the Chronicler simply invented an earlier reform, most scholars are now inclined to accept a connection between religious reform and the expectation or hope of political emancipation.

The situation in Judah during the decades preceding the Josian reforms is reflected in a small collection of sayings attributed to Zephaniah, a prophet identified in the title as active during the reign of Josiah (Zeph. 1:1). Exceptionally, Zephaniah is also provided with a four-generation genealogy beginning with a certain Hezekiah. Since Zephaniah seems to be familiar with activities at the court and refers to members of the royal family (1:8), it is still common to assume that the Hezekiah in question must be the Judean king who ruled before Manasseh. This is chronologically possible but quite uncertain. Another chronological possibility is that the Cushi listed as his father is identical with the great-grandfather of Jehudi, a courtier active during the reign of Jehoiakim (Jer. 36:14). The genealogy, alternatively, may have been occasioned precisely by the need to demonstrate native descent, in view of the fact that "Cushi" is also a gentilic meaning Ethiopian or Sudanese. This would be especially cogent if the title is of Deuteronomic origin, since native descent was an essential requirement for a prophet according to this school (Deut. 18:15, 18).[1] But it would be hazardous to draw any firm biographical conclusions from the superscription, and the rest of the book is no more forthcoming on the prophet himself than are most of the other books in Latter Prophets.

This little book exhibits relatively few of the usual formulae marking individual sayings. The opening diatribe against Judah and Jerusalem is bracketed by hyperbolic threat of cosmic proportions to be realized on the "Day of Yahweh" (1:2–18), a theme introduced by Amos. There follow denunciations of foreign peoples—Philistines, Moabites, Ammonites, and, further afield, Ethiopians and Assyrians (2:1–15)[2]—of a type found in most prophetic books. The expected transition from denunciation to promise of better things to come is delayed by a woe-saying directed against an unnamed city, presumably Jerusalem, that had failed to learn from the experience of disaster or near-disaster in the immediate past—perhaps with reference to the crisis of 701 B.C.E. under Hezekiah (3:1–7). The description of the future reversal (3:8–13) exploits the pseudo-Isaian themes of a final showdown in Jerusalem, the ingathering of both Jews and foreigners for worship in that city, and the emergence of a purified remnant, "a people humble and lowly."[3] This kind of language is notoriously difficult to place with any accuracy; together with the final apostrophe to Zion with which the book concludes (3:14–20), it makes a good fit with aspirations for return to the homeland and reconstruction in the late Neo-Babylonian or early Persian period.

In the first section (1:2–18) diatribe is directed at the syncretist party at the court. Since those who stand accused include the king's sons (1:8), the court can hardly be that of either Amon who was killed at age twenty-four or of Josiah during his minority. The political elite is indicted for engaging in the worship of Baal (2 Kings 21:3; 23:4–5), Assyrian-type cults of sun, moon, and stars (cf. 2 Kings 21:5; 23:4, 5, 11–12; Deut. 4:19), and the Ammonite deity Milcom alongside Yahweh (2 Kings 23:13).[4] The apostates are further identified as members of the aristocracy and the royal family who have adopted foreign customs and dress and profess an enlightened skepticism about the traditional religion and its prophetic representatives (1:7–13). Judges, prophets, and priests, adherents of the pro-Assyrian party, are also included in the indictment.[5] On the other side, that of Zephaniah himself, are ranged the "humble of the land" who fulfill the requirements of divine justice, seek righteousness, and live in obedient submission to God (2:3). At this point both theme and expression are remarkably close to the well-known "program" in Micah 6:8, namely, that what God requires of us is to act justly, be faithful to our commitments, and walk humbly with God. This, in effect, summarizes the ethical and religious ideal of the "humble of the land" with whom Zephaniah identifies.

The influence of Amos is apparent at several points in the book,[6] and demonstrates the strength and consistency of the tradition of prophetic preaching against social and political corruption. As in Amos, these evils are seen as premonitory hints of a universal judgment described in the traditional language of the "Day of Yahweh"—a final reckoning involving not just Israel, or even the nations, but the entire cosmos in a catastrophic act of uncreation (Zeph. 1:2–3; cf. Jer. 4:23–26). There are also hints of the traditional theme of the "foe from the north" (Zeph. 1:10–11), which will feature significantly in the early career of Jeremiah (Jer. 1:13–15; 4:6, etc).[7]

This is the right time to note that much of the last part of Micah (chapters 6—7) appears to have been edited and brought up to date during the time of Zephaniah's activity. Micah 6:9–16 reflects a situation of social disorder such as obtained during the reigns of Manasseh and Amon and probably also during the early years of Josiah's reign (2 Kings 21:16; 24:4). The allusion to "statutes of Omri" and "deeds of Ahab" (Micah 6:16) recalls the condemnation of Manasseh for imitating the much-maligned Ahab in setting up syncretist cults (2 Kings 21:3; cf. 23:4–14). Micah 6:9–16 also parallels Zephaniah in several respects. Both condemn an unnamed city, which must be Jerusalem (Micah 6:9; Zeph. 3:1), and expatiate on the evils of idolatry in general and the cult of Baal in particular. Both Micah and Zephaniah are unsparing in their condemnation of corrupt officeholders, listing princes, judges, prophets, and priests (Micah 3:9–12; Zeph. 3:3–5). The contrast between pride and humility is also a noteworthy feature of both, and we have seen that the much-quoted ethical summation of Micah 6:8 could have served as a program for the "humble of the land" of Zeph. 2:3; 3:11–13.[8] Here too, then, we note the persistence of a prophetic tradition of ethical teaching and protest against social abuses that shows signs of increasing consolidation and formalization as time passes. We now go on to inquire whether this tradition received a degree of official recognition by being incorporated into, or at least directly influencing, the Deuteronomic law considered as a state document.

Dtr's account of Josiah's reign (2 Kings 22:1–23:30) contains a fairly detailed account of religious reforms following on the discovery of a law book during repairs on the temple fabric. Close literary analysis of this account suggests the conclusion that two versions have been juxtaposed. The first (23:4–20) deals with the destruction of objectionable cult shrines and cult paraphernalia around the country, and especially the purification of the Jerusalem temple from non-Yahwistic personnel and objects; the second (23:21–24) prescribes a national celebration of Passover in Jerusalem and proscribes mediums, wizards, and associated "abominations." Only the latter refers the measures taken back to the finding of the lawbook, which is not so much as mentioned in the first account.

This feature of the narrative, together with others, has given rise to a protracted and ongoing debate as to what historical reality, if any, lies behind this entire chapter of the history.[9] Readers of a more conservative mindset will take the narrative more or less at face value. What the priest Hilkiah found in the temple was indeed the law contained in Deuteronomy and promulgated by Moses that, after a long period of neglect, was rediscovered, was verified by the prophetess Huldah, and provided the blueprint for a thoroughgoing religious reform. An alternative scenario would start out from the chronology provided in the parallel version in Chronicles (2 Chron. 34:1–18), according to which the reform got underway six years earlier, in Josiah's twelfth year, and the discovery took place some time later. But in view of the very persuasive arguments for dating Deuteronomy much later than the time of Moses, many critical readers have embraced the pious fraud theory first propounded by de Wette in the early nineteenth century. According to this hypothesis the book, recently composed, was "planted" by members of the reform party with access to the temple shortly before its discovery.

It is at least clear that for the author of the narrative (Dtr) the lawbook on which the reforms were based is the book of Deuteronomy or the Deuteronomic law (chaps. 12—26) in whatever form it existed at the time of writing.[10] Dtr wishes the reader to accept that this law was given by Moses, was available to Joshua, who is exhorted to meditate on it while annihilating the Canaanites (Josh. 1:8; cf. 8:30–31, 34; 23:6), was implemented in one particular instance by King Amaziah of Judah a century and a half before Josiah (2 Kings 14:5–6; cf. Deut. 24:16), but is not heard of between that point in time and its rediscovery during Josiah's reign. Critical scholarship is, however, unanimous in reading Deuteronomy as a pseudepigraphal work composed long after the time of Moses, though there is a wide range of opinion on the editorial history and authorship of the book. It is agreed that it attained its final form after the Judean monarchy had passed from the scene, but it contains enough indications of a linguistic and thematic nature to justify a seventh century date for the first draft. The story, if not the historical reality, of the discovery of an ancient book also makes a good fit with the renewal of interest in antiquity at that time, reflected in the collecting and preserving of ancient texts by Assurbanipal in the great library at Nineveh and the revival of ancient art forms under Psammeticus (Psamtik) I in Egypt.[11]

Returning to 2 Kings 22—23: we must take seriously the possibility that the account of the discovery of the book in the temple is a free composition of the author written to explain how the law came to be neglected during the preceding reigns of Manasseh and Amon. The main point would be to present a favorable profile of Josiah as an observant and zealous devotee of Yahweh. Pointing in this direction is the reaction of the young king, but not of those around him, on hearing the law read to him (22:11), and the favorable verdict of Huldah on Josiah, but not on his contemporaries (22:15–20). It also appears likely that the narrative about the repair of the temple is based on the account of repairs carried out earlier by Joash following on the execution of the Baalist queen Athaliah (2 Kings 12:4–16). The dating of the reform to the king's twentieth year in 2 Chron. 34:3 is probably meant to reinforce this positive image of Josiah by suggesting that he initiated the reform immediately on attaining his majority.

We can therefore accept, as a critical minimum, that Dtr's account of this event in the reign of Josiah (640–609) was elaborated on the basis of measures taken in Judah at that time to achieve independence from Assyria, in rapid decline following on the death of Ashurbanipal. These measures would have included the rejection of Assyrian-type cults—solar, lunar, and planetary (2 Kings 23:4,11–12; cf. Deut. 17:3)—and, in general, insistence on the worship of the national deity to the exclusion of competing cults, even those practiced in Israel for centuries. The extension of Josiah's reforming activity into the Assyrian provinces to the north (2 Kings 23:15–20) would have signaled even more clearly the intent to throw off the Assyrian yolk.

We must now go on to ask whether the prophetic figures active during the period of Assyrian hegemony influenced official policies and movements for reform in any way. Dtr records sporadic attempts at reform throughout the history of Judah. Asa, third to rule after Solomon, is credited with getting rid of idolatrous images, attempting to suppress the goddess cult, and putting the male cult prostitutes out of business (1 Kings 15:9–15). The limited success attending these measures may be gauged by the number of times they were repeated by later rulers— Jehoshaphat, Joash, Hezekiah, and, finally, Josiah (1 Kings 22:43–46; 2 Kings 11:17–18; 18:1–8). But what might easily be overlooked is that these reforms deal exclusively with cultic matters. Nowhere does the historian record official attempts to remedy the kinds of social abuses excoriated by the prophets, and the final disaster is explained solely in terms of cultic aberration (e.g., in Huldah's oracle, 2 Kings 22:15–17), never with reference to social injustices. And this is all the more puzzling in view of the juxtaposition of laws concerning cult and social ethics in Deuteronomy. Linked with this is another puzzle referred to earlier, namely, the failure of the historian to so much as mention the prophets active during the Assyrian period to whom books are attributed, with the exception of an Isaiah very different from the author of the sayings in Isaiah 1—35 who is represented as working in close collaboration with Hezekiah (2 Kings 19:1–7, 20–34; 20:1–19).

We can only speculate about what the solution to this puzzle might be. The historian could have assumed that the social message was implied in his many allusions to the preaching of "his (God's) servants the prophets,"[12] or in reference to the law that was, in the Deuteronomist view, the raison d'être of prophetic preaching. He seems in any case to be convinced that cultic aberration was the decisive factor in bringing about the political disasters that his history purported to explain.

If there is little evidence of prophetic influence on the history, the same is not the case with Deuteronomy and the Deuteronomic law or program. Like several prophetic books (Jer. 1:1; Amos 1:1), Deuteronomy is presented as "words of Moses" (Deut. 1:1) and in the form of public address to the entire people. Moses himself is described in the book as a prophet (Deut. 18:15–18; 34:10), and the true prophet, the one who continues the mission and work of Moses, is invested with the highest authority. There can be no doubt that Deuteronomy was deeply influenced by the prophetic movement, even while taking up a cautious attitude to the kind of apodictic claims advanced by those prophets who denounced public officeholders for their immorality or indifference to the common good.

Prophetic influence is most clearly discerned in the social legislation of Deuteronomy, which is, in some respects, quite advanced. Though marked by a certain utopian character, apparent in its abolition of poverty in principle (Deut. 15:4), it laid down precise provisions in favor of the marginal and disadvantaged, including resident aliens, the fatherless, widows, and unemployed clergy, which amount to a kind of social security system. Examples are the triennial tithe destined for these classes of people (14:28–29; 24:17–22; 26:12–15), remission of debts every seventh year (15:1–3) with appropriate safeguards against abuses (15:7–11), the prohibition of usury (23:19–20) and abusive debt collection (24:6, 10–13, 17), and insistence on the proper administration of justice (16:18–20). There are also provisions for the protection and, in some cases, the emancipation of slaves (15:12–18; 23:15–16; 24:7), and for fair treatment in the case of involuntary homicide (19:1–13).

One of the most distinctive features of the Deuteronomic legislation is the concern to preserve a traditional agrarian way of life together with the rights of the small farmer. Care for property, one's own and that of others, even extends to birds' nests (Deut. 22:6–7). The prohibition against removing boundary marks (19:14) struck at the practice of enclosure denounced by the prophets (e.g., Micah 2:2), and the provisions for release from military service (Deut. 20:5–9; 24:5) highlight a long-standing source of bitterness between the agrarian class and the monarchy. It is also noteworthy that the priestly tithe is quite restricted (18:1–8) and that support of the cult, an increasingly onerous burden as its operation became more and more complex, is to be proportionate to the individual's means (16:16–17). The monarchy itself is not condemned, but it is to be subject to the law and therefore, in effect, a constitutional monarchy (17:14–20).

These examples suggest that Deuteronomy contains not so much a law code as a program or polity, and it is apparent that such programs emanate from distinct parties or interest groups. Few issues in Old Testament studies have been debated as intensely and inconclusively as the provenance of the Deuteronomic program of cultic and social reform. At one time it seemed well established that its origins were to be sought in the Northern Kingdom, either in the period of its independent existence or during the century between the fall of Samaria and the finding of the lawbook in the Jerusalem temple.[13] However, one of the main supports of this hypothesis, namely, affinity between Deuteronomy and the Elohist source in the Pentateuch (E), is problematic not only because of the elusive nature of this strand but also on account of the difficulty of establishing its "northern" character with a reasonable degree of probability. Deuteronomy certainly betrays some affinity with the Ephraimite prophet Hosea, but Hosea shows little interest in the social abuses against which Deuteronomy legislates.[14] Moreover, diatribe against Baal and Ashera worship is by no means confined to Hosea.

A more promising approach, first proposed by Bentzen and given wide currency by von Rad,[15] focuses attention on the Levites as the class responsible for both the homiletic form and the content of the Deuteronomic lawbook. This line of inquiry has proved to be productive in several respects, but its Achilles' heel is the dearth of usable historical information on priests and Levites and the need to rely heavily on information provided by the Chronicler, not the most reliable of sources. In his history the Chronicler introduces Levites at several points as instructors in Torah, judges, and reformers—in other words, as discharging the functions proper to their office in the period of the Second Temple. But these Levites form a distinct clerical class inferior and ancillary to the sacrificing priests, and in this sense they are not attested during the period prior to the Babylonian exile.[16] Deuteronomy speaks throughout of "levitical priests," implying that ideally all priests are of Levitical descent, and Dtr records that such priests were excluded from gainful employment in the state sanctuaries of Bethel and Dan set up by Jeroboam (1 Kings 12:31). This may provide a useful clue since it is quite likely that, as the Chronicler informs us (2 Chron. 11:13–17; 13:9), these unemployed priests found their way into the kingdom of Judah where they were the object of charitable attention by the Deuteronomic legislators. But there is really no evidence that they brought with them a distinctive theological tradition that left its mark on Deuteronomy.

Several commentators have correctly emphasized the homiletic style of Deuteronomy, have taken it as evidence for Levitical preaching during the period of the monarchy, and have identified a later form of the Deuteronomic homily in Chronicles.[17] This is an attractive theory, but unfortunately unsupported by evidence. In fact, the verb in classical Hebrew that comes closest to our sense of preaching, *ntp* (hiphil), occurs generally in parallelism with "prophesy" and refers always to a prophetic activity. During the period in question, therefore, it is the prophet, not the Levite, who is the preacher (*maṭṭîp*).[18]

With all due regard for multiple uncertainties, this Deuteronomic chapter in the religious history of Israel may be summarized as follows. Movements of reform had been a constant feature of the history as narrated by Dtr since the time of Asa and his son Jehoshaphat in the late tenth and early ninth centuries (1 Kings 15:11–15; 22:43–46). The attempt to disestablish the high places (*bāmôt*) was first made by Hezekiah (2 Kings 18:4,22) as part of a reform whose purpose was to avoid a repetition of the fate visited on the Northern Kingdom. Impressive parallels between the preaching of Micah and the Deuteronomic legislation[19] suggest further that the class referred to as "the people of the land," whose interests and ethos found expression in Micah's preaching, played a significant role in the reform movement both then and in the next century under Josiah. We should also allow for a significant contribution from a pietist group responsive to prophetic preaching described as the "humble of the land" in Zephaniah. It may be suggested that such groups formed the conduit by means of which prophetic protest achieved a degree of official recognition by being incorporated in a state document. The scribal or sapiential character of Deuteronomy, to which several scholars have rightly drawn attention,[20] does not contradict this conclusion, since Deuteronomy was a state document (whether promulgated or not) drafted by specialists trained in the scribal and legal traditions. These scribes appear to have been active during Hezekiah's reign, and by the time of Josiah they had begun to assume responsibility for the writing and probably also the interpreting of the laws.[21]

Rules governing warfare (Deut. 20:1–20), treaty formulations including curses (Deut. 27:15–26; 28:15–68), and a rather consistent xenophobia are aspects of Deuteronomy that reflect the aspirations for independence from the Assyrians under Josiah and perhaps also Hezekiah. It was therefore natural that the book should emphasize the specifically Israelite character of prophecy. Prophecy is pointedly contrasted with foreign modes of mediation (18:14), and it is insisted that the prophet, no less than the ruler, must be a native Israelite (18:15, 18). The prophet who speaks in the name of a foreign deity is guilty of sedition and subject to the death penalty (13:1–5; 18:20), a stipulation that is readily intelligible in the context of the anti-Assyrian measures pursued, once the occasion offered, during the last century of Judah's existence.

14. THE PERSPECTIVE
OF CULT PROPHECY ON INTERNATIONAL AFFAIRS:
NAHUM AND HABAKKUK

W. F. **Albright,** "The Psalm of Habakkuk," in H. H. Rowley, ed., *Studies in Old Testament Prophecy,* Edinburgh: T. & T. Clark, 1950, 1–18; W. **Brownlee,** *The Text of Habakkuk in the Ancient Commentary from Qumran,* JBL Monograph Series 11, Philadelphia: Society of Biblical Literature and Exegesis, 1959; K. **Budde,** "Habakuk," *ZDMG* 84 (1930): 139–47; K. J. **Cathcart,** *Nahum in the Light of Northwest Semitic,* Rome: Biblical Institute Press, 1973; "Treaty Curses in the Book of Nahum," *CBQ* 35 (1973): 179–87; "More Philological Studies in Nahum," *JNSL* 7 (1979): 1–12; A. **George,** "Nahoum, Le Livre de," *SDB* 6: 291–301; D. E. **Gowan,** *The Triumph of Faith in Habakkuk,* Atlanta: John Knox Press, 1976; H. **Gunkel,** "Nahum 1," *ZAW* 13 (1893): 223–44; A. **Haldar,** *Studies in the Book of Nahum,* Uppsala: Almqvist & Wiksell, 1947; P. **Haupt,** "The Book of Nahum," *JBL* 26 (1907): 1–53; T. **Hiebert,** *God of My Victory: The Ancient Hymn in Habakkuk 3,* Atlanta: Scholars Press, 1986; P. **Humbert,** "Le Problème du livre de Nahoum," *RHPR* 12 (1932): 1–15; *Problèmes du Livre d'Habacuc,* Neuchâtel: Secrétariat de l'Université, 1944; J. G. **Janzen,** "Eschatological Symbol and Existence in Habakkuk," *CBQ* 44 (1982): 394–414; J. **Jeremias,** *Kultprophetie und Gerichtsverkündigung in der später Königszeit Israels,* Neukirchen-Vluyn: Neukirchener Verlag, 1969; P. **Jöcken,** *Das Buch Habakuk,* Cologne: Peter Hanstein, 1977; C.-A. **Keller,** "Die theologische Bewältigung der geschichtlichen Wirklichkeit in der Prophetie Nahums," *VT* 22 (1972): 399–419; "Die Eigenart des Propheten Habakuks," *ZAW* 85 (1973): 156–67; E. **Nielsen,** "The Righteous and the Wicked in Habaqquq," *StTh* 6 (1953): 54–78; E. **Otto,** "Die Stellung der Wehe-Worte in der Verkündigung des Propheten Habakuk," *ZAW* 89 (1977): 73–107; "Die Theologie des Buches Habakuk," *VT* 35 (1985): 274–95; B. **Peckham,** "The Vision of Habakkuk," *CBQ* 48 (1986): 617–36; B. **Renaud,** "La Composition du Livre de Nahum," *ZAW* 99 (1987): 198–219; J.J.M. **Roberts,** *Nahum, Habakkuk and Zephaniah,* 37–158; W. **Rudolph,** *Micha-Nahum-Habakuk-Zephanja,* 143–254; H. **Schulz,** *Das Buch Nahum,* Berlin: Walter de Gruyter, 1973; J.M.P. **Smith,** in J.M.P. Smith, W. H. Ward, and J. A. Bewer, *Micah, Zephaniah, Nahum, Habakkuk, Obadiah and Joel,* Edinburgh: T. & T. Clark, 1911,

267–360; W. **Soll**, "Babylonian and Biblical Acrostics," *Bib* 68 (1988): 305–23; M. A. **Sweeney**, "Concerning the Structure and Generic Character of the Book of Nahum," *ZAW* 104 (1992): 364–77; C. C. **Torrey**, "Alexander the Great in the Old Testament Prophecies," BZAW 41 (1925): 281–86; H. H. **Walker** and N. W. **Lund**, "The Literary Structure of the Book of Habakkuk," *JBL* 53 (1934): 355–70; A. S. **van der Woude**, "The Book of Nahum: A Letter Written in Exile," *OTS* 20 (1977): 108–26.

Max Weber's contention that prophecy in Israel was essentially concerned with international affairs[22] is confirmed by the history of the last decades of Judean independence. The books of Nahum and Habakkuk span the period of the decline and collapse of Assyria and the rise of Babylonian power under Nebuchadrezzar. Nahum is a composite work and, as we would expect, has been adjusted to fit later scenarios down into the Hellenistic period—not a difficult operation since the city, Nineveh, is mentioned by name only twice. The book seems to have been of special interest to those sectarians of the Hasmonean period who produced the Qumran Nahum *pešer* (4QpNah or 4Q169) and read it as a coded message referring to contemporary events.[23] But it is not a pseudepigraphal work, and its original nucleus can be dated with some assurance as the early decades of Josiah's reign.[24] We shall see shortly that Habakkuk dates from the end of the period in question, that is, from the time of Babylonian ascendancy following on the death of Josiah.

The centerpiece of Nahum is the oracle[25] against Nineveh (Nahum 1:15–2:12 [MT 2:1–13]) rounded out with a short prose comment (2:13 [MT 2:14]). There follows a woe oracle also directed against Nineveh, the Assyrian capital, concluding with the general rejoicing anticipated, with good reason, at the collapse of the Assyrian empire (3:1–19). These poems are introduced by an acrostic psalm in which the alphabetic sequence can be traced, with the help of a little text-critical surgery, from aleph to kaph. Added at some point to the anti-Assyrian poems to locate them in a liturgical setting, the acrostic psalm celebrates the theophany of the national warrior god using familiar motifs in a well-established tradition of cultic hymnography.[26]

The three short sayings following (Nahum 1:9–14), the text of which is not well preserved, may represent surviving fragments of cultic prophecy from the period of nationalistic revival following the death of Ashurbanipal. It is now impossible to say whether they come from the prophet of the title, Nahum of Elkosh, about whom nothing is known.[27] The first of these sayings (vv. 9–11) may be taking issue with a group opposed to the anti-Assyrian policy of Josiah and his supporters and, in that group, to one described as an "evil counselor," presumably a high official at the court. The second (vv. 12–13) is addressed to Jerusalem and, in the manner characteristic of official court and cult prophets, promises an end to Assyrian rule. The last (v. 14) is addressed to an individual, probably Ashurbanipal, recently deceased, predicting the destruction of his gods and the end of his line.

The anti-Assyrian poem is introduced by the herald (*m^ebaśśēr*), the one who brings good news. This kind of language would be particularly appropriate for the kind of optimistic prophet Nahum is taken to be, though its occurrence in Second Isaiah (Isa. 40:9; 52:7) suggests a shared editorial history. The poem describes with brutal realism the presumably anticipated capture and sack of Nineveh, which was in fact captured and "turned into hills of ruins and heaps of debris" by the Medes and Babylonians in 612 B.C.E. (ANET, 304–5). The herald bringing good news may have been a cult prophet acting on behalf of the anti-Assyrian party in the early years of the reign. We do not know whether it circulated surreptitiously or was published openly. At any rate, the seer's call to celebrate festivals and fulfill vows (1:15 [MT 2:1]) was in fact answered by Josiah when he convoked a great Passover of liberation a few years later (2 Kings 23:21–23).

The woe oracle against the "bloody city" (Nahum 3:1–19)[28] continues the description of its annihilation, and with this the book comes to an end. The tone of these poems will not easily find sympathetic resonance in the mind of the modern reader, or at least the modern reader who has not suffered under such conditions as the Assyrians imposed on their subject provinces. But it may help to recall that what was at stake for the poet and his audience was the reality of divine power and the possibility of justice in the world of international affairs. These issues will come to clearer expression in Habakkuk, to be considered shortly.

The most difficult issue with this book is to situate it on the spectrum of prophetic phenomena. Oracles against foreign nations are among the oldest and best established of prophetic types of discourse. The genre is present in most prophetic books, it occurs in a variety of contexts, but it is accepted that it originated and continued in use—though not exclusively—within the official cult and as a function of national policy. Nahum is, in essence, an oracle against a foreign nation, which would imply that its author was a central intermediary and that he presents us with cultic and nationalistic prophecy in a fairly pure state. The presence of hymnic and psalmlike material in the book, the mythological language of theophany (Nahum 1:4; cf. Amos 1:2; Joel 3:16 [MT 4:16]), the title "Yahweh of the hosts" (Nahum 2:13; 3:5), and the absence of criticism of the cult and other state institutions all point in this direction. While, therefore, the book cannot be read as a coherent liturgy, it seems that Nahum was the spokesman for the temple cult and

its personnel in the service of nationalistic revival after a century of subjugation to Assyria.[29]

In spite of the impressive territorial gains resulting from Josiah's bid for
independence (2 Kings 23:4; 2 Chron. 34:6–7),[30] a perceptive observer
of the international scene would have been obliged to make a rather cautious assessment of future possibilities. Egypt, which had regained its
independence in 655 B.C.E., was already on its way to bringing Syria and
Palestine back into its sphere of influence a decade before the death of
Ashurbanipal with the conquest of the Philistine city of Ashdod in 639.
Once it became apparent that Assyria was finished as a great power, this
goal was pursued more vigorously by Psammeticus I and Necho II of the
twenty-sixth Saitic dynasty. Josiah decided, correctly in the event, that the
future lay with the Babylonians; but his attempt to win their favor by opposing the Egyptian penetration into Syria cost him his life (2 Kings
23:29–30). The "people of the land" chose as his successor his younger
son Shallum whose throne-name was Jehoahaz (Jer. 22:11; 1 Chron.
3:15), no doubt because he opposed the new superpower. But the Egyptians deposed him after only three months on the throne and put Eliakim, Josiah's oldest son, in his place. Eliakim, renamed Jehoiakim by
the Egyptians, ruled as an Egyptian puppet with the task of keeping the
peace, suppressing movements of independence, and collecting the annual tribute routinely levied by the great empires (2 Kings 23:35). These
tasks did not make for popularity, and it is no surprise to hear of bloodshed, the execution of dissidents including prophets (Jer. 26:20–23),
and the opposition of those, including Jeremiah himself (Jer. 22:13–19;
26:1–19), who had supported at least some aspects of Josiah's policies.
    After the decisive defeat of the Egyptians at Carchemish on the Up-
per Euphrates in the summer of 605 B.C.E., control of the region passed
to the Babylonians, and Jehoiakim was forced to submit to a new master.
Shortly thereafter he made the mistake of withholding tribute, probably
as a result of the Babylonian failure to conquer Egypt in 600 B.C.E. As-
sisted by levies from neighboring states (2 Kings 24:2), the Babylonians
invested Jerusalem but Jehoiakim died, or was killed, before they could
occupy the city.[31] After a brief siege his son Jehoiachin was forced to submit and was deported together with the royal family, members of the
court, and a significant number of the professional classes. Many people
in Judah continued to regard the exiled king as monarch de jure, and
the Babylonians themselves may have encouraged this as a means of
keeping their appointee, Mattaniah, renamed Zedekiah, in line. During
the latter's reign the struggle between the pro-Babylonian and anti-
Babylonian parties in Jerusalem reached a level of great intensity, creating

a situation that Zedekiah, who comes through as a weak individual, was clearly unable to control. The outcome was a further bid for independence that predictably failed and led to the destruction of the capital city and the temple, another deportation, and the final loss of national independence (587 or 586 B.C.E.).

Shortly after the death of Josiah, a Jerusalemite prophet proclaimed, in the manner of Amos and Isaiah, the advent of a new world conqueror as the instrument of Yahweh's purpose in history. The proclamation comes as part of a dialogue between the prophet and his god (Hab. 1:2–2:5), an innovation in the prophetic literature that will be used in the second part of Isaiah (Isa. 40:1–11; 49:1–18) but that occurs in or is implied by certain cultic hymns that feature a complaint addressed to God followed by an assurance of a positive response delivered through a cultic intermediary (e.g., Pss. 20; 28; 60; 108). Like the lamentation psalms, this conversation begins with a complaint that the wicked and violent appear to triumph while the innocent are persecuted (Hab. 1: 2–4) . Using traditional language to describe an invading force (cf. Isa. 5:26–30), the divine response points to a new initiative of Yahweh in world history, the rousing of the Babylonians (*kaśdîm*—Chaldeans, Hab. 1:6), who, though themselves reprobates, will serve as instruments of punishment for the "wicked" in Judah (1:5–11). This reply does not entirely still the prophet's doubts since he continues to complain about the triumph of the wicked over the righteous, and he does so in a way suggesting that he himself is personally involved. But as he continues, the target of his denunciations shifts to the pitiless conqueror who devours nations, and to this a satisfactory answer can only lie in the future (1:12–2:1). The final response from Yahweh does not provide this answer. It will come, but in the meantime the righteous must persevere, believing that the salvation, the promise of which is communicated through prophetic revelation, will eventually be theirs (2:2–5).

This brief summary of the first part of Habakkuk has passed over some serious problems of interpretation that have proved remarkably resistant to solution and that must now be briefly mentioned.

The first concerns the date and historical reference of the dialogue. The allusion to Chaldeans would seem to place it firmly in the late Assyrian or early Neo-Babylonian period. Beginning with Duhm, who read "Kittim" for "Chaldeans" at Hab. 1:6, however, commentators have from time to time speculated that *hakkaśdîm* (1:6) is a gloss.[32] If this were so, the text would provide no clue to the identity of the "bitter and hasty nation" and its leader, especially in view of the conventional military language (the so-called *Völkerkampf* theme) employed.

Speculation, therefore, has been free to range from the Assyrians toward the end of the seventh century to the Macedonians and Alexander the Great in the fourth.[33] Closely related is the identity of "the wicked" (vv. 4, 13), opinion on which oscillates between internal opponents of the prophet and the new aggressors on the international scene.[34] It would be no surprise if this text had been reused and reapplied to changing political situations, but that would not exclude an origin in the years following the death of Josiah (609 B.C.E.), a time of profound political and religious disorientation in Judah. "The wicked" would then be the supporters of Jehoiakim (609–598) who, our historian tells us, shed innocent blood, executed prophets, and disregarded the claims of social justice (2 Kings 23:35; cf. Jer. 22:13–19; 26:1–23). The threat from the Babylonians and Nebuchadrezzar their ruler would make best sense sometime between the battle of Carchemish (605) and the first deportation (598). We have a close thematic parallel in Jer. 25:8–14 dated to that time. Yahweh is sending for the tribes of the north and for Nebuchadrezzar his servant as an instrument of Judah's chastisement. In due course, however, these two also would be punished for overstepping the bounds of their commission in fulfillment of prophetic prediction.

Habakkuk is the only preexilic prophet identified as a *nābî'* in the title, which could plausibly be taken to imply that he was a professional or prebendary prophet connected with the temple cult. The same conclusion is suggested by the term *maśśā',* oracle, used more often than not for curses or comminations against hostile nations, a genre that also featured in temple liturgies when the occasion called for it (cf. Pss. 60; 83; 108). We saw that the dialogue in the first section is based on a liturgical model and the psalm in Habakkuk 3 has its own liturgical rubrics. As a central intermediary, Habakkuk would be expected to deliver oracles especially at a time of political crisis, and we have an excellent example of the process by which such oracles were solicited at the end of Habakkuk's second complaint (2:1). The passage may be translated as follows:

> At my guard post let me take my stand
>   and station myself on the watchtower[35]
> to watch and see what he will say through me,
>   and what answer he will give to my complaint.

An anonymous seer, probably active during the Babylonian exile, has left behind a similar account of soliciting an oracle announcing the fall of Babylon (Isa. 21:6–8):

> Go, set a watchman,
>   let him announce what he sees.

> When he sees horsemen, riders in pairs,
>   riders on asses, riders on camels,
> let him listen hard, very hard.
> Then the seer cried out:
> "On a watchtower, O Lord, I stand
>   continually by day;
> at my guard post I take my station
>   every night."

While the precise significance of the terms "watchtower" and "guard post" escapes us, the passages provide a valuable glimpse of a process analogous to incubation rituals (e.g., Gen. 28:11; 1 Sam. 3:3) whereby oracles were solicited. The psalm in the third chapter completes the picture by a vivid description of the psychological and physiological changes that could occur during this preparatory process:

> I listen, I tremble inwardly,
>   my lips quiver at the sound.
> Rottenness enters my bones
>   my footsteps tremble beneath me.
>   (Habbakuk 3:16)

Habakkuk's patience was rewarded when he received a reply, doubtless in an state of transformed or disturbed consciousness, in which he was commanded to write the vision on tablets in large characters, like a highway sign, so that it could be read on the run. The reply, therefore, was not the kind that the analogy of the lamentation psalms would lead us to expect. And it leaves us asking what the vision was that the prophet was commanded to write so large that it could not be ignored even by those who hurried past without stopping.

From the answer of Yahweh it is at least clear that the vision writ large contained a prediction of well-being the truth of which many, the prophet among them, had reason to doubt (Hab. 3:3). No such vision has been mentioned in the book up to this point, so that some commentators have wondered whether the psalm in chap. 3, describing in magnificent language the coming of the warrior-god to save his people, is intended. It does indeed speak of the defeat of transgressors and enemies of Israel (Hab. 3:13–14). It describes in impressive terms the onset of prophetic ecstasy and records the prophet waiting quietly, that is, without doubt or perturbation, for the divine intervention (Hab. 3:16). But since we have no assurance that the dialogue and the psalm come from the same hand, we have to reckon with the possibility that the vision and prediction in question are those of an earlier prophet that remained unfulfilled and thus gave rise to the crisis of faith through which Habakkuk and his contemporaries were passing. In that case we might consider the prophecy that Isaiah was commanded to write as a warranty of its truth against a future fulfillment (Isa. 8:16–17; 30:8–10; cf. 29:11–12). Isaiah too spoke of the need for a positive endurance in faith when present circumstances seemed to contradict the prophetic promise of divine intervention (Isa. 7:9; 30:15). And since the words of Isaiah seem to have been given a new lease of life with Josiah's reforms and the expectation of freedom from the Assyrian yoke that inspired the reforms, a crisis of faith in prophecy, and therefore in the possibility of divine intervention, may well have occurred when those hopes died with the tragic and premature death of Josiah at Megiddo (2 Kings 23:29–30).[36]

The faith that is called for in the interim between prophecy and fulfillment is faith in the possibility and reality of divine intervention in human affairs (Hab. 2:4; cf. 1:5), a faith no easier then than it is now after the Holocaust. By means of a rather different reading, "he who is righteous by faith shall live" (Rom. 1:17; Gal. 3:11), Paul made this celebrated text serve as scriptural support for his polemic about the respective roles of faith and works. The Qumran Habakkuk *pešer,* on the other hand, referred it to both observance of the laws and faith in the Teacher of Righteousness (1QpHab viii. 1–3). Habakkuk's differentiation between the wicked and the righteous on the basis of faith does in fact constitute a bridge between earlier prophetic teaching, especially that of Isaiah, and certain developments during the period of the Second Temple that would lead to the emergence of the sects, inclusive of early Christianity.

The second and quite distinct section of the book consists in five woes against an unnamed tyrant (Hab. 2:6–20).[37] While it would be natural to identify the tyrant with the Babylonian king spoken of earlier, the language used provides no certain clues. He is a ruler guilty of plunder, bloodshed, and violence; he has founded a city on blood, has brought shame on his house, and inhabits a high and inaccessible fortress. Such a description could fit any one of several candidates throughout the history of the book's transmission. It bears repeating that prophetic books were not copyrighted and that sayings against foreign nations and rulers were particularly subject to reinterpretation in the light of new situations.

If it is true, as it seems to be, that Habakkuk is a central rather than peripheral prophetic figure, a *nābî'* in the officially sanctioned meaning of the term, it is equally true that by that time, the late seventh and early sixth century, such prophets were finding themselves increasingly in the position of having to take sides. Also indicative of a changing situation is the prophet's solicitation not of an oracle of salvation, which would be expected of a central intermediary, but of divine assurance in a crisis of faith. While the psalm in chapter 3 does not appear to be the original answer to the prophet's complaint, in the final arrangement of the book it serves the same purpose as the theophanies in Psalm 73 and at the conclusion of the book of Job, both of which raise the question of theodicy—the question, that is, of the reality and, by implication, the ethical character of the god of traditional religion. Such questioning increased in intensity following on the cumulative disasters of the late seventh and early sixth centuries B.C.E. It also featured prominently in the sayings of and traditions about a most remarkable individual in the history of Israel, to whom we now turn.

15. JEREMIAH

P. R. **Ackroyd,** *Exile and Restoration,* Philadelphia: Westminster Press, 1968, 50–61; "The Book of Jeremiah—Some Recent Studies," *JSOT* 28 (1984): 47–59; J. D. **Ball,** "Towards a New Understanding of the Jeremiah Scroll: The Problem and Recent Scholarship," *Studia Biblica et Theologica* 13 (1983): 51–75; H. **Bardtke,** "Jeremia der Fremdvölkerprophet," *ZAW* 53 (1935): 209–39; 54 (1936): 240–62; J. L. **Berquist,** "Prophetic Legitimation in Jeremiah," *VT* 39 (1989): 129–39; J. **Bright,** *Jeremiah,* Garden City: Doubleday, 1965; R. P. **Carroll,** *From Chaos to Covenant: Uses of Prophecy in the Book of Jeremiah,* London: SCM Press, 1981; *Jeremiah: A Commentary,* Philadelphia: Westminster, 1986; "Arguing about Jeremiah: Recent Studies and the Nature of a Prophetic Book," *VTS* 43 (1991): 222–35; J. L. **Crenshaw,** "A Living Tradition: The Book of Jeremiah in Current Research," *Int* 37 (1983): 117–29; T. R. **Hobbs,** "Some Remarks on the Composition and Structure of the Book of Jeremiah," *CBQ* 34 (1974): 257–75; W. L. **Holladay,** "The Background of Jeremiah's Self-Understanding," *JBL* 83 (1964): 153–64; *Jeremiah 1,* Philadelphia: Fortress Press, 1986; *Jeremiah 2,* Minneapolis: Augsburg Fortress, 1989; J. P. **Hyatt,** "Torah in the Book of Jeremiah," *JBL* 60 (1941): 381–96; "The Book of Jeremiah: Introduction and Exegesis," *IB* 5:77–1142; P. J. **King,** *Jeremiah: An Archaeological Companion,* Louisville: Westminster/John Knox Press, 1993; G. C. **Macholz,** "Jeremia in der Kontinuität der Prophetie," in H. W. Wolff, ed., *Probleme biblischer Theologie: Gerhard von Rad zum 70. Geburtstag,* Munich: Kaiser Verlag, 1971, 306–34; H. G. **May,** "The Chronology of Jeremiah's Oracles," *JNES* 4 (1945): 217–27; J. G. **McConville,** "Jeremiah: Prophet and Book," *TB* 42 (1991): 80–95; *Judgement and Promise: An Interpretation of the Book of Jeremiah,* Leicester: Apollos, 1993; W. **McKane,** *A Critical and Exegetical Commentary on Jeremiah,* vol. 1, Edinburgh: T. & T. Clark, 1986; S. **Mowinckel,** *Zur Komposition des Buches Jeremia,* Oslo: Dybwad, 1914; E. W. **Nicholson,** *Deuteronomy and Tradition,* Philadelphia: Fortress Press, 1967; *Preaching to the Exiles,* New York: Schocken Books, 1970; *The Book of the Prophet Jeremiah: Chapters 26–52,* Cambridge: Cambridge University Press, 1975; T. W. **Overholt,** "Remarks on the Continuity of the Jeremiah Tradition," *JBL* 91 (1972): 457–62; "Jeremiah and the Nature of the Prophetic Process," in *Essays in Honor of J. Coert Rylaarsdam*, Pittsburgh: Pickwick Press, 1977, 129–50; L. G. **Perdue** and B. W. **Kovacs**, eds., *A Prophet to the Nations: Essays in Jeremiah Studies*, Winona Lake, Ind.: Eisenbrauns, 1984; K.-F. **Pohlmann,** *Studien zum Jeremiabuch*, Göttingen: Vandenhoeck & Ruprecht, 1978; T. **Polk,** *The Prophetic Persona: Jeremiah and the Language of the Self*, Sheffield: JSOT Press, 1984; T. M. **Raitt,** "The Prophetic Summons to Repentance," *ZAW* 83 (1971): 30–49; *A Theology of Exile: Judgment/Deliverance in Jeremiah and Ezekiel*, Philadelphia: Fortress Press, 1977; A. **Rofé,** "The Arrangement of the Book of Jeremiah," *ZAW* 101 (1991) 390–98; H. H. **Rowley,** "The Early Prophecies of Jeremiah in Their Setting," *BJRL* 45 (1962–63): 198–234 (= *Men of God*, London: Nelson & Sons, 1963, 133–68); W. **Rudolph,** *Jeremia*, Tübingen: J.C.B. Mohr (Paul Siebeck), 1968; C. R. **Seitz,** "The Crisis of Interpretation over the Meaning and Purpose of the Exile," *VT* 35 (1985): 78–97; M. **Sekine,** "Davidsbund und Sinaibund bei Jeremia," *VT* 9 (1959): 47–57; K. **Seybold,** *Der Prophet Jeremia: Leben und Werk*, Stuttgart: Kohlhammer, 1993; J. **Skinner,** *Prophecy and Religion: Studies in the Life of Jeremiah*, Cambridge: Cambridge University Press, 1922; W. **Thiel,** *Die Deuteronomistische Redaktion von Jeremiah 1—25*, Neukirchen-Vluyn: Neukirchener Verlag, 1973; J. **Thompson,** *The Book of Jeremiah*, Grand Rapids: Eerdmans, 1980; E. **Tov,** "L'incidence de le critique textuelle sur la critique littéraire dans le livre de Jérémie," *RB* 79 (1972): 189–99; J. **Unterman,** *From Repentance to Redemption: Jeremiah's Thought in Transition*, Sheffield: JSOT Press, 1987; J. W. **Watts,** "Text and Redaction in Jeremiah's Oracles against the Nations," *CBQ* 54 (1992): 432–47; M. **Weinfeld,** "Jeremiah and the Spiritual Metamorphosis of Israel," *ZAW* 88 (1976): 17–56; H. **Weippert,** *Die Prosareden des Jeremiabuches*, Berlin: Walter de Gruyter, 1973; A. C. **Welch,** *Jeremiah: His Time and His Work*, Oxford: Blackwell, 1951; C. F. **Whitley,** *The Exilic Age*, Philadelphia: Fortress Press, 1957; "Carchemish and Jeremiah," *ZAW* 80 (1968): 38–49; M. J. **Williams,** "An Investigation of the Legitimacy of Source Distinctions for the Prose Material in Jeremiah," *JBL* 112 (1993) 193–210; W. **Zimmerli,** "Visionary Experience in Jeremiah," in R. Coggins et al., *Israel's Prophetic Heritage*, 95–118.

The editorial history and transmission of this longest of prophetic books with its many different kinds of material create more than usually difficult problems for interpretation. To begin with, the Old Greek or Septuagint version (OG, LXX) not only is shorter than the Masoretic text (MT) by about an eighth but also arranges the material differently. The Qumran Jeremiah fragments (4QJer[a-e]; 2QJer) confirm the existence of two significantly different versions corresponding to the LXX and the MT, and it is now clear that the difference is not just a matter of textual criticism but marks important stages in the transmission of the Jeremiah material. The present consensus is that the MT represents a later and more expansive version than the LXX, and the same conclusion is suggested by the location of the oracles against foreign nations at the center of the book in the LXX, as in Isaiah and Ezekiel, rather than at the end where—exceptionally—they are located in the MT. The interpreter's task, therefore, is complicated by the need to explain distinctive features and developments in one version vis-à-vis the other. Several commentators have noted, for example, the much more frequent allusion to Jeremiah as *nābî'* in the longer and presumed later version, which confirms a point made earlier about the semantic expansion in the use and scope of this term. Another example would be the promise of a righteous Davidic scion supported by equally righteous Levitical priests in Jer. 33:14–26. This passage, missing from the LXX but represented at Qumran (4QJer^c), reads like a commentary on 23:5–6, and bears comparison with certain ideas in Haggai, Zechariah 1—8, and even with the Testament of Levi (8:1–15) and the Testament of Judah (21:1–5; 24:1–6) from the Hasmonaean period.

As noted a moment ago, the oracles against foreign nations occur at the end of the book in the MT (chaps. 46—51) but are located at Jer. 25:13, and are arranged in a different order, in the LXX. A location at this point in the middle of the book is not surprising in view of the allusion in 25:13 to a distinct book containing such material, and we have seen that in other prophetic books judgment on the nations follows judgment on Israel (Isaiah 13—27; Ezekiel 25—32). The location of the foreign nation sayings at the end of the MT Jeremiah, immediately preceding the historical appendix of chapter 52, also disguises what appears to be the original *excipit* or envoi to the book, a word of assurance to the faithful scribe Baruch who got it all down in writing (Jer. 45:1–5), therefore a kind of colophon. However, it is impossible to say what the more original position would have been, since oracles against foreign nations do not have to be at the center of a prophetic book (they are at the beginning in Amos), and mention of a book of such oracles (25:13) could have led an editor to move them from the end to the center.

The foreign nation sayings cannot have been compiled before the Babylonian exile, and the most we can say about their authorship is that some of them may have their point of departure in sayings or fragments of sayings passed on from Jeremiah himself. This possibility might best be argued with respect to the anti-Babylonian oracles in chapters 50—51, which may have formed a distinct collection. We are informed that King Zedekiah went to Babylon in 594 B.C.E., probably to protest his loyalty after the abortive plotting of that year. Among his retinue was a royal official named Seraiah, brother of the scribe Baruch, who was charged by Jeremiah with the dangerous mission of taking with him a scroll containing predictions of the fall of Babylon, reading it on arrival, and then dropping it in the Euphrates as a symbolic anticipation of the fall of Babylon (Jer. 51:59–64). Needless to say, it is no longer possible to reconstruct the contents of this scroll, and it seems unlikely that they are reproduced in chapters 50—51.

Jeremiah 25 serves as a kind of hinge on which the two major sections of the book are hung, and it is therefore extremely important for understanding the structure and organization of the book as a whole. Since the ground-breaking work of the Norwegian scholar Sigmund Mowinckel, it is generally accepted that the Deuteronom(ist)ic school has played an important part in the production of the book, though there are differences of opinion as to the extent of its activity and the criteria for determining what is and is not Deuteronomic.[38] In chapter 25, in which the prophet looks back over twenty-three years of unheeded prophesying, characteristic Deuteronomic language and ideas are not difficult to detect. The people have refused to listen to "his servants the prophets" who called them to repentance with special reference to the matter of idolatry, and the price to be paid for this refusal is political disaster culminating in exile; which, of course, corresponds to a familiar pattern in Dtr (e.g., 1 Kings 8:46–53; 2 Kings 17:7–23; 21:10–15; 24:2–4). But Jeremiah is also introduced as a prophet to the nations (1:5), and so the editor has combined Jeremiah's sayings against Judah, compiled in 605/4 B.C.E., with sayings against foreign nations. In fact, the account of the writing of the scroll read publicly in the temple by Baruch and subsequently destroyed by Jehoiakim lists its contents as sayings directed against Israel, Judah, and all the nations (Jer. 36:2).

Whereas the Hebrew *Vorlage* of the LXX inserts the oracles against foreign nations immediately after the mention of a book containing such material (25:13), the MT proceeds at this point with the symbolic action of the cup of divine anger from which first Judah and its cities and then foreign nations are forced to drink (25:15–29). Allusion to the divine anger has inspired additional sayings about judgment on the nations couched in the conventional cultic and prophetic language appropriate to this theme (25:30–31, 32, 33, 34–38). Taken as a whole, therefore, the chapter served the theological purpose of the editor who wished both to explain the disasters foretold by Jeremiah that had actually happened and to hold out hope for the future, including retribution on Judah's oppressors.

The sermon of Jeremiah in 25:3–14 is presented as concluding the first collection of sayings against Judah covering the twenty-three years from his commissioning as a prophet (1:2) to the fourth year of Jehoiakim, that is, 627–605 B.C.E. We have seen that 605 was the year of Nebuchadrezzar's decisive defeat of the Egyptians at Carchemish and his subsequent succession to the Babylonian throne, events of fateful import for Judah as we now know and as many then might have guessed. A fuller account of this turning point in the prophet's career is given in chapter 36.[39] Baruch, we are told, wrote down the sayings of the previous twenty-three years at Jeremiah's dictation and was told to read them publicly in the temple from which Jeremiah was at that time debarred—not surprisingly, since he had recently predicted its destruction (7:1–8:3; 26:1–19). Baruch did so on the occasion of a public fast in December of the following year, a fast occasioned either by Nebuchadrezzar's recent advance into the country or a terrible drought (cf. 14:2–6) or both. After this first public reading the scroll was read a second time in the presence of a group of officials, including members of the family of Shaphan, which supported the prophet. The third reading took place in the winter palace in the presence of the king and the royal court. The reader was a certain Yehudi, and as he read, the king tore off pieces of the scroll, threw them on the fire, and ordered the arrest of both author and transcriber. The writing and public recital of sayings, several of which had been composed and delivered many years earlier, were presumably intended as a way of affirming their present validity. Jehoiakim's destruction of the scroll, on the other hand, was meant to deny its validity and perhaps also render its predictions inoperative. Baruch, however, rewrote the sayings, again at Jeremiah's dictation; and since the rewritten scroll contained many additional sayings (36:32), it constituted a second and expanded edition of Jeremian material from the first half of the prophet's career.[40]

We will never know for sure whether the threefold reading of the scroll and the culminating scene in the winter palace took place exactly or even approximately as described in this masterpiece of dramatic Hebrew prose. Parallelism with the discovery of another book associated with the temple, its recital in the presence of another king, Josiah, and the contrast between his reaction to its contents and the reaction of Jehoiakim to Jeremiah's oeuvre (2 Kings 22–23) is instructive for the way the narrative in chapter 36 is shaped, but that need not lead to the conclusion that the latter is a fiction aimed at dramatizing the triumph of the *written* prophetic word over even the highest secular and religious authority.

We therefore hold that at least the nucleus of this second edition of the Jeremiah-Baruch scroll is to be found in the first section of the book (chapters 1—25), and that it consisted for the most part of sayings directed against Judah and Jerusalem. Some of these have survived more or less in their original poetic form; others have been paraphrased in prose by a Deuteronomistic editor; and there are additions and glosses of uncertain provenance and date.[41] One type of prose composition of frequent occurrence in chapters 1—36 is a paraphrase of a prophetic saying provided with a minimum of narrative framework. Comparison with similar prophetic discourses in Dtr's history of the monarchy confirms the impression that this unit belongs to the same pattern and embodies typically Deuteronomic procedures.[42]

This first section of the book (chapters 1—25) also contains several lamentations and complaints to God that have been known in the modern period as Jeremiah's "confessions." The designation is in fact quite inappropriate because, unlike Augustine's work from which it is borrowed, the passages in question (Jer. 11:18–12:6; 15:10–21; 17:14–18; 18:18–23; 20:7–18) are not at all autobiographically explicit or revealing. Like several of the monologues in Job, they betray rather close affinity in style and language with the psalms of individual lamentation, a circumstance that suggests caution in using them as biographical source material.[43] Even more caution is in order in arguing from a liturgical form to a cultic setting, in the sense that Jeremiah actually delivered himself of these lamentations during temple worship as a cultic official or self-appointed representative of the people.[44]

One of the most prominent features of this prophetic book when compared with others is the presence in it of a more or less continuous account of Jeremiah's activity and suffering, concentrated for the most part in chapters 37—44, and dealing primarily with the period immediately preceding and following the fall of Jerusalem. In contrast to prose passages in the first half of the book, most of which are couched in the first-person singular and serve as minimal narrative framing for sermons (e.g., 7:1–8:3; 19:1–20:6), these are genuine third-person narratives recording events with considerable attention to background and detail, some part of which can be corroborated from nonbiblical sources.[45] This *historia calamitatum* is often ascribed to Baruch, which is possible but unprovable. Whatever its origin, it has been put together as exemplifying an ideal biography, presenting Jeremiah as the model of the unheeded and persecuted prophet who remains faithful to his commission in the manner of Moses. The theme of the persecuted prophet, which will eventually make its contribution to the gospel presentation of Jesus, is only hinted at in the traditions about Moses. Its mature formulation owes a great deal to the Isaian servant poem (Isaiah 52—53) and the Jeremian passion narrative in these chapters (37—44).[46]

The origin of the so-called book of consolation in Jeremiah 30—31 (with some additions in chap. 33) poses a special problem since, exceptionally, it holds out the promise of a new order for a restored and reunited people under a Davidic dynast. While some recent attempts have been made to read it in the context of the Josian reforms, and therefore to attribute it directly to Jeremiah, it stands in such stark contrast to what

Jeremiah has to say elsewhere in the book about prospects for the future that this conclusion must be considered highly unlikely. Here, too, we find indications of Deuteronomic editing, especially in the passage promising a new covenant (31:31–34). The tone and sentiments also make a good fit with the exilic Deuteronomic perspective familiar from Dtr and the book of Deuteronomy itself.[47] In giving new prescriptions for the future that draw on the experience of past religious failure, both Jer. 31:31–34 and Deut. 30:14 speak of the law inscribed in or on the heart without, however, explaining how exactly this inscription will lead to a future different from the past.

The last part of Jeremiah consists in the sayings against foreign nations discussed earlier (chapters 46—51) and a concluding chapter dealing with the reign of Zedekiah and taking the story down to the paroling of Jehoiachin by the Babylonian king Evil-merodach (Amel-Marduk). With some minor additions and subtractions, the passage is parallel to the final chapter in Dtr (2 Kings 24:18–25:30). This *excipit* supports the view that the book as a whole was edited by adherents of the Deuteronomic school not earlier than ca. 560 B.C.E., the thirty-seventh year of King Jehoiachin's exile in Babylon. Its inclusion made it possible to end the book on the same note of hope as the history.

It will now be apparent that those who edited and transmitted the book of Jeremiah, over a period of several centuries, have been at pains to present him as fulfilling the paradigm of the prophetic role in Israel. According to the Deuteronomic perspective this implied, more than anything else, concern with law and covenant after the manner of Moses. On this reading Jeremiah was the last of "his servants the prophets" (*ʿabādāyw hannᵉbîʾîm*), a long line of emissaries sent to warn Israel of the consequences of religious infidelity.[48] Like that of Moses, prophet par excellence, Jeremiah's activity spanned forty years (1:2–3: from the thirteenth year of Josiah to the fall of Jerusalem, i.e., 627–587 B.C.E.), like Moses he proclaimed the law, interceded with God for the people in time of distress, or at least was expected as prophet to do so, accepted rejection as the price of fidelity to his calling, suffered persecution, and faced the challenge of those who did not accept his authority.[49] It is precisely the regularity and consistency with which these Deuteronomic perspectives inform the book that rule out an explanation of the similarities in terms of a style of public discourse or preaching characteristic of that time. There is also the fact that there are sayings of Jeremiah widely deemed to be genuine that differ in significant respects from the Deuteronomic theology. With all due regard for the danger of circular reasoning, it can be argued, for example, that while the Deuteronomists regularly offer alternatives, after the early period Jeremiah himself seldom if ever does. The call to repentance, "turning," is, in the Deuteronomist view, an important aspect of prophetic preaching (e.g., 2 Kings 17:13; cf. Jer. 25:5–6; 26:3; 35:15). It is heard at times in Jeremiah's early period (3:21–23; 4:1–2, 14), but at a certain point Jeremiah decided that intercession was no longer possible (7:16; 11:14–17; 14:11–12), and from that point Judah's fate was sealed as far as he was concerned.

An adequate appreciation of the pervasiveness of the Deuteronomic perspective in this prophetic book would call for detailed rhetorical and thematic analysis of the different kinds of material in it, and especially the longer prose passages. We have space for only two further examples, one rhetorical and the other thematic. At several points we find an explanation of the disasters that are to overtake Judah, or have already overtaken it, in the form of question and answer (Jer. 5:19; 9:12–14; 16:10–13; 22:8–9). The analogy is not so much with the query of the son answered by the father reminiscent of the Passover seder (cf. Ex. 13:14–15; Deut. 6:20–25) but with a rhetorical form employed by the Deuteronomists for explaining the prospect or reality of political disaster. The question is "why has Yahweh done this to his land?" and the answer details the different forms of transgression leading to disaster (Deut. 29:24–28 [MT 29:23–27]; 1 Kings 9:8–9). This particular question and answer form is not found elsewhere in the Hebrew Bible, though it does occur in Assyrian annals where a subject people ask why calamity has befallen them and the answer is found in the anger of an offended deity (*ANET*, 300).

A more substantive example would be the criteria for distinguishing between true and false prophecy and the characterization of false prophecy in general. In his diatribe against contemporary holders of the prophetic office (Jer. 23:9–40) and his dealings with specific prophetic representatives—Hananiah, Ahab, Zedekiah, and Shemaiah (chaps. 28—29)—Jeremiah reflects the Deuteronomic doctrine on prophecy and follows the school criteria and guidelines for prophetic testing. False prophecy is rebellion (Jer. 28:16; 29:32; cf. Deut. 13:5) and is punishable by death (Jer. 28:16–17; cf. Deut 18:20). The false prophet is, in the first place, the one who speaks in the name of another deity and thus tempts to idolatry (Deut. 13:1–3; 18:20), a situation that, for Jeremiah, was attested only in Samaria (Jer. 23:13, though the reference is perhaps to a previous age). Much more to the point is the case of prophets who speak in the name of Yahweh but who have not been commissioned to do so. In keeping with Deuteronomic doctrine (Deut. 18:20) these are condemned by Jeremiah. They speak their own words (Jer. 23:36), their visions are products of their own imaginations (23:16) because they have not received their commission in the divine council (23:18, 22). Prophets whose predictions do not come true are thereby proved to be false (cf. Deut. 18:21–22), a consideration that appears to govern Jeremiah's dealings with the optimistic prophet Hananiah, though Jeremiah tendentiously limits the application of the criterion to those who predict well-being (Jer. 28:8–9). It is also of interest to observe that in both Deuteronomy (Deut. 13:1–5) and Jeremiah (Jer. 23:25–28, 32; 29:8) prophecy is linked with the theologically dubious phenomenon of dreams and their interpretation.[50]

A particularly important aspect of this prophetic profile is the initial commissioning, which in the case of Jeremiah is remarkably similar to that of Moses as described in the earlier of the two versions in the Pentateuch (Jer. 1:4–19; cf. Ex. 3:1–4:17). Both narratives conform to the one basic structure or grid: divine address, expostulation of the one addressed, confirmation and encouragement designed to overcome hesitation, an act of installation accompanied by a form of words, specification of the mission entrusted to the prophet designate, and a visionary experience.[51] Unlike Jer. 1:5, the Moses narrative omits designation and consecration from the womb, though the preceding account of birth and miraculous escape from death as an infant (Ex. 2:1–10) might be said to fulfill the same function. Both Moses and Jeremiah are reluctant to answer the call and come up with similar excuses, including oratorical ineptitude (Ex. 4:10; Jer 1:6).Both are sent on a mission and the word of reassurance for both is the same: "I am [will be] with you" (Ex. 3:12; Jer. 1:8, 19). The touching of Jeremiah's mouth and the accompanying declaration, "I have put my words in your mouth" (Jer. 1:9), echo the assurance given to Moses that Yahweh will be "with his mouth" (Ex. 4:12) and will put his words in the mouth of Aaron his spokesman (Ex. 4:15). The vision of the burning thornbush, finally, leads into the commissioning of Moses, whereas Jeremiah's visions come at the end, at least in the present state of the text (Jer. 1:11–16). But a visual or visionary experience is part of the commissioning in both cases.

While there is clearly more than one way of explaining the close affinity between these commissioning accounts, the parallelism confirms the impression that Jeremiah is being presented from the beginning of his career as a prophet after the manner of Moses.[52] The account of Jeremiah's call also illustrates the Deuteronomic theory of prophecy as set out in Deut. 18:15–18. Following the Mosaic model, the true prophet is "raised up" by Yahweh, who puts his words in the prophet's mouth and commissions him to speak (Deut. 18:18; Jer. 1:7, 9, 17). For the Deuteronomistic editors, in fact, Jeremiah is the last of "his servants the prophets," bringing to an end a long history of prophetic emissaries beginning with the exodus: "from the day your ancestors left Egypt *to this day* I have persistently sent all my servants the prophets" (Jer. 7:25). This will explain why Jeremiah concludes at the same point as Dtr and why the indications of Deuteronomic editing are so much more in evidence in Jeremiah than in any other prophetic book.

If the Deuteronomic portrait of Jeremiah dominates in the book, the question arises whether we can recover anything of Jeremiah's real likeness by dint of a painstaking work of restoration. Here as elsewhere we are dealing in probabilities at best, and perhaps our safest plan is to steer a course between naive optimism and out-and-out skepticism.

We begin, then, with the superscription to the book (1:1–3), which informs us that Jeremiah ben-Hilkiah belonged to, or was descended from, a family of priests at Anathoth, a village about three kilometers north of Jerusalem, and that his prophetic career began in the thirteenth year of Josiah, that is, 627 B.C.E. As noted earlier, the same date is given in chapter 25, which encapsulates twenty-three years of prophetic activity. Doubts about whether Jeremiah functioned as a prophet during the reign of Josiah (640–609), first raised by Friedrich Horst in 1923, have not been stilled in spite of all the arguments and counterarguments produced since then. For if he was commissioned to prophesy in 627, he would have been active during eighteen years of Josiah's reign and therefore during the religious reforms and the final years of Assyrian hegemony with which the reforms were, as we have seen, closely connected. Yet there are no oracles that can be safely dated to that reign[53] and not the slightest allusion to the kind of dealings between prophet and ruler attested in the book for later reigns. The sayings in the first part of the book (Jeremiah 1—6), moreover, depict a situation of widespread apostasy involving the monarchy (2:26; cf. 2:8; 4:9), which does not fit what we are told about Josiah in Dtr, a fortiori, if we accept the Chronicler's point that the reforms began in the twelfth year of the reign, and therefore before Jeremiah's call (2 Chron. 34:3). It is therefore difficult to see how Jeremiah's comminations against kings and princes would have made sense at any time between his call and the death of Josiah in 609 B.C.E.

A related problem, especially given Jeremiah's commissioning as "prophet to the nations" (1:5), is that anti-Assyrian oracles are missing from these early chapters. Assyria is mentioned in this first section only with reference to past history (2:36) or in a context suggesting the short period of Egyptian hegemony during the early years of Jehoiakim's reign (2:14–19). Yet Assyria was to remain at the center of international affairs for about fifteen years after the date assigned to Jeremiah's call in the superscription.[54]

On this particular issue a question still awaiting a satisfactory answer has to do with Jeremiah's attitude toward Josiah's reforms. Assuming that the date at Jer. 1:2 (the thirteenth year of Josiah) is correct, the first period of his activity would have coincided with the reforms, and it would be strange indeed if he had nothing to say about them. He commends Josiah by way of contrast with the despised Jehoiakim (22:15–16), but the allusion is quite general and retrospective. An undated prose passage has him publicly endorsing a covenant (11:1–17) that some commentators have taken, not unreasonably, to refer to the Josian reform. But the passage in question is transparently a Deuteronomic composition,[55] so that all we can safely deduce from it is that the editor wished to present him as supporting the reform, which of course is no more than we would expect. For much the same reason the so-called book of consolation (chapters 30—31) cannot be read as Jeremiah's own reflections on the Josian covenant, as was indicated earlier. In short, there is no saying of Jeremiah that can with confidence be taken as proof that he supported the reform, and certainly none dating from the reign of Josiah.

On the other hand, we do not have the impression that Jeremiah emerged after the death of Josiah as a completely unknown figure on the Jerusalem political and religious scene. If his one-man picket of the temple in the first year of Jehoiakim (609 B.C.E.) is regarded as his *début*, it was important enough to be taken up at the highest level. He also enjoyed from the beginning the patronage of the powerful family of Shaphan, which had been active in the reform movement during the reign of Josiah.[56] But in the absence of reliable information it is impossible to say what role, if any, Jeremiah played in public life during the latter part of Josiah's reign.

In the present state of our ignorance all we can say is that, if Jeremiah did not inaugurate his prophetic career after the death of Josiah at Megiddo in 609, that event proved to be a decisive turning point for him, as for many others. The dating of the call to the thirteenth year of Josiah allowed the Deuteronomic editor to represent him as supporting the reform and also, as noted earlier, to credit Jeremiah with a ministry of forty years' duration, a number having obvious associations with the Mosaic tradition. Whatever Jeremiah may have thought of Josiah's reforms, it was not long before the promulgation of a written law produced its own bureaucracy, a corps of legal scribes, perhaps attached to the temple, whose claim to authority, to control the "redemptive media," would inevitably conflict with prophetic claims. It is in the light of this development that we are to understand Jeremiah's polemic against "handlers of the law" (Jer. 2:8) and scribes whose false pen had turned it into a lie (8:8–9). The reform movement, such as it was, died with Josiah, but the tension between prophets on the one hand and drafters and interpreters of the laws on the other would continue and produce a situation uncongenial to the exercise of institutionally unattached prophesying.[57]

The priestly clan established at Anathoth in Benjamin, with which the author of the superscription associates Jeremiah, traced its ancestry back to Abiathar, survivor of the Shiloh priesthood who was exiled there during Solomon's reign (1 Kings 2:26). This kind of background would make it easier to explain the influence of Ephraimite traditions on Jeremiah and his interest in the destiny of the former Northern Kingdom. If the collection of sayings in Jeremiah 2—6 represent a deposit from the early phase of his career, it would be noteworthy in this respect that they refer often to exodus and wilderness traditions, as well as to the temptation posed by the fertility cults to which Israel had succumbed since the occupation of the land. The metaphorical way of speaking of religious infidelity as sexual transgression suggests that Jeremiah had learned from the Ephraimite Hosea, though similar denunciations of the Baal cult occur in more recent Judean prophecy (e.g., Zeph. 1:4–5). The Josian reforms detailed in 2 Kings 23 may have had some effect in the capital, though rather less in the rest of the country. Following Josiah's death, at any rate, there seems to have been a widespread collapse of confidence in the national cult, accompanied by a strong recrudescence of native cults, which the ensuing political disasters did nothing to discourage (Jer. 7:9; 44:15–19; Ezekiel 8, etc.).

As we read these early sayings, we have the impression that Jeremiah is in the process of assimilating the prophetic tradition and bringing it to bear on the contemporary situation, that he has not yet found his own voice. At this early stage, moreover, he still holds out the possibility of repentance ("turning") on condition that Israel abandon idolatry (Jer. 3:21–23) and practice truthfulness and justice (4:1–2). Yet there is already the sense that this will not happen, that people have hardened their hearts too often (6:10). And so this first collection ends with the acknowledgment that his task of assayer and tester of the people has not been successful, that in fact it was destined to fail from the start (6:27–30).

Before leaving this first section of the book, we note repeated allusion to the threat of invasion from the north (Jer. 4:5–8; 6:1–5, 22–26; cf. 10:22; 13:20).[58] On the basis of a reference of uncertain interpretation in Herodotus (1: 103–5), these passages are occasionally taken to refer to the Scythians who are thought to have invaded Palestine shortly after 630 B.C.E. It has further been proposed that Jeremiah predicted such an invasion, that this prediction was not fulfilled, and that in consequence he retired from public life, emerging only after the death of Josiah to deliver the "temple sermon" (Jer. 7:1–8:3) after the accession of Jehoiakim. All of this is quite uncertain. If Jeremiah began his prophetic career only after the death of Josiah, the "enemy from the north" would most naturally refer to the Babylonians and their allies (including, incidentally, the Scythians), who constituted a threat to the area after its subjugation to Egypt. The same conclusion is suggested by the sermon summarizing the first half of his activity, which links Babylonians with "tribes of the north" (25:9, 26; cf. 1:15). The motif is further elaborated in the oracles against the nations, in which Babylon is itself threatened with annihilation at the hands of northern nations (50:3, 9, 41; 51:48).

After the death of Josiah at Megiddo the nationalist party put his younger son, Shallum, on the throne. The Egyptians, however, deposed him in favor of Eliakim (Jehoiakim), probably taking him to be a more accommodating representative of their interests. In addition to the revival of syncretist cults (especially the cult of the goddess Asherah) mentioned earlier, this move signaled an intensification of internal strife that lasted down to the destruction of Jerusalem. In the same year (609 B.C.E.) Jeremiah delivered a memorable diatribe in the temple precincts that led to his arrest and trial by the ruling party (Jer. 7:1–8:3; 26:1–24). In spite of insistence on the death penalty by the temple staff, he was acquitted following appeal to precedent by provincial elders who were present and with the help of support in high places. Nevertheless, his prediction that the temple would be gutted earned him the lasting opposition of the temple personnel, including prebendary prophets, who succeeded in having him debarred from the temple itself, at least for the next few years (36:5).[59]

During the first years of the reign, down to the decisive Babylonian victory at Carchemish (605), Jeremiah is recorded as continuing in opposition to king, court, and temple, attacking Jehoiakim mercilessly and predicting that he would come to a bad end (13:18; 22:13–23). We are told that he escaped the fate of other opposition prophets such as Uriah, who was extradicted from Egypt and executed, thanks to the protection of the powerful Shaphanite clan (26:20–24). From this point onward, Jeremiah's career, and the truncated career of Uriah, illustrate the political role of the prophet; and it is particularly unfortunate that, apart from the Lachish ostraca mentioned earlier, we have to rely exclusively on the biblical sources for an idea how this worked out. We might put it somewhat abstractly by saying that the self-appointed task of prophets like Jeremiah and Uriah, not excluding others branded as "false prophets" like Hananiah, Zedekiah, and Ahab, was that of interpreting the changing pattern of political events in the light of the tradition as they understood it and mediated through their own personal experience of God. That this interpretation was carried out through actual participation in the events is obvious from the opposition that it engendered, not to mention the attempt on his life by members of his own clan (11:18–23). The isolation and internal conflict connected with playing out this role seem to have intensified through the remaining years of his life.

After the battle of Carchemish the balance of power shifted decisively in favor of the Babylonians, who then took control of Syria and Palestine from the Egyptians. Jehoiakim was soon forced to submit to a new master who invaded the country in order to secure tribute and reduce isolated pockets of resistance, especially along the Mediterranean littoral (*ANET*, 563; perhaps Jer. 47:5, 7). These events may have occasioned the liturgy of fasting during which Jeremiah's scroll was read in the temple (Jer. 36:9). About the same time a bad situation was made worse by a drought of exceptional severity during which Jeremiah refused to discharge the prophetic function of intercession.[60] In the last year of the century the Babylonian army was once again in the country, this time on its way to Egypt, where its successful advance was temporarily halted. It was probably this setback that led Jehoiakim to refuse tribute, the predictable outcome of which was a punitive expedition in which levies from neighboring provinces, traditional enemies such as Damascus, Moab, and Ammon, took part (2 Kings 24:1–2). It may have been on this occasion that Jeremiah brought Rechabites into the temple precincts, offered them wine, which they naturally refused, and proposed them as a model of a community faithful to its traditions (Jeremiah 35).

The last years of Jehoiakim are left in some obscurity by both Dtr and the Babylonian Chronicle. Whatever the sequence of events during the first siege of Jerusalem in 598/597, the new king Jehoiachin lasted only three months, capitulated, and was deported together with several thousand of the aristocracy and artisan classes, among them a priest called Ezekiel.

The next eleven years, from the first to the second deportation, were the most intense of Jeremiah's life. Nebuchadrezzar's appointee, another son of Josiah called Mattaniah, who was given the throne name Zedekiah, was from the start under pressure to join neighboring states in rebellion, a policy supported by powerful elements at the court. He himself appears to have been doubtful about the prospects of success, and was therefore disposed to listen to Jeremiah even during the critical days of the siege (Jer. 37:3–10, 16–21; 38:14–28). Jeremiah, in his turn, was not without sympathy for him (34:1–5) and did not share the aspirations of those who looked for a speedy return of the exiled Jehoiachin, widely regarded both in Judah and the Diaspora as the legitimate ruler (22:24–30).

The situation in the capital and the court reached a climax four years into the reign when a revolt broke out in the Babylonian army and, a little later, Psammetichus II came to power in Egypt. From then on, the hopes of the war faction in Jerusalem focused on Egypt, which was soon busy fomenting revolt among the smaller western states. Delegates from these states met in Jerusalem where, during their conference, they were confronted by Jeremiah wearing the yoke-bar and thongs used to restrain prisoners of war and predicting the divinely willed ascendancy of Babylon (27:1–15). This message of appeasement, which went counter to that of numerous nationalistic prophets of the region (27:9), led to a confrontation in the temple with a Gibeonite prophet, Hananiah ben-Azzur, who predicted that in two years Judah would be independent and Jehoiachin back on the throne (28:1–4). After initial hesitation, understandable in view of the political situation, Jeremiah reappeared, this time with an iron yoke, and predicted the death of Hananiah (in keeping with the Deuteronomic law concerning false prophets), which is reported to have occurred within the year (28:10–17).

These disturbances also affected the Babylonian diaspora, which appears to have kept in close touch with developments in Judah. We hear of a certain Shemaiah, a prophet in Babylon, who wrote to the temple authorities in Jerusalem urging them to take action against Jeremiah (Jer. 29:24–28). Other Diaspora prophets are known to have been executed for fomenting sedition (29:21–23). Jeremiah's advice was for the deported to come to terms with their situation, in the conviction that the future lay with them rather than with those who had been left behind. However, it would be prudent to suspect that Jeremiah's preferential option for the deportees, the "good figs" (chap. 24), may represent a contribution to the narrative by Judeo-Babylonian elements during or shortly before the period of resettlement.

We can at least say that, in assuming the role of spokesman for the party of appeasement, Jeremiah was not courting popularity. We hear of opposition from many quarters—the royal entourage (where, however, he seems to have had some influential friends), his hometown, and especially the temple bureaucracy. One incident, undated, led to his arrest by Pashhur, chief of the temple police, and exposure in the stocks at one of the temple gates. This came after the smashing of an earthenware jar at the Potsherd Gate (later the Dung Gate) facing the Valley of Hinnom to symbolize publicly the fate of the city (Jer. 19:1–20:6). The deepening alienation of the prophet is seen in his refusal to take part in rites of mourning or celebration, perhaps also his refusal to marry or remarry (16:1–9),[61] and especially to discharge the crucial prophetic function of intercession (11:14–17; 14:11–12). Recognition of the prophetic role did not necessarily imply acceptance or prevent people from thinking of such persons as strange, forbidding, dangerous, even deranged (e.g., Jer. 29:26). From the account of his trial, it seems that his support group was limited to members of one or two upper-class families (26:24; 32:12; 51:59) together with some of the country elders and rural nobility, the so-called people of the land who had supported Josiah's reforms.

Revolt, backed by Egypt, began in 589 B.C.E., and is referred to in Jer. 37:5 and, indirectly, in one of the Lachish ostraca recording a visit to Egypt by the army commander Coniah (*ANET,* 322). The predictable Babylonian reaction came the beginning of the following year. The desperate situation in Jerusalem is reflected in the manumission of slaves to fill the manpower shortage during the siege of the city, which lasted for at least a year and a half (Jer. 34:8–10). Meanwhile other Babylonian units were ranging the country, reducing and devastating the few cities that chose to resist. The siege was lifted briefly as a result of Egyptian intervention after the accession of Apries in Egypt (Jer. 37:5), but the relief was short-lived and the Babylonians were soon back in front of the walls. The population of the city, swollen by refugees from the countryside, suffered extremes of starvation until the walls were finally breached and city and temple torched by the army commander Nebuzaradan. Zedekiah himself was captured while trying to escape and, after seeing his children slaughtered before his eyes, was blinded and led into captivity.

The record of events in Jeremiah 32—34 and 37—39, together with 2 Kings 25, leaves us the impression of Zedekiah as a pathetic figure, uncertain of what to do, fearful for his life from the pro-Egyptian faction at the court, hoping for a last-minute miracle. He sent a delegation to Jeremiah urging him to intercede, only to be told that he had run out of options and had no choice but to surrender (37:3–10). After the temporary raising of the siege resulting from the approach of the Egyptian army (Jer. 37:3), Jeremiah left the city to visit Anathoth, perhaps to initiate negotiations for the purchase of the field. Not surprisingly, he was arrested on a charge of desertion, beaten, and thrown into prison. There he was visited by the king to whom he gave the same message as before (37:11–21). Transferred to better prison quarters, he received a visit from his uncle Shallum, the person from whom he bought the field (chapter 32); an act presented as an affirmation of faith in the future of the people and their devastated land.[62] As the situation deteriorated, with houses being torn down to expedite defense (33:4), the Babylonians masters of the entire country with the exception of Lachish and Azekah (cf. Lachish ostracon 4; *ANET,* 322), and the Babylonian army preparing to breach the walls, Jeremiah's plight deteriorated with it. The pro-Egyptian party demanded the death penalty for treason and had him put in a cistern, presumably leaving him to die. Released by a palace eunuch, he had a final meeting with the king with whom he pleaded in vain to surrender the city (chapter 38).

After the inevitable fall of the city and subsequent mayhem, as a prominent member of the appeasement party, Jeremiah was protected by a special decree and given the choice of staying in Judah or accompanying the exiles to Babylon (39:11–14). Choosing the former alternative, he was entrusted to the new governor and puppet king Gedaliah, another member of the Shaphan family. Following on Gedaliah's assassination by the nationalist faction, Jeremiah was taken forcibly to Egypt by the insurgents or their sympathizers (chapters 40—43). The last we hear of him, he is still preaching the same message and his hearers, among whom the women are given special mention, are still rejecting it (Jeremiah 44). If this is the way it really ended, a truly sad way, he must have died in one of the Jewish settlements in the Nile delta some time after the fall of Jerusalem.

Looking back over Jeremiah's place in the development of prophecy, we discern lines of continuity with a tradition that by his time was well established. His Benjaminite origins, the probable descent of his family from the Shiloh priesthood, and the affinities with the teaching and language of Hosea of the early sayings, have suggested the conclusion that his roots lay in the Ephraimite prophetic tradition.[63] There is some truth to this, but it cannot be pressed. To what extent a distinct, identifiable Ephraimite tradition survived after half a millennium in Anathoth, especially in view of its proximity to Jerusalem, is debatable to begin with. Moreover, Jeremiah drew his support not from his circle at Anathoth—which he condemned—but from certain families at the court and from the "elders of the land," who, to judge by their intervention in his trial, were more in line with the Judean Micah than with the Ephraimite Hosea (Jer. 26:17–19). In the previous chapter we noted affinities between sayings emanating from the Micah circle and the Deuteronomic program which, in consideration of the Deuteronomic predilection for Jeremiah, may be another indication that the book of Jeremiah represents more than one segment of prophetic experience and preaching.

While Jeremiah obviously has features in common with earlier prophetic figures like Amos, Hosea, and Micah, even a casual reader will notice some equally striking differences. At the linguistic and literary level, Gerhard von Rad has observed how, beginning with Jeremiah, the traditional forms of prophetic speech are breaking up and dissolving into longer and less clearly structured discourses. There is also greater emphasis on biographical narrations corresponding to an enhanced interest in the messenger as against the message.[64] Thus, Amos contains only one short biographical memoir (7:10–17) whereas (leaving aside the issue of historicity) we have something approaching a biography-cum-autobiography of Jeremiah from conception to his last days in Egypt. The frequent parallels between the Deuteronom(ist)ic "biography" of Moses and that of Jeremiah have often been noted, and the book of Deuteronomy itself is a prophetic discourse of Moses presented within a historical and biographical-autobiographical (in the third and first person) context.

What seems to be happening is that the basic prophetic idea of instrumentality, being called and used for a transcendent purpose, is becoming increasingly a matter not just of speaking but of a service tending toward a total life investment. While we do not detect a straight trajectory toward this point, the increased emphasis in Jeremiah on prayer, lamentation, suffering, interiority, identification with the grief and anger of God, are indicative in this sense and suggest a notable broadening in the way the prophetic function is perceived.

A further indication is the frequency of mimetic and symbolic actions recorded in the book.[65] Grounded as it is in homeopathic magic, this type of act has been routinized in various specialized areas of public activity such as warfare, medicine, law, and art. In its prophetic form, the intent was not just to supplement the spoken word with a kind of visual aid but to enhance its force and strengthen its efficacy. In early ecstatic prophecy the performance of such mimetic acts, for example, butting with iron horns or shooting arrows to simulate victory (1 Kings 22:10–12; 2 Kings 13:14–19), does not appear to have had any further impact on or implications for the performer. In Jeremiah, however, the range of such acts has increased to the point of drawing the consciousness of the actor more deeply into identification with his mission. Here again, then, we are approaching the point where the person, as much as the spoken word, is the message.

At almost any point of contact, a reading of Jeremiah—the Jeremiah presented in the many-faceted and many-layered literary portrait in the book—affronts our liberal assumptions about the nature of interpersonal relations, politics and, above all, religion. We see a person whose career took him into the public arena and who spent his life trying to influence decision-making at the highest level. Yet precisely here where we look for nuance, acknowledgment of political realities, willingness, and ability to compromise, we find only uncompromising assurance: "is not my word like fire, and like a hammer which breaks up rocks?" (23:29). We would be inclined to think that self-assurance combined with a deep sense of isolation and rejection makes for a bad psychological profile. In

Jeremiah, the Jeremiah of the book, it led to an overwhelming conviction of human bondage to sin. He speaks, among other things, of the inability to exorcise evil and of the desperate sickness of the human heart (13:23; 17:9). The nation that believes itself to be the elect of God stands under a divine judgment no less real for being unacknowledged. Its people are clay in the hands of the potter, who makes or breaks as he wills (18:1–11). It is indeed possible to know the divine will—for Jeremiah preeminently through the prophetic word—but there are many ways of evading the consequences of that knowledge. There are—fortunately, we may say—other emphases in the Hebrew Bible, including that of the editors who mitigated Jeremiah's preaching in the light of subsequent and different situations. But Jeremiah's teaching and life as presented in this book proved to be a major factor in the formation of the religious consciousness of early Judaism and the movements that arose within it, including in due course early Christianity.

V

BETWEEN THE OLD ORDER
AND THE NEW

16. PROPHECY IN CRISIS

P. R. **Ackroyd,** *Exile and Restoration,* Philadelphia: Westminster Press, 1968, 17–38; "The History of Israel in the Exilic and Post-exilic Periods," in G. W. Anderson, ed., *Tradition and Interpretation,* Oxford: Clarendon Press, 1979, 320–28; "An Interpretation of the Babylonian Exile: A Study of 2 Kings 20 and Isaiah 38—39," *Studies in the Religious Tradition of the Old Testament,* London: SCM Press, 1987, 152–71; L. C. **Allen,** *The Books of Joel, Obadiah, Jonah and Micah,* Grand Rapids: Eerdmans, 1974, 127–72; J. **Blenkinsopp,** "Abraham and the Righteous of Sodom," *JJS* 33 (1982): 119–32; E. **Bonnart,** "Abdias," *SDB* 8:693–701; J. L. **Crenshaw,** *Prophetic Conflict,* Berlin: de Gruyter, 1971; S. J. **De Vries,** *Prophet against Prophet: The Role of the Micaiah Narrative (1 Kings 22) in the Development of Early Prophetic Tradition,* Grand Rapids: Eerdmans, 1978; G. **Fohrer,** "Die Sprüche Obadjas," *Studia Biblica et Semitica Theodoro Christiano Vriezen,* Wageningen: H. Veenman, 1966, 81–93; S. **Herrmann,** "Prophetie und Wirklichkeit in der Epoche des Babylonischen Exils," *Arbeiten zur Theologie* 1 (1967): 32; E. **Janssen,** *Juda in der Exilzeit,* Göttingen: Vandenhoeck & Ruprecht, 1956; R. W. **Klein,** *Israel in Exile,* Philadelphia: Fortress, 1979; K. **Koch,** *The Prophets,* vol.2, *The Babylonian and Persian Periods,* Philadelphia: Fortress, 1982 [1978]; A. **Lods,** *The Prophets and the Rise of Judaism,* London: Kegan Paul, Trench, Trubner & Co., 1937, 173–83, 205–10; J. **Muilenburg,** "Obadiah, the Book of," *IDB* 3, 578–79; J. M. **Myers,** "Edom and Judah in the Sixth-Fifth Centuries B.C.E.," *Near Eastern Studies in Honor of W. F. Albright,* Baltimore: Johns Hopkins University Press, 1971, 377–92; E. W. **Nicholson,** *Preaching to the Exiles,* New York: Schocken Books, 1970; T. H. **Robinson,** "The Structure of the Book of Obadiah," *JTS* 17 (1916): 402–8; W. **Rudolph,** "Obadja," *ZAW* 49 (1931): 222–31; *Joel-Amos-Obadja-Jona,* Gütersloh: Gütersloher Verlagshaus/Gerd Mohn, 1971, 295–322; J.D.W. **Watts,** *Obadiah,* Grand Rapids: Eerdmans, 1969; H. W. **Wolff,** *Obadja, Jona,* Neukirchen-Vluyn: Neukirchener Verlag, 1977; "Obadja—ein Kultprophet als Interpret," *EvTh*

37 (1977): 273–84; "Prophecy from the Eighth through the Fifth Century," *Int* 32 (1978): 17–30.

The sixth century B.C.E. must be considered one of the cardinal epochs in antiquity, if not in human history. It witnessed the eclipse of the Semitic empires in the Middle East after two millennia of dominance, the rise of Greek philosophy, Jewish origins, Zoroastrianism and, further afield, Buddhism and Confucianism.[1] The first decades of the century saw the extinction of Judah as an independent state, though the nation had been in vassalage to one great empire after another for about half its existence. In the normal course of events the extinction of dynasty and national cult would have meant the end of the nation and its religion, as had happened when the kingdom of Samaria became part of the Assyrian empire a century and a half earlier. That this did not happen after the fall of Jerusalem and destruction of the national sanctuary is one of the more interesting circumstances of ancient history, the effects of which are still very much with us. It can be explained, in part, by the Babylonian policy of permitting, for administrative and fiscal rather than humanitarian reasons, the different ethnic groups resettled in Babylonia to maintain their separate identity, thereby keeping alive their historical, legal, and cultic traditions. Then again, during the long process of founding a new commonwealth, the Persian imperial authorities protected the province from being taken over by hostile neighbors, especially Samarians to the north and Arabs to the east and south.

Our first concern in this chapter is with the impact of these events on prophetic activity and the understanding of prophecy in general. We can set aside the idea that prophecy came to an end with the exilic period or shortly thereafter, an idea that evolved into something like a rabbinic dogma (e.g., *b. B. Bat.* 12b), while paradoxically contributing, in the modern period, to a prejudicial view of postexilic religion. The older view of classical prophecy as the apex of religious development generally went in tandem with a low view of Second Temple Judaism as formalistic, legalistic, ritualistic, etc. and a scholarly disinclination to spend much time studying the postexilic period.[2] This prejudicial approach is now widely abandoned. If we let the texts speak for themselves, one of the things they tell us is that prophecy did not come to an end during or shortly after the Babylonian exile, though it did undergo rather profound transformations. But before examining these changes, we must take a brief look at the political and social transformations of that time that affected every aspect of religious life.

It is unfortunate that the sixty years from the first deportation to the edict of Cyrus (598–538 B.C.E.) are so poorly documented. The

Babylonian conquest and subsequent deportations obviously resulted in widespread destruction, disruption of daily life, and some depopulation. This situation is reflected, no doubt hyperbolically, in prophetic texts that can be dated to that time and in the book of Lamentations. It is also reflected in the archaeological record—always partial and subject to revision—which indicates much more destruction in the south than in the north of the province, together with Edomite encroachments on Judean territory.[3] Edomite eagerness to profit by the Babylonian conquest of Judah has left its imprint on the biblical record, with the result that quite a chapter of anti-Edomite polemic can be assembled from biblical texts. Recall that "Edom" still served in the Roman period as a code name for unjust oppression (e.g., in *Mekilta*, the Tannaitic commentary on Exodus).[4]

Prominent in this anti-Edomite literature is the book of Obadiah, the shortest in the Hebrew Bible. Presented as a vision (cf. Isa. 1:1; Nahum 1:1), it contains three brief anti-Edomite sayings (Obad. 1b–4, 5–7, 8–14 plus 15b) rounded off with a typical finale threatening all hostile nations, including Edom, with divine judgment (Obad. 15a, 16–18). An editor has added supplementary verses promising the return of dispersed Israel to the homeland from as far away as Mesopotamia and Asia Minor and the establishment of God's kingdom in Jerusalem (19–21).[5]

The usual task of determining date and authorship is complicated by parallels to the first two sayings and some of the rest of the book in an anti-Edomite oracle in Jeremiah (Jer. 49:9–10, 14–16). Since neither version refers to the fall of Judah, which is clearly alluded to in the third saying (Obad. 11–14), it seems that both are drawing on a traditional stock of anti-Edomite oracles which, incidentally, have also found their way into the Jacob cycle (Gen. 25:23; 27:39–40). The cultic character and provenance of this category of saying have suggested to several scholars that Obadiah was, like Nahum, one of the surviving central cult prophets. But the Jeremiah parallels also suggest the possibility that this briefest of books and its author are artificial creations, rather like Malachi created out of a reference in the book itself (*mal'ākî*, "my messenger," 3:1). The name Obadiah means "servant of Yahweh," which, as noted earlier, is a common designation for a prophetic figure.

To understand what happened to prophecy at that time it will help to trace briefly the lines of continuity and assess the degree of discontinuity between the fall of Jerusalem in 587/586 and the fall of Babylon in 539 B.C.E. After the Babylonians took over, they installed Gedaliah of the family of Shaphan as puppet king in Mizpah (probably Tell en-Naṣbeh, about twelve kilometers north of Jerusalem), no doubt because of the devastation in the former capital.[6] Whether the appointment of a native, although not a member of the royal family, implied the intent to eventually restore the exiled Jehoiachin to the throne as a client king we do not know. If so, the idea would not have survived the assassination of Gedaliah and his "court" by the remnant of the nationalist party led by Ishmael, a member of the Davidic royal house (2 Kings 25:22–26; Jeremiah 40—41). Ishmael's terrorist act led to further deportations and population movements in the course of which Jeremiah was taken forcibly to Egypt (Jeremiah 42—44).

For fairly transparent ideological reasons, several biblical texts give the impression that Judah was almost entirely depopulated after the Babylonian conquest, with the result that on their return from Babylon the founders of the new commonwealth were presented with a political, social, and demographic tabula rasa.[7] This was certainly not the case. There was widespread destruction, especially in Jerusalem and the southern part of the province, but much less so in the former territory of Benjamin, and the Babylonians did not destroy the social substructure, for example, the institution of tribal elders and local judiciaries. Cultic activity also continued, possibly in Jerusalem on or near the site of the temple, more likely in Bethel and at other locations in the province.[8] With benefit of hindsight, we can say that the most disruptive aspect of this new colonial status was the expropriation of the landholdings of the deportees, which were turned over to the peasantry, the "poor of the land" (2 Kings 25:12; Jer. 40:7), for cultivation. This hardly amounted to a social revolution, as some have claimed, but it helped to exacerbate relations between Palestinian and Babylonian Jews after some of the latter repatriated in the early Persian period (see the arguments back and forth reflected in Ezek. 11:14–17; 33:23–25; Lev. 25:23).

Almost without exception, prophetic writings that have survived from that time of transition support the Diaspora Jews as the legitimate heirs of the old Israel, from Jeremiah who described them as the "good figs" (Jer. 24:1–10) to Haggai who condemned their Palestinian counterparts as ritually defiled (Hag. 2:10–14). The reason for this ideological slant in our sources is the obvious one that Judeo-Babylonians formed the socioeconomically and culturally dominant element in the Judean temple-community under Iranian rule. The crucial factor was their control, with the blessing of the imperial authorities, of the temple and its considerable resources, which translated into a very considerable amount of social and political control as well. It is likely, in any case, that conditions in the Jewish settlements in Babylonia were more conducive to the production of religious writing. On the other hand, scholars have from time to time argued for the Judean-Palestinian origin of the final edition of

Dtr, the so-called Deutero-Isaiah, and a number of smaller units including Isaiah 21, Jeremiah 30—31, and Ezekiel 34—37.[9]

The history of the Diaspora can be traced back to successive deportations by the Assyrians in the eighth and seventh centuries. Most of these
deportees were from the Northern Kingdom, and after their relocation
on the upper reaches of the Tigris and Euphrates they disappeared from
history. Judean deportees, on the contrary, were able to stay together
and organize some form of community life, settling in such southern
Mesopotamian centers as Tel-Abib, Nippur, and Babylon itself (Ezek.
1:3; 3:15; Ezra 2:59 = Neh. 7:61; Ezra 8:15–23). Many would have worked
the land; craftsmen would presumably have found work, or been put to
work, in the cities; some made a successful career in commerce.[10] Whatever their conditions in the early years of resettlement, they were soon
in a position to purchase property and send gifts back to the homeland.
Leadership was exercised by elders (Jer. 29:1; Ezek. 8:1, etc.), no doubt
also by priests, who would have been concerned to maintain links with the
past, not least by preserving genealogical records. In spite of the favorable sociological structure provided by separate settlements, resistance
to assimilation no doubt called for great vigilance, which will help explain why circumcision, sabbath observance, and dietary prescriptions
achieved during that time the confessional status they have preserved
ever since.

Several categories of cult personnel, from priests to temple servants
($n^e t \hat{i} n \hat{i} m$) maintained their identity and status in the Babylonian settlements over several generations (Ezra 2:36–58 = Neh. 7:39–60; Ezra
8:15–20), which seems to suggest a fairly well-developed social, economic,
and organizational substructure. With respect to religious organization,
an old suggestion is that it took the form of a network of synagogues serving the purposes of both prayer and education. At that stage such an institution, if it existed, would have involved nothing more than meeting together in a house of adequate size; we recall that the Diaspora elders were
in the habit of conferring with Ezekiel in his house (Ezek. 8:1; 14:1; 20:1).
Another possibility, perhaps not incompatible with the first, is that the deportees built their own temple at Casiphia, one of the principal centers
of the Diaspora. In Ezra's day, it was home to a certain Iddo (a priestly
name) and it was from there that Ezra was able to recruit cultic personnel.[11] However, neither of these conclusions is beyond question, depending as they do on inference rather than actual historical data.

We are also reduced to speculation when we go on to ask how these
Babylonian Jews were affected by state policy during this long period of
time. They may have thrown in their lot with the opposition to
Nabonidus (556–539), last of the Babylonian kings, who neglected the

state cult of Marduk for that of the North Mesopotamian moon deity Sin, and they may also have suffered for it. It seems tolerably clear, at any rate, that they supported the Persians during the final eclipse of Babylonian power. The payoff came in the form of Persian benevolence manifested in political and religious control when some of them returned to Judah and were installed by the imperial authorities as the dominant elite in the province.

We must now go on to ask how this situation, disorienting as it must have been, affected prophecy in its institutional forms and socially idiosyncratic manifestations. While it is obvious that prophecy did not come to an end at that time, the sense that one long phase of its history now belonged to the past is reflected in the Deuteronomic editing of Jeremiah as last in line of the prophetic servants and also in allusions to "the former prophets" that we begin to hear soon after the return from exile (Zech. 1:1–6; 7:7). Vague references to the drying up of inspiration will not suffice as an explanation of this state of affairs, since they do not explain why inspiration wilted then and not at another time. Optimistic prophets of the Hananiah type (Jeremiah 28), who functioned primarily but probably not exclusively in the cult, were obviously proved wrong and discredited. Ezekiel predicted that they would no longer have a place in the register of the house of Israel (Ezek. 13:9), and in fact none appear in the carefully preserved lists of cultic officials from the early Persian period. But even prophets of doom like Jeremiah would not necessarily have come through these experiences unscathed. It could be argued that, either by actually predicting disaster, or refusing to perform the prophetic role of intercession, they had contributed to bringing it about. So, for example, we find the deportees in Egypt after the fall of Jerusalem, among whom women were prominent and vocal, rejecting Jeremiah's often-repeated explanation of why it had all ended in this way (Jer. 44:15–19).

With all due allowance for the polemical cast of the literature, the decline in the quality of official, public prophecy, and the increase in confusion caused by conflicting prophetic claims, is already apparent between the first and the second deportation. Both Jeremiah (29:8) and Ezekiel (13:7–9, 23; 22:28) bracket prophecy with divination. Ezekiel also extends his polemic to women prophets who were practicing the magical arts by tying bands around the wrists of their clients and covering their heads with shawls while pronouncing spells (13:17–23). This may suggest that more traditionally Israelite forms of prophecy were waging a losing battle against the allure of Babylonian magic, divination by a variety of techniques, and dream interpretation.[12] Ezekiel follows up his assault on false prophecy with a condemnation of syncretism (14:1–11), with the obvious implication of a connection between them, and the same connection is made by the exilic Deuteronomist (Deut. 18:9–14, 15–22; cf. 13:1–5, 6–18). In the absence of an operative national cult under royal patronage such a situation of anomie and confusion is hardly surprising.

Given the close association of all forms of prophecy with the monarchy, either for or against, it is odd that the loss of royal patronage has been so seldom acknowledged as a basic factor in creating a situation fatal to the exercise of the kinds of prophecy attested while the monarchy was still in existence. A closely related factor is the dominance of the priestly and scribal classes during the Babylonian and early Persian periods. Contact with Babylonian scholarship favored the written word over oral delivery and the wisdom of the past over intermittent inspiration in the present. The priestly classes who edited and expanded existing narrative traditions, and who we may also presume were familiar with the Sumero-Akkadian scribal-intellectual tradition, elaborated a theology in which the prophetic functions of revelation and intercession were subsumed in and reabsorbed by the cult.[13] And, not least important, the Persian imperial authorities supported the Jerusalem cult and its leaders, a policy tending to inhibit the kind of public dissent characteristic of some forms of prophecy under the monarchy.

After the extinction of the monarchy, the same close association between prophet and king can be seen in the expressions of hope in prophetic texts from the late Babylonian and early Persian periods for a Davidic restoration. From time to time during those years the political situation must have seemed to justify such hopes. Though Jehoiachin, exiled in 598, had joined dignitaries from other subject lands in enforced exile in Babylon, he was still widely recognized as the legitimate king and is even referred to as "king of Judah" (*Ya'ukin šar Yaudaya*) on a tablet from the time of Nebuchadrezzar, which also refers to, but unfortunately does not name, his five sons.[14] Dates appear to have been calculated from his accession (Ezek. 1:2), and the exilic historian ends his work, certainly by design, with the notice that he was set free at the beginning of the reign of Nebuchadrezzar's successor Amel-Marduk (2 Kings 25:27–30). Perhaps the Babylonians intended to restore Jehoiachin to the throne as a client king at an opportune moment. Be that as it may, his grandson Zerubbabel (*Zer-Babili*, "seed" of Babylon), appointed provincial governor by the Persians, did become the focus of nationalistic aspirations during the disturbances following on the death of Cambyses (Hag. 1:12–15; 2:21–23; Zech. 4:6–8).

Prophetic texts datable to the Neo-Babylonian or early Persian period suggest that there focused on Jehoiachin and his descendants a messianic fervor based on the assumption that the dynastic promise was still valid and that therefore the dynasty was still the indispensable instrument of well-being and salvation. A passage in Jeremiah (33:14–16 = 23:5–6) speaks of a future in which Yahweh will raise up a "righteous Branch" (*ṣemaḥ ṣaddîq*) whose name will be "Yahweh our righteousness" or perhaps "Yahweh our victory" (*YHWH ṣidqēnû*). This symbolic title may, in addition, conceal an ironic pun on the name of the reprobate Zedekiah (*ṣidqiyāhû*, meaning "Yahweh is my righteousness"), who is contrasted with "the righteous Branch," the deposed Jehoiachin and his family, as the legitimate descendants of David. The same title, "the Branch," would later be conferred on Zerubbabel (Zech. 3:8; 6:12), following a well-established poetic tradition of exalted titulary applied to an ideal ruler (cf. the "messianic" poem in Isa. 9:2–7 [MT 9:1–6]).

Another title applied to the ideal or future dynast is "servant" (*'ebed*), a designation that has achieved notoriety from the mistitled "servant songs" in Isaiah 40—55. This usage is Deuteronomic,[15] and a Deuteronomic addition to the Jeremiah text discussed a moment ago (33:14–16) uses this title of the Davidic king and affirms the indefectibility of the dynastic promise. The same title occurs in Ezekiel 34—37, which, as suggested earlier, may represent a distinct exilic collection of material (Ezek. 34:23–24; 37:24–25). It is also conferred on Zerubbabel who is therefore designated both Branch and Servant (Zech. 3:8–10). The Deuteronomic use of this term for both ruler and prophet, with its emphasis on service and instrumentality, marked the furthest point reached to that time in the understanding of the function and purpose of institution and office.

So far in this section we have been talking about social and political changes as they affected the exercise of prophecy in its different forms. We now go on to consider how these changes precipitated an inner crisis in prophecy, bringing to the surface unresolved conflicts and antinomies that seem to be inseparable from its exercise. Something of this is already apparent in the polemic of Jeremiah and Ezekiel against those whom they took to be false prophets. Their major point was that these prophets were deceiving people with a false message of assurance originating in self-induced visions and dreams.[16] The content of the message, similar to that of prophets in neighboring states (Jer. 27:9), can be deduced from quotations attributed to these opponents of Jeremiah and Ezekiel: assurance of national well-being (*šālôm*), freedom from invasion and related evils, successful rebellion against the oppressor, and the like.[17] They are not condemned as apostates or devotees of alien deities, for they worshiped the same deity, used the same traditional forms of prophetic speech (for example, "thus says Yahweh"; Jer. 23:38; 28:2) and were presumably indistinguishable from Jeremiah or Ezekiel in appearance and demeanor. While some were attached to the temple, others may have been employed in more mundane capacities, for example, as messengers and couriers on behalf of the king and court. Jeremiah seems to refer to this function on one occasion (23:21), and we have seen that a *nābî'* functioned as a courier in one of the Lachish ostraca (III:19–21; *ANET*, 322).

We do not need to be psychologists to suspect that the violence of Jeremiah's attack on contemporary *nᵉbî'îm*, when taken in conjunction with his own doubts and self-questioning, suggests that the task of refuting these "false prophets" and establishing his own credentials was far from easy. Accusations of venality and immorality (Jer. 14:18; 23:11–15; 29:23) are routine ways of discrediting opposition, and even if true as stated do not get to the heart of the matter. The allegation that they were not divinely commissioned (Jer. 14:14; 23:18–22) is equally ineffective since unverifiable, and the same applies to the argument that their visions were of human not divine origin (Jer. 23:16; Ezek. 13:2–3). Doubts about the propriety of certain ways of obtaining a revelation, for example, by dreams, also seem to be unjustified in the light of prophetic history as a whole. The charge that they stole sayings from one another, practiced plagiarism in other words, may simply reflect that they appealed like their forebears to a well-established tradition of prophetic discourse and exhibited a strong sense of solidarity, neither of which is a matter of reproach.

This appeal to tradition, mediated or filtered through intense personal experience and brought to bear on the interpretation of contemporary events, is of course a crucial aspect of the complex phenomenon of prophecy. If we take the trouble to reconstruct what we can of the theology of the optimistic prophets, we shall see that they set great store on the covenant fidelity of Yahweh, divine promises made to the reigning dynasty (2 Samuel 7), and a special providence for Jerusalem—all established on the best prophetic precedent (Isa. 37:33–35, etc.). The counterargument that this is a selective reading of the tradition is not in itself entirely persuasive. In response to Hananiah's prediction of freedom from Babylonian domination within two years (Jer. 28:1–4), Jeremiah appealed to prophetic tradition to make the point that the burden of proof rests with the prophet of well-being rather than with the one who, like himself, predicted disaster (28:5–9). The argument, however, is far from cogent, since it is simply not the case that prophets whom Jeremiah would have accepted as genuine predicted only doom. And, in a more general sense, it is unclear why the criterion of falsification should apply only to optimistic predictions.

What it seems to amount to is that, in the last resort, the prophet can count only on the prophet's own ability to communicate the quality of a unique vision, a unique sense of absolute certitude, the self-authenticating character of discourse that can be compared to fire, to wheat compared with chaff, to a hammer that breaks up rocks (Jer. 5:14; 23:28–29). The indications are that Jeremiah himself managed to convince only a relatively small number of people, and it is particularly significant that this was so even after the destruction of Jerusalem, which he had successfully predicted.

Jeremiah's career illustrates, more than Jeremiah himself or his editors intended, the destabilizing influence of prophetic dissent. It also exemplifies the official need to control prophetic dissidents and how difficult it proved to do so, even in times of national crisis. The confrontation between Amos and Amaziah (Amos 7:10–17) and the letter of complaint about Jeremiah addressed to the Jerusalemite priests (Jer. 29:24–28) suggest that prophetic activity came under the jurisdiction of temple authorities, a circumstance that also helps to explain prophetic diatribe directed against priests. From the time of Amos we hear of frequent attempts to silence prophets or to bring them into line with state policies and the expectations associated with official prophetic role performance.[18] These attempts at controlling dissent were much less successful than was the case in contemporary Assyria or Babylonia, and therefore dissident prophetic activity had a much broader scope in Israel than in the great empires.

But the most grievous problem did not originate with state authorities, including the priesthood, in their attempts to control prophetic activity. More serious was the inability of the prophets' audience to distinguish between conflicting claims and predictions, leading not only to a breakdown of prophetic authority in general but to widespread questioning of the religious premises on the basis of which the prophetic message claimed a hearing. The contribution of optimistic prophets to this crisis is easier to assess, since it could be argued, *post factum*, that they had deceived the people into fatally misreading the contemporary political situation.[19] This is more obviously the case with short-term and high-risk predictions of the kind made by Hananiah (the Babylonian yoke would be broken within two years, Jer. 28:2–4) so that, had he lived a year or so longer, his credibility would presumably have been damaged beyond repair. But we have seen that it could also be argued that prophets like Jeremiah had actually contributed to bringing about the disasters that they foretold, both by their effect on public morale ("weakening the hands of all the people," Jer. 38:4) and by virtue of the belief that such prophecies, especially when accompanied by symbolic acts, had a performative and self-fulfilling character. The failure of his preaching to the small diaspora in Egypt in the postdisaster period (Jer. 44:1–19) is an important indication that prophets who predicted disaster were not automatically vindicated after the event.

We are led to conclude that the criterion of historical verification or falsification does not do justice to the complex phenomenon of prophecy as practiced in Israel. In its Deuteronomic formulation (Deut. 18:21–22), it cannot be applied by the prophet's contemporaries except for short-term predictions, which in fact the Deuteronomic "doctrine" on prophecy seems designed to discourage. Taken by itself, this criterion also threatens to reduce the prophetic function to that of predicting the future, by the very fact of suggesting that a prophet can lose his credentials by getting one such prediction wrong. But such a ruling, if applied strictly, would have discredited not only Hananiah but also Huldah, Amos, and perhaps Jeremiah himself. Once again, therefore, we come up against the impossibility of discriminating between true and false prophecy on the basis of objective and verifiable criteria.

The broader implications of the decline of confidence in prophecy can be seen in the widespread malaise, reflected in the literature produced shortly before and shortly after the fall of Jerusalem, concerning the intentions and even the ethical character of the god in whose name the prophets, whether optimistic or pessimistic, claimed to speak.

The problem may first be illustrated by two well-known incidents recorded by Dtr. The first, dealing with a Judean man of God who fell foul of an old prophet at Bethel (1 Kings 13:1–32), is a locus classicus of conflicting prophetic revelations, and also a fine example of classical Hebrew prose that deserves close reading. Since it presupposes the extension of Josiah's reforms to the Bethel area (the man of God mentions Josiah by name) and has unmistakable echoes of the mission of Amos to Bethel under a later Jeroboam, this narrative appears to be a free composition of the historian. It should therefore be read as a reflection on the problematic nature of prophetic revelation in the last days of the kingdom of Judah. The first part of the narrative (13:1–10) predicts the destruction of the Bethel altar by Josiah and the execution by him of the priests who serve it. The Judean man of God gives a miraculous sign guaranteeing the fulfillment of this prediction, and he discharges the prophetic role of intercessor by healing the king's withered hand. The story then takes an odd turn with the appearance on the scene of an old prophet surrounded by his "sons" (disciples). This local prophet persuades the Judean man of God, on the basis of a divine oracle that he claims mendaciously to have received, to partake of a meal in violation of a command received from God before leaving Judah. In the course of the meal the Bethel prophet pronounces an oracle, a genuine one this time, which condemns his Judean counterpart to death for disobeying the divine command. The story ends with the impressive scene of the body of the Judean man of God lying on the road, with the donkey and lion standing impassively on either side.

At the most obvious level, the story might be interpreted as making the point that an earlier oracle has precedence over a later one. But it also illustrates the Deuteronomic idea that prophecy also can serve as a kind of testing of the prophet's audience (Deut. 13:3). In this instance, however, we would have to say that the line between testing and deception is very thin indeed. There is no hint of disapproval of the mendacious oracle that led to the Judean prophet's death, and it was Yahweh, after all, who stationed that uncharacteristic lion in the prophet's path as he was on his way home.[20]

The second incident also deals with conflicting prophetic revelations, this time between the ecstatic prophets of a king of Samaria and Micaiah ben-Imlah (1 Kings 22:1–38). Whatever its historical basis, it seems to have been put together as a kind of test case to justify a minority revelation that is unfavorable over against a prophetic consensus that is optimistic and corroborative of official policy. Looking beyond this intention of the writer, however, we can detect a new and disturbing element, namely, the explanation of false prophecy as the outcome of a divine purpose to deceive by means of a supernatural agent (called simply the Spirit), functionally similar to the Satan who will emerge at a somewhat later stage (Job 1—2; Zech. 3:1; 1 Chron. 21:1). The correspondence with the situation during the last days of Judah is unmistakable. Both Jeremiah (4:10) and Ezekiel (14:9), in effect, accuse Yahweh of deceiving the people and leading them to ruin by means of false prophets. No one doubted that the disasters were the work of Yahweh—indeed, the result of a deliberate decision on his part (Lam. 2:8; cf. Amos 3:6). While the all-important question why he chose to do so remained in doubt, there was no doubt at all that conflicting prophetic revelations and claims played an important part in bringing the final disaster about (Lam. 2:14, etc.).

Anxious questions about the moral character of the god of traditional religion, reflecting the impact of the disasters of that time, may have left more of a mark on the literary record than is generally acknowledged. To pursue this theological issue in detail would take us too far afield, but one or two examples may be given. The identification of Jerusalem with Sodom in prophetic diatribe (Isa. 3:9; Jer. 23:14; Ezek. 16:43–58), for example, suggests the possibility that the dialogue of Abraham with Yahweh over the fate of Sodom in Gen. 18:22–33 is a late addition to the story reflecting the religious crisis of the sixth century B.C.E.[21] The dialogue deals with two related issues: the fate of the righteous caught in the destructive flow of events directly attributable to divine causality; the possibility that, at a certain critical mass, the righteous can save the wicked from the fate that they deserve. That these were issues of great moment both before and after the fall of Jerusalem is apparent in the writings that have survived from that time. Jeremiah asserted, no doubt with rhetorical exaggeration, that the presence of one righteous person would have saved Jerusalem (Jer. 5:1). Ezekiel, on the contrary, argued that if a land (Judah, for example) suffered the disasters of war, even those models of righteousness Noah, Daniel, and Job would, if present, save only themselves (Ezek. 14:12–20). In keeping with this rigorously individualistic approach to culpability and retribution, Ezekiel also rejected the traditional idea of solidarity in the kinship group, and thus sought to answer the charge that his contemporaries were being punished for the sins of their ancestors (Ezek. 18:1–20). The same position is taken by a Jeremian editor (Jer. 31:29), and it also comes to expression in one of the later strands of Deuteronomy (Deut. 24:16; cf. 2 Kings 14:6).

Reading Gen. 18:22–33 as a kind of midrash inspired by the fate of Jerusalem and the theological problems to which it gave rise also sets in higher relief some interesting and neglected parallels between this passage and the book of Job. Both protagonists know that they have no right to question God, but they do so notwithstanding (Job 9:12). Both presume to speak, while confessing that they are but dust and ashes (Job 42:6), and both raise the question of how a just God can destroy the righteous with the wicked (Job 9:22). Both narratives, finally, illustrate the limitations of the prophetic function of intercession. Like Jeremiah, Abraham intercedes with God, but once his intercession comes to an end the fate of the city is sealed.

In summary, then, prophecy did not come to an end with the loss of independence and exile but was forced by the pressure of social and political change into different directions that will occupy us in the remainder of this book. For those who, after the destruction, still had the faith and courage to pick up the pieces and build a future it must have appeared that the older forms of prophecy, in spite of their religious and ethical achievements, were no longer adequate to the needs of a new and quite different situation. It is in fact unlikely that the older prophetic writings would have survived the catastrophes of the early sixth century if they had not been made available and serviceable by appropriate reinterpretation and recontextualization. We now go on to see what can be known or reasonably conjectured about this process of transmission and interpretation that bridged the gap between state and colonial dependency, between Israel and Judaism, the old order and the new.

17. THE EXILIC-DEUTERONOMIC RESPONSE

P. R. **Ackroyd,** *Exile and Restoration,* 62–83; R. **Albertz,** *A History of Israelite Religion in the Old Testament Period,* vol. 2, *From the Exile to the Maccabees,* Louisville: Westminster/John Knox Press, 1994 [1992], 375–99; E. **Auerbach,** "Die grosse Überarbeitung der biblischen Bücher," *SVT* 1 (1953): 1–10; J. **Blenkinsopp,** *Prophecy and Canon,* 46–53, 80–89; W. **Brueggemann,** "The Kerygma of the Deuteronomistic Historian," *Int* 22 (1968): 387–402; M. **Cogan,** "Israel in Exile—The View of a Josianic Historian," *JBL* 97 (1978): 40–44; F. M. **Cross,** "The Themes of the Book of Kings and the Structure of the Deuteronomistic History," *Canaanite Myth and Hebrew Epic,* Cambridge, Mass.: Harvard University Press, 1973, 274–89; W. **Dietrich,** *Prophetie und Geschichte,* Göttingen: Vandenhoeck & Ruprecht, 1972; J. D. **Levenson,** "Who Inserted the Book of the Torah?" *HTR* 68 (1975): 203–33; A.D.H. **Mayes,** *The Story of Israel between Settlement and Exile,* London: SCM Press, 1983; R. D. **Nelson,** *The Double Redaction of the Deuteronomistic History,* Sheffield: JSOT Press, 1981; E. W. **Nicholson,** *Deuteronomy and Tradition,* Oxford: Basil Blackwell, 1967, 107–18; *Preaching to the Exiles,* New York: Schocken Books, 1970; M. **Noth,** *Überlieferungsgeschichtliche Studien,* Tübingen: Max Niemeyer, 1967[3] (= *The Deuteronomistic History,* Sheffield: JSOT Press, 1981); J. A. **Soggin,** "Deuteronomistische Geschichtsauslegung während des babylonischen Exils," in F. Christ, ed., *Oikonomia: Oscar Cullmann zum 65. Geburtstag gewidmet,* Hamburg-Bergstedt: Reich, 1967, 11–17; H. W. **Wolff,** "Das Kerygma des deuteronomistischen Geschichtswerk," *ZAW* 73 (1961): 171–85 (= "The Kerygma of the Deuteronomic Historical Work," in W. Brueggemann and H. W. Wolff, *The Vitality of Old Testament Traditions,* Atlanta: John Knox Press, 1975, 83–100.

There seems to be a consensus that the history of the Israelite nation from the death of Moses to the Babylonian exile (= Dtr) was composed around the middle of the sixth century B.C.E., either in Babylon among the deportees, or in the province of Judah, or less probably in Egypt. There is also substantial agreement that this exilic composition incorporates an earlier draft, or drafts, from the last decades of the Judean monarchy (Noth, Cross, Nelson, Mayes). The historian was certainly aware of the erosion of confidence in prophetic authority, the doubts being raised about the special relationship between Israel and its God, and the conditions necessary for securing God's cooperation. The response is written clearly into the history: both kingdoms were destroyed because of neglect of the laws (2 Kings 21:10–15), and the destruction could have been avoided had ruler and people heeded the prophets sent to them by God (2 Kings 17:13, 23; 20:16–18; 22:15–20; 24:2, 13). The historian thereby clears God of the charge of injustice or indifference, puts the blame where it belongs, and in doing so provides an overall theological rationale for prophecy.

The book of Deuteronomy had also gone through more than one edition, reaching its final form (with the exception of late additions in the Priestly style) at the same time as Dtr, and perhaps as an integral part of it. The book adopts a reflective approach to the phenomenon of prophecy and contains what might be called a first sketch for a doctrine of prophecy (Deut. 18:9–22; 13:1–5 deals with the prophet only incidentally). In keeping with the book's strongly integrationist ideology, major emphasis is on prophecy as a native Israelite phenomenon, contrasted with the different forms of divination and mediation practiced among the nations. (The author does not add that they were also practiced in Israel.) The principle of historical falsification applies to all prophets (18:21–22), but the ability to predict correctly is not enough to authenticate a prophet and his message. He must also, on penalty of death, speak in the name of Israel's God (13:1–5). Prophecy in Israel originated as God's answer to the people's request for mediation at Sinai-Horeb. It is therefore modeled on the ministry of Moses, which means that it is concerned essentially with covenant and law. When the prophet acts in that capacity, and only then, he or she does so with full divine authorization and must be obeyed.

The programmatic statement at the end of the book (Deut. 34:10–12), which denies parity between the mode of revelation proper to Moses ("face to face") and prophetic mediation, seems to be designed as a warning against a possible misunderstanding of Deut. 18:15–18, the promise of a "prophet like Moses," in the sense that prophetic communications throughout the history are on the same level as the Mosaic revelation. For the Deuteronomists this is decidedly not the case. The book concludes, therefore, by setting aside the epoch ending with the death of Moses as normative for all subsequent expressions of religious life including prophecy. Read in this way, the concluding statement of Deuteronomy also serves as a finale to the Pentateuch as a whole.[22]

The attribution of Deuteronomy to Moses allowed the pseudonymous author to look at prophecy from the perspective of origins, while Dtr views it retrospectively from the end of an epoch. In recording events, the historian is faithful to the Deuteronomic "doctrine" on prophecy, for example, in assigning prophets the role of preaching the law (2 Kings 17:13) and in the death penalty assessed on false prophets (e.g., 1 Kings 18:40). There is also concern to illustrate and justify the prophetic function of warning against the consequences of religious infidelity. Deuteronomy, in effect, redefines prophecy and does so in such a way as to restrict and circumscribe the potentially disruptive aspects of prophetic activity. The passage dealing with prophecy (Deut. 18:9–22) occurs in a section dedicated to public offices—monarchy, priesthood, prophecy, judiciary (17:14–19:21)—suggesting a concern to bring it within an institutional grid, and thus to define and limit its scope. If this is so, it would agree with the indications, noted earlier, that the Deuteronomic editor of Jeremiah viewed this prophet as recapitulating and bringing to an end the series of prophetic "servants" beginning with Moses the protoprophet. Given this view of the matter, we would want to pose the question: Did the exilic authors of this literature foresee any future for prophecy in the postdisaster period?

The answer to this question would call for a close reading of passages of Deuteronomic origin or inspiration referring explicitly or by implication to the exilic situation, and more specifically to the appropriate response of the people to this situation.[23] Although we hear of the need to listen to Yahweh's voice, which could be taken to refer to prophecy (Deut. 4:30; cf. 18:15), the emphasis seems to be on the action of the people as a whole. They are urged to seek Yahweh, to return to him, to pray, supplicate, and confess their sins, and in no case is mention made of prophetic intercession (e.g., Deut. 4:29–31; 30:1–5,10). We also hear of the law now written on the heart (Deut. 30:11–14; Jer. 31:31–34), again with no allusion to the mediating role of the prophet, and certainly with no diminution of the importance of the written law. That law is now presented as the equivalent of the vaunted intellectual tradition of Babylon and other foreign lands renowned for wisdom (Deut. 4:6–8, 32–35; 30:11–14). It is unclear what we are to conclude from this, and it is possible that the Deuteronomists themselves were not entirely clear on the forms of religious life appropriate for the new situation. Uncertainty may have extended to the most appropriate forms of mediation, especially in view of the ambiguities and antinomies besetting prophecy in the last years of the kingdom and the early years of the exile.

There is broad agreement that the same school was responsible for compiling and editing prophetic material during the exilic period. As noted earlier, Dtr mentions none of the canonical prophets by name with the exception of Isaiah and Jonah. Since it is unlikely that the historian was unaware of their existence, it may be that this exilic prophetic anthology was intended as a kind of supplement to the history, though by itself this does not provide a completely adequate explanation of the historian's silence. Another issue is the extent of this hypothetical exilic-Deuteronomic collection. We would need to find evidence in prophetic books of Deuteronomic editing, not an easy task nor one likely to lead to assured results. The prudent course will be to risk error on the side of less rather than more; in other words, to assign editorial expansions to this source only when there is clear evidence of Deuteronomic language or a point of view that is unambiguously characteristic of the Deuteronomists.

We begin with superscriptions to prophetic books containing chronological indications according to reigns, especially where there is the kind of synchrony between the two kingdoms occurring routinely in the history. Synchronized reigns occur only in the superscriptions to Amos and Hosea, but Isaiah, Micah, possibly Zephaniah, and certainly Jeremiah out of the fifteen books of the Latter Prophets are dated according to the reigns of Judean rulers. The *possibility* of Deuteronomic editorial expansions of prophetic sayings is also enhanced by the tendency of Dtr to expand predictions of individual prophets to take in more distant events. So, for example, the unnamed man of God who prophesied the end of the Shiloh priesthood is also made to predict the rise of the Zadokites and the destitution of the provincial priests as a result of Josiah's reforms (1 Sam. 2:27–36). The man of God from Judah who condemned the Bethel sanctuary also went on to predict Josiah's activity in the northern territories (1 Kings 13:1–2). Ahijah's condemnation of Jeroboam, which originally dealt only with the dynasty founded by that king, was extended to take in the fall of Samaria (1 Kings 14:15–16). Huldah, finally, uttered an oracle of good omen concerning Josiah, but is presented by the historian as the Hebrew Cassandra predicting the fall and destruction of Jerusalem (2 Kings 22:14–20).

This literary procedure in Dtr suggests that something of the same may have happened with the prophetic books, perhaps with specific reference to the Josian reforms and the exile. If so, the indications are not (leaving aside Jeremiah) exactly overwhelming. At this point we will briefly summarize conclusions reached in previous chapters, and it will be unnecessary to add that many of them are tentative. In Amos, references to the fate of Bethel may have been added, or modified, in the light of Josiah's action against that sanctuary in the seventh century (Amos 3:14; 5:6). The oracle against Judah, predicting the destruction of Jerusalem on account of sin (2:4–5), is probably Deuteronomic. In the poem or riddle about prophecy in the following chapter (3: 3–8), there occurs an explanatory gloss ("surely Yahweh God does nothing without revealing his plan to his servants the prophets") the purpose of which is to exonerate Yahweh of responsibility for the fate of Jerusalem, in keeping with the apologetic intent of Dtr. Allusions to the exodus, wilderness period, and occupation of the land (2:9–12) may be from the same source, as also the prose addition to the prophet's condemnation of contemporary worship (5:25–27).

Of importance for understanding the reformulation of prophecy in the light of the exilic experience are the passages in Amos enjoining a seeking of Yahweh that can lead through judgment to salvation (Amos 5:4–5, 6, 14–15). We are now in a better position to compare these "seek passages" with the message of the Deuteronomists addressed to the exiles couched in much the same terms (e.g., Deut. 4:27–31; Jer. 29:10–14). The conclusion suggests itself that the Deuteronomists made prophecy serviceable to their contemporaries by reading a message of judgment (e.g., in Amos) as one of *salvation through and subsequent to judgment.* In embracing this alternative, they may well have followed the lead of an earlier editor who was unable to accept Amos' message of total rejection (see the addition at Amos 9:8b). We also note that even with respect to the kingdom of Samaria the historian's attitude is not uniformly negative (2 Kings 13:5, 23; 14:27).

Apart from the titles, there is little in either Hosea or Micah attributable with the same degree of probability to a Deuteronomic editor. Affinities there certainly are, especially where Hosea speaks of the broken covenant (Hos. 6:7; 8:1), but we do not know that they derive from Deuteronom(ist)ic editing. The allusion to the reunification of the kingdoms under a Davidic king in Hosea (3:4–5) is also a well-attested exilic theme and may derive from the same Deuteronomic source. As suggested earlier, Isaian sayings, especially those dealing with Assyria, seem to have been edited and expanded during the reign of Josiah, but they betray few characteristically Deuteronomic features.[24] The historian had access to biographical traditions about this prophet that, however, convey a rather different impression from the sayings (Isaiah 36—39). It would not be surprising, in view of the interest of the school in prophetic biography, if these hagiographical narratives were added to the sayings by a member of the school during the exile. Biographical interest is also much in evidence in the Deuteronomic edition of Jeremiah that, as noted earlier, parallels in some important respects the Deuteronomic portrait of Moses. The point has been made that the Deuteronomic concentration on Jeremiah arose out of the conviction that with him a definite phase in the history of prophecy had come to an end.

In an age of disorientation and discontinuity, of endings and beginnings, the exilic Deuteronomists summoned the remnant of Israel to return to its origins in the belief that the God of the exodus, the God of Moses, though hidden, would again reveal his face: "From there you will seek Yahweh your God, and you will find him if you search after him . . . for Yahweh your God is a merciful God; he will not fail you or destroy you or forget the covenant with your fathers which he swore to them" (Deut. 4:29, 31).[25]

18. EZEKIEL

P. R. **Ackroyd,** *Exile and Restoration,* 103–17; L. C. **Allen,** *Ezekiel 20—48,* Waco, Tex.: Word Books, 1990; J. **Blenkinsopp,** *Ezekiel,* Louisville: John Knox Press, 1990; L. **Boadt,** "Ezekiel, Book of," *ABD* 2:711–22; W. H. **Brownlee,** *Ezekiel 1—19,* Waco, Tex.: Word Books, 1986; K. W. **Carley,** *Ezekiel among the Prophets,* London:

SCM Press, 1975; R. E. **Clements,** "The Ezekiel Tradition: Prophecy in a Time of Crisis"; R. **Coggins** et al., *Israel's Prophetic Tradition,* 119–36; G. A. **Cooke,** *The Book of Ezekiel,* Edinburgh: T. & T. Clark, 1936; W. **Eichrodt,** *Ezekiel: A Commentary,* Philadelphia: Westminster Press, 1970; M. **Fishbane,** "Sin and Judgement in the Prophecies of Ezekiel," *Int* 38 (1984): 131–50; G. **Fohrer,** *Die Hauptprobleme des Buches Ezechiel,* Berlin: de Gruyter, 1952; F. S. **Freedy,** "The Glosses in Ezekiel 1–24," *VT* 20 (1970): 129–32; M. **Greenberg,** *Ezekiel 1—20,* Garden City, N.Y.: Doubleday, 1983; G. **Hölscher,** *Hesekiel: Der Dichter und das Buch,* Berlin: de Gruyter, 1924; C. G. **Howie,** "Ezekiel," *IDB* 2 (1962): 203–13; W. A. **Irwin,** *The Problem of Ezekiel,* Chicago: University of Chicago Press, 1943; P. **Joyce,** *Divine Initiative and Human Response in Ezekiel,* Sheffield: JSOT Press, 1989; J. D. **Levenson,** *Theology of the Program of Restoration of Ezekiel 40—48,* Missoula, Mont.: Scholars Press, 1976; J. **Lust,** ed., *Ezekiel and His Book: Textual and Literary Criticism and Their Interrelation,* Louvain: Louvain University Press, 1986; L. J. **McGregor,** *The Greek Text of Ezekiel,* Atlanta: Scholars Press, 1985; K-F. **Pohlmann,** *Ezechielstudien,* Berlin: de Gruyter, 1992; H. Graf **Reventlow,** *Wächter über Israel: Ezekiel und seine Tradition,* Berlin: de Gruyter, 1962; H. H. **Rowley,** "The Book of Ezekiel in Modern Study," *BJRL* 36 (1953–54): 146–90 (= *Men of God,* 169–210); S. **Talmon** and M. **Fishbane,** "The Structuring of Biblical Books: Studies in the Book of Ezekiel," *ASTI* 10 (1976): 129–53; C. C. **Torrey,** *Pseudo-Ezekiel and the Original Prophecy,* New Haven: Yale University Press, 1930; M. **Tsevat,** "The Neo-Assyrian and Neo-Babylonian Vassal Oaths and the Prophet Ezekiel," *JBL* 78 (1959): 199–204; J. W. **Wevers,** *Ezekiel,* London: Thomas Nelson & Sons, 1969; W. **Zimmerli,** "Das Gotteswort des Ezechiel," *ZTK* 48 (1951): 249–62 (= *Gottes Offenbarung: Gesammelte Aufsätze,* Munich: Kaiser Verlag, 1963, 133–47; see also 148–77, 178–91); "Israel im Buche Ezechiel," *VT* 8 (1958): 75–90; "The Special Form- and Traditio-Historical Character of Ezekiel's Prophecy," *VT* 15 (1965): 515–27; "The Message of the Prophet Ezekiel," *Int* 23 (1969): 134–36; *Ezekiel 1,* Philadelphia: Fortress Press, 1979 [1969]; *Ezekiel 2,* Philadelphia: Fortress Press, 1983 [1969].

The book of Ezekiel seems to have gone through difficult times in reaching the finished state in which we now have it. The Greek version (LXX) is more compact than the MT and perhaps represents, on the whole, an earlier stage of transmission. The Greek text reconstructed from Papyrus 967 from the Chester Beatty collection shows significant differences from both the standard LXX text and the MT. The relatively few fragments recovered from the first, third, fourth, and eleventh caves at Qumran, covering about seventy-four verses, are said to be close to the MT. (Unfortunately, the Ezekiel scroll from the eleventh cave had deteriorated too badly to allow unrolling). The text of some chapters of the book—especially 7, 21, and 28—is in poor shape, and there are numerous glosses throughout, but the overall condition of the text is no worse than we would expect.

The zealous work of glossators and scholiasts attests to the significance attached to the book, especially in circles of an apocalyptic or mystical tendency, but it has aggravated the problem of working back from book to author. If we begin by simply collating the information that the book provides, we learn from the superscription (1:1–3) that it is ascribed to a certain Ezekiel ben-Buzi, of a priestly family, who had an extraordinary vision in Babylon in the year 593 B.C.E. It is generally assumed that he arrived there with the first batch of deportees in 598, though we are not told this, and there was more than one deportation. Indications are that he was active for a time in Judah before going to Babylon, so that he may have had the visionary experience immediately or shortly after arriving in the Diaspora. According to the dates attached to thirteen sections in the book,[26] he remained active at least until 571. He was married, and his wife died during the siege of Jerusalem (24:15–18). That is about all that we learn, taking the information in the book at face value, and we have no other sources of biographical information. The often bizarre symbolic mimes and gestures that he is described as performing (see especially chaps. 4, 5, and 12); the often extremely emotional language, sometimes verging on the pathological and pornographic (chaps. 16 and 23), he employs; the ecstatic experiences to which he was subject; the loss of speech and perhaps also movement (3:25–27); have given rise to the suspicion that he suffered from some physical or psychological disorder—aphasia, catatonia, epilepsy, and schizophrenia have all been suggested, the last in a remarkable essay by Karl Jaspers.[27] While one or other of these conditions is quite possible, especially in view of the frequent association between sickness and possession, such suggestions are speculative and often vitiated by ignorance or neglect of the editorial history of the book.

The debate on that history has been going on since the beginning of the century and will doubtless continue. There is no consensus, but the following summary statement would probably find broad acceptance. While not a late Second Temple pseudepigraphal work, as suggested by C. C. Torrey,[28] the book is essentially the product of a school or circle that owed allegiance to Ezekiel, was closely associated with the cult, and inhabited the highly literate, quasi-esoteric priestly tradition well represented at a somewhat later time in some of the Qumran writings. The difficulty of distinguishing between the contribution of Ezekiel and that of his school, while real enough, is not so great that we cannot detect signs of elaboration. In the great vision of the *merkaba* or chariot throne in chapter 1, for example, the complicated description of the wheels (1:15–21) is probably the product of learned speculation among the prophet's following, a first stage in the process that will eventually endow the wheels with a life of their own as independent angelic beings—the *ophannim* of the mystical schools.

Commentators have found more substantial, but more questionable, evidence of editorial elaboration and expansion in those passages that speak of new possibilities and a new order for the future. In this respect the fall of Jerusalem is the great divide between the early career of the prophet (593–587/586) and the later period of his activity and that of his discipleship. The first part of the book, therefore, ends with Jerusalem invested by Nebuchadrezzar (chapters 1—24), the oracles against foreign nations occupy the space between the beginning of the siege and the fall of the city (25—32), and the announcement of the disaster (33) is followed by the proclamation of hope and new life (34—39) and the vision of the new temple and commonwealth (40—48).

Not surprisingly, questions of attribution and date are more severe with respect to material from this postdisaster period. As is the case with the formation of the Gospels, spanning the second destruction in 70 C.E., the fall of Jerusalem and cessation of temple worship have left their mark on the book, in that sayings that may have been composed and delivered before 587/586 have been revised in the light of the experience of disaster. To take only one small-scale example, it seems that predictions of exile have been expanded to take in the terrible fate of Zedekiah, last king of Judah, blinded and led off in shackles to captivity in Babylon (Ezek. 12:12–13). More generally, there is a marked shift from indictment of the nation, one of the most radical in prophetic writings, to emphasis on a new dispensation. Ezekiel himself may, of course, have re-edited and expanded his earlier preaching, as Jeremiah appears to have done with his (Jer. 36:32). Yet it remains extremely difficult to give an account of the book as we have it without positing a school that continued his work, adapting his teaching to new situations as they arose.[29]

It is no doubt to this school that we owe the striking architectonic unity of the book. We have just seen that it is organized according to a familiar triadic pattern: judgment on Israel (chapters 1—24), judgment on hostile nations (25—32), salvation for Israel (33—48). At a different level, a more complex pattern is detectable from which we may be able to distill useful information about the production of the work. The book opens with a detailed description of a vision in which Ezekiel saw what, in the final summing up, is identified as "the glory of YHWH" (Ezek. 1:28). This "glory" or divine effulgence (*kābôd* in Hebrew) is a technical term in Priestly tradition for the mysterious manifestation of the divine presence in worship. It seems to have been originally connected with the ark housed at the sanctuary of Shiloh and taken into battle as the visible guarantee of the presence of Yahweh of the hosts. We recall that, after it was captured by the Philistines, the daughter-in-law of the priest Eli died in giving birth to a son with a name of ill omen. The name, Ichabod,

meaning "alas, the Glory!" or "where is the Glory?" is explained with reference to the disaster: "the Glory has gone into exile from Israel, for the
ark of God is taken" (1 Sam. 4:21–22). Perhaps inevitably, this theological topos came to be associated in Priestly lore with the mobile sanctuary
in the wilderness (e.g., Ex. 16:7, 10–12) and in due course with the Jerusalem temple and its inner sanctuary, the Holy of Holies.

In a second vision (chaps. 8—11) the prophet witnessed the *kābôd*
abandoning the Jerusalem temple five years before the latter was destroyed, moving first to the main entrance of the building (9:3; 10:3–5),
then to the east gate (10:18–19), thence finally to the Mount of Olives to
the east (11:22–23).[30] Since it was the same manifestation that appeared
to Ezekiel in Babylon, this must be the first stage in its relocation among
the exiles there. The writer is therefore giving new meaning to the exile
of the *kābôd* in the care of Eli, and in doing so providing an explanation
of how worship is possible in a land polluted with idols, now that Yahweh's presence is manifested in it. In the final vision (chaps. 40—48),
dated to the twenty-fifth year of the exile, that is, at the halfway mark to
the jubilee year of release, the prophet or a disciple saw it return by the
same way it had left (43:1–5), thus completing the cycle from exile to
restoration, from absence to return, from spiritual death to new life.

The reversal of order, following which the vision of the *kābôd* and the
merkaba vouchsafed to Ezekiel in Babylon now stands at the beginning of
the book, occurred when the vision was prefaced to the original account
of the prophet's commissioning in order to make the point that the commission issued from the Enthroned One. The actual commissioning,
which was originally quite distinct from the vision and of an entirely different order, features the command to eat a scroll containing an ominous message for the prophet's contemporaries (Ezek. 2:3–3:11). No entirely adequate explanation of the chronological confusion resulting
from this transposition, and reflected in the dates at the beginning of the
book (1:1–3), has been offered to date. One is tempted to explain the
thirtieth year (1:1) as the thirtieth year of the prophet's age, since according to a ritual ordinance thirty is the minimum age for ordination
to the priesthood (Num. 4:30). According to Priestly tradition, moreover, the *kābôd* was supposed to appear to the ordinands during this cer-
emony (Num. 9:4–6). But other proposals have been made, and the matter will no doubt continue to be discussed.[31]

The affinities of this theological-symbolic schema with Priestly-cultic
and Priestly-scribal tradition in the early books of the Bible are clearly detectable and important for the attempt to place Ezekiel and his following. According to this tradition, Moses also had a vision of the *kābôd* during which he was accompanied by a group of elders (Ex. 24:9–11,

15b–18a) as happened frequently to Ezekiel (e.g., Ezek. 8:1); and in both instances, Moses and Ezekiel, the vision led to a commissioning. It is noteworthy also that both Moses and Ezekiel are disinclined to penetrate the visible epiphenomena of the divine presence, the former in witnessing only the back of Yahweh (Ex. 33:18–23), the latter in the deliberate choice of language of indirection in describing the Enthroned One (Ezek. 1:26–28). The appearance of the *kābôd* in the wilderness often presaged judgment and death, as it does in Ezekiel (e.g., Ex. 16:7, 10–12; Num. 14:10b–12; 16:19, 42). But the most distinctive feature of the throne in Ezekiel is its *mobility*, a characteristic that occasioned much learned speculation among the prophet's disciples (e.g., the hubs and spokes of the wheels), not to mention among later readers (e.g., the fantastic suggestion that it describes a spaceship). The point is that mobility is also the salient characteristic of the ark-sanctuary in the wilderness according to Priestly tradition (e.g., Ex. 40:34–38), and here too, in the Priestly History, this characteristic is a function of Israel's absence from and eventual return to the land.

These affinities between Ezekiel and the Priestly narrative strand in the Pentateuch (or, including Joshua, the Hexateuch) are consonant with the narrative structure of the Priestly source (P) as a whole. P begins with the creation of the world, understood as a kind of cosmic temple, reaches its climax with the establishment of the mobile wilderness sanctuary (Exodus 39—40), and ends with the setting up of that sanctuary at Shiloh in the Promised Land (Joshua 18—19).[32] Since no one doubts that there is a close affinity between Ezekiel and P, it seems that the teaching of Ezekiel, as transmitted by his disciples, has been set up to move thematically between the poles of exile and return, divine absence and presence, spiritual death and new life. The concentration by the school of Ezekiel on the central issue of cult and divine presence, on which many other matters both spiritual (e.g., freedom from sin and guilt) and temporal (e.g., land tenure, Ezek. 11:14–21) depended, their familiarity with cultic law, their polemic in favor of Diaspora Judaism and of the Zadokite priesthood (e.g., Ezek. 40:46; 43:19; 44:15–31; 48:11),[33] suggest that we are dealing with a priestly-scribal and probably Judeo-Babylonian elite, and one that was actively preparing for an eventual return to Judah.

The further conclusion seems unavoidable that this group overlapped with the authors of the exilic or early postexilic rewriting of the ancient traditions and drafting of the laws known to modern biblical scholarship as the Priestly source (P). We speak of partial overlap not of identity, because there are some significant differences between cultic laws expressed or implied in Ezekiel and those set out in P. In Ezekiel the roles of prophet and priest are deployed by the same individual, a first stage in the process by which prophecy would eventually be absorbed, or reabsorbed, into the priesthood and the cult.

It will be useful at this stage to summarize the contents of the book. The first section (Ezekiel 1—7) records the vision of the mobile throne in Babylon followed by the prophetic commission to preach to an obdurate people (2:1–3:11). Ezekiel then went to Tel-abib, one of the centers of the Babylonian diaspora, where he stayed in a catatonic state for a week (3:12–15). After receiving a further charge to act as watchman for Israel (3:16–22), he had another vision of the *kābôd* in a plain, during which he was told that he must remain secluded in his house and would be temporarily deprived of speech (3:22–27).[34] He was also commanded to perform certain acts presaging the coming disaster (4:1–5:4). The section ends with comminations against Jerusalem and Judah and what appears to be a short sermon based on Amos' fourth vision (Ezek. 5:5–7:27; cf. Amos 8:1–3).

If Ezekiel's call to proclaim a message of doom is to be found in the scroll vision, it may have taken place before his departure for Babylon, since it concludes with a command to go to the *gôlâ* (Ezek. 3:11), though the term *gôlâ* can refer to a collectivity as well as a state or place, and could therefore also refer to his fellow-expatriates in Babylonia. But it is still difficult to avoid the conclusion that some part of Ezekiel's early activity took place in Judah. He records the death of a certain prince Pelatiah in Jerusalem while he was actually prophesying (11:13), and the symbolic carrying of an exile's baggage could not very well have been intended for people already in Babylon (12:1–7).

Ezekiel's editors linked the original call with the vision of the chariot-throne by making the commission emanate from the One on the throne: On seeing the vision the prophet falls on his face and hears a voice addressing him (1:28). Since practically all the sayings and discourses attributed to Ezekiel are, in one way or another, responses to events in the real world, the call itself may have taken place in reaction to the political disturbances following on Zedekiah's plotting against Nebuchadrezzar in 594 (cf. Jeremiah 28). The failure of these conspiratorial activities led to the dispatch of a diplomatic mission to Babylon (Jer. 51:59), an event dated a year before Ezekiel's vision in Babylonia (Jer. 51:59; Ezek. 1:2).

The next section of the book (Ezekiel 8—11) records another vision, dated a year later in 592, in which he was transported in the spirit to Jerusalem and given a supernaturally guided tour of the temple and its precincts. What he saw there shows the extent of the triumph of the syncretists under Zedekiah and the total failure of whatever religious reforms had been carried out by Josiah thirty years earlier. The "lustful image which provokes to lust" shown to him near a gate of the inner court of the temple (8:3) was no doubt a nude representation of the Canaanite goddess, of a kind well attested in the archaeological record. The animal and reptile figures were of Egyptian origin and bore witness to the pro-Egyptian policy pursued by Zedekiah during the last years of his reign. Further on there were women engaged in the Tammuz cult and a cult group worshiping the rising sun—all this in the temple itself. As he returned to the point where the tour began, he witnessed supernatural agents of destruction being sent out to annihilate the city with the exception of the faithful few who were marked with the letter *tav* (shaped like a cross) on their foreheads. After Ezekiel's failed attempt to intercede, the *kābôd* left its place and settled on the hill to the east of the city.

Located toward the end of this section there is a short sermon that takes issue with the claims of those who remained in Judah and supports the Babylonian *gôlâ* as the true Israel of the future (11:14–21). It seems that the homeland Jews were arguing that the deportees had been expelled from the cult community, or had left it of their own free will, and had thereby forfeited title to their land, which the survivors were now free to occupy (11:15; cf. 33:23–29; 36:2). Ezekiel countered this claim with the argument that the deportees were still within the jurisdiction of Yahweh since Yahweh had himself become a sanctuary for them, proving his presence beyond a doubt by appearing to a prophet in Babylon. It was the Palestinians who, by their apostasy, had forfeited a place in the future restoration. We note how here, as in the Priestly history (cf. Gen. 17:8; Ex. 6:7–8), what is important is divine presence rather than making and keeping covenants.

The final and longest section of the predisaster part of the book (chaps. 12—24) consists of about twenty-five discourses most of them beginning with the formula: "the word of Yahweh came to me." It starts off with a defense of Ezekiel's prophetic activity, acting out the predicted future by dramatic miming (12:1–20), attacking the self-deceptive indifference of his audience (12:21–13:16), and polemicizing against alternative contemporary forms of prophetic activity, including activity by female prophets that sounds more like witchcraft (13:17–14:11). Ezekiel's antiprophetic polemic draws heavily on his older contemporary Jeremiah (cf. Jer. 23:9–40; 27–29). The line of argument is much the same. While using an identical form of words, these other prophets see their task as fulfilling the expectation of their audience, thereby promoting an attitude of self-deceptive complacency. Even more than Jeremiah, Ezekiel emphasizes, here and elsewhere (Ezek. 3:16–22; 33:1–9), the grave responsibility of the prophet to the community that he must serve. He is also more aware of the likelihood of collusion between the prophet and his public that disingenuously solicits his guidance (14:1–11).

The political disasters through which Ezekiel and his contemporaries were living called into question all sorts of traditional religious ideas and apparently gave rise to an intense debate. Typical reactions, expressed in the book in direct quotes, are to the effect that Yahweh neither sees, knows, nor cares what is going on (8:12), that his way of dealing with people is unjust (18:25, 29), that he is visiting the sins of the ancestors on their descendants (18:2). The old idea that God imputes the guilt of parents to their descendants in a multigenerational linkage (Ex. 34:7; Num. 14:18) is countered by Ezekiel with a strong insistence on personal responsibility and accountability. Since Ezekiel was a priest, and therefore presumably expert in sacral law, he expounds his teaching on this point in the form of a case history, similar to the formulation of the case laws, involving three generations—father, son, grandson—in which there is no transmission of guilt from one to the other (Ezekiel 18). The practical and pastoral conclusion is that the person remains free to "turn" from one way of life to another. This "turning" (the literal meaning of the Hebrew *tᵉšûbâ*, usually translated "conversion"), meaning a decisive redirection of one's life, is one of the most important aspects of Ezekiel's teaching.

The other side of the problem of divine justice and the ethical character of the God of traditional religion is dealt with in an earlier passage (Ezek. 14:12–23) in the same section. Like the author of Abraham's pleading with God to spare the Cities of the Plain (Gen. 18:23–32), Ezekiel raises the question whether the presence of a few righteous people could save a sinful land. Unlike the author of the Genesis text, Ezekiel denies this possibility. Noah, Daniel, and Job, those traditional paradigms of righteousness, would, if present in a sinful land on which divine punishment is visited, save no one but themselves, not even their sons and daughters.[35] Here too, therefore, Ezekiel is at pains to emphasize personal responsibility and dispel the idea that its place can be taken by prophetic or priestly intercession, that there can be any kind of salvation by proxy.

These two passages (Ezek. 18:1–32; 14:12–23) exemplify the ethical teaching of Ezekiel and his school, but it will be clear that elements of this teaching are to be found in all parts of the book. The general impression is that moral guidelines are related directly to the kind of community Israel was intended to be. Hence the starting point is the special relationship with Israel's God and therefore the primary imperative is the rejection of idolatry (e.g., 5:11; 6—8; 14:1–11; 16; 23). In keeping with the priestly ethic in the Pentateuch, and the so-called Holiness Code (Leviticus 17—26) in particular, there is no distinguishing in principle between ethical and ritual. Idolatry is directly connected with violence, murder, adultery, and other crimes or disorders. One of the most specific indictments in Ezekiel (22:6–12) lists incest and coition during the woman's menses alongside murder, adultery, perjury, and the like. This does not mean, of course, that all of these were put on the same level, but it does imply that the concern was to outline a way of life not in general but one consonant with being this particular and unique community. The tie-in between land tenure and participation in the cult, noted earlier, is also significant in this respect, since participation in the cult was itself contingent on the pursuit of a common ideal of the moral life. The ethical teaching of Ezekiel, and prophetic teaching in general, presupposes an intrinsic relationship between morality and worship.

The long series of discourses or sermons in Ezekiel 12—24 also contains a number of striking and, in some cases, remarkably sustained figurative or allegorical narratives: the vine that is good only for burning (15:1–8), the nymphomaniac bride (16:1–63), the great eagles (17:1–24), the lioness and her cubs (19:1–9), the ravished vineyard (19:10–14), the two sisters who become prostitutes (23:1–49). These passages in verse and prose are self-consciously literary in character, in keeping with Ezekiel's reputation as skillful with words (Ezek. 33:30–33), a "parable monger," as he was called, adept at figurative speech (20:49). The protracted parable about the female foundling who is rescued from death, weds her rescuer, and eventually ascends to queenly estate is probably based on a romantic folktale. If so, it has been developed into a raw tale of sexual transgression narrated in such unsavory detail that modern versions have felt obliged at several points to fall back on paraphrase and circumlocution and some rabbis forbade its liturgical use.

With the exception of the first (15:1–8), all these compositions are figurative retellings of the history of Israel. While the time span of the allegories about eagles and lions is restricted to the last years of the kingdom of Judah, the remaining two cover the entire history: Israel in Egypt; Jerusalem brought under the covenant relationship; the divided monarchy; dealings with Philistines, Assyrians, and Babylonians; the end of nationhood. Ezekiel's verdict on the monarchy is radically negative. It went wrong right from the start, and it was the principal cause of Israel's ruin. Here too we detect affinity with Priestly tradition that brings the history to an end with entrance into the land and completely ignores the subsequent history. But Ezekiel differs from both the Priestly narrative and prophetic predecessors in one significant aspect, namely, in tracing Israel's spiritual failure back beyond the wilderness wandering and occupation of the land to the very beginning of the story in Egypt (20:8; 23:3).

The Egyptian sojourn is the first chapter in the theological review of Israel's history in 20:1–44. Both this chapter and the figurative narratives already discussed are reminiscent of a type of psalm in which the history of unfaithful Israel is presented as a kind of parable or riddle (Ps. 78:2; cf. Ezek. 17:2). The historical review itself is also structurally similar to the historical recital in Ps. 106, which ends with a prayer for the ingathering of the people. The setting for Ezek. 20:1–44 is a consultation of the prophet by elders whose request, whatever it was, was refused. Perhaps they anticipated a proximate return to the homeland, following on recently delivered optimistic prophecies.[36] Perhaps they were seeking prophetic approval of a separate cult establishment for the Jewish ethnic minority in Babylon; and it is even possible, as was suggested earlier, that such a sanctuary was actually built, at Casiphia or elsewhere. At any rate, the historical review reveals sin and infidelity from the very beginnings of the history in Egypt and ends, unexpectedly, with a reaffirmation of the special relationship in spite of everything, couched in the familiar exodus language: "with a mighty hand and an outstretched arm, with wrath poured out, I will be king over you" (20:33). Some have seen here, not inappropriately, an anticipation of the Reformation doctrine of *sola gratia*.[37]

The diatribes, mock laments, taunt songs, and the like directed against hostile nations (Ezekiel 25—32) form a distinct compilation similar to those found in other prophetic books, especially Isaiah 13—23 and Jeremiah 46—51. It is made up of three blocks of material: sayings directed against Judah's immediate neighbors (Ezekiel 25), a collection of material in verse and prose against Tyre (26:1–28:19), and a longer series of anti-Egyptian sayings (29—32). As indicated by the dates, the nucleus of the collection goes back to a political commentary by Ezekiel on events associated with Nebuchadrezzar's campaigns in Syria, Palestine, and Egypt. These have been expanded in the light of subsequent history, as is the case with similar sayings in other prophetic books. The oracle against Ammon (25:1–7; cf. 21:28–32), for example, alludes to Arab encroachments in the middle of the sixth century that brought the kingdom of Ammon to an end. Inevitably, the poems announcing the destruction of Tyre look beyond the unsuccessful siege by the Babylonians, which lasted thirteen years according to Josephus (*Ant.* 10:228), to its conquest by Alexander in 332.[38] Similarly, the sayings about Egypt go beyond Hophra's unsuccessful attempt to raise the siege of Jerusalem in 588 (Jer. 37:1–10) to Babylonian campaigns against Egypt in the last years of Nebuchadrezzar's reign.

This kind of oracular utterance, which can be traced back to the ritual curse pronounced by the seer on the eve of hostilities, was a remarkably durable weapon in the prophetic armory. It helps keep us mindful that the prophet operated not in a timeless world but in the public arena, including the sphere of international affairs. In the final analysis, the impetus for Ezekiel's prophetic activity stemmed from a religious experience through which the tradition in which he stood was mediated and reformed. Since, however, religion and politics were facets of the same reality, this particular appropriation of the tradition came to expression as a decision in the political sphere, one that more often than not happened to be at odds with official policy.

This collection of political sayings originally formed a quite distinct book. It was located after the sermons and visions (chapters 1—24) as a counterweight to the indictment of Israel and to prepare for the projection of a new order in the last part of the compilation. This structuring device is apparent from the dramatic ending to the first part of the book—the arrival of a courier with the news that Jerusalem had fallen and the sudden unloosening of the prophet's tongue—which is taken up again after the oracles against foreign nations (24:25–27; 33:21–22). Chapter 33 appears to be little more than a recapitulation, or alternative version, of some of the more important teachings in the first part of the book: the responsibility of the watchman (33:1–9; cf. 3:16–21), the possibility and necessity of conversion (33:10–20; cf. 18:5–32), the conditions for secure possession of the land (33:23–29; cf. 11:14–21). At the same time, the chapter prepares the reader for the last section of the book (chaps. 34—48) in which is to be found the answer to the agonizing question put to Ezekiel by his contemporaries: "How then are we to live?" (33:10).

Whatever the origin of the temple blueprint in Ezekiel 40—48, it would be mistaken to think of it as a quite distinct block with no organic connection with the rest of the book. It records the return of the *kābôd* as the final stage of a movement begun much earlier (9:3; 10:3–5, 18–19; 11:22–23). Moreover, the last of the sermons in chapters 34—37 prepares explicitly for the vision by referring to the future temple that will sanctify Israel (37:28). Both here and elsewhere in the prophetic literature it is possible to uncover a unity of theme and structure without having to establish unity of authorship.

Chapters 40—48, therefore, may not derive from Ezekiel himself. Parts of the preceding chapters (34—39) also provide at different points reasonably clear indications of different authorship. So, for example, the condemnation of the shepherds of Israel in chapter 34—an indictment of the monarchy—appears to be an elaboration of Jer. 23:1–8 and ends with the promise of a Davidic ruler in terms closer to those of Jeremiah and Deuteronomy than to the genuine sayings of Ezekiel in 1—24. The address to the mountains of Israel (36:1–15), which has drawn along the saying against Mount Seir (Edom) as a kind of counterweight (35), also has little of Ezekiel in it. The sermon that promises a new heart and spirit (36:16–38) has made generous use of earlier Ezekiel sayings. There are clear echoes of the review of Israel's history of infidelity in chapter 20, and the promise of repatriation and a new heart and spirit, a kind of spiritual heart transplant, follows the same lines and uses the same language as the saying at 11:14–21. Leaving aside for the moment the vision of dry bones (37:1–14), the last of these sermons in 34—37, which holds out the prospect of the two kingdoms reunified under a Davidic ruler (37:15–28), appears to come from the same source as chapter 34. It seems likely, then, that all of chapters 34—37, with the exception of the two sermons in 36:16–37:14, derives from individuals or groups outside the school of Ezekiel who cherished the hope of a new national and ecumenical unity under the rule of a Davidic dynast.

The vision of the dry bones in the plain (Ezek. 37:1–14) is quite distinctive in form and content. It begins not with the conventional "The word of Yahweh came to me" (as in 34:1; 35:1; 36:16; 37:15) but with the narrative introduction of the earlier visions. Like the vision of the *kābôd* (3:22; 8:4), it took place in the plain, and it uses the same language of the hand and spirit of God (cf. 1:3; 3:22, 24; 8:1). The vision narrative may be read as an elaboration on the quote of the dispirited deportees— "Our bones are dried up, our hope has perished, our life thread has been cut" (37:11). It is also possible that it echoes the posthumous miracle of Elisha when the dead man was restored to life after coming in contact with the bones of the prophet (2 Kings 13:20–21). The latter suggestion would be consonant with an aspect of Ezekiel's prophetic self-understanding that is worth noting. It is a remarkable fact that, while he is clearly familiar with the prophetic tradition as a whole, Ezekiel is, at several points, more in line with the "primitive" prophecy of the early period. The extraordinary behavioral effects of possession, including levitation and second sight, bring to mind the careers of Elijah, Elisha, and their colleagues. Both the mobile throne and the chariot of Elijah are powered by the whirlwind surrounded by fire (cf. 2 Kings 2:1, 11). Much of the language of spirit possession and the hand of Yahweh is also borrowed from these narratives (e.g., 1 Kings 18:46; 2 Kings 3:15). Like Elisha, Ezekiel is consulted by the elders in his house (2 Kings 6:32); and even the familiar "You shall know that I am Yahweh" already occurs in these early prophetic legends (1 Kings 20:13, 28; cf. 2 Kings 5:8). While the major prophetic books have little to say about the spirit, for Ezekiel, as for the "primitives," it is the decisive agent, being not only the principle of movement and renewal but the dynamic factor in prophetic possession (Ezek. 2:2; 3:24; 11:5; 37:1).[39]

This remarkable narrative of the valley of bones (Ezekiel 37) has provided a powerful visual symbol of the reversal of the life-death process, or the belief in physical resurrection, or the vivifying power of God, throughout Jewish and Christian history. It also epitomizes the function of prophecy at a crucial moment of history. The *gôlâ* community, which has lost its will to survive, is vivified by the spirit activated through the word of God addressed to the community. This happens in two stages. First, the prophetic summons brings the disiecta membra together into a community. Only then can the spirit come into them, bringing the will to live and accept the future. In the explanation of the vision (37:11–14) that future is identified as settlement in the land, and the further point is made that, when that happens, they will at last acknowledge the truth of the prophetic word.

The long and rather rambling prophecy about Gog and the land of Magog (Ezekiel 38—39) has been spliced into the book at this point. This is clear from the connection between the end of the prediction immediately preceding (37:28) and the vision of the future temple (40—48). This apocalyptic fantasy of the final, miraculous defeat of the forces of evil in the land of Israel has given rise to a great deal of labored and even bizarre speculation. So, for example, it was read during the Cold War as a coded prophecy about historical events that were taking place or about to take place; after all, the words *roʾš mešek* (ruler of Meshech, 38:2) sound suspiciously like Russia and Moscow. More surprisingly, a great deal of effort has gone into determining the historical identity of the places mentioned in the text. We must begin, however, from the observation that all of them, with the exception of Persia (38:5), occur in the so-called Table of the Nations in Genesis 10. In other words the apocalypticist, who probably knew less about their location than we do, has put together his piece as a kind of mosaic of biblical references and motifs, including such familiar phrases as "seize spoil, carry off plunder" (Isa. 8:1–4), "I will send fire on Magog" (cf. Amos 1:4), and the like. What we have, then, is an apocalyptic tract from long after the time of Ezekiel inspired by the prophetic topos of the Day of Yahweh (Ezek. 39:8) and, more specifically, the prediction in Jeremiah and elsewhere of the coming of a foe from the north (Ezek. 38:17).[40]

The last section of the book (chapters 40—48) is presented as a vision of the future temple, though it will be obvious as we read on that at several points this visionary context has been overlooked. The nucleus of the vision, dated to the year 573 B.C.E., is a description of the temple to be built according to a heavenly model—a common motif in the ancient Near East. This detailed architectural survey leads up to the return of the *kābôd* and the assurance of the permanent presence of God with his people (40:1–43:11a). So far this is entirely consonant with and indeed integral to the book as a whole. To this nucleus, however, there have been added not only several supplements (43:13–17; 44:1–3; 46:19–24) but a substantial amount of cultic and ritual prescription and instruction dealing with the altar (43:18–27), the duties and prerogatives of cultic personnel (44:4–31), and the role in the temple cult of the secular ruler (45:9–46:18). The present state of the text, especially where the law of the temple is announced but not followed up (43:11b–12), suggests that some of this legislation has fallen out, possibly because of discrepancies with cultic law in the Pentateuch. The Babylonian Talmud (*b. Shab.* 13b) has preserved an engaging story about a certain Hananiah who burnt the midnight oil with a vengeance, three hundred jars of it, while attempting to harmonize Ezekiel 40—48 with Pentateuchal law.

Different again is the quite schematic and utopian account of the allotment of land (45:1–8; 47:13–48:35). This part of the blueprint brings to mind the assignment of tribal territories after the setting up of the sanctuary at Shiloh in Josh. 18:1–19:51, basically a P narrative. Toward the end of this final section (Ezek. 47:1–12) the Eden myth emerges once again (cf. 28:12–19),[41] with the powerful image of the stream that issues from the temple and becomes a great river bringing life and healing to the barren wastes of the Judean wilderness. There seems to be no good reason to doubt that this goes back, directly or indirectly, to Ezekiel himself. The expansion of Ezekiel's vision to accommodate material unique in the prophetic literature was clearly dictated by polemical factors. Stipulations concerning the civic ruler, who is referred to as prince (*nāśî'*) but never as king (*melek*) in this section, have several features in common with "the law of the king" in Deuteronomy (Deut. 17:14–20). They are not, however, essentially at variance with Ezekiel's own critical attitude to monarchy, and in any case the more modest title of "prince" is found earlier in the book (12:10; 21:25).

The situation is quite different with the priesthood, however. For here it is clear that a Zadokite priestly glossarist has used the prophetic vision to further the claims of the faction to which he belonged. His claim is that only those descendants of Levi who belonged to the Zadokite group could function as priests, while all others claimants, from now on called simply Levites, must serve as adjutant, nonsacrificing clergy, and this as punishment for religious infidelity (40:46b; 43:19; 44:10–16; 45:1–8;

47:10–11). Nothing of this goes back to Ezekiel, who never refers to Zadokites and even criticizes the Jerusalem priesthood for neglect of its responsibilities (7:26; 22:26) and presumably also practicing, or at least condoning the practice of alien cults, including the goddess cult (Ezekiel 8).

Tension and strife among different factions or families of priests was going on from at least the time of the secessionist cult set up by Jeroboam in Bethel and Dan. The details, and even the main lines, are obscure, and need not concern us. The principal issue during the late Babylonian and early Persian periods focused on the project of rebuilding the Jerusalem temple and who should control its operations and substantial revenues. The result seems to have been a compromise between factions named after their respective eponyms, Aaron and Zadok. It was the "sons of Zadok" who annexed the prophetic authority of Ezekiel to further their own claims, and who apparently retained their leading position to the time of the Hasomaeans. The Zadokite strand in Ezekiel 40—48 is, therefore, one of several examples of the close associations between prophecy and priesthood in the Second Temple period.

In spite of the complicated editorial history of the book, we can discern something of the complex and many-sided figure who gave his name to it. The historian will view him as one of the leading opponents of the war party in the last years of Zedekiah and a major force for survival among the deportees in Babylon, where the urge to rebel was by no means extinguished. (We recall, for example, the two diaspora prophets who were executed by the Babylonians shortly after the first deportation, Jer. 29:21–22.) As a polemicist, he represented the claims of the diaspora Jews that would shape the future down to Ezra and beyond. As a prophet, he defies classification, combining the mantic features of the primitives with membership in the central cultic elite. He was not, as Hölscher maintained, a visionary who was transformed into a *littérateur* by his editors. He was a visionary priest who also happened to have an extraordinary breadth of learning seen, for example, in his interest in the archaic period of history, his use of mythological themes, and his expertise in the forms and substance of sanctuary law. Moreover, both aspects were at the service of his contemporaries over a period of at least two decades. He therefore exemplifies prophecy as a form of pastoral ministry and community leadership. While it may be oversimplified to speak of him, with Wellhausen, as the father of Judaism, his capacity to generate a following, demonstrated in the editorial history of the book, and to project a new form of life for communities that doubted their ability to survive, was certainly a significant factor in the emergence of Judaism in the early Persian period.

19. EXILIC PROPHECY
IN THE ISAIAN TRADITION

(See also bibliography pp. 97–98.)

K. **Baltzer,** "Zur formgeschichtlichen Bestimmung der Texte vom Gottesknecht im Deutero-Jesaja-Buch," in H. W. Wolff, ed., *Probleme biblischer Theologie: Gerhard von Rad zum 70. Geburtstag,* Munich: Chr. Kaiser, 1971, 27–43; H. M. **Barstad,** "On the So-Called Babylonian Influence in Second Isaiah," *SJOT* 2 (1987): 90–110; *A Way in the Wilderness: The "Second Exodus" in the Message of Second Isaiah,* Manchester: University of Manchester: Journal of Semitic Studies, 1989; "The Future of the 'Servant Songs': Some Reflections on the Relationship of Biblical Scholarship to Its Own Tradition," in S. E. Balentine and J. Barton, *Language, Theology and the Bible: Essays in Honour of James Barr,* Oxford: Clarendon Press, 1994, 261–70; J. **Begrich,** *Studien zu Deuterojesaja,* Munich: Kaiser Verlag, 1963; S. H. **Blank,** "Studies in Deutero-Isaiah," *HUCA* 15 (1940): 1–46; J. **Blenkinsopp,** "Second Isaiah—Prophet of Universalism?" *JSOT* 41 (1988): 83–103; P.-E. **Bonnard,** *Le Second Isaïe: Ses Disciples et Leur Éditeurs, Isaïe 40—66,* Paris: J. Gabalda, 1972; R. E. **Clements,** "Beyond Tradition History: Deutero-Isaianic Development of First Isaiah's Themes," *JSOT* 31 (1985): 95–113; R. J. **Clifford,** *Fair Spoken and Persuading: An Interpretation of Second Isaiah,* New York: Paulist Press, 1984; D.J.A. **Clines,** *I, He, We, and They: A Literary Approach to Isaiah 53,* Sheffield: JSOT Press, 1976; P.A.H. **de Boer,** *Second Isaiah's Message,* Leiden: E. J. Brill, 1956; G. R. **Driver,** "Isaiah 52:13–53:12: The Servant of the Lord," in M. Black and G. Fohrer, eds., *In Memoriam Paul Kahle,* Berlin: de Gruyter, 1968, 90–105; B. **Duhm,** *Das Buch Jesaja,* Göttingen: Vandenhoeck & Ruprecht, 1968[5] [1892]; K. **Elliger,** *Deuterojesaja,* Neukirchen-Vluyn: Neukirchener Verlag, 1970; M. **Haran,** "The Literary Structure and Chronological Framework of the Prophecies in Is. 40–48," *SVT* 9 (1963): 127–55; G. H. **Jones,** "Abraham and Cyrus: Type and Anti-type?" *VT* 22 (1972): 304–19; A. S. **Kapelrud,** "The Main Concern of Second Isaiah," *VT* 32 (1982): 50–58; K. **Koch,** "Die Stellung des Kyros im Geschichtsbild Deuterojesajas und ihre überlieferungsgeschichtliche Verankerung," *ZAW* 84 (1972): 352–56; *The Prophets,* 2, *The Babylonian and Persian Periods,* 118–51; A. **Laato,** *The Servant of YHWH and Cyrus: A Reinterpretation of the Exilic Messianic Programme in Isaiah 40—55,* Stockholm: Almqvist & Wiksell, 1992; J. L. **McKenzie,** *Second Isaiah,* Garden City: Doubleday, 1968; R. F. **Melugin,** *The Formation of Isaiah 40—55,* Berlin: de Gruyter, 1976; S. **Mowinckel,** "Die Komposition des deuterojesajanischen Buches," *ZAW* 49 (1931): 87–112, 242–60; *He That Cometh,* Oxford: Clarendon Press, 1959, 187–260; J. **Muilenburg,** "Isaiah, Chapters 40—66," *IB* 4 (1966): 381–651; C. R. **North,** *The Suffering Servant in Second Isaiah,* Oxford: Oxford University Press, 1956[2]; *The Second Isaiah,* Oxford: Clarendon Press, 1964; H. M. **Orlinsky,** "The So-Called 'Servant of the Lord' and 'Suffering Servant' in Second Isaiah," *VTS* 14 (1967): 1–133; G. **von Rad,** *Old Testament Theology,* vol. 2, 238–62; H. H. **Rowley,** *The Servant of*

the Lord and Other Essays on the Old Testament, Oxford: Blackwell, 1965[2], 1–93;
J. D. **Smart,** *History and Theology in Second Isaiah,* Philadelphia: Westminster
Press, 1965; C. **Stuhlmueller,** "Deutero-Isaiah (chaps. 40—55): Major Transi-
tions in the Prophet's Theology and in Contemporary Scholarship," *CBQ* 42
(1980): 1–29; H. E. **von Waldow,** "The Message of Deutero-Isaiah," *Int* 22
(1968): 259–87; C. **Westermann,** *Isaiah 40—66: A Commentary,* Philadelphia:
Westminster Press, 1969; R. N. **Whybray,** *The Heavenly Counsellor in Isaiah
40:13—14: A Study of the Sources of the Theology of Deutero-Isaiah,* Cambridge:
Cambridge University Press, 1971; *Isaiah 40—66,* London: Oliphants, 1975;
Thanksgiving for a Liberated Prophet, Sheffield: JSOT Press, 1978; P. **Wilcox** and
D. **Paton-Williams,** "The Servant Songs in Deutero-Isaiah," *JSOT* 42 (1988):
79–102; H.G.M. **Williamson,** *The Book Called Isaiah: Deutero-Isaiah's Role in Com-
position and Redaction,* Oxford: Clarendon Press, 1994, 1; W. **Zimmerli,** *"Pais
Theou,"* TDNT, 4:654–77; "Jahwes Wort bei Deuterojesaja," *VT* 32 (1982):
104–24.

Ezekiel's vision of the new temple is dated to the twenty-fifth year of
the exile (573 B.C.E.). After the passage of another quarter of a century
or so a new generation of prophets was announcing emancipation to
take place in the jubilee year, which featured return to ancestral land
(Isa. 40:2; 61:2; cf. Lev. 25:8–24). By then, Nebuchadrezzar was long
dead, Nabonidus had left Babylon for seclusion at the oasis of Tema in
northwest Arabia, and the Iranian Cyrus of Anshan had conquered Ecbatana, capital of the Medes, and was extending his rule into Asia Minor.
With the collapse of the Babylonian empire only a matter of time, it was
possible to entertain hopes for repatriation and the restoration of political autonomy in the homeland.

The biblical record contains quite a dossier of prophetic oracles from
that time, celebrating proleptically or *post factum* the fall of Babylon,[42]
the return to the homeland of the deportees or their descendants, the
restoration of the native dynasty, and general well-being.[43] By far the
most important of these seers active during the last decade of Babylonian rule is the anonymous author of sayings and sermons preserved in
Isaiah 35 and 40—55, the so-called Second Isaiah.

Since the end of the eighteenth century, Isaiah 40—66 has been
widely acknowledged to be a separate collection of later date than the
eighth century Isaiah whose sayings are recorded in chapters 1—39. This
conclusion still stands, and it is not inconsistent with the emphasis in recent scholarship on elements of thematic and structural unity throughout the entire book. Bernhard Duhm's distinction between exilic 40—
55 and postexilic 56—66, designated Deutero-Isaiah and Trito-Isaiah
respectively, is less assured, and alternative divisions in these last twenty-
six chapters of the book have been proposed.[44] Duhm was also the first

to draw attention to the four so-called Servant Songs (42:1–4; 49:1–6; 50:4–11; 52:13–53:12) as deriving from a source other than the author of Isaiah 40—55. Though recently under attack, we shall see that this proposal still merits consideration.

It may be helpful to remind the reader again at this point that the book of Isaiah does not contain a straightforward sequence of preexilic (1—39), exilic (40—55), and postexilic (56—66) material. As noted earlier, significant additions were made to the first part during and after the Babylonian exile. The anti-Babylonian poems, for example (13:1–22; 14:3–21; 21:1–10), could not very well have been written before the death of Nebuchadrezzar in 562 B.C.E. and may even be later. Other sayings predicting repatriation, the subjugation of the nations including Edom, the reestablishment of the dynasty, and the preeminence of Jerusalem/Zion also make best sense if read in the historical context of the late exilic or early postexilic period. While the second part of the book is much more of a unity in both style and theme, it too shows signs of editorial expansion. In addition, its latter section (49—55) has some distinctive characteristics that set it apart from the preceding chapters (40—48). And finally, we shall see that the last part of the book (generally taken to be 56—66) cannot be from one author, has its own editorial history, and may have taken over older prophetic sayings from the time of the First Temple.

One corollary of these elementary observations about the structure and organization of the book is that the break between the first and second parts is not as clean as is sometimes thought. The historical appendix (36—39) ends with a prediction of exile in Babylon (39:5–8) and thereby sets up a contrast between this prophetic word of Isaiah and the assurance of emancipation and repatriation conveyed in chapters 40—55. It also sets the scene for the "proof from prophecy," which is such an important feature of Isaiah 40—55, in the sense that the god who, through his prophets, foretold these "former things" and then brought them about (41:22; 43:9, 18–19; 46:9; 48:3–5), has thereby demonstrated his ability to bring about the "new thing" (43:19) now being announced. The book of Isaiah, therefore, exhibits the same pattern of judgment followed by well-being that we have observed in other prophetic books, with the difference that here the juxtaposition carries a more explicit and sustained theological message.

The chapter immediately preceding the historical appendix (Isaiah 35) also belongs thematically and linguistically with the poems of Second Isaiah. Suffice it to note the theme of Zion restored, Israel as blind and deaf, the new miracles in the wilderness, and the *via sacra* over which the exiles are to return home (35:8–10; cf. 40:3–5). The connection was broken by the insertion of the historical narrative of chapters 36—39, which established a different connection, namely, the connection between a prediction made by Isaiah during the reign of Hezekiah and its fulfillment viewed as the essential prerequisite for a new phase in the religious history of the Israelite community.

Not much needs to be said in support of the proposition that these chapters date from a later epoch than that of Isaiah of Jerusalem. The historical context is no longer the kingdom of Judah during the period of Assyrian supremacy but the Jewish diaspora in the last years of Babylonian rule. Reference to the Iranian Cyrus king of Anshan (44:28; 45:1), to Babylonian deities, to the anticipated fall of Babylon, to the repatriation of the exiles, put this conclusion beyond any reasonable doubt. There are indeed links with the eighth-century Isaiah—e.g., the frequent use of the title "the Holy One of Israel"—but the differences in form and literary texture are more in evidence than the similarities. We cannot explain why chapters 40—55 were attached to 1—39 by appealing to an Isian "school" active over the intervening two centuries—a hypothesis for which there is absolutely no evidence. The ardent commitment of the first Isaiah to Zion as political reality and symbol of a beleaguered people would certainly be part of an eventual explanation, but the main point would be the perceived connection between prophecy and fulfillment to which we have just referred.

We note, parenthetically, that the broad agreement among biblical scholars that these chapters were composed in Babylon rather than in late Neo-Babylonian Judah is challenged from time to time.[45] While it is true that there is no conclusive indication in chapters 40—55 leading us in one direction or the other, the polemic against Babylonian deities, cults, and practices (e.g., astrology, 46:1; 47:13), as well as the theme of repatriation from Babylon (e.g., 48:20), strongly suggest a Babylonian location.

Prophetic books are not lavish in providing biographical information, and Isaiah 40—55 is no exception. That the author is anonymous is hardly exceptional in the context of antiquity, though at least one scholar claimed to find the author's name at Isa. 42:19 where *mᵉšullām* ("dedicated one" in the RSV but also a personal name Meshullam) is in apposition to "the servant of Yahweh".[46] A more specific reason for anonymity could be the political situation at the time of writing or oral delivery. Predictions of the victory of Cyrus and the fall of Babylon, together with satire directed at the Babylonian imperial cult, even when circulating in the restricted ambient of the Jewish ethnic deportees, could not have been free of risk. Earlier prophets who preached sedition had been tortured and executed by the authorities (Jer. 29:21–22).

Whether the author of all or part of Isaiah 40—55 met a similar fate must remain an open question, depending as it does on the uncertain interpretation of the third and fourth of the so-called Servant Songs—to which we shall return.

The opening verses of this section (40:1–11) have been taken to reflect a prophetic commissioning from Yahweh in the heavenly assembly after the manner of the earlier Isaiah (6:1–13).[47] In the opening apostrophe (40:1–2) the verbs are in the plural but there is no allusion to a divine council, as there is, indirectly, in Isaiah's great vision in the (heavenly) temple. The command to comfort Israel and proclaim the end of exile represented as penal servitude is therefore addressed to a plurality of seers to which the author presumably belongs. In Isa. 35:3–4 (occurring in a passage that belongs with the same exilic material) the same plurality is commissioned to comfort the people with the good news of imminent salvation, and in Isa. 52:7–10 an individual herald is linked with a prophetic group that rejoices in anticipation of the same event. The command to prepare the way of Yahweh in preparation for his parousia (40:3–5) is also addressed to a prophetic plurality, and only then (40: 6–8) do we hear the seer himself speaking, in a passage that seems to allude cryptically to the end of Babylonian rule. The interpretation of the fourth apostrophe (vv. 9–11) is complicated by the feminine form *mᵉbasśeret* (herald), which is often taken to be in apposition to Zion-Jerusalem (as in the NRSV). But the point of the commission is precisely to bring good news *to* Zion (40:1; cf. 52:7–8); and there is also something rather forced in the image of Jerusalem climbing up a high mountain to make a proclamation.[48]

In summary, then, the commission to proclaim the termination of exile following on the end of Babylonian rule and leading to a new era of well-being appears to have been addressed to an individual seer with his prophetic following. It would be natural to assume that the seer in question, whom we hear from time to time speaking in his own name (Isa. 40:6; 48:16; 49:1–6), is the author of much of the material in Isaiah 40—55. It is also a reasonable working hypothesis that the last part of the book (chapters 56—66) derives, at least in part, from this seer's disciples who perpetuated his message after his death. We shall go on to suggest that the identity of the Isaian "Servant," in dispute since antiquity (see, for example, the question of the Ethiopian eunuch to Philip, Acts 8:34), may best be approached by working back from the disciples to the master, from the "servants of Yahweh" of the last eleven chapters of the book to the prophetic "Servant" commemorated in chapters 49—55.

To make this connection more clearly we may note again the distinction between chapters 40—48 and 49—55, a distinction not necessarily of authorship but of theme and content. The first section, beginning and ending with an exodus from Babylon (40:1–5; 48:20–22), focuses on the expectation of a new era to be inaugurated by Cyrus, with polemic against the Babylonian imperial cult an important subsidiary theme. The following section, on the other hand, says nothing about Cyrus or Babylon, and it is in general much less concerned with the contemporary political situation than with the internal situation of the community.

It was to be expected that the campaigns of Cyrus and the growing internal opposition to Nabonidus, the last of the Babylonian kings (556–539), should have occasioned a flare-up of prophetic activity in the Diaspora. By 550 B.C.E. Cyrus had united the Persian tribes under him and occupied Ecbatana, capital city of the Medes. In the course of the next three years his campaigns in Armenia and Asia Minor had been crowned by the capture of Sardis, capital of the Lydian kingdom ruled by the legendary Croesus, and the annexation of the Greek cities on the Ionian seaboard. These stirring events were the "new thing" proclaimed by the seer (43:19) and are referred to here and there throughout these chapters (41:2–4, 25–29; 45:1–7). Support for Cyrus must have been strong, though perhaps not unanimous, among the ethnic minorities settled in the cities and countryside of the alluvial plain of southern Mesopotamia. From this point of view Isaiah 40—48 could be read as propaganda for the pro-Cyrus party at a point in time when his conquest of Babylon could be reasonably predicted (see especially 43:14–17; 47:1–15; 48:14).

In view of this situation it is understandable that a long oracle about Cyrus should form the centerpiece of this section (Isa. 44:24–45:13). In it he is designated as shepherd and anointed (*māšîaḥ*), both well-attested synonyms for king, and the remarkable claim is made that Yahweh was responsible for his success, that his actions were intended to serve the purposes of the dispersed Jewish communities, and that he would see to the repatriation of Jewish exiles and the rebuilding of their destroyed city. For good measure the seer even predicted his future conquest of Egypt, an event however, that took place only under his son and successor Cambyses (45:14). In other sayings (43:14–17; 47:1–15; 48:14) the author prophesied the fall of Babylon and engaged in polemic against the Babylonian state religion in a manner not unlike that of his contemporary, the Ionian philosopher Xenophanes.[49]

Given the dismal record of optimistic prophets in the last years of the monarchy, it would be surprising if this prophet's proclamation of good news had not been greeted with skepticism. No doubt anticipating such a response, he attempted to disarm criticism by claiming that he spoke in the name of a god who had already demonstrated his ability to inspire predictions of the future and then make them happen. This is a cardinal point in Second Isaiah's apologetic. The proof of divinity is to predict the future and then bring it about. Unlike the Babylonian deities, Yahweh stood behind his prophets (Isa. 44:26). The very disasters through which the people had passed were turned into occasions for faith, in that they had happened in fulfillment of prophecy and therefore provided grounds for confidence now that judgment lay in the past (48:3–8). Repeatedly the seer called his contemporaries, understandably reluctant to put themselves on the line once again, to witness that this reading of contemporary events was the only one that made sense for them, that in effect they had no alternative but the one now being held out to them.

By the very nature of its claims, prophecy raises the issue of the reality and power of the deity who validates the message. Many of the survivors of the disaster must have concluded that the God of Israel had been discredited along with his prophets, and for the deportees the spectacle of ceremonies and processions in honor of Marduk, city god of Babylon, would have been a constant reminder of Yahweh's defeat. This situation will help to explain why, beginning about that time, Israel's tribal and national God was increasingly represented as a cosmic deity residing in the circle of the heavens and presiding over the destinies of all nations.[50] The shift in emphasis was clearly intended to counter the allure of Babylonian religion and the cult of Marduk, the imperial deity, in particular. To take only one example, the claim of Isa. 43:10 that

> Before me no god was formed,
>   nor shall there be any after me

seems to take aim at the Babylonian theogony according to which Marduk (also known as Bel, Isa. 46:1) was born of the gods Ea and Damkina.

The ultimate act of divine power would be the creation of the world, and among the Babylonians it was celebrated in the canonical creation myth *enuma elish* (*ANET*, 60–72). Recited in the course of the New Year *akitu* festival, this text opens with a theogony according to which the gods, descended from a primordial couple Apsu and Tiamat, caused a disturbance that led Apsu to plan their destruction. On hearing this the god Ea took preemptive action by slaying Apsu, after which he begot Marduk, wisest and strongest of the gods. As a first step toward avenging her dead spouse, Tiamat created a corps of monsters under the command of a certain Kingu to whom were entrusted the tablets of destiny. Since the high gods, called the Anunnaki, felt unequal to taking on Tiamat, they entrusted the task to Marduk. As the price for his acceptance, Marduk insisted on supremacy in the pantheon, with which went the prerogative of establishing the destinies. After defeating Tiamat in single

combat, Marduk took the tablets of destiny from Kingu, created earth
and sky out of the dismembered body of Tiamat, fixed the stations of the
gods in the zodiacal band and, finally, created mankind out of the blood
of Kingu mixed with slime. This last act relieved the lesser gods of the
onus of cultic service, and in return for this favor they built the Esagila
ziggurat-temple in Babylon for him. After gathering there in solemn procession, they recited his fifty names in a paean of praise and proclaimed
his universal kingship.

This myth, clearly, conveys a message about power, one that encapsulates the themes of creation, kingship, and cult. Since Marduk was the
city-god of Babylon and patron of the empire, its recital also served as a
form of political propaganda. As we read Isaiah 40—55, it is difficult to
avoid the impression that the author set himself the task of countering
this ideology of power. All the elements are present, with the result that
we can reconstruct a kind of mirror image of the myth with Yahweh in
the place of Marduk. There is the cosmogonic war resulting in the defeat of Tehom (Tiamat), the Great Deep (Isa. 51:9–11); the creation of
light and darkness (45:7), and of the sky, the celestial bodies, and the
earth (40:12, 26; 44:24, etc.). The triumphal procession over the *via sacra*
(40:3–5; cf. 35:8–10), like the one over which Marduk and Nabu were
carried (46:1–2, 5–7), was represented as leading to the sanctuary
(44:28) in which the epiphany of the god was to take place (40:10;
51:7–10). The climax is the proclamation of the kingship of Yahweh
bringing the assurance of a favorable destiny:[51]

> How beautiful upon the mountains
>   are the feet of the messenger who announces peace,
> who brings good news,
>   who announces salvation,
>   who says to Zion, "your God reigns!"
>
>   (52:7)

The reversal of current assumptions about the location of power is
carried over from the act of creation into the historical events of Israel's
founding. By creating Israel (Isa. 43:1, 15) Yahweh won the right to be
its king (44:6). The first exercise of this right was the rescue from Egypt
and the destruction of Israel's enemies at the sea. Now, in these latter
days, this act is about to be replicated with the end of captivity and return to the land (43:16–17; 50:2), but without the haste that marked the
earlier departure (52:12). The miraculous interventions by which Israel
was sustained in the wilderness also will be repeated (35:5–7). The theme
of cosmogonic victory is shifted therefore from the time of creation to
that of the exodus from Egypt (51:9–10); the mythological sea-deity

Yamm, familiar from Late Bronze Age Canaanite epic, becomes the Red Sea or Reed Sea (*yam-sûp*).[52] The implication is that the creative power expressed in the symbolic language of myth is also the redemptive power that now, as in the beginnings of its history, is available to a subjugated and humiliated people; and this in spite of current assumptions about the location of power in the "real world."

The activity of this exilic seer and his support group (both alluded to, as we have seen, in the introductory verses) was aimed therefore at persuading their Jewish contemporaries that, in spite of appearances to the contrary, their god was still in control of the flow of historical events. The frequent use of rhetorical questions, the form of disputation increasingly in evidence from that time,[53] may be taken to reflect preaching that was actually going on in the *gôlâ* assemblies. Perhaps also much of the anti-idolatry diatribe in this part of Isaiah originated in synagogal or proto-synagogal preaching in Diaspora communities at that time. The thrust of this preaching about the reality of divine power in the political realm was to prepare for the statement that the same god who had guided Israel's destiny from the beginning was behind the meteoric rise to power of Cyrus (Isa. 41:1–4, 25–29; 44:24–45:13). As we have seen, this is the central affirmation of chapters 40—48. The contrast between these theological affirmations and the actual political insignificance of the Jewish ethnic minority in Babylon (alluded to at one point as "the servant of rulers," 49:7) has probably suggested the use of the term "servant of Yahweh" for the community. To be more precise, we should observe that where it occurs in this first section (40—48) it refers in practically every case to the Jewish community as a whole, whereas in the second section (49—55) this broader connotation is the exception.[54] Before drawing out some of the implications of this observation, we should first briefly examine the broader context of usage with which the exilic author would certainly have been familiar.[55]

The term "servant of Yahweh" (*'ebed YHWH*) was used in Deuteronomic circles for a specially designated intermediary, the paradigm being Moses himself (Num. 12:7–8; Deut. 34:5). Since Joshua was the first to replicate this Mosaic role, he too bears the title (Josh. 24:29; Judg. 2:8). Prophets were also seen to perpetuate the work of Moses throughout the subsequent history, so it is understandable that individual holders of the prophetic office and the prophetic succession as a whole should be described in terms of servanthood or mediatorial service.[56] The representative of the Davidic dynasty is also described as Yahweh's servant because the monarchy was also considered, ideally, to perpetuate the mediatorial role of Moses, prophecy and monarchy being viewed as parallel embodiments of the Mosaic office.[57] This aspect of the monarchy could, however, be more easily perceived once the imperfect reality had passed from the scene. Hence the frequent allusions in exilic writings to the ideal king of the future as Yahweh's servant.[58] By the time of the exile, then, the parallelism between prophecy and monarchy as executors of the divine will and mediators between God and the people was well established.

The language of servanthood, therefore, connotes a role or function performed on behalf of Israel. Consequently, Deuteronomic writings do not refer to the Israelite community as a whole by this term. Where the designation occurs elsewhere in exilic writings with reference to the collectivity (Jer. 30:10; 46:27–28; Ezek. 28:25), the latter goes under the name Jacob, a usage also found in a few chapters of Isaiah (41:8; 44:1–2, 21; 45:4; 48:20). In these instances the intent is clearly to recall the election of the great ancestor who was chosen after many tribulations to bring a numerous people into existence and who, like his descendants, was exiled in Mesopotamia, entered into servitude there and, in the course of time, returned to his own land.

In Isaiah 40—48, then, it is generally Israel represented by the diasporic "remnant" that is the servant of Yahweh. At this point we recall that the German scholar Bernhard Duhm, writing about a century ago, identified four passages (42:1–4; 49:1–6; 50:4–9; 52:13–53:12) that he claimed derived from a source other than Deutero-Isaiah and in which the *'ebed* who speaks or is spoken of is an individual with a special mission, not Israel as a whole as elsewhere in this section of the book.[59] Now the one passage in chapters 40—48 that does not fit the collective interpretation is the first of Duhm's "Servant Songs," that is, 42:1–4. Here the speaker is Yahweh, who designates an individual as his servant and chosen one, endowing him with the spirit so that he may fulfill his mission of dispensing justice and law to the nations. He will persevere in this task until successful and will discharge it without violence and brutality. This job description cannot easily refer to a prophet, since prophets do not dispense justice, least of all to the nations. Confirmation that the author is here referring to a royal rather than a prophetic figure is the poem about the once and future Davidic ruler in Isa. 11:1–9. He too is endowed with the spirit, is charged with bringing justice to the nations, and will put an end to the violence and brutality so often characteristic, then as now, of international relations. The same perspective informs other texts that allude to an ideal ruler to come (e.g., Jer. 33:15), and it is especially noteworthy that in the only reference to the Davidic line in chapters 40—55 (Isa. 55:3–4) the king is also charged with international responsibilities.

If this much is accepted, the context in which this first *'ebed* passage occurs, and specifically the lines immediately preceding it (41:25–29), would suggest that the ruler in question is Cyrus, and that it is he who is to carry out on behalf of Israel those tasks that would, in normal circumstances, be discharged by Israel's own charismatic leaders. That he, a pagan ruler, is described as Yahweh's servant would by no means rule out this identification because the same designation is bestowed even on the tyrant Nebuchadrezzar (Jer. 25:9; 27:6; 43:10). Moreover, the title "my servant" is no more remarkable than "my shepherd" (Isa. 44:28) or "Yahweh's anointed" (45:1), also used of Cyrus.

In discussing these questions of reference and identification it is, however, always prudent to allow for multiple, cumulative, or serial interpretation. Hence, in this instance, an original allusion to Cyrus of Anshan may, in the light of disappointing historical developments, have been displaced somewhat later by reference to either Jehoiachin, the Judean ruler in exile, or one of his sons. We know that after the return of the first immigrants to Judah another descendant of Jehoiachin, Zerubbabel, is referred to in prophetic texts as Yahweh's servant (Hag. 2:23; Zech. 3:8). While the Davidic dynasty does not play an important role in Isaiah 40—66, it would be strange if it were not somehow part of the projected future opened up by the momentous events that were taking place at that time on the international scene.

The second section of the book (chapters 49—55) opens with a speaker addressing the nations. Using the language of prophetic commissioning, he speaks of being called and given a name from the womb, being equipped for his task as a weapon in Yahweh's hand, and designated Yahweh's servant through whom he (Yahweh) will be glorified (49:1–6). Practically everything that the speaker says of himself is said elsewhere in Second Isaiah of the community: the sense of failure and rejection (40:27) to which Yahweh responds with the promise of renewed help (41:10), being formed and called from the womb (43:1; 44:1), the provision of necessary equipment (41:15–16), the glorification of Yahweh by means of the one called (44:23). For good measure, this "servant of Yahweh" is actually identified with Israel (49:3), and the following passages are also most readily understood as referring to the people as a whole (49:7–26). But the problem is that the mission assigned to the speaker includes the task of bringing Israel back to its God, which task must be ascribed to an individual or collectivity within Israel, not to Israel itself. It seems, then, that the passage has been expanded to allow for a certain identification between the prophet and Israel, while still describing the prophet's own sense of mission to Israel.

The explicit identification of the "servant" with Israel in this text (49:3) illustrates that often the first stages in the history of interpretation of biblical texts are incorporated into the texts themselves. The powerful appeal of these so-called Servant Songs has, paradoxically, rendered them almost immune to interpretation precisely for this reason. Yet in spite of the many uncertainties, some modest progress can be made in delimiting the boundaries within which these texts open up their meaning. One approach that will be proposed at a later point of our study starts out from the indications in the last section of the book (56—66) of the existence of a prophetic group rejected by the majority and calling themselves "servants of Yahweh." That these last chapters have been added to the section in which the "Servant Songs" occur itself suggests a connection between "the Servant" and "the servants of Yahweh"; and the link is further strengthened by editorial additions to the last two of the "Servant Songs." We will note these briefly, deferring further discussion of the matter to the next section.[60]

The first of these (Isa. 50:10–11) follows one of the rare passages in these chapters in which a speaker addresses his public in the first person (50:4–9). While he is identified as "the servant of Yahweh" only in the comment added to his words, the language of "opening" or "wakening" the ear strongly suggests prophetic inspiration. It appears that in carrying out his mission to his fellow exiles he has suffered violence and contumely and has been wrongly accused. He is therefore certain of his ultimate vindication by Yahweh who will stand by him. The comment added by one of his followers at least makes it clear that the community is divided between those who adhere to and those who reject this prophet and his teaching. While the precise circumstances can no longer be recovered, the kind of language used (walking in darkness without light) suggests that he has been arrested and imprisoned by the authorities, and for that reason discredited in the eyes of many of his fellow exiles.

It appears to be the same individual who complains of the failure of his mission while affirming the assurance of vindication by Yahweh in the earlier "servant" passage in the first person (49:1–6). Clearer still is the connection with the later and longer passage in which a servant of Yahweh passes from suffering, humiliation, and rejection to ultimate vindication (52:13–53:12). Here especially, where the difficulties of interpretation have proved well-nigh insuperable to generations of commentators (see North, 1956), we can aspire only to present in outline a plausible reading consonant with the approach outlined so far. We begin with the observation that the speaker at the beginning and end of the passage is Yahweh (52:13–15; 53:11–12),[61] and that this address in the divine first-person frames the words of another speaker who, at one time one of those who rejected the "servant," has now come to understand and accept the significance of his ministry (53:1–11). The intensity of the language in this lament, almost unparalleled in the Hebrew Bible, arises out of the profoundly moving experience of conversion to discipleship and prepares us for what we will be told about the suffering and rejection of the "servants of Yahweh" in the last chapters of the book. It is not surprising that this commemorative lament has continued to reverberate throughout Jewish history, and that it came to have such a decisive influence on the early Christian understanding of the prophetic ministry of Jesus.

We need only add that the language in which the fate of this anonymous prophet is described is in several respects ambiguous and patient of more than one interpretation. That he is compared to a lamb led to the slaughter (53:7), that he is taken away and cut off from the land of the living (v. 8), that he has his sepulcher with the wicked (v. 9) would seem most naturally to imply that he was put to death.[62] If this is so, the final promise that he will see his offspring and that his work will bear fruit in the end would imply that he lives on in the prophetic following dedicated to perpetuating his message. It remains for us to see what was made of that message in the new situation opened up by the prospect and reality of return to the homeland.

VI
PROPHETS AND PROPHECY
IN THE
SECOND COMMONWEALTH

20. JUDEAN PROPHECY
IN THE EARLY PERSIAN PERIOD

P. R. **Ackroyd,** "Studies in the Book of Haggai," *JJS* 2 (1951): 163–76; 3 (1952): 1–13; "The Book of Haggai and Zechariah 1–8," *JJS* 3 (1952): 151–56; *Exile and Restoration*, 138–217; "The History of Israel in the Exilic and Post-exilic Periods," in G. W. Anderson, ed., *Tradition and Interpretation*, Oxford: Clarendon Press, 1979, 320–50; S. **Amsler,** "Zacharie et l'origine d'apocalyptique," *SVT* 22 (1972): 227–31; J. L. **Berquist,** "The Social Setting of Malachi," *BTB* 19 (1989): 121–26; W.A.M. **Beuken,** Haggai-Sacharja 1—8, Assen: Van Gorcum, 1967; M. **Bič,** *Die Nachtgesichte des Sacharja*, Neukirchen-Vluyn: Neukirchener Verlag, 1964; E. J. **Bickerman,** "The Historical Foundations of Postbiblical Judaism," in L. Finkelstein, ed., *The Jews: Their History, Culture and Religion*, 70–114; J. **Blenkinsopp,** *Ezra-Nehemiah: A Commentary*, Philadelphia: Westminster Press, 1988; "Temple and Society in Achaemenid Judah," in P. R. Davies, ed., *Second Temple Studies*, vol. 1, *Persian Period*, Sheffield: Sheffield Academic Press, 1991, 22–53; R. P. **Carroll,** "Twilight of Prophecy or Dawn of Apocalyptic?" *JSOT* 14 (1979): 3–35; T. **Chary,** *Les Prophètes et le Culte à partir de l'Exil*, Paris: Desclée, 1955, 119–59; R. J. **Coggins,** *Haggai, Zechariah, Malachi*, Sheffield: JSOT Press, 1987; J. J. **Collins,** "The Message of Malachi," *BTB* 22 (1984): 209–15; J. M. **Cook,** *The Persian Empire*, London: J. M. Dent & Sons, 1983; P. R. **Davies,** ed., *Second Temple Studies*, vol. 1, *Persian Period*, Sheffield: Sheffield Academic Press, 1991; W. D. **Davies** and L. **Finkelstein,** eds., *The Cambridge History of Judaism*, vol. 1, *Introduction: The Persian Period*, London & New York: Cambridge University Press, 1984; J. A. **Fischer,** "Notes on the Literary Form and Message of Malachi," *CBQ* 34 (1972): 315–20; K. **Galling,** "Die Exilwende in der Sicht des Propheten Sacharja," *VT* 2 (1952): 19–36; *Studien zur Geschichte Israels im persischen Zeitalter*, Tübingen: J.C.B. Mohr (Paul Siebeck), 1964; "Serubbabel und die Wiederaufnahme des Tempels in

Jerusalem," in A. Kuschke, ed., *Verbannung und Heimkehr: Festschrift W. Rudolph*, Tübingen: J.C.B. Mohr (Paul Siebeck), 1961, 67–96; B. **Glazier-McDonald**, *Malachi: The Divine Messenger*, Atlanta: Scholars Press, 1987; L. L. **Grabbe**, *Judaism from Cyrus to Hadrian*, vol. 1, *The Persian and Greek Periods*, Minneapolis: Fortress Press, 1992; E. **Hammershaimb**, *Some Aspects of Old Testament Prophecy from Isaiah to Malachi*, Copenhagen: Rosenkilde & Bagger, 1966; R. **Hanhart**, *Sacharja*, Neukirchen-Vluyn: Neukirchener Verlag, 1992; P. D. **Hanson**, *The Dawn of Apocalyptic*, Philadelphia: Fortress Press, 1975; F. **Hesse**, "Haggai," *Verbannung und Heimkehr*, 109–34; J. **Jeremias**, *Die Nachtgesichte des Sacharja*, Göttingen: Vandenhoeck & Ruprecht, 1977; K. **Koch**, *The Prophets: The Babylonian and Persian Periods*, 152–207; T. **Lescow**, *Das Buch Maleachi: Texttheorie—Auslegung—Kanontheorie*, Stuttgart: Calwer, 1993; A. **Lods**, *The Prophets and the Rise of Judaism*, London: Kegan Paul, Trench, Trubner & Co., 1937, 184–99, 265–80; R. **Mason**, *The Books of Haggai, Zechariah, and Malachi*, Cambridge: Cambridge University Press, 1977; S. L. **McKenzie** and H. N. **Wallace**, "Covenant Themes in Malachi," *CBQ* 45 (1984): 549–63; C. L. **Meyers** and E. M. **Meyers**, *Haggai, Zechariah 1—8: A New Translation with Introduction and Commentary*, Garden City, N.Y.: Doubleday, 1987; H. G. **Mitchell**, J.M.P. **Smith**, J. A. **Bewer**, *A Critical and Exegetical Commentary on Haggai, Zechariah, Malachi, and Jonah*, Edinburgh: T. & T. Clark, 1912; F. S. **North**, "Critical Analysis of the Book of Haggai," *ZAW* 68 (1956): 25–46; J. M. **O'Brien**, *Priest and Levite in Malachi*, Atlanta: Scholars Press, 1990; R. **Pautriel**, "Malachie, Le Livre de," *SDB*, 5: 739–46; D. L. **Petersen**, *Haggai and Zechariah 1—8: A Commentary*, Philadelphia: Westminster, 1984; A. **Petitjean**, *Les Oracles du Proto-Sacharie*, Paris: J. Gabalda, 1969; L. G. **Rignell**, *Die Nachtgesichte des Sacharja*, Lund: Gleerup, 1950; W. **Rudolph**, *Haggai-Sacharja 1–8—Sacharja 9–14—Maleachi*, Gütersloh: Gütersloher Verlagshaus Gerd Mohn, 1976; M. **Smith**, *Palestinian Parties and Politics*, 82–98; E. **Stern**, *The Material Culture of the Land of the Bible in the Persian Period 538–332 B.C.*, Warminster: Aris & Phillips and Jerusalem: Israel Exploration Society, 1982; A. S. **Van der Woude**, "Zerubbabel und die messianischen Erwartungen des Propheten Sacharja," *ZAW* 100 (1988): 138–56; P. A. **Verhoef**, *The Books of Haggai and Malachi*, Grand Rapids: Eerdmans, 1987; G. **Widengren**, "The Persians," in D. J. Wiseman, ed., *Peoples of Old Testament Times*, Oxford: Clarendon Press, 1973, 312–57; "The Persian Period," in J. H. Hayes and J. M. Miller, eds., *Israelite and Judaean History*, 489–538; H. W. **Wolff**, "Prophecy from the Eighth Through the Fifth Century," *Int* 32 (1978): 17–30; *Haggai: A Commentary*, Minneapolis: Augsburg, 1988; E. M. **Yamauchi**, *Persia and the Bible*, Grand Rapids: Baker Book House, 1990.

A great deal of misunderstanding has arisen from the once commonly accepted assumption that for all practical purposes prophecy came to an end with the Babylonian exile. At the risk of laboring the obvious, we begin by noting that five of the fifteen books in Latter Prophets (Joel, Jonah, Haggai, Zechariah, Malachi) are entirely postexilic compositions and that numerous additions to the remaining books are also of late origin, including such substantial sections as Isaiah 24—27 and

56—66. Despite laments that prophetic guidance was no longer available (Lam. 2:9), prophetic activity was in evidence from the earliest years of the return (Ezra 5:1–2; Zech. 7:2–7; 8:9). But in order to understand how prophecy functioned in this later period and in what ways it was different from earlier forms we must first take stock of the political situation in the province of Judah after the transition from Babylonian to Persian rule.

At first the change did not make much difference. Palestinian Jews[1] came within the satrapal system of the Persian empire, which reproduced major aspects of Assyrian and Babylonian imperial administration. Since Syria and Palestine had most recently been ruled from Babylon, they formed part of the satrapy that included Babylon and the Trans-Euphrates region (Babili-Ebirnari). Only after the revolt of Babylon in 482 B.C.E., suppressed with exceptional brutality by Xerxes, did these regions come to form a separate administrative entity known as the "Beyond the River" satrapy (Ezra 5:6, etc.). The center of imperial administration was the old Median capital of Ecbatana (Hamadan) until Darius moved it to Susa and Persepolis. Jerusalem and the surrounding area of Judah (Yehud) formed one of several provinces, together with Syria, Samaria, Megiddo, and others, under the jurisdiction of the local satrap, probably resident in Damascus. The thesis that Judah was controlled and administered from Samaria during the Neo-Babylonian and Persian periods down to the governorship of Nehemiah, proposed half a century ago by Albrecht Alt, is now generally abandoned.[2]

As long as they kept the peace and paid tribute, provinces under Persian imperial control enjoyed a fair degree of autonomy, issuing their own coinage, policing their own territory, and collecting tribute and taxes. It seems to have been Persian policy to respect the juridical status of local political entities, to give their support to a local elite that promised to be cooperative and preserve the *pax Persica*, and to put such an elite in place where it was not locally available. This last appears to have been the policy implemented in the repatriation of Babylonian Jews and the offer of imperial subsidy for the rebuilding of the Jerusalem temple.

Judah was one of several provinces the status of which was determined by its temple and temple personnel; other examples are known from Mesopotamia, Egypt, and Asia Minor. In these instances the central government sponsored, subsidized, and, where necessary, restored such politically significant local cults. Cyrus II (Kurush), founder of the Achaemenid empire, claimed to have restored the Marduk cult in Babylon after the neglect that it had suffered under the last Babylonian king, Nabonidus. He also restored the cult of the moon god Sin at Ur, and his successor Cambyses claimed to have purified the great sanctuary of Sais in Egypt. Later still, we find Darius reproving the satrap Gadatas for imposing tribute on the shrine of Apollo in Magnesia.[3] It is therefore by no means implausible that the same monarch should have subsidized the rebuilding of the Yahweh temple in Jerusalem (Ezra 6:8).

Another aspect of imperial policy was the insistence that local law codes remain in force, backed by the coercive power of the central government. Darius mandated a codification of ancient Egyptian laws and enjoined their observance, and in the same spirit a later king commissioned Ezra to enforce "the law of the God of heaven" among Jews in the Trans-Euphrates satrapy (Ezra 7:14, 25–26). Concern for law observance also extended to prescriptions mandating the proper carrying out of the local cult. Complaints of royal commissioners under Cyrus about the laxity of temple officials in Babylon have come down to us, and among the Elephantine papyri there is a letter from the satrap in Egypt ordering the Jewish settlers to observe one of their festivals according to the traditional order.[4] It is by no means improbable that Darius' interest in the codification and implementation of local laws extended to the Jewish community, and that much of the legislation in the Pentateuch formed the civil constitution of the Jewish ethnos under Persian imperial control.[5]

The province of Judah can therefore be described as a temple-community comparable to others in the Persian empire. The function of such temples was not confined to sacrifice, prayer, and other cultic acts. The larger temples also served as administrative centers with their own bureaucracies; they issued loans, controlled and collected revenues from real estate, supported colleges of scholars and scribes, not to mention hordes of temple servants including butchers, bakers, keepers of sacrificial herds, and the like. Supreme authority over this organization was, of course, vested ultimately in the monarch. It was in his capacity as legal successor to the Babylonian kings that Cyrus restored the Esagila shrine in Babylon, and it was the same kind of juridical claim that underpinned imperial control of the Jerusalem temple, formerly a dynastic shrine. An important reminder of this status was the requirement that prayers for the well-being of the imperial family be incorporated into the daily liturgy (Ezra 6:10).

In the provinces, royal authority was normally exercised through officials and commissioners appointed by the central government. One of their tasks was to oversee the financial management of the temple and its considerable assets. Expediency and good sense dictated the appointment, where possible, of local people to discharge these functions. Cyrus, for example, appointed a Lydian to oversee the Sardis treasury, while under Darius a Davidite, Zerubbabel, was sent out as governor of Yehud. Under normal circumstances, however, the day-to-day task of temple administration devolved on the priesthood.

This last point is particularly important for understanding the situation in Judah as the Babylonian-Jewish element was beginning to assume administrative and economic control, including control of the rebuilt temple. The authority of the temple clergy was not confined to control of the sacrificial cult, as important as that was. The legal, or at least social, standing of residents was contingent on participation in and support of the cult, which meant that, in a real sense, their civic existence depended on the priesthood. Title to real estate was also contingent on good standing in the cultic community, a circumstance that inevitably sowed the seeds of conflict once the descendants of former residents began to trickle back to the province. The priesthood, therefore, wielded considerable power not only in the religious sphere—the cult being the primary and indispensable means of salvation—but also in the economic and political spheres.

The quite unique importance of the Jerusalem temple and its operations in the early Persian period was bound to generate conflict, and it is important for understanding prophetic texts from that time to see how conflict developed. Our principal source, the author of Chronicles-Ezra-Nehemiah, is committed to the view that the Babylonian immigrants alone, and not those who had never left the province, were in direct line of succession to the old Israel and, as such, had to assume responsibility for the reestablishment of the sacrificial cult. We may well choose to discount this slanted view of the situation, but there can be no doubt that such claims were being staked, and that would have led to acrimonious disputes over control of the temple and its revenues, title to property expropriated after the Babylonian conquest, genealogical claims, and related matters. The situation would also have been exacerbated by accusations of religious infidelity passed back and forth between Babylonians and Palestinians and between different priestly factions. Here, too, the Chronicler's view of the Diaspora Jews as alone remaining faithful to the religious traditions is certainly oversimplified.

From the beginning of the Persian period a basic issue was to decide how one qualified for membership in the Jerusalem temple-community. Since the passing of the nation-state, which retained its political institutions though in vassalage to foreign powers, the matter could not be decided purely on grounds of national identity. Other factors entered into play including, for the first time, laws governing ritual purity (e.g., Hag. 2:10–14). It is therefore no surprise to find disagreement on the status of specific categories of people, including those who had defiled themselves with idolatry, resident aliens (*gērîm*), and eunuchs. With respect to this last category, for example, Isa. 56:3–5 expresses an inclusive attitude quite at variance with the Deuteronomic law that excludes from the community the sexually mutilated as well as certain ethnic categories (Deut. 23:1). For the same reason, marriage with women outside the group became increasingly problematic and emerged as a major issue at the time of Ezra and Nehemiah.

Conflict was also going on at that time within the ranks of the priesthood over issues of legitimacy, control of the temple and its considerable resources, and the status of temple personnel. Some who claimed priestly lineage but could not substantiate their claim were excluded "until there should be a priest to consult Urim and Thummim" (Ezra 2:59–63).[6] The ruling was clearly handed down by other priests already installed in office who were anxious to control recruitment into the priesthood. The revival of even the idea of this ancient form of divination would, moreover, indicate a degree of assimilation of prophetic-divinatory functions into the priesthood. The process by which the Aaronite branch of the priesthood achieved dominance and other branches were reduced to a subservient position is obscure and is not our present concern. It will suffice to note that the distinction between sacrificing priests and adjutant Levites was unknown during the time of the monarchy, is attested only in the very latest editorial stratum of Deuteronomy (27:14),[7] but was fully in operation by the time the Priestly source (P) came to be written. The circumstance that only 74 Levites are listed in the census of repatriates in Ezra 2 (= Nehemiah 7) as against 973 priests, and that Ezra had difficulty recruiting Levites for his mission as he prepared to leave Babylon (Ezra 8:15–20), would perhaps indicate that the creation of a distinct Levitical order was of fairly recent occurrence.

The Chronicler has it that Cyrus issued a rescript informing all and sundry that Yahweh, having put him in power, commanded him to see to the rebuilding of the temple in Jerusalem (2 Chron. 36:22–23; Ezra 1:1–4). While the authenticity of this text is not entirely above suspicion, the permission granted to the deportees to return and the subsidizing of the cult (Ezra 6:4) were entirely consistent with Persian policy.[8] The Chronicler goes on to describe the enthusiastic response to the rescript among Babylonian Jews who left en masse for the homeland under the leadership of a certain Sheshbazzar, described as prince (*nāśî'*) and governor (*peḥâ*) of Judah (Ezra 1:5–11; 2:63; 5:14). The same Sheshbazzar, bearer of a good Babylonian name, is also credited with having laid the foundations of the temple (Ezra 5:16), though elsewhere we hear that this happened only several years later (Ezra 3:1–13). Information provided by the biblical sources for this period is for the most part confused and self-contradictory, and it is especially doubtful whether there was such a large-scale aliyah at that time as is suggested by the register at Ezra

2:1–70 (= Neh. 7:6–73). The statistics for different categories in this list add up to around 50,000, which suggests that the list refers to the demographics of a much later time than the reign of Cyrus. It seems likely that initially only a small number trickled back, and that these early repatriates were joined by others at intervals thereafter, for example, in connection with Cambyses's campaign against Egypt in 525 B.C.E. If the response had been as enthusiastic as the Chronicler would have us believe, it is difficult to understand why it took almost a quarter of a century to complete work on the temple.

After Cambyses died in Palestine on his way back from Egypt, his place was taken by another son of Cyrus, Bardiya (known to the Greeks as Smerdis), who had himself proclaimed king and won acceptance throughout most of the empire, especially after suspending taxes for three years (Herodotus 3:67). After reigning only a few months, however, he was captured and executed by Darius, descendant of a cadet line of the Achaemenids, who for the next two years was engaged in a desperate struggle to secure his rather shaky claim to the throne, put down rebellions, and restore law and order. The official version put out by Darius, in the famous rock inscription of Behistun, was that Bardiya was killed by Cambyses and that the person killed by Darius was a look-alike of Bardiya, a pretender whose name was Gaumata; which version most historians recognize to be transparently propagandistic, designed to legitimize Darius's assumption of power. His usurpation resulted in rebellions in many parts of the empire, particularly in Egypt and the satrapy of Babylon to which Judah belonged. The last of the revolts in Babylon was instigated by a certain Arakha who claimed royal descent and called himself Nebuchadrezzar IV. He held out until the winter of 521 B.C.E., at which time he was captured and impaled together with his Babylonian supporters.[9]

It is unlikely that these nationalist uprisings at both ends of the satrapy would have left the intervening provinces unaffected. The Chronicler's version of events in Judah during this period (Ezra 3—6) raises a host of problems, but he at least testifies that the rebuilding of the temple was carried out in response to prophetic preaching and was even mandated by a prophetic oracle (Ezra 5:1–2; 6:14). Among these prophets involved in the work from the beginning, two are known by name: Haggai and Zechariah.

The oracles of Haggai have been provided with dates, put into a narrative framework (Hag. 1:1, 12–14), and interspersed with traditional prophetic formulae, perhaps by the circle or school that goes under the name of the Chronicler.[10] The numerous occurrences of "oracle of Yahweh" (n^e'um YHWH) are meant to give the impression of a prophet in the classical mold, but in both form and content Haggai is quite distinctive. Much of the material in this short book belongs rather to the category of disputation. The indications include admonitions to pay attention (Hag. 1:5, 7; 2:15, 18), rhetorical questions (1:4; 2:3, 16, 19), anticipating objections and then answering them (1:2–6)—rhetorical devices that will appear in a more developed form in Malachi. The use of ritual law to make a point (Hag. 2:10–14) is also unique in this respect.

While the distinction between prophets of doom and prophets of well-being is rarely if ever absolute, the frequent occurrence of words of assurance—"fear not" (2:5), "I am with you" (1:13; 2:4), "take courage" (2:4)—suggests that Haggai stands rather in the tradition of optimistic prophecy associated with the state cult. The prediction addressed to the Davidite Zerubbabel of an imminent end to the contemporary political order, meaning concretely the breakup of the Persian empire (Hag. 2:6–9, 20–23), is not different in essence from Hananiah's prophecy of emancipation from the Babylonian empire, a prophecy delivered in the temple (Jer. 28:1–4).

The close association between priests and prophets is illustrated in the account of a delegation sent by a certain Sarezer in 518 B.C.E. to inquire about the proper time for fasting to commemorate the destruction of Solomon's temple (Zech. 7:1–7). The question was put to both priests and prophets at "the house of Yahweh of the hosts,"[11] but the real agenda behind the request was revealed to Zechariah by prophetic inspiration. The Chronicler associates Haggai with Zechariah as fervent advocates of the rebuilding of the temple (Ezra 5:1; 6:14), which suggests that, whatever their origin, whether Palestinian or Babylonian, both were in the tradition of cult prophecy. The same conclusion is suggested by the halakah on a point of ritual purity recorded by Haggai (Hag. 2:10–14; cf. Lev. 22:4–7). The point, which concerned the entire community in Judah at that time (520 B.C.E.),[12] seems to be that whatever cult had been carried out since the destruction of the Jerusalem temple had not rendered them acceptable to God but that, on the contrary, their polluted state had rendered that cult unacceptable. In view of similar prophetic denunciations elsewhere, the reference is most likely to syncretic practices at cult centers other than Jerusalem, perhaps especially at Bethel ("what they offer *there* is unclean," 2:14). It therefore seems tolerably clear that both Haggai and Zechariah (the author of chapters 1—8) were central cult prophets, in the line of those who functioned in the Jerusalem temple in close association with the priesthood under the monarchy (e.g., 2 Kings 23:2).

The editorial framework to Haggai's preaching, especially the dates, turns this little book into a kind of diary covering several stages marking the work of temple building. To this extent it is comparable to the

Chronicler's somewhat garbled account of the same event in Ezra 3—6. The latter is also punctuated by dates from the seventh month of the first year of a presumed return under Zerubbabel to the sixth year of Darius, when the work was eventually finished (Ezra 3:1, 6, 8, 10; 6:15, 19). In Haggai the dates cover the short period from the sixth to the ninth month, that is, autumn and early winter, of Darius' second year, and to each one there corresponds a prophetic oracle or short discourse.

In the *first* of these (1:2–11), Haggai addressed a reproach to the governor Zerubbabel, the high priest Joshua ben Jehozadak, and the community in general. People were saying that the time was not ripe for the rebuilding, perhaps with reference to the seventy years of Jeremiah (Jer. 25:11–14; 29:10–14), to which Zechariah also alludes (Zech. 1:12).[13] The miserable economic and social condition of the community (cf. Zech. 8:10, which adds social unrest and political strife) are attributed to lack of enthusiasm for the work of rebuilding. The temple must be built before Yahweh can manifest his glory, in other words, show his hand in the political arena. The rebuilding is therefore the necessary precondition for the world-shaking events that will usher in the new age proclaimed by the prophets. We see already that in this respect the message of Haggai is not essentially different from the eschatological teaching in the last chapters of Isaiah, which will be discussed in the next section. Haggai therefore proclaimed the eschatological hope at the center of the cultic establishment, and his editor notes the positive response to this preaching (1:12–14; cf. Ezra 5:1–2; 6:14).

The *second* discourse seems to have been displaced and to have lost its date, resulting in some chronological confusion. Most commentators, however, reattach 2:15–19 to the date at 1:15. In 2:15–19, at any rate, the peripeteia, the turning point from curse to blessing, is the laying of the foundation stone on the twenty-fourth day of the sixth month (late September 520 B.C.E.)—"from this day on I will bless you" (2:19). The *third* sermon or discourse, following about a month later (2:2–9), confronts discouragement in prosecuting the work expressed in unfavorable comparisons with Solomon's temple which, incidentally, only the oldest of Haggai's contemporaries would have seen (cf. Ezra 3:12–13). The guarantee of political and social well-being is the presence of the divine Spirit manifested in eschatological prophecy. In a short while, the prophet's audience is told, a great political upheaval will result in the restoration of the temple to its former splendor. The *fourth* discourse, exactly three months after the laying of the foundation stone, condemns cult practice that had been going on in the province since the destruction of the temple (2:11–14). The prediction of the overthrow of the Persian empire and the restoration of the native dynasty is made more clearly and specifically in the *fifth* and last of the recorded oracles on the twenty-fourth day of an unspecified month (2:21–23). There are to be world-shaking events bringing the present political order to an end, at which time Zerubbabel will reign as messiah and God's elect. The point is made with the help of the symbolic icon of Yahweh's signet ring (*ḥôtām*), the same image of royalty used by Jeremiah with reference to the exiled Jehoiachin, Zerubbabel's grandfather (Jer. 22:24).

The language used in the third and fifth sayings makes it clear that we are dealing with a messianic movement in Judah, comparable with movements in contemporary Babylonia, triggered by political turmoil throughout the Persian empire between the death of Cambyses in July 522 and the final restoration of order by Darius two years later. As noted earlier, the Chronicler's account is vitiated by a tendency to telescope events in the reign of Cyrus with later developments in Darius' reign. One aspect of this perhaps willful confusion in the Chronicler's account of events is uncertainty about the respective roles of Sheshbazzar and Zerubbabel. The Chronicler does, however, provide one interesting piece of information, namely, the intervention of Tattenai, administrator of the Trans-Euphrates region, who put a stop to the work of rebuilding pending confirmation of Zerubbabel's work permit (Ezra 5:3–17). The dates in Haggai run from about August to December of the second year of Darius. Since the latter seized power in the autumn of 522, the second year of his reign would be 520. As early as the Greek historians, however, there has been uncertainty about the calculation of regnal years of several of the Persian kings including Darius I. Since the revolt of Arakha (a.k.a. Nebuchadrezzar IV), referred to earlier, may have coincided with the activity of Haggai (i.e., August to November, allowing some time for news to travel), it is possible that the messianic movement in Judah, which focused on the person of the Davidite Zerubbabel, was part of the larger disturbance in the satrapy.

What happened to this Jewish messiah we do not know. We do know that Darius eventually came out on top, and he had the details of his struggles and triumphs engraved for posterity in the propagandistic Behistun inscription.[14] Zechariah 6:9–14 has been taken to imply that Zerubbabel was recalled and his place taken by the high priest. The night visions of Zechariah, at any rate, provide an interesting test case of the disconfirmation of eschatological hopes and the process of adjustment that it entailed.

Zechariah's account of the delegation about fasting (Zech. 7:1–7), mentioned earlier, suggests association with cult and priesthood. He is identified as a *nābî'* in the superscription to the book that, however, confuses him with the Zechariah ben-Jeberechiah mentioned at Isa. 8:2. A priest named Zechariah son of Iddo, contemporary of the high priest Joiakim, successor to Joshua (Jeshua), is listed in a census at Neh. 12:16. It is conceivable that this is the same person, but Iddo and Zechariah are both quite common names. The book of Zechariah consists of eight vision reports sandwiched between a sermonlike introduction (1:1–6) and a concluding section dealing with fasting and prospects for the future (chapters 7—8). The dates affixed to the introduction and conclusion (Zech. 1:1; 7:1) span the period from the second to the fourth year of Darius, while the night visions, or at least the first of them, date to the eleventh month of Darius' second year. In other words, they are said to occur two months after the last dated oracles of Haggai (Zech. 1:7; cf. Hag. 2:10, 20).

In spite of some editorial deletions and additions, the vision reports in Zechariah exhibit a clear structural unity. If we assume that these reports go back to the time indicated and the person to whom they are attributed, the same would not be the case with the homiletic framework to the visions, which shows clear signs of later compilation. The preface (Zech. 1:1–6) is in effect a short sermon on repentance or "turning" (*t⁵ûbâ*), along the same lines as Mal. 3:7:

> From the days of your fathers you have turned aside from my statutes and have not kept them. Return to me, and I will return to you, says Yahweh of hosts.

This is the message and the language of the exilic Deuteronomists, and there are indications that both Malachi and the author of Zech. 1:1–6 have modeled themselves on this source. Zechariah 1:1–6 reminds the reader that "the former prophets" (1:4; cf. 7:7, 12) or "my servants the prophets" (1:6, a Deuteronomic expression, as we have seen) preached repentance to the Israel of an earlier day, that their message fell on deaf ears, and that the result was disaster. Their predictions were verified, and it was left to the forefathers to acknowledge the justice of God and lament their mistakes during the exile. This is nothing else but a summary of Deuteronomic preaching addressed to the survivors of the Babylonian conquest.

The concluding section of Zechariah (chapters 7—8), on the other hand, looks forward to a new future when the curse will be turned to blessing. Here there are two distinct but related themes. The first is introduced by the delegation on fasting, which provided the occasion to distinguish between authentic and inauthentic penitential exercises. The same theme is pursued, and in the same way, in Isa. 58:1–9, the conclusion to which provides the resolution to the situation set out in Zechariah:

You shall call, and Yahweh will answer;
You shall cry, and he will say, "Here I am."

Cf. Zech. 7:13:

Just as when I called they would not hear, so when they called I would not hear.

The point is that fasting is worse than useless if unaccompanied by active concern for others, especially socially marginalized classes such as widows, the fatherless, resident aliens, and the poor (Zech. 7:8–10; cf. Isa. 58:6–7). The forefathers neglected this message and the result was exile. In the age to come, however, the fasts that commemorate the destruction of city and temple will be turned into festivals of rejoicing (Zech. 8:18–19).

The sermon on true fasting, therefore, broadens out into the theme of eschatological reversal, projecting an age when Yahweh, on his return to Zion, will confer a new name on the city and temple. Here too the perspective is identical with that of the so-called Third Isaiah (Isa. 60:14; 62:1–5, 12), who also speaks of the temple as "my holy mountain" (*har qodší*, 56:7; 57:13; 65:11, 25; 66:20). The population of Jerusalem will overflow, it will be augmented by a faithful people returned from the Diaspora, the land will be fertile, foreigners will come to worship Yahweh in the temple, and the religious prestige of the Jew will be such as to attract a host of proselytes. As in Haggai, the turning point, the peripeteia, is the laying of the foundation stone of the temple. Henceforth, whatever the uncertainties of the present time, it only remains for the people to grasp the opportunity, responding to the divine initiative by a life of religious fidelity (Zech. 8:14–17).

This, then, is the homiletic framework of the night vision sequence. We have seen that this sequence is dated two months after Haggai's proclamation of the imminent messianic reign of Zerubbabel. There is no indication of where the visions are supposed to have taken place. It could be Judah, but it could also be Babylon shortly after the collapse of the last revolt in that city. The *first* of the night visions (1:7–17) features a supernatural courier on horseback to whom a cavalry patrol reports that all is quiet in the land. This was bad news, since messianic hopes depended for their fulfillment on the collapse of Persian rule when faced with movements of nationalist revival. On hearing the news, the angel interpreter, who appears to be identical with the courier, intercedes with Yahweh to take pity on Jerusalem now that the seventy years foretold by Jeremiah are coming to an end. The result is positive, and the seer is commissioned to proclaim that Yahweh has indeed returned from

Babylon, that in spite of everything the temple must be rebuilt, after which the promised reversal of fortune would take place.

Like other examples of the disconfirmation of eschatological predictions, in the Bible as elsewhere, the disappointing outcome of all this was not the complete collapse of group expectations but rather a reassertion of goals, a rescheduling of the expected millennium.[15] The promised reversal of fortune was initially connected with the laying of the foundation stone of the temple; when the predictions went unfulfilled, expectations were refocused on the completion of the building several years later. The temple was in fact completed and dedicated in the sixth year of Darius (Ezra 6:15), but again without bringing closure to the expectations associated with it. We hear of prophetically supported messianic movements in the reign of Artaxerxes I (445/4 B.C.E.) focused on the person of Nehemiah. Though they appear in the form of allegations directed at Nehemiah by his enemies (Neh. 6:6–7), they provide a plausible indication that the hopes aroused by the building of the temple were rekindled seventy years later—the same interval of time as that of the exile—this time with the prospect of the rebuilding and repopulation of Jerusalem. Thus the messianic movement in the early Persian period, initially concentrated on the Davidite Jehoiachin and his family, had an essential point of reference in the rebuilding of temple and city; a fact not unimportant for understanding later developments, including Jewish and Christian messianic movements.

The *second* vision, of four horns cast down by four smiths (Zech. 1:18–21 [MT 2:1–4]), is generally taken to refer to the succession of imperial powers (Assyria, Babylonia, Persia, Media) at whose hands Judah had suffered, and their past or, in the case of Persia, imminent destruction. But this leaves us with the problem that only the first two of these "horns" could be said to have scattered the people of Judah, while the Persians, far from scattering them, allowed them to come together. The symbolism may therefore encrypt an allusion to the recent suppression of the Babylonian revolts led by Nidintu-Bel and Arakha, respectively. Whatever hopes may have focused on these revolts while they were in progress, the memory of the hated conqueror of Jerusalem, whose name both rebels claimed, would have facilitated a reinterpretation after resistance collapsed. In the *third* vision (Zech. 2:1–5 [MT 2:5–9]) the prophet sees a man with a measuring line who explains that he is going to measure Jerusalem, presumably with a view to the rebuilding of the walls. Through another heavenly intermediary the angel interpreter repeats the message of the first vision about the future state of Jerusalem. Reuse of the Isaian topos of Yahweh as a wall of fire around the city (Isa. 4:5) may have served as a warning against building the walls at that time—an act that could have been interpreted as the first stage of a plan to rebel. The vision has been expanded by an address to Jews still in Babylon to leave quickly for *ereṣ yiśrā'ēl* in order to escape the retribution about to fall on the rebellious city after the failed rebellions (2:6–7).

The *fourth* in the series is introduced in a different way (3:1) and is the only one in which the angel interpreter does not speak with the seer. It is also out of chronological order because it looks forward to the coming of a messianic figure known under the code-name of the Branch (3:8; cf. 6:12). We should probably take chapters 3 and 4 as a continuous symbolic narrative serving as the centerpiece of seven rather than eight visions, with a marked correspondence between the first (1:7–17) and the seventh (6:1–8). The logical order in this centerpiece is difficult to determine and is complicated by oracles addressed to Zerubbabel (4:6–10a) affirming that he is the one to complete the rebuilding of the temple, but emphasizing the need for spiritual rather than military resistance (4:6).

In the opening scene revealed to the seer the accusation brought against Joshua the high priest by the Satan[16] is dismissed by Yahweh presiding over a judicial session in heaven. Though soiled and barely saved from destruction—a veiled reference to lapse into apostasy—the Zadokite Joshua and his colleagues are to be given control of the temple and thus play an important role in the coming messianic age (3:1–10). The stone with seven eyes, later explained as the eyes of Yahweh that survey the whole earth (3:9a; 4:10b), doubtless refers to the zodiacal band and the seven planets and indicates that, despite appearances to the contrary, nothing that happens in the sphere of international events escapes Yahweh's surveillance and control.

The golden lampstand supporting a bowl with seven lamps and flanked by two olive trees represents the temple and the dyarchy of civil rule and high priesthood (4:1–3, 11–14).[17] The problematic nature of this kind of dual leadership and the disappointment of hopes placed in Zerubbabel can also be read between the lines of the oracle with which the visions are rounded off (6:9–15). The prophet is commissioned to take silver and gold from certain wealthy Jews newly returned from Babylon, make a crown (the Hebrew has "crowns"), and put it on the head of Joshua the high priest. However, the portentous saying (Zech. 6:12–13) with which this act is to be accompanied makes it quite clear that the crown is intended not for Joshua but Zerubbabel:

> Behold the man whose name is Branch; he will "branch" from where he is; he will build the temple of Yahweh; . . . he will assume royal honor, He will ascend the throne and reign!

The substitution of the high priest Joshua for the Davidite Zerubbabel, and the insistence on the high status of the priest that follows, are understandable in view of the enhanced role of the temple clergy after Zerubbabel had disappeared from the scene.

The *fifth* vision (5:1–4) features a flying scroll on which, as the angel interpreter explains, is written a curse on theft and perjury. Since its dimensions are identical with those of the vestibule of Solomon's temple (1 Kings 6:3), the audience is to understand that this document of improbable size emanated from the Jerusalem temple. In view of the connection between the temple and ownership of land, discussed earlier, it may be conjectured that the condemnation of theft and perjury had to do with illegal expropriation of real estate that had been going on in Judah during the captivity. Equally fantastic appears to be the imagery of the *sixth* vision (5:5–11), in which the prophet saw a barrel or basket with a woman (or, more likely, a female figurine) in it being transported out of Judah by two birdlike females. Since the woman represents the people's iniquity, the action may be taken to symbolize the purging of idolatry with special reference to the addictive cult of the Canaanite goddess of fertility (cf. Ezek. 8:3; Jer. 44:15–19). It also seems to imply that a temple to this goddess was either planned or actually built in Babylon, recalling the cult of Anath-bethel among Jewish colonists settled on the island of Elephantine in Upper Egypt, perhaps about this time.[18] The *seventh* and last vision (6:1–8), reminiscent of the first, has four chariots setting off to the four corners of the earth on patrol. The reference to the chariot drawn by black horses bringing the spirit of Yahweh to the north country (i.e., Babylon, as at 2:6) is obscure. In view of the passage immediately following, it may refer to a prophetically inspired movement in the Diaspora that led a group of Jews to return. On this uncertain note the visions come to an end.

While in general faithful to a well-established prophetic genre, the vision reports of Zechariah introduce a new element symptomatic of what was happening to prophecy at that time. While previous visions, for example, those of Micaiah and Isaiah, had supernatural beings speaking to one another and to the seer, Zechariah for the first time introduces an *angelus interpres*, a supernatural agent who explains what was going on. The significance of this move will appear more clearly if we recall that the term *ma'lāk* (angel, messenger) had come to be used as a synonym for prophet (Isa. 42:19; 44:26; Hag. 1:13; Mal. 3:1; 2 Chron. 36:15–16). And in fact the interpreter of the visions from within also assumes the prophetic role of intercession (Zech. 1:12) and the giving of oracles (1:14–17; 2:4–5). But since the principal function of this personage is to *interpret,* we have a shift from direct inspiration to the interpretation of previous prophetic sayings. This is no doubt the most important aspect of these visions for the historical development of Israelite prophecy.

While much of the symbolism of the night visions remains obscure, there is enough evidence of the reuse and reinterpretation of prophetic topoi to put this conclusion beyond reasonable doubt. These include the seventy years of Jeremiah (Zech. 1:12; Jer. 25:11; 29:10), the blacksmiths (Isa. 54:16–17), the measuring line (Ezek. 42:20), the north country (Jer. 1:13–16), the designation Branch (Jer. 23:5; 33:15), the wall of fire (Isa. 4:5), perhaps also the horsemen who brought news of the fall of Babylon (Isa. 21:9). From this point on, the eschatological reinterpretation of the "former prophets" (Zech. 1:4; 7:7, 12) will be an important factor in the religious history of the Second Temple period.

The same term has been used to provide a title to the last book in the prophetic corpus (Malachi = my messenger). This short collection of prophetic sayings is the last of three anonymous booklets of roughly equal length, all of which are introduced under the rubric "oracle" (*maśśā'*) and begin "The word of Yahweh . . ." (Zech. 9:1; 12:1; Mal. 1:1). The name, however, has clearly been borrowed from the reference to the eschatological precursor within the book ("Behold, I send my messenger," 3:1)—incongruously, since the anonymous seer did not think of himself in that role. The reason for this sectioning at the end of the prophetic collection, one would suppose, was the need to arrive at the number twelve and thus permit the entire prophetic corpus to fall into a three plus twelve pattern, thereby symbolizing the three great ancestors and the twelve sons of Jacob/Israel, in other words, the totality of the house of Israel in light of which the reader is invited to read the prophets. This proposal is, as we shall see shortly, congruous with the last verses of Malachi (4:4–6 [MT 3:22–24]), which serve as the finale to the prophetic corpus as a whole, perhaps even to Torah and Prophets together.

The book of Malachi provides no biographical information on the author. The content, and what little it tells us about the social background against which the book was written,[19] suggests that it dates from sometime between the reestablishment of the Jerusalem cult (515) and the mission of Nehemiah (445), therefore probably during the reign of Xerxes (486–464) or early in the reign of Artaxerxes I, nicknamed Long Hand (464–425), a period about which we know very little indeed as far as Judah is concerned. The author's intense concern with the cult, together with his ferocious attack on the priesthood, suggests that he may have been either a dissident priest turned prophet or a Levite. But of even greater interest is the evidence provided by the book for a quite remarkable collapse of religious enthusiasm in the community, and especially in the temple priesthood, within the half-century or so following the dedication of the temple.

As in Haggai and Zechariah, the prose of Malachi has been worked over to bring it into line with preexilic prophecy. But the frequent and tedious insertion of "oracle of Yahweh (of hosts)" fails to disguise the quite distinctive category of disputation and polemic featuring question and answer, objection and refutation.[20] We have the impression of a much-compressed account of real disputes going on in the temple precincts during the period prior to and perhaps during Nehemiah's administration. Thus, skepticism about the reality of God's love and providence seems to have been occasioned by a miserable economic situation aggravated by natural disasters (Mal. 2:13–16; 3:10–11). It is answered with reference to Yahweh's predilection for Jacob over Esau manifested by current disasters visited on Edom, the traditional enemy, perhaps as a result of Kedarite Arab expansion (1:2–5).

The main point of contention, however, is neglect of the cult, manifested in offering sick animals, and failure to tithe. While both of these could be explained by the economic hardships that seem to have been endemic during the first half of the fifth century, the prevalent sense of boredom (1:13) and religious skepticism (1:2; 2:17; 3:14–15) was probably due to the disconfirmation of the hopes aroused by completion of the temple and official restoration of the cult. In view of the high expectations with which the $b^e n\hat{e}$ $hagg\hat{o}l\hat{a}$ returned to the homeland, it is ironic that Malachi should contrast the miserable state of affairs in Jerusalem with the cult of Yahweh in the Diaspora, which was even then attracting proselytes (1:11; cf. Zeph. 3:9–10; Isa. 56:3–8).

An issue of equally serious import was the tendency of Jewish men to marry non-Jewish women and take over the cults of their gods. This tendency was a major headache for the reform party during the missions of Ezra and Nehemiah (Ezra 9:1–2; 10:2–5; Neh. 10:30 [MT 10:31]; 13:23–27). Malachi, in fact, ends with a passage in which those who feared Yahweh covenanted together and had their names written in a "book of remembrance" ($s\bar{e}per$ $zikk\bar{a}r\hat{o}n$) in a way strikingly reminiscent of the covenanting that took place during Nehemiah's administration (Mal. 3:16–18; cf. Neh. 9:38–10:1 [MT 10:1–2]). While this passage does not speak explicitly of covenant making, the conferring together ($nidb^e r\hat{u}$) strongly suggests it, and the abuses against which Malachi preaches (neglect of the cult, lack of economic support for the clergy, marriage with foreign women) are the same as those whose removal Nehemiah insisted upon in a signed covenant. As the context makes clear, the "Yahweh fearers" and "servants of God" whose names appear on the document are seen to constitute the true eschatological community as distinct from the reprobates destined for destruction at the final judgment.[21]

In answer to the question "where is the God of justice?" (Mal. 2:17) the seer announced the imminent advent of a messenger, called the messenger of the covenant, who would prepare for the final temple theophany by purifying the sons of Levi and thus preparing the community for the eschatological judgment (3:1–4). The final paragraph of the book, which is also the conclusion to the prophetic corpus as a whole, identifies this eschatological precursor as Elijah who is to return from heaven before the end to reunite divided Israel (cf. Sir. 48:10). The much disputed identity of this eschatological messenger[22] will be somewhat clarified by the close parallel in Ex. 23:20:

> Behold, I send my messenger[23] before you to guard you on the way
> and to bring you to the place which I have prepared.

The possibility of reading "place" (*māqôm*) as a synonym for "temple," in keeping with well-established usage, renders this text particularly adaptable to the situation at the end of the last prophetic book. According to one interpretation (Hos. 12:13), the guardian messenger was none other than Moses himself, and Moses qua prophet. The author of Mal. 3:1 seems to have taken up this tradition, associating it with the promise of a prophet like Moses at Deut. 18:15–18 interpreted eschatologically. In this form the expectation of such a prophet of the end days persisted down to the end of the Second Temple period, and it is attested in the Qumran texts and early Christian writings.[24]

The dependence of Malachi on Deuteronomic language and thought is not restricted to this particular instance; it is pervasive throughout the book. Important Deuteronomic themes such as the love of Yahweh for Israel (Deut. 7:7–8; cf. Mal. 1:2), the father-son relationship (Deut. 1:21; 32:5–6; cf. Mal. 1:6; 2:10; 3:17), the name of Yahweh (Deut. 12:5; cf. Mal. 1:6, 11, 14; 2:2, 5; 3:16; 4:2 [MT 3:20]), the acknowledgment of Yahweh as the one God (Deut. 6:4; cf. Mal. 2:15), appear throughout. The same goes for stipulations of law to which the book refers that draw not so much, if at all, on the Priestly legislation but on the Deuteronomic lawbook; laws concerning sacrificial offerings (Mal. 1:8, 13–14, based on Deut. 15:21; 17:1) and tithing in particular (Mal. 3:10; cf. Deut. 18:1–8). The religious transgressiveness of Judah is referred to comprehensively as "abomination" (*tô'ēbâ*, Mal. 2:11), an important legal term for the Deuteronomists (e.g., Deut. 14:3; 17:1, 4; 23:17–18). Also, the distinctive Deuteronomic style is much in evidence throughout the book (e.g., Mal. 2:2–3; 3:7).

Dependence on Deuteronomy is also apparent in the author's emphasis on the priesthood as Levitical and the conspicuous absence from the book of any allusion to Aaron or Aaronite priests.[25] Over against the current corruption of the priesthood he presents an ideal portrait of Levi, drawing on features emphasized in Deuteronomy (Deut. 21:5; 33:10). We recall that Deuteronomy, unlike P, makes no distinction between priest and Levite (with the exception of the late Deut. 27:14) but assigns the same status to all as Levitical priests. The covenant with Levi to which Mal. 2:4–7 appeals does not go back to the incident of the apostasy at Baal-peor (Num. 25:10–13), as is often assumed, but to the oracle of Moses on Levi in which the latter is praised for having kept the covenant, as a result of which the sons of Levi "shall teach Jacob your ordinances and Israel your law" (Deut. 33:10). It is also possible that the author of Malachi had in mind the apostasy of Aaron at Sinai, the counteraction of Levites, and their subsequent "ordination" for divine service (Ex. 32:25–29; cf. Deut. 33:9)—especially since this account ends with a reference to the angel-messenger and a day of judgment (Ex. 32:34).

21. FROM PROPHECY TO APOCALYPTIC: FURTHER DEVELOPMENTS IN THE ISAIAN TRADITION

(See also bibliographies pp. 97–98 and 181–82.)

W.A.M. **Beuken,** "The Main Theme of Trito-Isaiah—'The Servants of Yahweh,'" *JSOT* 47 (1990): 67–87; J. **Blenkinsopp,** "Interpretation and the Tendency to Sectarianism: An Aspect of Second Temple History," in E. P. Sanders, ed., *Jewish and Christian Self-Definition,* vol. 2, *Aspects of Judaism in the Graeco-Roman Period,* Philadelphia: Fortress Press, 1981, 1–26; "A Jewish Sect in the Persian Period," *CBQ* 52 (1990): 5–20; R. P. **Carroll,** *When Prophecy Failed,* 150–56; K. **Elliger,** "Der Prophet Tritojesaja," *ZAW* 49 (1931): 112–40; P. D. **Hanson,** *The Dawn of Apocalyptic,* 32–208; W. **Kessler,** "Zur Auslegung von Jes. 56—66," *TLZ* 81 (1956): 335–38; *Gott geht es um das Ganze: Jesaja 56—66 und Jesaja 24—27 übersetzt und ausgelegt,* Stuttgart: Calwer, 1960; H.-J. **Kraus,** "Die ausgebliebene Endtheophanie: Eine Studie zu Jes. 56—66," *ZAW* 78 (1966): 317–32; F. **Maass,** "Tritojesaja?" in F. Maass, ed., *Das ferne und nahe Wort: Festschrift Leonhard Rost,* Berlin: Töpelmann, 1967, 151–63; J. **Muilenburg,** *IB* 5 (1956): 381–419, 652–773; O. **Plöger,** *Theocracy and Eschatology,* Richmond: John Knox Press, 1968 [1962[2]]; A. **Rofé,** "Isaiah 66:1–4: Judean Sects in the Persian Period as Viewed by Trito-Isaiah," A. Kort and S. Morschauer, eds., *Biblical and Related Studies Presented to Samuel Iwry,* Winona Lake, Ind.: Eisenbrauns, 1985, 205–17; B. **Schramm,** *The Opponents of Third Isaiah: Reconstructing the Cultic History of the Restoration,* Sheffield: Sheffield Academic Press, 1995; J. **Schreiner,** *Sion-Jerusalem, Jahwes Königssitz: Theologie der heiligen Stadt im Alten Testament,* Munich: Kosel, 1963; E. **Sehmsdorf,** "Studien zur Redaktionsgeschichte von Jesaja 56—66," *ZAW* 84 (1972): 517–76; S. **Sekine,** *Die Tritojesajanische Sammlung (Jes. 56—66) redaktionsgeschichtlich untersucht,* Berlin: de

Gruyter, 1989; M. **Smith,** *Palestinian Parties and Politics,* 99–147; P. A. **Smith,** *Rhetoric and Redaction in Trito-Isaiah,* Leiden: E. J. Brill, 1995; O. H. **Steck,** *Studien zu Tritojesaja,* Berlin: de Gruyter, 1991; S. **Talmon,** "The Emergence of Jewish Sectarianism in the Early Second Temple Period," in *King, Cult and Calendar in Ancient Israel,* Jerusalem: Magnes, 1986, 165–201; J. **Vermeylen,** *Du prophète Isaïe à l'apocalyptique,* 2 vols., Paris: J. Gabalda, 1977–78; C. **Westermann,** *Isaiah 40— 66: A Commentary,* Philadelphia: Westminster Press, 1969 [1966]; R. N. **Whybray,** *Isaiah 40—66,* London: Oliphants, 1975; W. **Zimmerli,** "Zur Sprache Tritojesajas," *Gottes Offenbarung,* Munich: Kaiser Verlag, 1963, 217–33.

One of the most difficult tasks of the historian of the Second Commonwealth is to assess the impact of events, international and internal to Jewish communities, on developments within these communities as these are reflected in the surviving texts. The problem of correlating event or social situation with text is especially in evidence with respect to millenarian and messianic movements and the emergence and development of sectarianism within Judaism. Until recently the conventional wisdom stayed close to the well-known description of the Jewish "philosophies" in Josephus, and therefore traced the origin of the sects no further back than the Hasmonaean period. In recent decades, however, the opinion has begun to take hold that the first emergence of sectarianism can be detected much earlier, even that it was a practically inevitable outcome of religious and social conflict in the early years of *šîbat ṣiyyôn* (the Return to Zion).

One approach to this issue, represented by Plöger's *Theocracy and Eschatology* and Hanson's *The Dawn of Apocalyptic,* assumes a correlation between a certain literary mode (eschatological or apocalyptic writing) and the social phenomenon of sect formation. It also postulates a gradual development within prophetic and allegedly related circles (Levites) in the direction of fully formed apocalyptic as it comes to paradigmatic expression in the Enoch material and Daniel. Working back from Daniel and the *asidaioi* of 1 Macc. 2:42 (cf. 1 Macc. 7:13; 2 Macc. 14:6), Plöger traced a trajectory of increasing alienation between the hierocratic leadership and pietistic groups by way of Joel 3, Zechariah 12—14, and Isaiah 24—27, the so-called Isaian apocalypse. Somewhat similar is Hanson's view of tension between anti-eschatological Zadokite clergy and a prophetic-visionary group that included disenfranchised Levites, significant differences being his discovery of what he calls proto-apocalyptic in Isaiah 40—55 and an interpretation of the greater part of Isaiah 56—66 as antipriestly polemic, one that most reviewers have found forced and unconvincing.[26]

One of the most problematic aspects of both these essays in religious history is the attempt to create a trajectory covering some four centuries with generally inadequate data. Both authors also write as if millenarian, messianic, and apocalyptic movements are peculiar to Judaism, which of course is not the case. A rather different approach, inspired by Max Weber's understanding of early Judaism, is taken by Talmon, who locates the origins of sectarianism in the passage from monocentricity to pluricentricity, in other words, from the one entity of the nation state to the different centers in the Diaspora and homeland, especially the self-segregating *bᵉnê haggôlâ*, the Judeo-Babylonian elite in the Persian province of Judah.[27] Along somewhat similar lines, Morton Smith suggested that the covenanting together of the integrationist, Yahweh-alone party under Nehemiah (Neh. 9:38–10:39 [10:1–40]), in some respects an anticipation of covenant making at Qumran, betrays indications of incipient sectarianism. Other proposals, to be considered shortly, have been made on the basis of a close reading of the final chapters of Isaiah.

We begin by assuming that certain political and social situations, not restricted to any one epoch, will tend to precipitate or encourage messianic, millenarian, or apocalyptic thinking, that this kind of thinking will tend to affect some segments of society more than others, and that it will in any case introduce tension or conflict in the society in question. The transition from Neo-Babylonian to Persian rule was such a juncture, and we have seen that it gave rise to a messianic (i.e., nationalist and royalist) movement in Jewish communities. Concentrating even before the ascendancy of Cyrus on the exiled Jehoiachin, it was transferred in time to his grandson Zerubbabel. We also noted that this movement was closely associated with plans for rebuilding both the temple and the city. Successive stages, marked by alternating hope and disillusionment, can be observed: the expectation of returning to the homeland, the laying of the foundations of the temple, the resumption of work during the revolts against Darius, and the completion of temple building a few years later. That it did not end there is suggested by the complaint made against the Jerusalemites at the beginning of Xerxes' reign (486–484 B.C.E.) noted at Ezra 4:6. The mission of Ezra, which probably took place in the seventh year of Artaxerxes I (therefore 458 B.C.E.),[28] was almost certainly contemporary with an even more serious uprising in Egypt, this time with the backing of Athenian land and sea forces (460–454). While we do not know that Palestinian Jews took part in the uprising, another letter from the satrapal authorities to the central government, complaining that the city walls were being rebuilt as a prelude to revolt, resulted in a decree forbidding the work to continue (Ezra 4:7–23).

When Nehemiah arrived on his first mission in 445 B.C.E., perhaps significantly seventy years after the completion of work on the temple, he found the walls torn down and the gates gutted by fire. We do not know whether this resulted from an overenthusiastic implementation of the rescript of Artaxerxes; from Jewish participation in the revolt of the satrap Megabyzus, which took place about this time; or from hostile action by Kedarite Arabs or other neighboring groups. When Nehemiah in his turn set about rebuilding, the action was again interpreted as a preparation for rebellion (Neh. 2:19; 6:6), and it was even alleged that he himself harbored messianic pretensions. While these allegations were probably fabricated by the opposition, and while there is no evidence that Nehemiah was a Davidite,[29] they serve to show that messianism was still a live issue and that prophets continued to play an important role in these events, as at the time of the rebuilding of the temple. Two of them, Shemaiah and Noadiah, are in fact named in our source (Neh. 6:6–14). Nothing that we are told about either Nehemiah or Ezra obliges us to believe that they were consciously anti-eschatological. We might also bear in mind that the Chronicler, who transmitted and edited this material, had absolutely no interest in highlighting messianic disturbances.

Since messianic movements find a more sympathetic hearing among the economically marginalized, it should be added that social conditions in Judah during the early Persian period appear to have been generally bad and occasionally disastrous. Heavy tribute was levied by the central government, little if any of it benefiting the provinces that were systematically drained of bullion. The resulting inflation and large-scale insolvency drove farmers off their land and benefited no one except the moneylenders. Bad as it was from the beginning, this situation got much worse after the accession of Xerxes (486), who levied taxes of a confiscatory magnitude to finance his crusade in Europe. We see from Nehemiah 5, in which the peasantry complain of economic exploitation by the elite of Babylonian origin, that both religious and economic factors had by then created a deep rift within the population of the province.[30]

Like messianic movements under Roman rule, those which we know of during the Persian period were not all of one kind. Some opted for armed rebellion with a view to regaining independence under a Davidic ruler. Others disavowed direct military action (e.g., Zech. 4:6; 9:9–10) in the belief that God would himself intervene, and that this intervention could be hastened by fidelity to the laws, proper worship, and penitential practices. While this issue of engaging in or abstaining from military action has been much discussed apropos of the Asidaeans in resistance to the Seleucids,[31] it is equally relevant for the Persian period. There were also forms of millenarian prophecy for which the Davidic ruler played either a minor role or none at all. At several points the last eleven chapters of Isaiah, for example, manifest a throughgoing eschatological perspective, yet we hear no laments for the passing of the monarchy or allusions to its future restoration.[32]

We now look briefly at these last eleven chapters of Isaiah to see whether they provide information on religious movements and groups during the Persian period. We saw in an earlier section[33] that Isaiah 56—66, conventionally designated Trito-Isaiah, is in several respects closely related to Isaiah 40—55, especially the latter part of it (chapters 49—55). One of these connecting strands links disciples with the prophetic figure designated "the Servant" who speaks and is spoken of in the last three of Duhm's "Servant Songs." It seems likely that these disciples formed a prophetic-eschatological group within the postexilic community under a leader whose voice is heard proclaiming his mission in the Spirit (Isa. 59:21; 61:1–4). It was also suggested earlier that the editorial expansions to the third and fourth of the "Servant Songs" (the relevant texts are Isa. 50:10–11; 53:1–11) provide an important literary link between the central and last part of Isaiah and, correspondingly, between the anonymous exilic "Servant" and his following.

This last section of the book opens with a remarkably liberal statement on membership in the community, assuring adherents of the Yahweh cult of foreign descent (*ben-hannēkār*), as well as eunuchs, of their good standing in the community, thus permitting them to participate in the cult on condition of observing the community's covenant requirements, especially Sabbath (Isa. 56:1–8). The same broad perspective is apparent in the final section (66:18–23) dealing with proselytism, missionary preaching, the ingathering of the nations and dispersed Jews to participate in the parousia in Jerusalem. The open admissions policy stated or implied in these two passages is at variance with the Deuteronomic law of the community (Deut. 23:2–9), as also with some aspects of the program of Ezekiel in chapters 40—48 (especially 44:7–8) and that of Ezra and Nehemiah (Ezra 9:1–4; Neh. 9:2). They may therefore have been added as "book ends" at a later date according to an editorial technique found in other biblical compositions (Westermann, 295–308). Comparison with Zech. 14:16–21, which refers to people coming to Jerusalem to celebrate the Feast of Tabernacles, and with Jonah, which pioneers a new understanding of prophecy, suggests the century between the administrations of Nehemiah and the conquests of Alexander. These passages presage later developments, including the early Christian belief that a Gentile mission must precede the parousia. The final verse (Isa. 66:24) foresees the defeat and destruction of rebellious elements in the community in a way meant to recall the opening verses of the Isaiah book and thus affirm its essential unity.[34] It brings the book to an end on such a somber note that it became customary to read it in synagogue before the preceding verse.

The first "book end" is followed by diatribe against negligent prophets ("watchmen"[35]) and rulers (shepherds) reminiscent of the gloss on Isa. 9:14 ("So Yahweh cut off from Israel both head and tail"), which identifies rulers as the head and lying prophets as the tail. Polemic is also directed against the syncretists who take part in fertility cults and sexual rites and who are contrasted with the devout who are suffering persecution. The righteous one (*ṣaddîq*) who has perished and whose death has gone unlamented (57:1) is generally given a collective interpretation but may in fact refer back to the righteous Servant (*ṣaddîq 'abdî*, 53:11) whose disciples perpetuated his message. This, in its turn, puts one in mind of Isa. 30:20–21, which seems to allude to a teacher now hidden (deceased?) who will be seen once again, whose message will be heard, and who continues to provide guidance for those who follow him.

The message of the prophetic mentor is restated in the following section (Isa. 57:14–21). The way is to be prepared for the final showdown when God, who dwells in the heavenly temple, will take up his residence with the lowly and humble, those who mourn among his people. Preparing for this consummation was doubtless understood by these "mourners" to consist in faithful observance of the covenant requirements. The theme of eschatological reversal, familiar from the Gospels, foresees that those who now mourn will rejoice when the great day dawns.[36] The section ends with a phrase repeated from 48:22—"there is no peace for the wicked"—which, though often quoted facetiously since, was intended as a verdict of eschatological judgment on the reprobates, those who reject the prophetic message.

The nucleus of the collection, containing a compendium of the eschatological teachings of the group, is found in Isaiah 60—62. Like 57:14–21, this compendium of eschatological doctrine best fits either the last years of the exile or the early years after the return (the temple and city are still in ruins, 60:13; 61:4) and shows no sign of the opposition and conflict to which these teachings were to give rise with the passing of time. It begins with an apostrophe to Jerusalem: the glory of God will appear in Zion bringing salvation to an oppressed people, those scattered abroad will return, the nations will be subject to Israel, will bring tribute and work as *Gastarbeiter* in rebuilding the city. Above all, the temple will once again be glorious and shine at the center of the earth. The prospect of a renewal of the heavens and the earth, a cosmic *apokatastasis* that comes to expression here and elsewhere in these chapters, is often taken to represent a later and more explicitly apocalyptic development (Westermann, 298–99, 363–64, 427–28). This is possible, though there is no overwhelming argument to support it, and there are good grounds for distrusting theories of development based solely on thematic arguments.

It is worth noting that throughout these last eleven chapters prophetic-eschatological faith is focused on temple and altar: the temple will be glorified, rich gifts will be brought to it, the faithful will partake of their sacrificial goods in peace in the temple precincts (Isa. 60:7, 13; 61:6; 62:9). There is therefore no opposition in principle between the bearers of this eschatological faith and the temple authorities and supporters (Hanson's Zadokite-hierocratic party) and no evidence that the former were anticultic. The seer who speaks for them in fact goes on to expound a teaching not unlike the priesthood of all the faithful. The entire people will in the last days be relieved of servile labor, as are the priests, and will receive tithes from the nations. In this way the covenant to the house of Levi will be extended to all (cf. Num. 25:10–13).

At one point in this extended apostrophe, admittedly an obscure one, we catch a glimpse of the prophetic group in whose name the anonymous seer is speaking (Isa. 62:6–7). Addressing Jerusalem, he speaks of watchmen stationed on the walls whose task is to remind Yahweh continually of his promise to liberate the city. These *mazkîrîm* (the title suggests the function of reminding God to intervene) are therefore charged with the task of intercession and prayer on behalf of the entire community, functions that have long been associated with the prophetic office.

Commentators have often noted the strongly liturgical flavor of much of the material in these chapters, but they have not always drawn the correct conclusions from this observation. It does not follow that a passage like Isa. 58:1–14 originated in a cultic setting, since the author may simply have adopted a traditional cultic form for his own purposes. The passage in question is a prophetic answer to those who could not understand how their communal fasts were failing to influence Yahweh to do something about the disastrous economic conditions then prevailing. The same conditions are presupposed in Isa. 59:1–20 in which the change of tone and the alternation between speakers (second, third, and first person) suggest that the saying has been modeled on a communal lament of a cultic nature. The same appears to be the case with the long passage 63:1–65:7, which reflects a kind of drama celebrating proleptically the event of salvation in response to the community's plea. Like several psalms (Pss. 44; 74; 77; 79) this one opens with praise, continues with confession of sin, and ends with petition. The strangely worded appeal at 63:16 seems to be saying that, though the ancestors who enjoyed God's favor are dead and gone, God is still their father and must look on the miserable condition of his children.[37] According to the traditional model a positive response would come at this point, but in this instance the divine readiness to act is thwarted by the false worship in which the prophet's contemporaries were indulging (65:1–7). The response is addressed to the people as a whole and not just to the priesthood who controlled the temple.[38] This is not to deny that the latter also indulged in such practices, but the author of these sayings, unlike Malachi, does not make a special point of polemicizing against the priesthood.

In the last two chapters we come upon the clearest indications of internal conflict, beginning with 66:5 in which an oracle of assurance is addressed to those who "tremble at his word." From this saying of an anonymous seer we learn that these "quakers" (*hᵃrēdîm*) are hated and cast out, in effect, excommunicated by their "brethren," that is, their fellow-Jews.[39] This has happened "for my name's sake" (*lᵉma'an šᵉmî*), that is, by virtue of their association with the seer who is addressing them, whom we must presume to be their leader. (Matt. 10:18, 22 is based on this text.) A further reason is implied in the taunt directed at them by their "brethren": "Let Yahweh manifest his glory that we may see your joy." The taunt is not directed at their eschatological beliefs as such, but at the typically sectarian conviction that they, and they alone, will share in the rejoicing accompanying the parousia. In an earlier passage (65:8–12) Yahweh's servants and chosen ones are contrasted with the apostates (i.e., syncretists) who worship Gad and Meni, gods of good luck, following which judgment is pronounced on the reprobates (65:13–14). The language is that of eschatological reversal familiar to readers of the Gospels. It suggests that the taunt of the "brethren" is their answer to the claim, put forward here, that the "servants" will rejoice at the coming of God to save and to judge while their opponents will be put to shame. This impression is confirmed as we go on to read that the name of these opponents will serve as a curse for Yahweh's servants, while the latter will be called by a new name, one appropriate to the new age about to dawn.[40]

The first two sayings in the last chapter (66:1–4) seem to deal with quite different matters. The first (vv. 1–2) has generally been interpreted as a rejection of the proposal to rebuild the temple, and therefore as representing a position directly opposed to Haggai and Zechariah, and the second (vv. 3–4) as a brutally explicit condemnation of animal sacrifice.[41] If, however, the one who "trembles at my word" in the first saying (v. 2) belongs to the same category as the "quakers" of verse 5 who look with eager anticipation to the parousia, an event which, if it is not to take place in the temple, is at least inseparable from it (cf. Isa. 60:7, 13; 62:9; 66:6, 20–21, 23), this interpretation can hardly be correct. It would be pertinent to refer to Solomon's prayer at the dedication of the First Temple (1 Kings 8:27–30), since it shows that support of the temple is compatible with disavowal of popular misunderstandings of its place in the religious life of the community. In these last chapters of Isaiah the idea of heaven as God's dwelling is linked with his being present to the faithful in the community: "I dwell in a high and holy place, and with the one who is broken and lowly of spirit" (57:15; cf. also 63:15 and 40:22). As for the saying about the sacrificial cult, it should be noted that the juxtaposition of legitimate with illegitimate cult acts (e.g., the slaughtering of an ox with human sacrifice) refers to acts performed by those who have chosen their own ways and delight in their idols (66:3), that is, those addicted to syncretic cults whose basic attitude vitiates even the legitimate cultic acts that they perform (cf. 57:5–13; 65:1–7, 11; 66:17).

Isaiah 66:1–5, then, testifies to a rift within Palestinian Judaism of the early Persian period involving a prophetic-eschatological minority led by a seer who understood his mission, and that of his followers, in terms of servanthood as exhibited in the life and teaching of the anonymous Servant of chapters 49; 50; and 52—53. This group described itself as "those who tremble at his word" (66:1–5), implying a reverential and fearful attention to eschatological prophecy as passed on in the exilic and postexilic "Isaian school." Other self-descriptions occurring in these chapters are "servants of Yahweh" ('*abādîm*, 65:8–9, 13–16) and "mourners" ('*abēlîm, mit'abbelîm*, 57:18; 61:2; 66:10). They appear to have been excluded at some point from participation in the temple cult, which, given the political and social importance of the cult in a temple-state like Judah, would help to explain their miserable social and economic status. While not necessarily opposed to their eschatological teaching in itself, their opponents rejected their exclusivist claims, were addicted to syncretic cults, and included at least some of the temple authorities. While the designations occurring in these chapters are not exactly analogous to Asideans, Pharisees, and Essenes, the group that appropriated them to itself marks an important point of transition from prophetic discipleship to sect.

On this issue we note the curious fact, passed over in the commentaries, that Ezra was supported in his mission by a group described as "those who tremble at the word (commandment) of the God of Israel" (Ezra 9:4; 10:3), essentially the same self-description as in Isa. 66:2, 5.[42] Shortly after his arrival in Jerusalem, Ezra was confronted with the need to do something about the regrettable addiction of Diaspora Jews to marriage with foreign women (Ezra 9:1–2). After his initial and somewhat intemperate reaction, the initiative was taken by these "quakers" (*harēdîm*, 9:4), who from then on were closely associated with Ezra in fasting, penitential prayer, and keeping vigil in preparation for the covenant, which was carried out according to their counsel (10:3).

At first sight there would appear to be nothing in common between the group so designated in Isaiah 66, which was ostracized and disowned by the majority, and Ezra's support group, which appears to constitute a kind of religious elite within the *gôlâ* community, which itself was the dominant religious, political, and social group in the province. It also seems that what caused the latter to tremble was solicitude for the law rather than prophetic revelations (Ezra 10:3). But we have seen that it is misleading to make a sharp distinction between a prophetic-eschatological orientation and strict attention to the observance of the law. We might also note in these chapters of Isaiah that mourning is associated with fasting in the same way that eschatological joy is with feasting (65:13–14, etc.), and the same association occurs where the Ezra narrative speaks of those who supported the reform program. Parallelism between "all who trembled at the words of the God of Israel because of the faithlessness of the returned exiles" (Ezra 9:4) and Ezra "mourning over the faithlessness of the exiles" (10:6) suggests that trembling and mourning are being predicated of a penitential group within the community among whose members Ezra found his principal support. We therefore have a kind of anticipation of the milieu in which the book of Daniel circulated during the Seleucid persecution: mourning, fasting, penitential prayer, intense concern with the law and with prophecy (e.g., Dan. 10:2–3).

Also, marriage with foreign women, the main problem confronting Ezra, brought with it involvement in non-Yahwistic and syncretic cults (Ezra 9:1) to which priests and Levites were by no means immune (9:1–2; cf. 10:18–24). This is precisely the situation against which the Isaian "quakers" and "servants" protested, obviously with very limited success. Confirmation is at hand in Malachi, the anonymous author of which is clearly concerned with the same issues. It was noted earlier that in Mal. 3:16–18 it is those who fear and serve God who enter into covenant, presumably to remove the abuses castigated by the prophet. We are now in a better position to suggest that the covenant alluded to in this passage in Malachi is in all probability identical with the one initiated by the *hᵃrēdîm* of Ezra 9—10.

The conclusion toward which these considerations converge, namely, that Ezra's program was accepted and enforced not only by a minority group but by one that derived its inspiration from prophetic-eschatological teaching, and that *on that basis* supported his work, will appear paradoxical in view of conventional scholarly representations of Ezra and his mission. It would imply that Ezra's mission resulted in a temporary setback for the civic and religious leadership of the community, which had compromised itself by syncretism, while bringing about a no-less-temporary enhancement of status for his prophetic support group. It would also help to explain the apparently limited success of his mission, to judge by the situation confronting Nehemiah on his arrival in Jerusalem.[43]

Whatever the later vicissitudes of this prophetic group, which owed allegiance to the person and teaching of the anonymous prophet of the exile, it presages in important ways the emergence of sects in the Roman period, not excluding early Palestinian Christianity, and it will help to contextualize the profound influence of Isaiah 40—66 on how these early Christians thought about their identity and that of Jesus. It also illustrates the social dynamics involved in the formation of prophetic subgroups and their consolidation around the teaching and memory of a charismatic figure. In these respects its significance for the future can hardly be exaggerated.

22. JERUSALEM TEMPLE PROPHECY

G. W. **Ahlström**, "Some Remarks on Prophets and Cult," in J. C. Rylaarsdam, ed., *Transitions in Biblical Scholarship*, Chicago: University of Chicago Press, 1968, 113–29; *Joel and the Temple Cult of Jerusalem*, Leiden: Brill, 1971; L. C. **Allen**, *The Books of Joel, Obadiah, Jonah, and Micah*, Grand Rapids: Eerdmans, 1976; C. T. **Begg**, "The Classical Prophets in the Chronistic History," *BZ* 32 (1988): 100–7; W. **Bellinger**, *Psalmody and Prophecy*, Sheffield: JSOT Press, 1984; T. **Chary**, *Les Prophètes et le culte à partir de l'exil*, Paris: Desclée, 1955; H. **Gese**, "Zur Geschichte der Kultsänger am zweiten Tempel," in *Abraham unser Vater: Juden und Christen im Gespräch über die Bibel*, Leiden: Brill, 1963, 222–34; A. B. **Johnson**, *The Cultic Prophet in Ancient Israel*, Cardiff: University of Wales Press, 1962; *The Cultic Prophet and Israel's Psalmody*, Cardiff: University of Wales Press, 1979; A. S. **Kapelrud**, *Joel Studies*, Uppsala: Lundequist, 1948; H.-J. **Kraus**, *Worship in Israel*, Richmond: John Knox Press, 1966, 101–12, 229–36; R. **Mosis**, *Untersuchungen zur Theologie des chronistischen Geschichtswerkes*, Freiburg: Herder, 1972; S. **Mowinckel**, *The Psalms in Israel's Worship*, vol. 2, Nashville: Abingdon Press, 1967, 53–73; J. **Newsome**, "Toward a New Understanding of the Chronicler and His Purposes," *JBL* 94 (1975): 210–12; D. L. **Petersen**, *Late Israelite Prophecy*, Missoula, Mont.: Scholars Press, 1977; W. **Prinsloo**, *The Theology of Joel*, Berlin: de Gruyter, 1985; H. H. **Rowley**, *Worship in Ancient Israel*, London: S.P.C.K., 1967, 144–75, 176–212; W. **Rudolph**, *Joel-Amos-Obadja-Jona*, Gütersloh: Gütersloher Verlagshaus Gerd Mohn, 1971; A. **Welch**, *The Work of the Chronicler*, London: Oxford University Press, 1939, 42–54; T. **Willi**, *Die Chronik als Auslegung: Untersuchungen zur literarischen Gestaltung der historischen Überlieferung Israels*, Göttingen: Vandenhoeck & Ruprecht, 1972; H.G.M. **Williamson**, *1 and 2 Chronicles*, Grand Rapids: Eerdmans, 1982; H. W. **Wolff**, *Joel and Amos*, Philadelphia: Fortress Press, 1977.

In Israel, as elsewhere in the Near East, prophets were attached to temples and carried out specific functions there including intercessory prayer and the giving of oracles, especially in critical situations. It is for this reason that prophets are so often linked with the official priesthood in prophetic diatribe (e.g., Jer. 23:11). Much prophetic activity went on in temples, and even prophetic figures who were not on the temple staff would have more easily found an audience in the temple precincts (e.g., Amos 7:10–17; Jer. 7:1–8:3; 36:4–8). We have seen that one or other of the canonical prophets may have belonged to this cult category, at least initially, but it does not follow that prophets who chose to address their public in a temple did so as cult functionaries. At the literary level, the existence of temple prophecy has been deduced from what appear to be prophetic oracles embedded in psalms (e.g., Pss. 20:8; 28:6; 60:6; 81:5; 110:1) as well as psalms embedded in prophetic books, for example, Habakkuk and Jonah.

One of the most important aspects of the transformation of Israelite prophecy after the loss of national independence was its reabsorption into the cult. The Priestly source (P), which comes from this period of transition and reflects a concern for the reestablishment of genuine worship, provides some interesting clues to this process. During the wilderness period, which for P served a paradigmatic function, divine communications were received in the mobile sanctuary where Moses heard the voice of God addressing him from above the "mercy seat" (Ex. 25:22; Num. 7:89). While this *theologoumenon* still preserves something of the ancient oracle tent, it also anticipates the *bat qôl* (heavenly voice), later to serve as a substitute or surrogate for prophecy, now considered a thing of the past.[44] The transmission of prophetic charisma, the clearest illustration of which is the succession of Elisha to Elijah, also undergoes a transformation in the worldview of the priest-theologians. According to P the transference of leadership charisma from Moses to Joshua is effected by an act comparable to the ordination of priests. In Num. 27:15–23 (P) we note that Joshua possesses the spirit before the laying on of hands, but in Deut. 34:9, from a later priestly hand, he is full of spirit by virtue of the act—an interesting case of progress toward the institutionalizing of charisma.[45] We also observe how in the P narrative guidance in the wilderness is effected not by means of the prophetic word but by the fire and cloud hovering over the sanctuary (Num. 9:15–23, etc.). According to the Priestly version of Moses' call, finally, we see that Aaron acts as his *nābî'*, and does so in such a way as to suggest that the prophetic task of confronting the king had passed by default to the eponym of the priesthood (Ex. 7:1).

This shift in the location and consequent understanding of prophecy is apparent in the early Persian period with the predominance of liturgical forms and cultic concerns in Haggai, Zechariah 1—8, Isaiah 56—66, and Malachi. It is also much in evidence in the preaching of a certain Joel ben-Pethuel to the congregation, which included farmers and vintners, on the occasion of a national crisis. The four swarms of locusts, each with its own specialized way of wreaking havoc (Joel 1:4), are often read as metaphoric for successive military invasions (1:6–7), but it seems more likely that a devasting plague of locusts is being appropriately described in military terms. Such sporadic ecological disasters have been a familiar feature of life in the Levant from the earliest times to the recent past. The setting is Judah in the Persian period, and since the author is greatly concerned with the impact of the disaster on the temple economy (1:9–10, 13, 16; 2:14), some time after 515 B.C.E.[46] The problem of dating the book as a whole is compounded by the fact that the plague was read at a later time as a harbinger of the last days and the consummation of history (2:28–3:21 [MT 3:1–4:21]). Leaving this eschatological expansion aside for the moment, we have, if not the outline, at least the main elements of a penitential liturgy in which the cult prophet played an important role.

The opening address to the congregation (1:2–12) concludes with a call to the priests to convoke a solemn service of fasting and repentance (1:13–18) to which the people were summoned by the blowing of the shofar (2:1, 15). There follow the prayer of petition (1:19–20) and the call to fast and repent (2:1–17), and the liturgical action ends with an oracle of assurance delivered by the prophet (2:18–27). As in the psalms referred to earlier, this oracle of well-being (beginning 2:19) marks the peripeteia, the turning point in the liturgical act. In view of the many verbal and thematic contacts of Joel with Amos (which may help to explain the place of Joel in the Dodekapropheton), it is worth noting that the first two visions of Amos (7:1–6) also deal with locusts and drought, often using the same language, and that these disasters also are averted by prophetic intercession. We are not told, and we cannot simply assume, that this function was discharged by Amos in the course of a cultic act. But by the time of Joel there can be no doubt that the averting of disaster could be achieved, if at all, only by such a cult act in which the entire community participated. For Joel, whose criticism of his contemporaries is mild in comparison with that of Amos (1:5; 2:12), the current threat to the economic existence of the community can be turned aside only by means of acts of worship performed in the temple, acts in which the prophet seems to have played a leading role.

In the course of our study we often have had occasion to regret the absence of usable source material because of the Palestinian climate, the decision of the final editors, or the vagaries of archaeology. We can only imagine how different our image of the past would be had we been able to recover the archives of the Jerusalem temple. In the absence of such a direct source of information on the Second Temple, and of other reliable contemporary source material prior to the Herodian period, we have to rely almost exclusively on the work of the Chronicler (1 and 2 Chronicles with Ezra-Nehemiah), which represents the final stage of a rewriting of the history from the perspective of the Jerusalem cult-community. The dating of this work is one of the many issues in Second Temple studies on which there is no consensus and no likelihood of reaching one in the foreseeable future. On the assumption that it takes in the activity of Ezra and Nehemiah, it could not very well have appeared in its final form earlier than the first decades of the fourth century B.C.E., and could be later.[47]

Using the technique of genealogical linkage, much favored by P, the author traces the history of the postexilic cult community to the beginnings of history (1 Chronicles 1—9), beginning the actual narrative with the death of Saul and the accession of David. For the Chronicler it was David rather than Moses who founded the cultic establishment and the different orders of Levites, though this act had to be repeated more than once throughout a long history marked by frequent apostasy (1 Chron. 23:2–32; 2 Chron. 29:25–30; 31:2; Ezra 6:18). The author gives pride of place to the guilds of temple musicians who are described as founded by David in his capacity as inspired musician and as themselves discharging their functions by virtue of prophetic inspiration (1 Chron. 25:1–8). It was probably among these temple musicians that the tradition of a prophetic David originated. This tradition is reflected in the "last words of David" (2 Sam. 23:1–7), added to the story at a late date, and presented as oracular and therefore as the product of divine revelation. The Qumran Psalms scroll (11QPs[a]) attributes to him 4,050 hymns composed by virtue of his prophetic gift (*n^{e}bû'â*),[48] and among the first Christians the psalms of David were read as predictive of Christ and the church (e.g., Acts 1:16; 2:25–31, 34).

For the Chronicler, then, the composition and rendition of liturgical music was a form of prophecy. Prophecy and poetry coalesce in many ancient cultures; in Israel they came together in the act of worship. It is tempting to think of the "prophetic" Levitical musicians of the Second Temple as the descendants in direct line of the cult prophets of the First Temple, but the linkage is tenuous. (One indication may be the substitution of "Levites," meaning "Levitical musicians" in 2 Chron. 34:30 for "prophets" in 2 Kings 23:2.) There are indications that these musicians or poets (*m^{e}šor^{e}rîm*, 1 Chron. 15:16, 27; 2 Chron. 5:12–13; 35:15) achieved a progressively more important place in the hierarchy of the Second Temple, in which process the attribution of prophetic gifts no doubt played a legitimating role. Whatever their origin, they also usurped the oracular function of earlier cult prophecy, discharging this task not only in the temple but on the battlefield (2 Chron. 20:13–23), reminiscent of the role of Levites in the Qumran War Scroll (1QM). One of the Levitical leaders, Chenaniah by name, has a title that seems to connote a role both musical and oracular (1 Chron. 15:22, 27).[49]

The bringing of liturgical music under the rubric of prophecy, in liturgies in which God was acknowledged, thanked, and praised, continued into the Roman period and beyond. Not only is it well represented in early Christianity and the Qumran community, but its traces can be detected in Jewish liturgical practice long after the destruction of the Second Temple.[50]

Before leaving this subject, we note another aspect of the reinterpretation of prophecy in the Chronicler's work, namely, the transformation of the preexilic prophets into historians. We see this in the author's allusion to chronicles attributed to Samuel, Nathan, Isaiah, and other prophetic figures, some of them otherwise unattested (1 Chron. 7:41; 16:4; 23:5, 30; 2 Chron. 5:13; 7:6; 8:14). This idea of prophetic historiography also continued down into the Roman period, is exploited by Josephus,[51] and explains the inclusion of the history under the rubric of Former Prophets in the Hebrew Bible.

23. THE ESCHATOLOGICAL
REINTERPRETATION OF PROPHECY

G. W. **Anderson,** "Isaiah 24—27 Reconsidered," *SVT* 9 (1963): 118–26; R. E. **Clements,** *Isaiah 1—39,* Grand Rapids: Eerdmans, 1981, 196–224; R. J. **Coggins,** "The Problem of Isaiah 24—27," *ExpT* 90 (1979): 328–33; F. M. **Cross,** *Canaanite Myth and Hebrew Epic,* Cambridge, Mass.: Harvard University Press, 1973, 343–46; M. **Delcor,** "Les Sources du Deutero-Zacharie et ses procédés d'emprunt," *RB* 59 (1952): 385–411; H. **Gese,** "Anfang und Ende der Apokalyptik dargestellt am Sacharjabuch," *ZTK* 70 (1973): 20–49; P. D. **Hanson,** "Jewish Apocalyptic Against Its Near-Eastern Environment," *RB* 78 (1971): 31–58; "Zechariah 9 and the Recapitulation of an Ancient Ritual Pattern," *JBL* 92 (1973): 37–59; D. G. **Johnson,** *From Chaos to Restoration: An Integrative Reading of Isaiah 24—27,* Sheffield: JSOT Press, 1988; O. **Kaiser,** *Isaiah 13—39: A Commentary,* Philadelphia: Westminster Press, 1974 [1973], 173–233; M. A. **Knibb,** "Prophecy and the Emergence of the Jewish Apocalypses," in R. Coggins et al., *Israel's Prophetic Tradition,* 155–80; K. J. **Larkin,** *The Eschatology of Second Zechariah: A Study of the Formation of a Mantological Wisdom Anthology,* Kampen: Kok Pharos, 1994; W. R. **Millar,** *Isaiah 24—27 and the Origin of Apocalyptic,* Missoula, Mont.: Scholars Press, 1976; R. **North,** "Prophecy to Apocalyptic via Zechariah," *SVT* 22 (1972): 47–72; B. **Otzen,** "Traditions and Structures of Isaiah 24—27," *VT* 24 (1974): 196–206; R. F. **Person,** *Second Zechariah and the Deuteronomic School,* Sheffield: JSOT Press, 1993; D. L. **Pe-**

tersen, *Late Israelite Prophecy,* 1—54; O. **Plöger**, *Theocracy and Eschatology,* Richmond: John Knox Press, 1968; "Prophetisches Erbe in den Sekten des frühen Judentums," *TLZ* 79 (1954): 291–96; C. **Rowland,** *The Open Heaven,* London: S.P.C.K., 1982, 193–213; W. **Rudolph,** *Haggai-Sacharja 1–8—Sacharja 9–14—Maleachi,* Gütersloh: Gütersloher Verlagshaus-Gerd Mohn, 1976, 159–246; M. **Saebo,** *Sacharja 9—14,* Neukirchen-Vluyn: Neukirchener Verlag, 1969; O. **Steck,** "Das Problem theologischer Strömungen in nachexilischer Zeit," *EvTh* 28 (1968): 447–48; M. A. **Sweeney,** "Textual Citations in Isaiah 24—27: Towards an Understanding of the Redactional Function of Chapters 24—27 in the Book of Isaiah," *JBL* 107 (1988): 39–52; J. **Vermeylen,** "La Composition littéraire de l'apocalypse d'Isaïe," *ETL* 50 (1974): 5–38; H. **Wildberger,** *Jesaja 2,* Neukirchen-Vluyn: Neukirchener Verlag, 1978, 885–1026; H.-W. **Wolff,** *Joel and Amos,* 57–86.

Thus far in the present section we have noted some aspects of the transformation that prophecy underwent after the loss of national independence and royal patronage. If prophetic activity was to continue in the basically different social and political circumstances obtaining in the postdisaster period, it would necessarily be of a different kind and would be perceived differently among the survivors of the disaster. Increasing reference to former prophets, occasional laments for the absence of prophetic guidance and, not least, the well-attested practice of adapting earlier prophetic sayings to new situations—for example, in the vision reports of Zechariah 1—8—are symptomatic of this new situation. Once prophecies delivered in an earlier epoch were available in writing, the emphasis would tend to be less on direct inspired utterance and more on the inspired interpretation of past prophecy. Contact with the scribal and intellectual tradition of Mesopotamia may have encouraged this shift in emphasis, but the main influence was the greatly increased insistence on law and the Deuteronomic redefinition of the prophetic role discussed earlier. What it amounted to was a much stronger conviction that, at least in the normal course of events, God does not communicate directly but has revealed his will and purpose in past communications whose bearing on the present situation remains to be elucidated.

With this shift in emphasis the role of biblical interpretation, as understood in Judaism and Christianity, began to be decisive for the self-understanding of the community in which the writings were preserved and passed on. And since texts can be interpreted in more than one way, control of this interpretative function was also a powerful political factor in defining the "redemptive media" available within the community and controlling access to them. As the history of the Second Commonwealth unfolds, we detect on the one hand a tendency toward the institutionalization of exegesis that, in the case that concerns us here, reached classical formulation in the view of the prophets as tradents of the law. On the other hand, however, there were those who, while not necessarily denying them this function, chose to emphasize the projection through the prophetic role of a future reality quite different from the present.

It may still be necessary to add that this transformation should not be viewed—as it has been routinely in Christian scholarship—as symptomatic of religious decline, the "drying up of inspiration" (whatever that means), or the triumph of the letter over the spirit. One could illustrate this pejorative view of postexilic developments from any number of commentators from Wellhausen down to the present. Alfred Lods, for example, in a work bearing the significant title *The Prophets and the Rise of Judaism,* comments that "the fate of prophecy was sealed when, side by side with the living word of the messenger of Yahweh, there appeared a new authority, that of the written word." At this point he was speaking about developments in late seventh-century Judah; but as we move into the Second Temple period we are invited to note how "the inward flame which had inspired the movement until now is growing dim, and may soon be extinguished."[52] Tension between "the written word" and oral communications delivered to prophets is certainly a feature of religious life beginning in the last decades of the kingdom of Judah, but it is not very helpful to speak of prophetic inspiration dying out without explaining why it happened then and not at some other time. It is also misleading to assume that the preexilic canonical prophets represent the apogee of religious development so that whatever followed would inevitably be construed as a declension from that high ideal. In one sense, the change in the forms and understanding of prophecy in the Second Commonwealth resulted from the failure of earlier prophecy to solve certain crucial problems, especially the problem of discriminating between true and false prophecy. It also became increasingly apparent that prophecy is incapable of providing a firm basis for the ongoing life of the community. And finally, it is not self-evident that the consolidation of scribalism in the Second Temple period, with the emergence of an intellectual and theological tradition into which prophecy was inevitably drawn, must be viewed as a symptom of decline.

Simply put, the problem for those who preserved these texts and took them seriously was: How can the word of God addressed to our ancestors who lived in a different age and faced different problems become a word of God for us today? Since, as far as we know, prophetic books did not generate commentaries before the Roman period (the earliest extant come from Qumran), we have to reconstruct the solutions to this problem from the editorial history of the texts themselves. We have noted at more than one point in our study the difficulties attending this task of reconstruction, for the process of editing began long before the time of

which we are speaking. General doctrinaire theories (e.g., a prosodic ty-
pology rigidly applied) and general thematic treatments (e.g., the degree of mythological over against historical reference) are perhaps less
likely to succeed than a strategy of starting out from the clearest, most
concrete and specific indications. These would include glosses, texts that
manifest an explicit intent of expanding or commenting on a previous
passage (e.g., Isa. 16:13–14a as updating the oracle on Moab immediately preceding), or those in which certain regularly recurring formal
and literary features strongly suggest such an intent. By prudent use of
such an approach we may hope to fill in some of the many gaps in our
knowledge of the editorial history of prophetic books, and therefore of
the religious history of the Jewish community in the Persian and early
Hellenistic periods.

Since constraints of space dictate a highly selective approach to this
task, we will limit ourselves in this section to a brief look at Joel 2:28–3:21
(3—4), Zechariah 9—14, and certain sections of the book of Isaiah, especially Isaiah 24—27, the so-called Isaian apocalypse.

In dealing earlier in this chapter with the preaching of Joel ben-
Pethuel, we noted that a later hand had transformed the plague of locusts into a proleptic symbol of final judgment to take place on the Day
of Yahweh. Many commentators therefore assume that even in the first
part of this booklet all references to the Day (Joel 1:15; 2:1b–2a, 11b)
are editorial. While this is certainly possible, it is by no means certain because, whatever its origin, the idea of the Day of Yahweh was a familiar
topos in preexilic prophecy (e.g., Amos 5:18–20; 8:9–14; Zeph. 1:14–18).
The second part of the book of Joel begins with a prediction that in the
latter days the Spirit will be poured out on the entire community (this is
the sense of the phrase "all flesh"), resulting in an eruption of prophetic
activity (Joel 2:28–29 [MT 3:1–2]). The closest parallels to this saying
about the creative and renewing power of the divine Spirit are to be
found in the address of Ezekiel, or one of his disciples, to a defeated and
dispirited people in exile (Ezek. 39:29; 36:26; 37:1–14). But it is only
here, in Joel, that the Spirit is spoken of as the source of prophetic activity, though there is perhaps more than an echo of the words of Moses
to Joshua in the episode, discussed earlier, of the ordination of elders at
the wilderness sanctuary: "Would that all Yahweh's people were
prophets, that Yahweh would put his spirit upon them!" (Num. 11:29).
The distinguishing factor is that an age is anticipated in which the Spirit
will endow not just designated individuals but the entire community, or
at least those in the community whose profession of faith matched that
of the anonymous seer. In the course of time both rabbinic Judaism (for
which the Holy Spirit is synonymous with the spirit of prophecy) and

early Christianity (Acts 2:16–21) would find in this passage an essential aspect of eschatological and messianic faith.

The following passage (Joel 2:30–32 [MT 3:3–5]), which goes on to speak of a cosmic upheaval, seems to be related to an earlier saying (2:10) about the effect of divine judgment on the earth and the heavenly bodies. Here, however, these cosmic events are reinterpreted as signs of the final judgment, a familiar representation in Jewish and early Christian apocalyptic. The effect of the final judgment will be to reveal the true Israel, those who call on the name of Yahweh or, in other words, those who share the writer's eschatological faith. It is important to note that in support of this belief the seer appeals to the authority of a prophetic word spoken in the past:

> On Mount Zion and in Jerusalem there will be a remnant which escapes, as Yahweh has said. (Joel 2:32)

The reference may be to Obadiah 17, where this assertion occurs in practically identical form. Much the same idea is expressed in Isa. 4:2–6, where the term "escaped remnant" ($p^e l\bar{e}t\hat{a}$) is also used, as it is elsewhere in the book of Isaiah (10:20; 37:31–32). The fuller description that follows of the judgment of the nations in the valley of Jehoshaphat (Joel 3:1–3 [MT 4:1–3]), to be preceded by the final showdown in Jerusalem (3:9–21 [MT 4:9–21]), also draws its inspiration from prophetic sources, especially the prophecy of Obadiah and the apocalyptic battle against the legendary Gog as described in Ezekiel 38—39. The oracle against Phoenician and Philistine cities, which refers to trading in Jewish slaves with the Greeks (Joel 3:4–8 [MT 4:4–8]), is often identified as a still later insertion from the time of the Diadochoi (successors of Alexander the Great), suggested by the general allusion to the slave trade at 3:3. This is probably correct, since it is only here that we have a specific political reference of any kind in the book.[53]

The difficulty of dating editorial expansions of prophetic books is well illustrated by the material we have just considered. Apart from the reference to the Greeks, which is not all that helpful and in any case applies only to the passage in which it occurs (Joel 3:4–8 [MT 4:4–8]), there are no datable historical allusions, despite the intensely political character of this kind of writing and the general probability that it was precipitated by real historical crises. All we can say is that the nucleus of the book has been expanded by a commentator closely familiar with the prophetic heritage, whose intent was to bring out more clearly its eschatological meaning. We would probably not be far wrong in dating the bulk of this material to the last century of Persian rule and the saying directed at the Philistine and Phoenician cities to the century that followed.[54]

The same problem confronts the reader of Zechariah 9—14 and is even more frustrating, since many of the sayings in this collection do refer to quite specific but also unidentifiable historical events. We recall that Zechariah chapters 9—11 and 12—14 and Malachi comprise the final three anonymous sections of the prophetic compilation, all introduced in the same way and of roughly equal length; and that the expedient of attaching the first two of these to Zechariah and giving the last a fictitious title had the purpose of rounding off the prophetic collection at twelve. This in itself would indicate an important stage in the formation of the prophetic corpus.

The first of these three "appendices" opens with an oracle of a Jewish seer against the cities of Phoenicia and Philistia (Zech. 9:1–8). The opening verse (9:1) is textually obscure, but if it is read as a title, the Masoretic text would suggest a location in Syria ("the word of Yahweh is in the land of Hadrach, and Damascus is its resting place"). While the language of this first section is not specific enough to enable us to pin down the historical reference, especially since the Phoenician and Philistine cities are linked elsewhere in prophetic diatribe (Amos 1:3–10; Joel 3:4 [MT 4:4]), the best fit would be with the campaigns of Alexander between the battle of Issus (333) and the conquest of Egypt, the highlights of which were the subjugation of Tyre and Gaza after lengthy sieges. If this is so, we would have an indication of the initial response of Jewish communities to the Macedonian conqueror: satisfaction at the discomfiting of traditional enemies mixed with apprehension for the fate of Jerusalem. In the event, Alexander continued on down the coastal plain delayed only by the five-month siege of Gaza whose king actually did perish (Zech. 9:5). Stories about Alexander's stopover in Jerusalem and encounter with Jaddua the high priest, picked up or invented by Josephus and reported in the Talmud, are evidently legendary.[55]

The apostrophe to Zion, which follows on quite naturally (Zech. 9:9–10), is of a type familiar to the tradition of prophetic discourse (cf. Zeph. 3:14–20). It proclaims the advent of the Davidic messiah who will bring war to an end, and it does so by recalling the ancient oracle of Judah pronounced by Jacob on his deathbed (Gen. 49:8–12). While it is often taken to be a later insertion, it fits in equally well by way of contrast with the Macedonian world conqueror and may therefore be seen as preparing for the much starker contrast in Daniel's vision between the beasts and the One in Human Form. The allusion to the setting free of Jewish prisoners and the promise of double recompense, modeled on the language of Second Isaiah (Isa. 40:1–2), leads to a prediction of victory over the Greeks (Zech. 9:13), which is probably a gloss, perhaps from as late as the struggle with the Seleucid rulers. The fiercely confident tone of the poem following (Zech. 10:3–12), which predicts ruin on foreign rulers, military victory for a reunited Jewish people, and the repatriation of their dispersed compatriots, provides no sure clue to its origin unless "Egypt" and "Assyria" are understood as code names for the Ptolemaic and Seleucid empires, respectively. The following short poem (11:1–3), which is a mock lament on the defeat or death of foreign rulers, also defies any attempt to place it historically.

Nowhere is the problem of finding historical coordinates more in evidence than in the extended and detailed narrative about the hiring of a shepherd, a narrative that appears to be an allegorization of a prophetic-symbolic action (Zech. 11:4–16).[56] The literary model is clearly Ezek. 37:15–28, the account of a symbolic mime involving sticks marked with the names Judah and Ephraim in which the prophet acts out the role of the Davidic king who is to unite them. In the Zechariah passage the seer is invited to take responsibility for a flock destined to be butchered, meaning presumably to rule over a people in place of their own corrupt leaders who allow them to be bought and sold—whether metaphorically or with reference to the slave trade is uncertain. He accepts the commission and carries it out with the help of two staffs called Noam (Favor) and Hoblim (Union), and in doing so disposes of three of their rulers, presumably the ones who were oppressing them. But then, for reasons unstated, he annuls the agreements into which he had entered with the foreign rulers who had put him in power. The contemptible sum he receives as payment for his trouble (equaling the monetary value of a slave, Ex. 21:32) ends up in the temple treasury, and the last act of the mimetic drama presages a successor who will resume the previous pattern of oppressive and predatory rule.

This strangest and most obscure of all prophetic texts continues to defy attempts to crack its narrative code. The most probable hypothesis is that it mirrors an episode in the history of Second Temple Judaism, but its details, sharply etched as they are, escape us. The allusion to the ties between Judah and Israel (11:14) brings to mind the troubled relations between the province of Judah and the Jews of the Samaria region during the Persian and early Hellenistic periods (cf. Ezek. 37:15–28 on which the metaphor is based), and there may be a hidden pointer in the same direction in the seer's reference to the sheep dealers "who were watching me" (*haššōmᵉrîm 'otî*, 11:11), since the participle can also be translated "Samarians."[57] While the long history of estrangement between Jews in the province of Judah and those in the region of Samaria goes back to the early days of the return from exile, indeed to the settlement of foreign elements in the territory of the central and northern tribes by Assyria, it entered a new phase with the establishment of a Macedonian colony in Samaria following on the unsuccessful rebellion of 332 B.C.E. The political and religious differences between Jerusalem and the supporters of the sanctuary at Gerizim continued to be an important factor in the history of the country down into Hasmonaean times, and the present narrative no doubt reflects an episode in that history about which we are entirely in the dark.[58]

The second section (Zechariah 12—14) is rather different in some important respects. For one thing it is entirely in prose, with the exception of 13:7–9, whereas the previous section is mostly in verse. It no longer deals with Judean-Samaritan relations but with matters concerning the Jerusalem community, and it draws largely for inspiration on Ezekiel, as with the fountain and the river flowing from Jerusalem (Zech. 13:1 and 14:8; cf. Ezek. 47:1–12). This last section of the book is composed for the most part of some sixteen short eschatological *logia* beginning with the formula "on that day" (*bayyôm hahû*`), which appears only once (9:16) in the previous section. This formula provides us with a distinct possibility of tracing a line of development in the editorial history of prophetic books. The phrase is, of course, used in all kinds of contexts, sometimes with reference to a past event (e.g., Jer. 39:16; Ezek. 20:6), but it also occurs throughout the prophetic books with reference to a particular event of judgment or salvation in the future. Among these instances, which are of different kinds, there is a type consisting in a short prose paragraph with the phrase at the beginning (in other types it can be in the middle or at the end) serving as commentary or *pešer* on an earlier, generally immediately preceding passage, and extending the horizon of this text into the future. It seems to have been especially favored by commentators on Isaiah, whether the perspective is merely futuristic (e.g., the series appended to an oracle on Tyre [Isa. 23:1–12] and one on Egypt [Isa. 19:1–15]) or eschatological in the commonly accepted sense of that term (e.g., Isa. 10:20–23; 11:10–11; 27:12–13). In some few instances (Isa. 4:2–6; 17:7–9; 27:1) there is no apparent link with the immediate context, at least not in the sense of text followed by commentary, and in these cases we are close to the kind of series we have identified in Zechariah 12—14. After the final redaction of the prophetic corpus around the beginning of the second century B.C.E. this process could no longer be incorporated into the text but was carried on in commentaries of which the earliest examples known to us are the Qumran *pešārîm* on prophetic books referred to earlier.

From all these "on that day" passages one could put together quite a compendium of eschatological teaching emanating from sages and seers of the Second Temple period, teaching that is backed by the authority of other prophetic words spoken in the past. The collection of these sayings in Zechariah 12—14 takes in a vast futuristic panorama: the destruction of foreign powers hostile to Israel; the exemption from judgment of a remnant that will join the Yahweh cult and take part in the great pilgrim feast of Sukkot; the preeminence of Jerusalem, where holiness will extend even to the harness bells on the horses; purification from sin and the end of idolatry; the restoration of the Davidic dynasty; theophany on the Mount of Olives ushering in an age of prosperity and fertility, etc. The only negative elements disturbing this eschatological fantasy are, first, the prospect of a terrible final battle that only a remnant, variously estimated at a third (Zech. 13:7–9) or a half (14:2), will survive, and second, a subdued note of tension between the city itself and the people of Judah (12:7; 14:14).

The passage describing mourning rites for a public figure in whose death the people had somehow been implicated (12:10–14) has given rise to a wide range of hypotheses from King Josiah (d. 609 B.C.E.) to Simon Maccabee (d. 134 B.C.E.).[59] It would be tempting to opt for the former since the text mentions the plain of Megiddo where Josiah met his death (2 Kings 23:29–30), and we know from 2 Chron. 35:25 that he was still being lamented at least as late as the fourth century. But since we have no evidence that his own people were implicated in his death, the temptation should probably be set aside. Simon is almost certainly too late, as is also a more popular candidate, Onias the high priest slain in 170 B.C.E. We have to bear in mind that names from the second century have been proposed only because we know this period quite well, whereas we know practically nothing of the internal history of the community during the fourth and third centuries. It is therefore an open question whether this passage refers to an unknown figure of that unknown period: either a martyred prophet or, more probably, given the allusions to the house of David, a casualty of Judean messianism, which we have no reason to believe died out after the time of Nehemiah. It is hardly surprising if early Christian preaching, especially touching the death of Jesus, has drawn so often on these chapters.

As we look back over these additions to Joel and Zechariah we cannot help asking who produced this work of commentary. We conclude that they drew their inspiration from written prophecy and claimed for themselves an inspiration comparable to that of the prophets. That is to say, they believed that God continued to speak through them not so much by virtue of direct inspiration as by means of their insight into the meaning of existing prophetic texts. At the same time, they dissociated themselves from contemporary prophetic practitioners whom they tended to dismiss together with such suspect forms of mediation as teraphim, divination, and dream interpretation (Zech. 10:2). In one extraordinary passage (Zech. 13:2–6) the contemporary profession of the *nābî'* has, in the opinion of the writer, sunk so low that the prophet will go to any lengths to hide his calling. He will not advertise his profession by donning prophetic garb or exhibiting self-inflicted lacerations (cf. 1 Kings 18:28; 20:35–43), perhaps even preferring to be mistaken for a male prostitute. In this view the professional prophet is, almost by definition, a purveyor of falsity, and therefore subject to the death penalty following Deut. 13:1–5 and 18:20.

These continuators of the old protest prophecy would therefore hardly have thought or spoken of themselves as *nᵉbî'îm*, and they probably thought of genuine prophecy as a phenomenon belonging either to the past or to the new age that God was even then preparing to usher in. It is possible, but no more, that they were in some way associated with the temple and its personnel; at least there is no evidence of alienation from the temple establishment. It is also possible, even probable, that this kind of work emanated from associations or conventicles similar to the disciples of the Isaian Servant discussed earlier, and was not entirely dissimilar from the associations and sects explicitly attested in the Greco-Roman period. In the absence of information we can say no more than this.

The Isaiah scroll itself testifies to prophecy written down for later generations:

> Now go, write it on a tablet,
>   inscribe it in a book
> that it may be for a later time,
>   as a witness for ever
> (Isa. 30:8)

—a perspective that will no doubt help to explain the vast expansion of the original core of Isaian sayings. It was understood that these sayings were not written just for the contemporaries of the prophet:

> In that day the deaf shall hear
>   the words of a book,
> and out of their gloom and darkness
>   the eyes of the blind shall see.
> (Isa. 29:18)

It was equally clear, however, that it required interpretation, but to decode it one had to have the key:

> And the vision of all this has become to you like the words of a book that is sealed. When they give it to one who can read, saying, "Read this," he says, "I cannot, for it is sealed." And when they give the book to one who cannot read, saying, "Read this," he says, "I don't know how to read." (Isa. 29:11–12)

One suspects that this cryptic saying has to do with the kind of insight required to read prophecy and, more specifically, the eschatological hermeneutic that provides the key to its understanding according to the schools that edited the scroll in the latter part of the Second Temple period. It is at least relevant to note that it follows a passage in verse in which the prophets are denounced as blind, drunk, and asleep; in other words, incapable of understanding. Once again, therefore, we have the contrast between those who called themselves prophets and those who believed that they had been designated to mediate the word of God through their interpretation of what God had spoken in the past.

In some Isaian texts the intent to expand an earlier saying, or to add to an existing saying a new saying to meet the different circumstances of the present, is explicitly stated. Such is the long oracle against Moab (Isa. 15:1- 16:12) to which a later hand has added the comment:

> This is the word which Yahweh spoke concerning Moab in the past.
> But now Yahweh says . . . (Isa. 16:13–14a)

—and there follows another oracle about Moab. Almost certainly the same hand has brought up to date the oracle dealing with Arabian tribes (Isa. 21:13–15) with a brief prediction beginning, "For thus Yahweh said to me" (vv. 16–17). Elsewhere it is fairly clear, even if not explicitly announced, that an earlier saying is being reinterpreted. The poem about the pleasant vineyard in the so-called Isaian apocalypse (27:2–5), for example, is clearly related to the song of the vineyard in the first part of the book (5:1–7), and is related as commentary to text.

The regular pattern, discussed earlier, of prose commentary introduced with the formulaic "on that day" points in the same direction. A good example of adapting, recycling, bringing up to date by successive commentary is the oracle against Shebna, a high official of Hezekiah (22:15–19). A first extension (vv. 20–24) reflects his replacement by a certain Eliakim, and when the latter also failed to live up to expectations, a further installment was called for (v. 25). Other examples of serial commentary would be Isaiah's prediction to King Ahaz about a young woman bearing a son to be called Immanuel (Isa. 7:10–17 plus 18–25) and the series of five additions to the oracle about Egypt (Isa. 19:1–15 plus 16–25) that take us down into the Hellenistic period. Such adjustments were especially in order with the oracles against foreign nations, occasioned by the need to respond to the changing international scene. An oracle against Sidon (23:1–14), for example, has been expanded to take in the sister city of Tyre after the latter's punishment at the hands of Artaxerxes III (343) and Alexander (332). The rehabilitation of Tyre about seventy years later by Ptolemy II called for a further extension, this time in the light of the eschatological teaching about the subjection of the nations to Israel (23:15–18).

To the extent that it is possible, the reconstruction of the editorial history must start out from concrete and specific features in the text illustrated by the examples given. Advantage should also be taken of parallels where they occur (e.g., Isa. 2:2–5 and its parallel at Micah 4:1–4), similarity in language and theme with passages known to be of later date than the eighth century (e.g., Isa. 14:1–2 compared with Zech. 8:20–22), and standard ways of introducing glosses (e.g., Isa. 6:13; 9:15). The conclusion that emerges from this kind of analysis is that the original nucleus of Isaiah has been interpreted and expanded so as to transform the book into a manual of eschatological teaching. Nowhere is this more in evidence than in chapters 24—27, the so-called Isaian apocalypse.

We saw earlier that the standard breakdown of the Isaiah scroll (chapters 1—39; 40—55; 56—66) is deceptive if it gives the impression of a simple sequence of preexilic, exilic, and postexilic. If we exclude the biographical supplement (chapters 36—39) much of the first part is editorial, and a significant proportion of it is clearly postexilic. This later material, moreover, includes some rather long sections; for example, most of the oracles against foreign nations (chapters 13—23) and the eschatological finale (chapters 33—35). While forming what looks like an independent booklet, chapters 24—27 have been positioned as a supplement to the oracles against the nations. Since the only concrete historical allusion in this section is to Moab (25:10–12), it has even been suggested that the point of departure for the so-called Isaian apocalypse was this passage that served as a supplement to the long oracle against Moab in the previous collection (15—16). This may be so, but the section 24—27 has undergone a development of its own, and not all the references in it to a doomed city (24:10, 12; 25:2; 26:5; 27:10)—the anonymity of which has caused exegetes such frustration—can be explained in this way.[60]

Isaiah 24—27 can be described as a compendium of mostly eschatological *logia*, addresses, and psalms with no very obvious internal arrangement or logical sequence. It opens with an announcement of a catastrophe affecting all classes of society equally (24:1–3). The address that follows (24:4–20) has something of the flavor of a liturgical lament for the condition of the earth, which is suffering (as we know it does) on account of its human inhabitants. There is a very definite shift of focus in the middle of this passage with what appears to be a reference to rejoicing throughout the Diaspora (24:14–16a), after which we hear a voice claiming a secret revelation that introduces a sobering note into the general euphoria, probably alluding to the vision referred to in 21:2.[61] There follows the first of several short passages introduced with the familiar "on that day" formula (24:21–23). It foresees the destruction of heavenly and earthly powers and the establishment of God's kingdom in Zion as adumbrated in the Sinai covenant (cf. Ex. 24:9–10).

An interesting feature of these chapters as a whole is the alternation of sayings with hymns, two of which celebrate the destruction of a hostile city (25:1–5; 26:1–6). Even a rapid glance at the history of interpretation will suggest that the problem of the city's identity is insoluble in the present state of our knowledge. Apart from our fairly comprehensive ignorance of events in the fourth and third centuries, we have to allow for the readaptation of a theme that in any case is highly stylized, following an ancient pattern. (See, e.g., the Sumerian lament over the destruction of Ur, *ANET,* 455–63.) Alternation with the theme of the final triumph of God in Jerusalem-Zion suggests, in any case, that the alien city has no one historical referent, that it is anti-Zion, a political symbol for opposition to the purpose of God in history.

The first of the hymns is followed by sayings in prose (25:6–12) about the eschatological banquet on Mount Zion, the abolition of suffering and death, and the advent of salvation. The second is linked with a prayer of petition and longing similar to the so-called wisdom psalms, one that looks forward to liberation from foreign rule and the final resurrection (26:7–19). It is followed by an injunction from an apocalyptic seer to his associates to hide from the coming judgment, in other words, to dissociate themselves from those who do not share their beliefs (26:20–21; cf. 2:10–11, 19, 21–22). Other eschatological sayings follow based on earlier prophetic and mythological themes. While the historical context remains obscure, the reference to Leviathan and Tannin at the beginning (27:1) and to Assyria and Egypt at the end (27:12–13) may contain a veiled allusion to the Seleucid and Ptolemaic empires, respectively, while the city of foolish people (27:10–11; cf. Sir. 50:26) may at this point allude to the fate of Samaria after the Macedonian conquest.

To avoid misunderstanding, it is worth recalling that eschatology, understood as a way of thinking or a complex of beliefs about the end of history in an absolute or relative sense, was not unknown during the period of the First Temple. What Amos, Zephaniah, and others say about the

Day of Yahweh (*yôm YHWH*) implies that it was a familiar idea to their contemporaries. It was to mark a great turning point, a time of salvation and victory for Israel (Zeph. 1:14–16), the banishing of darkness and insecurity (Amos 5:18–20; 8:9; Zeph. 1:15), the end of want and sorrow (Amos 8:10), etc. Structurally, it fit into a larger mythic scenario that can be partially reconstructed from psalms and hymns and according to which the end corresponds to the beginning; cosmogony provides the clue to eschatology. Thus the history of early humanity in Genesis 1—11, which draws heavily on the Sumero-Akkadian scribal tradition, presents a model of history beginning with creation and ending with uncreation and the emergence of a new order. Along much the same lines, but not necessarily in direct dependence on Genesis 1—11, Jeremiah draws a picture of divine judgment as a progressive undoing of creation into chaos:

> I looked on the earth, and lo, it was waste and void;
>   and to the heavens, and they had no light.
> I looked on the mountains, and lo, they were quaking,
>   and all the hills moved to and fro.
> I looked, and lo, there was no man,
>   and all the birds of the air had fled.
> I looked, and lo, the fruitful land was a desert,
>   and all its cities were laid in ruins
>   before Yahweh, before his fierce anger.
>
>   (Jer. 4:23–26)

Hence many of the elements in the teaching of those who edited and expanded the prophetic books in the late Persian and early Hellenistic periods were developments of thought patterns attested in earlier stages of the prophetic movement.

If, nevertheless, we look for new departures, we may find them at the points where this mythic construct was brought to bear on the ongoing theological problem created by Israel's subjection to foreign rule, as the hope for emancipation flowed or ebbed with the changing international situation. While the limitations of our historical knowledge rule out confident trajectories, it is possible to detect the gradual consolidation of what might be called an eschatological doctrine dealing with the destiny of Israel, the nations, and the entire created order. Increasingly in evidence is also schism within Jewish communities precipitated by the acceptance and interpretation of prophetic texts with a view to validating a certain type of eschatological doctrine. This is a crucial issue because it leads into the emergence of sects, including early Palestinian Christianity—a subject that, however, belongs to a later chapter of the history.

24. JONAH

T. D. **Alexander,** "Jonah and Genre," *TB* 36 (1985): 35–59; I. A. **Ben-Yosef,** "Jonas and the Fish as a Folk Motif," *Semitics* 7 (1980): 102–17; J. A. **Bewer,** *A Critical and Exegetical Commentary on Jonah,* Edinburgh: T. & T. Clark, 1912, 3–65; R. E. **Clements,** "The Purpose of the Book of Jonah," *SVT* 28 (1975): 16–28; K. M. **Craig,** "Jonah and the Reading Process," *JSOT* 47 (1990): 103–14; J. **Day,** "Problems in the Interpretation of the Book of Jonah," *OTS* 26 (1990): 32–47; T. E. **Fretheim,** *The Message of Jonah,* Minneapolis: Augsburg, 1977; "Jonah and Theodicy," *ZAW* 90 (1978): 227–37; H. **Gese,** "Jona ben Amittai und das Jonabuch," *Theologische Beiträge* 16 (1985): 256–72; S. **Goodhart,** "Prophecy, Sacrifice and Repentance in the Story of Jonah," *Semeia* 33 (1985): 43–63; J. C. **Holbert,** "'Deliverance Belongs to Yahweh!': Satire in the Book of Jonah," *JSOT* 21 (1981): 57–81; C. A. **Keller,** "Jonas, le portrait d'un prophète," *TZ* 21 (1965): 329–40; J. **Limburg,** *Jonah,* Louisville: Westminster/John Knox Press, 1993; D. P. **Payne,** "Jonah from the Perspective of Its Audience," *JSOT* 13 (1979): 3–12; J. M. **Sasson,** *Jonah: A New Translation with Introduction, Commentary, and Interpretations,* New York & London: Doubleday, 1990; A. **Soleh,** "The Story of Jonah's Reflective Adventures," *Beth Mikra* 24 (1979): 406–20 (Hebrew).

Jonah is fifth in the Dodekapropheton, between Obadiah and Micah. This position is one of several indications of editorial concern for chronological sequence, since a prophet named Jonah ben-Amittai was active during the reign of Jeroboam II (786–746 B.C.E.). The context (2 Kings 14:25) informs us that this prophet predicted the successful outcome of Jeroboam's campaigns to restore the borders of Israel. He was therefore an optimistic and nationalist prophet and, despite the generally negative verdict of the historian on the Northern Kingdom, his intervention is not condemned. Unlike the other prophetic books, however, the book of Jonah bears no title, does not consist of prophetic sayings, and begins at once with narrative. In some respects it resembles other legendary narratives about prophets (e.g., Elijah, Elisha, Isaiah), but its peculiar tone and style mark it as, at most, an imitation of this genre. For this reason alone, it is highly unlikely that, as Duhm argued, it stood originally after the allusion to the Northern prophet of the same name mentioned in Dtr (2 Kings 14:25). Nor can it be described as a midrash on that text. Though it does have some of the characteristics of haggadic midrash, its artfulness and complexity put it in a different category; and in any case, if it were to be regarded as narrative commentary, its textual point of departure would not be 2 Kings 14:25.

Early Christian writers read the book typologically, with reference to the descent into death and resurrection of Jesus (e.g., Matt. 12:39–41), and some modern authors have taken it to be an allegory referring to the exilic experience of Israel. The prophet's name has also been coerced to render an allegorical meaning, "dove, son of fidelity," or something of the sort. But if allegorical elements are to be found at all in the book they would be in the psalm (Jonah 2:2–9 [MT 2:3–10]), which is probably not native to this context, and which many scholars regard as a later and not entirely appropriate insertion into the narrative.

While the story makes use of well-attested folktale motifs (cf. Perseus, Sinbad), it achieves a level of sophistication in its use of ironic contrast, deliberate exaggeration and distortion, and deployment of key words that puts it well beyond the scope of folktale pure and simple. Its author was clearly a trained hand at writing, one who was well versed in the historical, scribal, and prophetic heritage of Israel, and whose intent was to make some specific points for the benefit of a specific audience. It will be our task to try to identify these, regretfully leaving aside any further discussion of the literary quality of this delightful narrative.[62]

The story begins with Yahweh's call to Jonah to preach in Nineveh, a task that Jonah avoids by taking a ship at Joppa (Yafo) bound for Tarshish, that is, in the opposite direction (Jonah 1:1–3). The scene then moves to shipboard, where it becomes obvious at once that it is not so easy to flee from the presence of Yahweh; for it is he who hurled a great wind at the sea (1:4) and thereafter stilled it (1:15). The point is transparently clear to the reader but apparently not to Jonah: Yahweh's action is not confined to the land of Israel, but is also experienced, and should be acknowledged, both at sea and in foreign lands (2:10 [MT 2:11]; 3:10; 4:6; etc.); and this in ironic contrast to Jonah's own profession of faith in Yahweh maker of the sea and the dry land (1:9).

In the second episode (1:4–16) we are invited to observe the behavior of the pagan sailors during the storm. They pray to their own gods and one of them, the captain or the first mate, constrains an unwilling Jonah to do the same. After casting lots, they hear his story and reluctantly follow his advice and pitch him overboard. Before doing so, however, they address a prayer to Yahweh and, after the storm is miraculously stilled, embrace Jonah's own profession of faith and carry out appropriate cultic acts, including sacrifice, there and then on shipboard.

The large fish appointed by Yahweh (Jonah 1:17 [MT 2:1]—the same verb (*mnh*) is used for the plant, the worm, and the east wind (4:6–8)— to serve as a novel form of transportation presumably got him back to his point of departure. There the commission was repeated, and this time Jonah performed, reluctantly, the prophetic role of divine messenger. Here, once again, we are invited to concentrate on the conduct of the pagans, inhabitants of a city that was a byword for oppression and god-lessness. They listened to the message, contemptuously brief as it was, and on hearing it they believed, proclaimed a ritual of fasting incumbent also on the animal world, prayed, and turned from evil (3:5–9). In other words, they underwent a thorough conversion that, given the identity of the god in whose name the prophet spoke, involved the acceptance by the entire city of the Jewish religion. The reaction of God was equally swift: he also "repented" of the evil that he thought to do to them, and he did not do it.

The reaction of Jonah was of a quite different nature. He had, of course, observed how the king of Nineveh (sic) and his subjects had responded to the message of doom, but it appears from the subsequent course of events that he at least was not quite sure how Yahweh would react to their repentance. The analogy of Abraham faced with the annihilation of Sodom (Gen. 18:16–33) would suggest that in this situation the prophetic role called for intercession. Instead, he in effect accused Yahweh of discrediting him by not fulfilling the prediction of doom precisely because of his mercy and compassion! To make it worse, he quoted at God the words of the theophany at Sinai (Ex. 34:6) ending with Elijah's despairing cry on his way to the same place (1 Kings 19:4).

The final scene (Jonah 4:6–11) leads rapidly to the concluding statement of Yahweh by way of three successive dispositions affecting Jonah as he sat outside the city waiting to see what would happen: a plant that grew overnight with preternatural rapidity to provide him shelter; a worm uncharacteristic of its kind in size and habits that gnawed the plant; a scorching east wind that, combined with the burning sun, made him once again want to die. There is something distinctly sapiential about this appeal to the world of nature to make a point about divine causality and divine freedom and then apply it to God's action in history. Jonah's concern for the plant (he was really concerned about himself, but this would not have served the purpose) leads a fortiori to the divine concern for the city with its many people and cattle, and at the same time illustrates the freedom of God to create and destroy, to threaten destruction and then be moved by compassion.

What we seem to have in this book is a kind of sapiential critique of prophecy and an attempt to deal with some of the theological problems to which, as we have seen, prophecy gave rise. For his protagonist the author chose a nationalist prophet who predicted success during Jeroboam II's border wars in the eighth century. There also appears to have existed a tradition that this Jonah predicted the fall of Nineveh (Tobit 14:4, 8). If he did he was wrong, since Nineveh was destroyed only a century and a half after the lifetime of the prophet; a circumstance that, if he had noted it, would have made it easier for the writer to take up the problem of unfulfilled prophecy. His critique is quite radical, since it implies that prophecy of this kind can easily conceal a basically inadequate understanding of God and God's purposes.

The most important implication of the story is that the freedom of God is not constrained even by the prophetic word. The fact that God can "repent," that is, in ordinary terms, change his mind, means that he is free even after the prophetic word has been spoken. More specifically and unexpectedly, he is free to respond graciously to true repentance and prayer on the part of Gentiles, even of traditional and archetypal enemies of Israel like the Assyrians. The irony is that they understand this but the prophet does not:

Perhaps God will give a thought to us, that we do not perish. (1:6)

Who knows, God may yet repent and turn from his fierce anger, so that we perish not. (3:9)

From this point of view the book is theologically crucial, since it breaks once and for all the bond of what might be called prophetic causality by its emphasis on the divine freedom.

There is another thing the prophet does not understand, and that is the divine will to save. Ironically again, this is the theme of the psalm that he sings in the fish's innards: "salvation belongs to Yahweh!" (2:9 [MT 2:10]). In this respect the author aligns himself with a current of thought the best expression of which is found in the Isaian Servant and his disciples. This does not, however, justify presenting the book of Jonah as a protest against the reforming measures taken by Ezra and Nehemiah, and therefore against integrationist tendencies in the Second Commonwealth. For one thing, Ezra and Nehemiah were concerned with matters internal to the Judean temple-community and not at all with the fate of the Gentiles. But we must also be careful in aligning Jonah with a universalist perspective. Universalism is a slippery term; the salvation offered to Gentiles in exilic prophetic writings (e.g., Isa. 45:22; 49:6; 52:10) implies an acknowledgment of the lordship of Israel's God (e.g., Isa. 45:23; 51:5) and is sometimes couched in the form of an offer they can't refuse. The point is that they are to embrace the religion of Israel when it is preached to them, which is in fact what happens to the pagans in the book of Jonah (1:16; 3:5) and what no doubt was actually happening in various parts of the Near East and the Levant at the time of writing.

If we must find a target for the writer's criticism, it would not be Ezra and Nehemiah but the kind of prophetic threat represented by the author of the so-called Isaian apocalypse, a threat directed, as we have seen, against an unnamed city. Of its inhabitants the author says:

> This is a people without discernment;
>> therefore he who made them will not have compassion on them,
>> he that formed them will show them no favor.

> (Isa. 27:11)

Nineveh, on the contrary, will be saved even though its people do not know their right hand from their left.

Both the freedom of God and his will to save had already been clearly affirmed in the ethical teaching of Ezekiel:

> If a wicked man turns away from all his sins which he has committed, . . . none of the transgressions which he has committed shall be remembered against him; for the righteousness which he has done he shall live. Have I any pleasure in the death of the wicked, . . . and not rather that he should turn from his way and live? (Ezek. 18:21–22)

In what appears to be a Deuteronomic expansion of the incident of Jeremiah's visit to the potter (Jer. 18:5–12), the same teaching is applied on the political level:

> If at any time I declare concerning a nation or a kingdom, that I will pluck up and break down and destroy it, and if that nation, concerning which I have spoken, turns from its evil, I will repent of the evil that I intended to do to it. (Jer. 18:7–8)

The declaration in question refers, of course, to judgment oracles addressed by prophets to foreign nations. That it is this teaching that the Jonah story purports to illustrate is as explicit as could be expected:

> When God saw what they did, how they turned from their evil way, God repented of the evil which he had said he would do to them; and he did not do it. (Jonah 3:10)

There is perhaps a further aspect to the author's critique concerning the matter of worship. As the story gets underway, it emphasizes the fact that the prophet is fleeing from the presence of Yahweh (*millipnē YHWH,* Jonah 1:3; cf. 1:10), a phrase with well-known cultic connotations. We note further that the psalm put into his mouth speaks of its author having been cast out from the divine presence (2:4 [MT 2:5]). Yet the story goes on to show that God is present elsewhere than in the sanctuary or in the land of Israel. His activity, and therefore his presence, is attested on the high seas and in the pagan land of Assyria. And just as the author of the psalm knows that his prayer reaches the temple even though he is far distant from it (Jonah 2:7 [MT 2:8]), the pagans themselves offer cult to Yahweh where they are, in their own habitat. The sailors even offer sacrifice on board ship in defiance of the Deuteronomic law. Here, too, the author of the book aligns himself with a view, certainly not uncontested, according to which God accepts and even enables worship directed to him by Gentiles (Zeph. 3:9–10; Mal. 1:11, 14).

The author, then, chooses as his protagonist a prophet who balks at his call for fear of being discredited by Yahweh's regrettable tendency to be moved by the repentant sinner (4:1–2; cf. Zech. 13:4–6). Consequently, he also refuses to discharge the prophetic function of intercession both during the storm and at Nineveh. In the first episode he sleeps instead of praying. And since the author at this point uses a word denoting not ordinary sleep but the preternatural kind put on the man in the garden of Eden and on Abraham during his covenant making (*tardēmâ,* Gen. 2:21; 15:12), perhaps there is more to this sleep than first appears. A clue to its meaning may be found in a critique of contemporary prophets in Isa. 29:10:

> Yahweh has poured out upon you
> a spirit of deep sleep (*tardēmâ*);
> he has closed your eyes, O prophets,
> and covered your heads, O seers.

This is the sleep of imperception and spiritual dullness. Jonah does not even appreciate the irony of confessing faith in the God of heaven, maker of the sea and dry land (1:9), while fleeing from his presence. Worse, he has closed his eyes and his mind to what is the will of God in this particular situation, misled as he is by his own rigid and unyielding view of the prophetic office.

The book, then, addresses itself to the problem of unfulfilled prophecy and the anger and frustration that it occasioned. By implication, it also offers a solution to the problem of theodicy, to which, as we saw earlier, prophecy, whether fulfilled or not, tends to give rise. By emphasizing the freedom of God, it interposes the possibility of salvation between the prophetic word and its anticipated effect. At the same time, it pioneers a new understanding of the prophetic office based on the profound and simple conviction that God's ultimate will is always and everywhere to save. This new form, which might be called apostolic prophecy, has implications that we have not yet worked out or perhaps even fully grasped.

NOTES

NOTES TO INTRODUCTION

1. David E. Aune, *Prophecy in Early Christianity and the Ancient Mediterranean World* (Grand Rapids: Eerdmans, 1983), contains an excellent survey of prophecy in the Greco-Roman world, early Christianity, and early Judaism.

2. A. W. Jenks, *The Elohist and North Israelite Traditions* (Missoula, Mont.: Scholars Press, 1977); R. R. Wilson, *Prophecy and Society in Ancient Israel* (Philadelphia: Fortress Press, 1980), 135–252.

3. On prophetic traditions see most recently my *Sage, Priest, Prophet. Religious and Intellectual Leadership in Ancient Israel* (Louisville, Ky.: Westminster/John Knox Press, 1995), 11–15, 148–57.

NOTES TO PART I: PROLEGOMENA

1. For a translation and brief comment on the Lachish ostraca see J.C.L. Gibson, *Textbook of Syrian Semitic Inscriptions*, vol. 1, *Hebrew and Moabite Inscriptions* (Oxford: Clarendon Press, 1971), 32–49, and K.A.D. Smelik, *Writings from Ancient Israel* (Edinburgh: T. & T. Clark, 1991), 116–31; a fuller account in A. Lemaire, *Inscriptions Hébraïques*, Tome 1, *Les Ostraca* (Paris: Les Editions du Cerf, 1977), 85–143; S. B. Parker, "The Lachish Letters and Official Reactions to Prophecies," in L. M. Hopfe, ed., *Uncovering Ancient Stones: Essays in Memory of H. Neil Richardson* (Winona Lake: Eisenbrauns, 1994), 65–78.

2. D. H. Johnson, *Nuer Prophets: A History of Prophecy from the Upper Nile in the Nineteenth and Twentieth Centuries* (Oxford: Clarendon Press, 1995); T. W. Overholt, *Prophecy in Cross-Cultural Perspective* (Atlanta: Scholars Press, 1986), 23–148; *Channels of Prophecy: The Social Dynamics of Prophetic Activity* (Minneapolis: Fortress Press, 1989).

3. See the contributions to the debate on the editing of prophetic books and the label *nābî'* by Auld, Carroll et al. in *JSOT* 27 (1983).

4. See my *Sage, Priest, Prophet*, 161–63.

5. J. Blenkinsopp, "Prophecy and Priesthood in Josephus," *JJS* 25 (1974): 239–62.

6. Second Kings 14:27, "but Yahweh had not said that he would blot out the name of Israel from under heaven" sounds polemical, and it may be directed against Amos (see especially Amos 9:8a: "See, the eyes of Yahweh God are upon the sinful kingdom, and I will destroy it from the surface of the ground"); see F. Crüsemann, "Kritik an Amos im deuteronomistischen Geschichtswerk," in H. W. Wolff, ed., *Probleme biblischer Theologie* (Munich: Kaiser, 1971), 57–63; C. Begg, "The Non-mention of Amos, Hosea and Micah in the Deuteronomistic History," *BN* 32 (1986): 41–53; "The Non-mention of Zephaniah, Nahum and Habakkuk in the Deuteronomistic History," *BN* 38/39 (1987): 19–25.

7. *Ancient Judaism* (New York: The Free Press, 1952 [1917–1919]), 395.

8. J. Barr, "Le Judaïsme postbiblique et la théologie de l'Ancien Testament," *RTP* 18 (1968): 209–17; J. Blenkinsopp, "Old Testament Studies and the Jewish-Christian Connection," *JSOT* 28 (1984): 3–15.

9. B. Duhm, *Das Buch Jesaia* (Göttingen: Vandenhoeck & Ruprecht, 1968[5] [1892]).

10. G. Hölscher, *Die Propheten: Untersuchungen zur Religionsgeschichte Israels* (Leipzig: J. C. Hinrichs, 1914).

11. The point was demonstrated in Hölscher's *Hesekiel: Der Dichter und das Buch* (Giessen: A. Töpelmann, 1924).

12. Gunkel's principal statement on prophecy was his introduction to Hans Schmidt, *Die Grossen Propheten*, in *Die Schriften des Alten Testaments II, 2* (Göttingen: Vandenhoeck & Ruprecht, 1923[2]). His form-critical method is exemplified in "Nahum 1," *ZAW* 13 (1893): 223–44 and "Der Micha-Schluss," *Zeitschrift für Semitistik und verwandte Gebiete*, 2 (1924): 145–78.

13. H. Gunkel, "Die geheimen Erfahrungen der Propheten," in *Die Grossen Propheten*, xvii–xxxiv (see previous note).

14. S. Mowinckel, *Zur Komposition des Buches Jeremia* (Oslo: Dybwad, 1914).

15. See especially his *Prophecy and Tradition: The Prophetic Books in the Light of the Study of the Growth and History of the Tradition* (Oslo: Dybwad, 1946).

16. I. Engnell, *The Call of Isaiah* (Uppsala: Lundquist, 1949), 54–60; "Methodological Aspects of Old Testament Study," *SVT* 7 (1960): 21; *A Rigid (sic) Scrutiny: Critical Essays on the Old Testament* (Nashville: Vanderbilt University Press, 1969).

17. H. S. Nyberg, *Studien zum Hoseabuch* (Uppsala: Lundquist, 1935); H. Birkeland, *Zum Hebräischen Traditionswesen: Die Komposition der prophetischen Bücher des Alten Testaments* (Oslo: Dybwad, 1938).

18. G. Widengren, *Literary and Psychological Aspects of the Hebrew Prophets* (Uppsala: Lundquist, 1948).

19. S. Mowinckel, *Psalmenstudien III: Die Kultprophetie und prophetische Psalmen* (Oslo: Dybwad, 1923); *The Psalms in Israel's Worship* (Nashville: Abingdon, 1967), 2:53–73.

20. See note 13. Other significant studies on cult prophecy are A. Haldar, *Associations of Cult Prophets among the Ancient Semites* (Uppsala: Almqvist & Wiksell, 1945); A. R. Johnson, *The Cultic Prophet in Ancient Israel* (Cardiff: University of Wales Press, 1962[2]); *The Cultic Prophet and Israel's Psalmody* (Cardiff: University of

Wales Press, 1979); W. H. Bellinger, Jr., *Psalmody and Prophecy* (Sheffield: JSOT Press, 1984).

21. The British branch of the "Myth and Ritual School" was represented by S. H. Hooke, *Essays on the Myth and Ritual of the Hebrews in Relation to the Culture Pattern of the Ancient Near East* (London: Oxford University Press, 1933); *Myth, Ritual and Kingship* (Oxford: Clarendon Press, 1958). One of the leading representatives of the Scandinavian branch was I. Engnell, *Studies in Divine Kingship in the Ancient Near East* (Oxford: Blackwell, 1967²).

22. The latter view, no longer in favor, was held by J. P. Hyatt, "The Prophetic Criticism of Israelite Worship," in H. M. Orlinsky, ed., *The Library of Biblical Studies* (Cincinnati: Hebrew Union College Press, 1969), 201–24 and C. F. Whitley, *The Prophetic Achievement* (London: A. R. Mowbray, 1963), 63–92.

23. The point is made succinctly by William McKane: "The assumption that there is an indissolubility of form and setting, on which the transition from form-critical observations to conclusions about the cultic functions of prophets sometimes rests, appears particularly fragile." "Prophecy and the Prophetic Literature," in G. W. Anderson, ed., *Tradition and Interpretation: Essays by Members of the Society for Old Testament Study* (Oxford: Clarendon Press, 1979), 164.

24. H. E. von Waldow, *Anlass und Hintergrund der Verkündigung des Deuterojesaia* (Ph.D. diss., Bonn, 1953). However, in *Der traditionsgeschichtliche Hintergrund der prophetischen Gerichtsreden* (Berlin: A. Töpelmann, 1963), he derived the prophetic pronouncement of judgment from the secular practice of law.

25. "Prophetenamt und Mittleramt," *ZTK* 58 (1961): 269–84; *Das Amt des Propheten bei Amos* (Göttingen: Vandenhoeck & Ruprecht, 1962); *Liturgie und prophetisches Amt bei Jeremia* (Gütersloh: Gütersloher Verlagshaus, 1963). A similar position was taken by J. Muilenburg, "The 'Office' of the Prophet in Ancient Israel," in J. P. Hyatt, ed., *The Bible in Modern Scholarship* (Nashville: Abingdon Press, 1965), 74–97.

26. E. Würthwein, "Amos Studien," *ZAW* 62 (1950): 10–52.

27. E. Würthwein, "Der Ursprung der prophetischen Gerichsrede," *ZTK* 49 (1952): 1–15. Cf. F. Hesse, "Wurzelt die prophetische Gerichtsrede im israelitischen Kult?" *ZAW* 65 (1953): 45–53.

28. H. W. Wolff, "Hoseas geistige Heimat," *TZ* 81 (1956): cols. 83–94. In *Amos' geistige Heimat* (Neukirchen-Vluyn: Neukirchener Verlag, 1964) (= *Amos the Prophet: The Man and His Background* [Philadelphia: Fortress Press, 1973]), Wolff argued that significant aspects of Amos' message derive from the sapiential tradition rooted in the old clan ethos; along the same lines S. Terrien, "Amos and Wisdom," in B. W. Anderson and W. Harrelson, eds., *Israel's Prophetic Heritage* (New York: Harper & Brothers, 1962), 108–15. The influence of the sapiential-scribal tradition also has been detected in Isaiah by J. Fichtner, "Jesaja unter den Weisen," *TLZ* 74 (1949): cols. 73–79, and J. W. Whedbee, *Isaiah and Wisdom* (Nashville: Abingdon, 1971).

29. J. L. Crenshaw, *Prophetic Conflict: Its Effect upon Israelite Religion* (Berlin: Walter de Gruyter, 1971); J. A. Sanders, "Hermeneutics in True and False Prophecy," in G. W. Coats and B. O. Long, eds., *Canon and Authority* (Philadelphia:

Fortress Press, 1977), 21–41; S. J. De Vries, *Prophet against Prophet* (Grand Rapids: Eerdmans, 1978), a study of 1 Kings 22.

30. H. M. Orlinsky, ed., *Interpreting the Prophetic Tradition* (New York: KTAV Publishing House, 1969); M. Buber, *The Prophetic Faith* (New York: Macmillan, 1949); U. E. Simon, "Martin Buber and the Interpretation of the Prophets," in R. Coggins et al., eds., *Israel's Prophetic Tradition* (Cambridge: Cambridge University Press, 1982), 250–61; A. J. Heschel, *The Prophets* (New York: Harper & Row, 1962); Y. Kaufmann, *The Religion of Israel from Its Beginnings to the Babylonian Exile*, trans. and abridged by Moshe Greenberg (New York: Schocken Books, 1972), 341–451.

31. In the eighteenth century both Robert Lowth, bishop of Oxford (1710–1787) and Johann Gottfried Herder (1744–1803) had a keen appreciation for the literary qualities of the Old Testament, and specifically for the poetry in the prophetic books. Hermann Gunkel also had a high esteem for the literary quality of the canonical prophets; see his "The Prophets as Writers and Poets," trans. J. L. Schaaf in D. L. Petersen, ed., *Prophecy in Israel* (Philadelphia: Fortress Press, 1987 [1923]), 22–73. See also L. Alonso-Schökel, *Estudios de poetica hebrea* (Barcelona: Herder, 1963).

32. J. Magonet, *Form and Meaning. Studies in Literary Techniques in the Book of Jonah* (Sheffield: Sheffield Academic Press, 1983 [1976]); J. S. Ackerman, "Jonah," in R. Alter and F. Kermode, eds., *The Literary Guide to the Bible* (Cambridge, Mass.: Belknap Press of Harvard University Press, 1987), 234–43.

33. For example, L. Festinger et al., *When Prophecy Fails* (New York: Harper & Row, 1964).

34. Akkadian *nabi'um*, a passive form, would, if relevant, emphasize the commissioning; others, however, relate the Hebrew word to the active voice, thereby emphasizing the prophet as speaker, e.g., T. J. Meek, *Hebrew Origins* (New York: Harper & Brothers, 1952[2]), 150–51.

35. Thus, niphal occurs some seventy times in Jeremiah and Ezekiel with reference to prophetic speech, while the hithpael is attested in the two books only seven times. In Amos 7:16 the niphal parallels the verb *ntp* in hiphil, with the meaning "preach" (*lo' taṭṭip*).

36. The term "legend" derives from Latin *legendum*, referring to edifying hagiography assigned for public reading in monastic settings (cf. *Legenda Sanctorum*). While not necessarily unhistorical, it is a genre that does not aspire to a high level of historicity. See the classic study of A. Jolles, *Einfache Formen* (Darmstadt: Wissenschaftliche Buchgesellschaft, 1958 [1930]), 23–61.

37. J. Ross, "The Prophet as Yahweh's Messenger," in B. W. Anderson and W. Harrelson, *Israel's Prophetic Heritage*, 98–107.

38. See the sober and rather pessimistic assessment of biblical texts as source material for reconstructing the social world of Israelite prophecy in R. P. Carroll, "Prophecy and Society," in R. E. Clements, ed., *The World of Ancient Israel* (Cambridge: Cambridge University Press, 1989), 203–25.

39. See further below, 178–79.

40. See the section on "Warfare and War Prophecy" in Weber's *Ancient Judaism*, 90–117.

41. "We shall understand 'prophet' to mean a purely individual bearer of charisma, who by virtue of his mission proclaims a religious doctrine or divine commandment," *The Sociology of Religion*, 46.

42. See Berger, 948–49; Emmett, 13–23; D. Little, "Max Weber and the Comparative Study of Religious Ethics," *JRE* 2 (1974): 5–40; D. L. Petersen, "Max Weber and the Sociological Study of Ancient Israel," in H. M. Johnson, ed., *Religious Change and Continuity* (San Francisco: Jossey-Bass, 1979), 117–49.

43. See note 2.

44. I. M. Lewis, *Ecstatic Religion*, 29.

45. In addition to R. P. Carroll and R. R. Wilson, see T. W. Overholt, "The Ghost Dance of 1890 and the Nature of the Prophetic Process," *Ethnohistory* 21 (1974): 37–63.

46. Norman Cohn, *The Pursuit of the Millennium* (New York: Oxford University Press, 1970² [1957]); *Cosmos, Chaos and the World to Come: The Ancient Roots of Apocalyptic Faith* (New Haven, Conn.: Yale University Press, 1993).

NOTES TO PART II: FROM THE BEGINNINGS TO AMOS

1. For the text of the Mesha stela and brief commentary see J.C.L. Gibson, *Textbook of Syrian Semitic Inscriptions. I. Hebrew and Moabite Inscriptions*, 71–83; C.A.D. Smelik, *Writings from Ancient Israel*, 29–50.

2. *ANET*, 501–2; F. Rosenthal, ed., *An Aramaic Handbook* vol. 1, no. 1 (Wiesbaden: Otto Harrassowitz, 1967), 1–2 (original text).

3. See A. Malamat, "A Mari Prophecy and Nathan's Dynastic Oracle," in J. A. Emerton, ed., *Prophecy: Essays Presented to Georg Fohrer on his Sixty-fifth Birthday* (Berlin: Walter de Gruyter, 1980), 68–82.

4. Discussed by M. Hengel, *Judaism and Hellenism*, vol. 1 (Philadelphia: Fortress Press, 1974), 184–85.

5. This suggestion calls for a thorough comparison between the social teaching of Israelite sages, with its indubitable contacts with Egyptian wisdom (e.g., Prov. 22:17 to 24:22), and the prophetic demand for social justice.

6. *ANET*, 625, and the note on *maškanum*; cf. Hebrew *miškān* (tent-shrine).

7. I owe this quotation to a paper delivered by Dr. Martti Nissinen at the Fifteenth Congress of the International Society for Old Testament Study, July 1955, with the title "References to Prophecy in Neo-Assyrian Sources."

8. On Neo-Assyrian prophecy see de Jong Ellis and Weippert (bibliog.); also H. B. Huffmon, "Ancient Near Eastern Prophecy," *ABD*, 5:477–82.

9. See Lindblom, *Prophecy in Ancient Israel*, 8–12, and G. Fohrer, *History of Israelite Religion* (Nashville: Abingdon Press, 1972), 223–29, who makes a clean distinction between nomadic seerdom and ecstatic prophecy.

10. M. Weber, *Ancient Judaism*, 90–117.

11. H. M. Barstad, "The Understanding of the Prophets in Deuteronomy," *SJOT* 8.2 (1994): 236–51, identifies the "prophet like Moses" with Joshua.

12. The last phase, *weloʾ yāsāpû*, may imply that elders were not known subsequently to act ecstatically.

13. On Karl Jaspers' concept of an axial age in the first millennium B.C.E., see S. N. Eisenstadt, ed., *The Origins and Diversity of Axial Age Civilizations* (Albany: State University of New York Press, 1986), especially part 2 dealing with Israel.

14. On Amos 2:11–12 as part of a Deuteronomic redaction of the book, see W. Schmidt, "Die deuteronomistische Redaktion des Amosbuches," *ZAW* 77 (1965): 178–83; H. W. Wolff, *Joel, Amos* (Neukirchen-Vluyn: Neukirchener Verlag, 1967), 137–38, 204–07 (= *Joel and Amos* [Philadelphia: Fortress Press, 1977], 170–71).

15. The date at the beginning (1:3) and the account of Moses' death at the end (34:1, 7–9) of Deuteronomy, both attributed to P, reflect the process by which this book was incorporated into the P-edited narrative of founding events.

16. Y. Kaufmann, *The Religion of Israel from Its Beginnings to the Babylonian Exile*, trans. and abridged by Moshe Greenberg (New York: Schocken Books, 1972), 227–28; M. Buber, *Moses: The Revelation and the Covenant* (New York: Harper & Brothers, 1958), 162–71.

17. On the oracular character of this tent, see M. Haran, "From Early to Classical Prophecy: Continuity and Change," *VT* 27 (1977): 385–97. He takes 1 Sam. 2:22b, which refers to the sons of Eli lying with the women who served at the entrance to the tent of meeting (at Shiloh!), to be a P editorial addition. Note that the term *mᵉšārēt*, "minister," is used of both Joshua (Ex. 33:11) and Samuel (1 Sam. 2:11). It may not be mere coincidence that both are also described as *naʿar*. In addition to the usual meaning "youth," this term may have become standard for "prophetic disciple"; see the curious repetition *wᵉhannaʿar naʿar* (1 Sam. 1:24) with reference to Samuel, and *wayyēlek hannaʿar hannaʿar hannābîʾ* (2 Kings 9:4) with reference to one of the "sons of the prophets" commissioned by Elisha to anoint Jehu. This last phrase may contain a lemma and gloss explaining the unfamiliar usage; cf. *nʿrm*, Ugaritic, with the meaning "members of a guild," C. H. Gordon, *Ugaritic Manual* (Rome: Pontifical Biblical Institute, 1955²), 297.

18. Moses is mentioned by name in only two prophetic texts that can claim to be preexilic, that is, Micah 6:4 and Jer. 15:1.

19. Judges 6:7–10 reports a brief sermon in the Deuteronomic style by an anonymous prophet.

20. First Samuel 9:1–10 speaks only of a "man of God," a term that is not used in the rest of the narrative, which speaks of a seer (*rōʾeh*) and identifies him with Samuel. The explanatory gloss at v. 9, which would follow more naturally v. 11, is designed to assure Samuel's status as *nābîʾ*.

21. The phrase "Do whatever your hand finds to do" (1 Sam. 10:7) connotes a military exploit, especially in view of Saul's commissioning by Samuel (10:1). His first military exploit appears to have been against the Ammonites rather than the Philistines (11:1–11). The reference could, however, be to an attack on the Philistine garrison (or the assassination of a Philistine commander) at Geba, 13:3–4 (cf. Gibeah, 10:5, 10), with the ecstatic rapture constituting a parallel tradition to the hewing up of the oxen and sending the parts to all the tribes in 11:6–7.

22. The biblical traditions have no doubt exaggerated the achievements of the United Monarchy, which has left practically no trace in the archaeological

record, but we can detect at least the beginnings of a state system (bureaucracy, taxation, forced labor, etc.) at that time.

23. On the Samarian ostraca see J.C.L. Gibson, *Textbook of Syrian Semitic Inscriptions*, 1:5–20, 71–83; A. Lemaire, *Inscriptions Hébraïques*, vol. 1, *Les Ostraca* (Paris: Editions du Cerf, 1977), 23–81, 245–50.

24. On the Kuntillet 'Ajrud graffiti see Z. Meshel in *ABD*, 4:103–9.

25. First Kings 18:18, 31–32, 36–37; 21:20–26; 22:37–53; 2 Kings 1:17–18.

26. For the view that the taunt is directed specifically at the Phoenician Baal, see R. de Vaux, *Les Livres des Rois* (Paris: Editions du Cerf, 1958), 13–16; *The Bible and the Ancient Near East*, 238–51.

27. J. Lindblom, *Prophecy in Ancient Israel*, 49.

28. E. Würthwein, *Proclamation and Presence*, 152–66.

29. Little is known of the Nazirite order apart from the Samson saga (Judges 13—16) and the late regulations in Num. 6:1–21. If *pᵉrāʿôt* in Judg. 5:2 (Song of Deborah) refers to long locks of hair (cf. Num. 6:5), there may be an indirect allusion to Nazirites here too.

30. The manner in which Rechabites are commended for their fidelity to their traditions in Jeremiah 35 is not easily reconciled with the alternative view that they formed a guild of metalworkers, as maintained by F. S. Frick, "Rechab, Rechabite," *ABD*, 5:630–32.

31. Parenthetically, the communal prophecy of this early period provided a model for sects of the late Second Temple period that regarded themselves as the heirs of the prophetic tradition, which may help to explain some of the more encratic and enthusiastic elements in early Christianity. The ideal of a prophetic fellowship sustaining the charismatic impulse of the beginnings keeps on emerging throughout Christian history, sometimes assuming forms as strange and bewildering as the "primitives" who looked to Elijah and Elisha for leadership.

32. For example, Luke 9:57–62 and Acts 1:6–11, where the taking up of Jesus and giving of the Spirit are modeled on the Elijah narrative, using the same vocabulary as in the LXX version in *Kingdoms*. The disciples are to be clothed with power and work miracles, reminiscent of the miraculous cloak of Elijah, and it is emphasized that they see Jesus being taken up, as Elisha must see his master, in order to receive the Spirit.

NOTES TO PART III: THE PERIOD OF ASSYRIAN EXPANSION

1. N. Gottwald, *All the Kingdoms of the Earth*, 94, has even referred to Tiglathpileser as "the father of Israelite eschatology."

2. While the dates of Assyrian rulers will generally have a margin of error of no more than a year or two, the chronology of the kings of Israel and Judah is still subject to debate and dates should be considered approximate; see the options listed in J. H. Hayes and J. M. Miller, *Israelite and Judaean History*, 682–83; J. H. Hayes and P. K. Hooker, *A New Chronology for the Kings of Israel and Judah* (Atlanta: John Knox Press, 1988).

3. Morton Smith in J. A. Garraty and Peter Gay, eds., *The Columbia History of the World* (New York: Harper & Row, 1972), 153.

4. See *ANET*, 321 for the Siloam inscription, cut after Hezekiah's engineers had completed the tunnel bringing water from the Gihon spring to the pool of Siloam.

5. On the Samarian ostraca see J.C.L. Gibson, *Textbook of Syrian Semitic Inscriptions*, vol. 1, 5–20, 71–83; A. Lemaire, *Inscriptions Hébraïques*, vol. 1, 23–81, 245–50; W. Shea, "The Date and Purpose of the Samaria Ostraca," *IEJ* 27 (1977): 21–22; A. Mazar, *Archaeology of the Land of the Bible*, 409–10.

6. On the prophets as poets, see H. Gunkel, "The Prophets as Writers and Poets," in D. L. Petersen, ed., *Prophecy in Israel* (Philadelphia: Fortress Press, 1986), 22–73 [1923]. On the prophet as pamphleteer and popular leader (*demagogos*), see Max Weber, *Economy and Society* (Berkeley, Calif.: University of California Press, 1968 [1956⁴]), 444–46.

7. J. S. Holladay, Jr., "Assyrian Statecraft and the Prophets of Israel," *HTR* 63 (1970): 29–51, argues a connection with the Assyrian practice of holding the entire people rather than the ruler alone responsible for maintaining treaty obligations.

8. See G. von Rad, *Old Testament Theology* 2:273–77.

9. See the remarks of E. Auerbach, "Die grosse Überarbeitung der biblischen Bücher," *SVT* 1 (1953): 8–9, on redactional activity during the exile; and, with reference to Amos, W. H. Schmidt, "Die deuteronomistische Redaktion des Amosbuches," *ZAW* 77 (1965): 168–93.

10. On the cultic background of the sayings against the nations see, in addition to the commentaries, A. Bentzen, "The Ritual Background of Amos 1:2–2:16," *OTS* 8 (1960): 85–99, and M. Weiss, "The Pattern of the 'Execration Texts' in the Prophetic Literature," *IEJ* 19 (1969): 150–157. Other aspects are discussed by M. Fishbane, "The Treaty Background of Amos 1:11 and Related Matters," *JBL* 89 (1970): 313–18; S. M. Paul, "Amos 1:3–2:3, a Concatenous Literary Pattern," *JBL* 90 (1971): 397–403; W. Rudolph, "Die angefochtenen Völkersprüche in Amos 1 und 2," in K.-H. Bernhardt, ed., *Schalom: Studien zu Glaube und Geschichte Israels. A. Jepsen zum 70. Geburtstag* (Stuttgart: Calwer Verlag, 1971), 45–49 (defends the authenticity of the sayings); M. E. Polley, *Amos and the Davidic Empire. A Socio-Historical Approach* (Oxford: Oxford University Press), 1989.

11. Corresponding to the original five sayings against foreign nations there are five sayings beginning "Hear [this word]" (Amos 3:1, 13; 4:1; 5:1; 8:4), five reproaches (4:6–11), and five visions; cf. the poem with the fivefold refrain in Isaiah (5:25; 9:8, 16, 20; 10:4), which has definite associations with Amos, and the opening verse of which ("Yahweh has sent a word against Jacob," Isa. 9:8 [MT 9:9]) may refer to the preaching of Amos. See R. Fey, *Amos und Jesaja* (Neukirchen-Vluyn: Neukirchener Verlag, 1963), 89–104.

12. H. W. Wolff, *Joel and Amos*, 168–71, and Schmidt, "Die deuteronomistische Redaktion," 172–74, assign vv. 10–12 to a Deuteronom(ist)ic editor, but the allusion in v. 9 to the destruction of the gigantic Transjordan Amorites is also a Deuteronomic theme; cf. Deut. 2:10, 20–21.

13. H. W. Wolff, *Amos the Prophet*, 6–16 (= *Amos geistige Heimat* [Neukirche-Vluyn: Neukirchener Verlag, 1964], 5–12); S. Terrien, "Amos and Wisdom," in

B. W. Anderson and W. Harrelson, eds., *Israel's Prophetic Heritage*, 106–14; J. L. Crenshaw, "The Influence of the Wise upon Amos," *ZAW* 79 (1969): 42–52.

14. "His servants the prophets" (*ʿăbādāyw hannᵉbîʾîm*) is the standard term for the prophetic succession in Deuteronomic writings (1 Kings 14:18; 15:29; 18:36; 2 Kings 9:7, 36; 10:10; 14:25; 17:13, 23; 21:10; 24:2; Jer. 7:25; 25:4; 26:5; 29:19; 35:15; 44:4).

15. In the context, a more appropriate translation of *lamed* than the RSV "for Bethel."

16. On the so-called doxologies (Amos 4:13; 5:8–9; 9:5–6) see, in addition to the commentaries, F. Horst, "Die Doxologien im Amosbuch," *ZAW* 47 (1929): 45–54; J.D.W. Watts, "An Old Hymn Preserved in the Book of Amos," *JNES* 15 (1956): 33–39; J. L. Crenshaw, "Amos and the Theophanic Tradition," *ZAW* 80 (1968): 203–215. G. W. Ramsey, "Amos 4—12—A New Perspective," *JBL* 89 (1970): 187–91, suggests the rather implausible translation, "Prepare to call your gods, O Israel!" for this verse. On the reproach form in vv. 6–11, see J. Blenkinsopp, "The Prophetic Reproach," *JBL* 90 (1971): 267–78, and on its relation to the covenant, W. Brueggemann, "Amos 4:9–13 and Israel's Covenant Worship," *VT* 15 (1965): 1–15, following Reventlow, *Das Amt des Propheten bei Amos*, 120–24.

17. See especially Deut. 4:27–31, seeking Yahweh in exile, and Deut. 12:2–7, which enjoins seeking him at the place that he shall choose rather than frequenting the native sanctuaries, which are to be destroyed (cf. 12:30). One should also bear in mind the typically Deuteronomic motivation clause, "that you may live . . ." (Deut. 4:1; etc.).

18. "Plumb line" for *ʿănāk* is doubtful, since this word, which occurs four times in Amos 7:7–8 and nowhere else, seems to be cognate to Akkadian *annaku*, tin. The matter is thoroughly discussed by S. Paul, *Amos*, 233–36.

19. If *hêkāl* at Amos 8:3 means "temple" rather than "palace," it would seem that a slight alteration has changed "female singers" (*šārôt*) to "songs," that is, hymns (*šîrôt*), more in keeping with the proprieties of worship in the Second Temple.

20. The interpretation of Amos 7:14 has long been a matter of dispute. There is a strongly represented opinion that the context calls for an affirmative statement by Amos in one of the following senses: (a) "I was not a prophet . . . but now I am"; see especially H. H. Rowley, "Was Amos a Nabi?" in J. Fück, ed., *Festschrift Otto Eissfeldt* (Halle: Max Niemeyer, 1947), 191–98; (b) "Am I not a prophet . . . ?"; see especially G. R. Driver, "Amos 7:14," *EvTh* 67 (1955–56): 91–92; P. R. Ackroyd, "Amos 7:14," *EvTh* 68 (1956–57): 94; "A Judgment Narrative Between Kings and Chronicles," in G. W. Coats and B. O. Long, eds., *Canon and Authority*, 83–84; (c) "Certainly I am a prophet . . . ," assuming emphatic *lamed*; S. Cohen, "Amos Was a Navi," *HUCA* 32 (1961): 175–78; H. N. Richardson, "A Critical Note on Amos 7:14," *JBL* 85 (1966): 89; H. Schmid, "'Nicht Prophet bin ich, noch bin ich Prophetensohn.' Zur Erklärung von Amos 7:14a," *Judaica* 23 (1967): 73. There is also the question whether the nominal sentence (i.e., with the verb understood) should be translated in the past (as Rowley above) or the present, as, for example, H.-J. Stoebe, "Der Prophet Amos und sein bürgerlicher Beruf," *Wort und Dienst* 5 (1957): 160–81; S. Lehming, "Erwägungen zu Amos," *ZTK* 55 (1958): 145–69; and many of the commentators. See also J. MacCormack, "Amos 7:14," *EvTh* 67 (1955–56): 318; A.H.J. Gunneweg, "Erwägungen

zu Amos 7:14," *ZTK* 57 (1960): 1–16. I have assumed that the most natural reading is in the present: "I am not a *nābî'* nor am I a *ben-nābî'*, for I am a herdsman
and a dresser of sycamore fig trees." The second part of the statement, "Yet Yahweh took me . . . ," does not contradict this. Amos is saying that he received an
ad hoc commission even though he was a layman, that is, not a professional or
prebendary prophet.

21. On Amos 7:10–17 as deriving from an alternative account of the reign of
Jeroboam II (2 Kings 14:23–29), see P. R. Ackroyd, "A Judgment Narrative" (n. 20).

22. H. Schulte, "Amos 7,15a und die Legitimation des Aussenseiters," in
H. W. Wolff, ed., *Probleme biblischer Theologie. G. Von Rad zum 70. Geburtstag* (Mu-
nich: Chr. Kaiser, 1971), 462–78; G. M. Tucker, "Prophetic Authenticity: A Form-
Critical Study of Amos 7:10–17," *Int* 27 (1973): 423–34.

23. These variants include Amos 8:4 (cf. 2:7; 5:11); 8:6 (cf. 2:6); 8:7 (cf. 4:2;
6:8); 8:8 (cf. 9:5); 8:9 (cf. 5:18); 8:10 (cf. 5:16–17); 8:13–14 (cf. 5:2). As H. W.
Wolff, *Joel and Amos,* 325, puts it, "Those who formulated these oracles still had
Amos' own words ringing in their ears."

24. Allusions to the earthquake have been identified in 4:11; 6:11; 7:7–8; 8:8; 9:1.

25. See Y. Yadin, *Hazor II: An Account of the Second Season of Excavations, 1956*
(Jerusalem: Magnes Press, 1960), 24–26, 36–37; J. A. Soggin, "Das Erdbeben von
Amos 1:1 und die Chronologie der Könige Ussia und Jotham von Juda," *ZAW* 82
(1970): 117–21. Needless to say, the precise date of 760 B.C.E., suggested elsewhere
by Yadin, cannot be established archaeologically and was based presumably on
the practice of several commentators of dating Amos to that time; an unfortunately not uncommon case of circularity. If Amos 8:9 ("I will make the sun go
down at noon/ and darken the earth in broad daylight") alludes to a solar
eclipse, it may be the one recorded for the eponym year of Bur-sagale in Assyria,
corresponding to June 15, 763 B.C.E. If so, it would have been almost total in
Northern Israel (magnitude .982) and would have taken place at 9:05 A.M. local
time. It would inevitably have made a profound impression and would have been
interpreted as boding no good for the future. See Y. Yadin, "Hazor," in M. Avi-
Yonah, ed., *Encyclopedia of Archaeological Excavations in the Holy Land* II, Jerusalem:
Israel Exploration Society & Massada Press, 1976, 485, 495. The more precise
date of 760 B.C.E. suggested earlier by Yadin was presumably based on the practice of several commentators of so dating Amos' ministry and not on the basis of
archaeological data; see J. L. Mays, *Amos, A Commentary,* 20.

26. On the name, see J. J. Stamm, "Der Name des Propheten Amos und sein
sprachlicher Hintergrund," in J. A. Emerton, ed., *Prophecy: Essays Presented to Georg
Fohrer on His Sixty-fifth Birthday* (Berlin: Walter de Gruyter, 1980), 137–42; S. Paul,
Amos, 33—34.

27. That Amos came from the kingdom of Samaria rather than from Judah
has been argued sporadically and is not ruled out by anything in the biblical
record; see H. Schmidt, *Die Herkunft des Propheten Amos* (Berlin: Walter de
Gruyter, 1920), 158–71; more recently, S. N. Rosenbaum, *Amos of Israel: A New Interpretation* (Macon, Ga.: Mercer University Press, 1990).

28. The term *bōqēr* (Amos 7:14), though a hapax legomenon, would most
naturally mean one who has the care of cattle or oxen. Its incompatibility with
"Yahweh took me from following the flock" (*ṣōʾn,* sheep and goats, v. 15) should not

be pressed, since this may be a conventional way of describing a call (cf. 2 Sam. 7:8). In Amos 1:1 he is described as one of the *nōqᵉdîm* of Tekoa. The most probable meaning of this term is still "herdsman" or "sheep rearer," and its only other occurrence in the Hebrew Bible, at 2 Kings 3:4 with reference to the king of Moab, and its use in a Ugaritic text (*ANET*, 141) in association with priests, do not suggest a lowly social status. Even if Amos did look after livestock destined for sacrifice, as suggested by Kapelrud, *Central Ideas in Amos*, 5–7, this would hardly make him a "cultic official," and no one, to my knowledge, has suggested that dressing sycamore figs was a cultic function. For the meaning of the term *nōqēd* see, in addition to the commentaries, S. Segert, "Zur Bedeutung des Wortes noqed," *SVT* 16 (1967): 279–83. The conjecture of M. Bič, "Der Prophet Amos—ein Haepatoskopos," *VT* 1 (1951): 293–96, that *nōqēd* connotes divination by inspection of livers, was refuted by A. Murtonen, *VT* 2 (1952): 170–71.

29. The account of Jeroboam's reign in 2 Kings 14:23–29 records his success in restoring Israel's boundaries to the north and the east as far as the Dead Sea (cf. Amos 6:13–14, alluding to victories east of the Jordan). While there is no mention in Dtr of hostilities with Judah, Uzziah was also pursuing an expansionist policy in various directions, including the Transjordan region according to 2 Chron. 26:6–8, which, if true, would have increased the likelihood of friction. Dtr also notes that Jeroboam's campaigns had prophetic support (2 Kings 14:25).

30. Amos 2:13; 3:11; 4:12; 5:11, 16; 6:7, 14; 8:11; 9:8, 9.

31. This can be seen especially in the vassal treaties of Esarhaddon (*ANET*, 537–38). It was the prediction of exile that brought Amos to the attention of the authorities (Amos 7:11), but it occurs as a major theme throughout the book (1:5,15; 4:2–3; 5:27; 6:7; 7:17; 9:4). Another standard curse form occurs at 5:11b (cf. 9:14 and Deut. 28:30, 39): "You have built houses of hewn stone but you shall not dwell in them; you have planted pleasant vineyards, but you shall not drink their wine." Also noteworthy in this respect is very frequent use of the term *pš'* (rebel, rebellion) for sinning. See D. R. Hillers, "Treaty-Curses and the Old Testament Prophets," *BibOr* 16 (1964): 1–101; F. C. Fensham, "Common Trends in Curses of the Near Eastern Treaties and Kudurru-Inscriptions Compared with the Maledictions of Amos and Isaiah," *ZAW* 75 (1963): 155–175; M. Fishbane, "The Treaty Background of Amos 1:11 and Related Matters," *JBL* 89 (1970): 313–18; J. S. Holladay, "Assyrian Statecraft and the Prophets of Israel," *HTR* 63 (1970): 29–51.

32. For a convenient summary of recent discussion see A. J. Everson, "Day of the Lord," *IDBS*, 209–10, and for an exhaustive analysis see S. J. De Vries, *Yesterday, Today and Tomorrow* (Grand Rapids: Eerdmans, 1975), 55–331. Given the nature and understanding of warfare in ancient Israel, there is no need to choose between a military and a cultic connotation. The war context of Amos 5:18–20, the first passage in the prophetic literature dealing explicitly with the "Day of Yahweh," is supported by 1:14 ("the day of battle") and 2:16 ("on that day," i.e., of defeat in battle).

33. Allusions to autumn and harvesting (Amos 4:9; 5:16–17; 8:1–3), cultic rejoicing and lamentation (5:16–17; 8:3, 10), and the hymn of praise to the creator God (4:13; 5:8–9; 9:5–6) have been taken to indicate that Amos addressed the people at Bethel gathered for the autumnal festival of ingathering. This may be so, but it does not in any case provide the key for interpreting the book as a

whole, as was claimed by J. Morgenstern, "Amos Studies," *HUCA* 11 (1936): 19–140.

34. The tax-exempt status of officiants of state cults was normal in antiquity and is explicitly attested for the Second Temple (Ezra 7:24).

35. See L. A. Sinclair, "The Courtroom Motif in the Book of Amos," *JBL* 85 (1966): 351–53, and on the *rîb* pattern (i.e., statement of the case against the accused): B. Gemser, "The *Rîb-* or Controversy-Pattern in Hebrew Mentality," *SVT* 3 (1955): 120–34; H. B. Huffmon, "The Covenant Lawsuit in the Prophets," *JBL* 78 (1959): 285–95; H.-J. Boecker, *Redeformen des Rechtsleben* (Neukirchen-Vluyn: Neukirchener Verlag, 1964); J. Harvey, "Le 'Rîb-Pattern,' réquisitoire prophétique sur la rupture de l'alliance," *Bib* 43 (1962): 172–96; *Le Plaidoyer prophétique contre Israël après la rupture de l'alliance* (Bruges and Montreal: Desclée de Brouwer, 1967); J. Blenkinsopp, "The Prophetic Reproach," *JBL* 90 (1971): 267–78; K. Nielsen, *Yahweh as Prosecutor and Judge: An Investigation of the Prophetic Lawsuit (Rîb-Pattern)* (Sheffield: JSOT Press, 1978).

36. On the Yavneh-Yam inscription see J.C.L. Gibson, *Textbook of Syrian Semitic Inscriptions*, vol. 1, 26–30; K.A.D. Smelik, *Writings from Ancient Israel*, 93–100.

37. It is noteworthy that Assyria is not mentioned in Amos, unless we read "Assyria" with the LXX for the MT "Ashdod" at 3:9, which is possible but hardly obligatory. The foreign power referred to as an enemy (*ṣar*, 3:11) and "a nation" (*gôy*, 6:14) is presumably Assyria, though this is not said. Assuming the conventional date for Amos, about a quarter of a century before the accession of Tiglath-pileser III, it is remarkable that he should have foreseen conquest by the Assyrians, since we know of no significant military threat from that quarter after the last western campaign of Adad-Nirari III in 796 B.C.E. (*ANET*, 281–82). So this whole matter of dating is still *sub iudice*. Add that we know very little of the long reign of Jeroboam II, and we can only speculate on the events that, according to Dtr (2 Kings 14:26), reduced Israel to desperate straits at that time.

38. Second Kings 18:1 puts Hezekiah's accession in the third year of Hoshea, but 18:13 dates Sennacherib's campaign (701 B.C.E.) in the fourteenth year of Hezekiah, which means he came to the throne in 715 B.C.E. (with a margin of error of no more than a year).

39. A. Alt, "Hosea 5:8–6:6: Ein Krieg und seine Folgen in prophetischer Beleuchtung," *Kleine Schriften*, vol. 2, 1953, 163–87; H. Donner in J. H. Hayes and J. M. Miller, eds., *Israelite and Judaean History*, 421–34; H. W. Wolff, *Hosea*, 103–21.

40. See especially Amos 3:11; 6:14; and the forecast of the end of Damascus, 1:3–5. Other indications of Hosea's acquaintance with Amos: the preference for loyalty and knowledge of God over sacrifice (6:6) is reminiscent of Amos 5:21–24 though verbally not very close; 10:2b, the destruction of altars and cultic pillars, echoes the language of the last vision (Amos 9:1); and it is particularly significant that the only mention in Amos of false or syncretic cults (8:14) appears to have evoked a response in Hosea (4:15). The latter speaks of Gilgal and Beth-aven (= Bethel) and those who swear "as Yahweh lives!" while Amos 8:14 refers to Ashima of Samaria, a deity also mentioned at 2 Kings 17:30 and probably in the Elephantine papyri.

41. The text is, however, obscure; see H. W. Wolff, *Hosea*, 151, 157–58. *ṣōpeh* = watchman is used of the prophets in Jer. 6:17; Ezek. 3:17; 33:2, 6, 7; Isa. 52:8; 56:10.

42. *'ᵃdammeh*, here translated "I gave parables," is obscure; cf. the NRSV "I will bring destruction." The latter is possible, but the former preferable because it fits the context better. However, "I give parables," in keeping with a well-attested frequentative or iterative sense (Gesenius-Kautsch, *Hebrew Grammar*, §112dd), is better still, and intimates that, for Hosea, this prophetic process is still going on.

43. H. W. Wolff, "Hoseas geistige Heimat," and *Hosea*, 75.

44. The hypothesis of a prophetic covenant mediator whose functions included the reading of the law in a solemn cultic assembly, was never widely accepted and is now abandoned. It was advanced by H.-J. Kraus, *Worship in Israel* (Richmond: John Knox Press, 1966), 102–12, and expanded by J. Muilenburg, "The 'Office' of the Prophet in Ancient Israel," in J. P. Hyatt, ed., *The Bible in Modern Scholarship* (Nashville: Abingdon Press, 1965), 74–97. It has often been criticized, for example, by R. E. Clements, *Prophecy and Covenant*, (1965), 80, and *Prophecy and Tradition* (Atlanta: John Knox Press, 1975), 8–14. The main point is that Deut. 18:15–18 does not describe an actual function but a theoretical ideal, an attempt to say how prophecy fits into the ideal commonwealth as projected by the authors.

45. H. H. Rowley, "The Marriage of Hosea," *BJRL* 39 (1956): 200–23 (= *Men of God* [New York: Thomas Nelson & Sons, 1963], 66–97) covered the spectrum of opinions up to the time of writing; see further the leisurely discussion in Andersen and Freedman, *Hosea*, 115–309, and, for Wolff's hypothesis of the premarital sexual rite (somewhat analogous to the medieval *ius primae noctis*), see Wolff, *Hosea*, 13–15. The hypothesis is contested by W. Rudolph, "Praparierte Jungfrauen?" *ZAW* 75 (1963): 65–73.

46. *'ôd* also could refer to Yahweh's addressing Hosea, as in the NRSV ("The LORD said to me again . . ."), which, however, makes it more difficult to explain the change from the third to the first person.

47. The name Gomer has resisted attempts to wrest a symbolic meaning from it. The dual form Diblaim is unusual as a patronymic, which has led some commentators to the conclusion that it conceals an allusion to the cult of Asherah or Anath that is no longer clearly understood, since *dᵉbelâ* means "fig cake," and cakes made of figs or raisins seem to have featured in the cult of these deities (cf. 3:1; Jer. 7:18; Isa. 16:7). This is perhaps too recondite, and in any case a feminine dual form would then be required.

48. This should not be emended to "I am not your God" as in the RSV and the NRSV; cf. *'ehyeh 'ᵃšer 'ehyeh*, Ex. 3:14.

49. It is therefore very difficult, if not impossible, to decide whether Hos. 8:1b is Hosean or Deuteronomic. The verb *'br* (transgress) is Deuteronomic but *pš'* (rebel) occurs often in early prophetic texts but not at all in Deuteronomy. The term *bᵉrît* occurs in Hosea with the meaning of an international treaty (10:4; 12:1 [MT 12:2]). The covenant with the animal world in 2:18 (MT 2:20) is of a different kind and occurs in a passage that we take to be editorial. The covenant transgressed at Adam (6:7) may refer to an event in the recent past unknown to

us. The rare occurrences of the key term *b'rît* in pre-Deuteronomic prophetic texts does not encourage the thesis, once widely held, of the high antiquity of either the language of covenant or its religious institutional embodiment.

50. A connecting link could be the anti-Canaanite measures of Hezekiah (2 Kings 18:4, 22). The associative link between the golden calf episode in Exodus 32 and Jeroboam I's cultic establishment (1 Kings 12) might lead us to find a further link between the measures taken after the apostasy at Sinai—the so-called cultic decalogue of Exodus 34—and the reforms of Hezekiah.

51. The biblical evidence for prostitution carried out in a cultic establishment and in association with cult acts is unassailable in spite of recent attempts, some quite desperate (e.g., E. A. Goodfriend, "Prostitution," *ABD* 5:505–10), to explain away the relevant texts, including Hos. 4:14.

52. In addition to numerous figurines of the fertility goddess and *maṣṣēbôt*, the graffiti from Kuntillet 'Ajrud in the Sinai, from the ninth or eighth centuries B.C.E., are of special interest. Some of these record blessings in the name of Yahweh and his Asherah. Pending publication of the material by the excavator, Zeev Meshel, see his *Kuntillet 'Ajrud: A Religious Centre from the Time of the Judaean Monarchy on the Border of Sinai* (Jerusalem: Israel Museum, 1978), Catalogue no. 175, and his article in *ABD* 4:103–09. Archaeological evidence for the survival of syncretism in the exilic and postexilic periods is surveyed in lively fashion by Morton Smith, *Palestinian Parties and Politics That Shaped the Old Testament* (New York: Columbia University Press, 1971), 90–93.

53. The allusion to Jacob in Hos. 12:3–4, 12 does not, of course, solve the currently much debated issue of the historicity of early Israelite traditions, but it puts the burden of proof more firmly with those who dismiss these narrative traditions as late fiction.

54. In addition to the commentaries see P. R. Ackroyd, "Hosea and Jacob," *VT* 13 (1963): 245–59; E. M. Good, "Hosea and the Jacob Tradition," *VT* 16 (1966): 137–51; C. Jeremias, "Die Erzväter in der Verkündigung der Propheten," in H. Zimmerli, ed., *Festschrift für W. Zimmerli* (Göttingen: Vandenhoeck & Ruprecht, 1977), 206–22; and the exhaustive study of F. Diedrich, *Die Aufspielungen auf die Jakob-Traditionen in Hosea 12:1–13:3* (Würzburg: Echter Verlag, 1977).

55. It is worthy of note that wherever the spirit (*rûaḥ*) is associated with prophecy in prophetic texts generally deemed to be early (i.e., preexilic) the connotation is pejorative; see Hos. 9:7, 12; Micah 2:11; Isa. 29:10(?); Jer. 5:13.

56. Micah 2:3–4 has been expanded editorially, and 2:12–13, dealing with the theme of the reunification of the remnant (*š'ērît*) under a king, is almost certainly exilic or early postexilic. Van der Woude (1969) takes it to be a quotation from Micah's prophetic opponents, with Micah's answer, beginning "but I said," in 3:1. This, however, is quite improbable since 3:1–4 is not addressed to prophets and the pattern of thought in 2:12–13 is not typical of optimistic prophecy, to judge by the little we know of it under the monarchy.

57. J. T. Willis, "The Structure of Micah 3—5 and the Function of Micah 5.9–14 in the Book," *ZAW* 81 (1969): 191–214.

58. A. S. van der Woude, "Deutero-Micha: ein Prophet aus Nord-Israel?" *NTT* 25 (1971): 365–378.

59. The discovery of an incense altar and a fertility stela in an Israelite sanctuary could perhaps be seen as confirmation, though the dating remains uncertain; see Y. Aharoni in M. Avi-Yonah, ed., *Encyclopedia of Archaeological Excavations in the Holy Land,* vol. 3, 747–49.

60. First suggested by B. Stade, "Micha 1:2–4 und 7:7–20, ein Psalm," *ZAW* 23 (1903): 163–77, the liturgical character of the chapter was developed by H. Gunkel (1928); see also B. Reicke, "Liturgical Traditions in Micah 7," *HTR* 60 (1967): 349–68, and, for the section in general, T. Lescow, "Redaktionsgeschichtliche Analyse von Micha 6—7," *ZAW* 84 (1972): 182–212.

61. On the meaning of the elusive term '*am hā`āreṣ.* during the monarchy, see S. Daiches, "The Meaning of 'Am-haaretz' in the Old Testament," *JTS* 30 (1929): 245–49; J. A. Soggin, "Der judäische 'am-ha'areṣ. und das Königtum in Juda," *VT* 13 (1963): 187–95; R. de Vaux, "Les Sens de l'expression 'peuple du pays' dans l'Ancien Testament et le rôle politique du peuple en Israël," *RA* 58 (1964): 167–72; E. W. Nicholson, "The Meaning of the Expression 'Am-ha'ares' in the Old Testament," *JSS* 10 (1965): 59–66; S. Talmon, "The Judean 'am ha'areṣ in Historical Perspective," *Fourth World Congress of Jewish Studies,* 1 (1967): 71–76; M. H. Pope, " 'Am Ha'arez," *IDB* 1 (1962), 106–7.

62. A. S. van der Woude, "Micah in Dispute with the Pseudo-Prophets," 247, on 2:7a, translates the difficult *he'āmûr bēt-ya'ᵃqōb:* "He [i.e., Yahweh] affirmed [what has been undertaken by] the house of Jacob," reading the first word as a hiphil, *he'ᵉmîr,* as in Deut. 26:17–18, with reference to Yahweh's covenant fidelity in which the people were blindly trusting. They may have done so, but this improbable emendation does not prove it.

63. I take *'et-rûaḥ YHWH* (Micah 3:8), absent in Symmachus, as a gloss on *koaḥ* inserted by an editor more familiar with the idea of an inspired person being filled with the Holy Spirit than the endowment as described here. The phrase is syntactically awkward and breaks up the rhythm of the line; cf. H. W. Wolff, "Wie verstand Micha von Moreschet sein prophetisches Amt?" 406–7.

64. The content of Micah's indictment and his preference for archaic terms (*rā'šîm, qᵉṣînîm, ḥēleq, ḥebel bᵉgôrāl, qᵉhal YHWH*) would seem to support Wolff's hypothesis. It is also interesting and possibly relevant that, as he points out, Num. 11:16–25 combines ecstatic prophecy with the institution of the elders (Wolff, 416).

65. Points of contact between Micah and Amos are numerous: e.g., Micah 1:2–7; cf. Amos 1:2; Micah 1:3; cf. Amos 4:13; Micah 2:3; cf. Amos 5:13. We noted earlier the parallels between Micah 2:6–7 and Amos 7:15–16, both using the verb *nṭp* (hiphil), "preach," for what the prophet does.

66. On the history of the interpretation of Isaiah see C. R. Seitz, "Isaiah, Book of," *ABD,* 3:472–88.

67. The editorial insertion at Isa. 7:8b refers to Esarhaddon's settling of a foreign ruling class in Samaria in 669 B.C.E. (cf. Ezra 4:2). It was inevitable that the message of assurance would be followed by threats after Ahaz invited in the Assyrians, and also, perhaps, at the time of Hezekiah's revolt, 705–701 B.C.E. (Isa. 7:17–25; cf. 8:5–10).

68. Among recent commentators who take this line see P. Auvray, *Isaïe 1–39* (Paris: Editions du Cerf, 1972), 104–8, and H. Wildberger, *Jesaja I,* 289–93; for

other references J. Vermeylen, *Du Prophète Isaïe à l'apocalyptique,* 216–21.
O. Kaiser, *Isaiah 1–12,* 96–106, defends the quite different hypothesis that
hāʿalmâ (v. 14) refers to any young woman in Judah of marriageable age, in the
sense that "the danger will disappear so rapidly that women who are now with
child will name their sons, in thankfulness for being saved, 'Immanuel,' 'God
with us'" (103). The article with *ʿalmâ* and the parallelism with the other symbolic names that attach to specific individuals create serious problems for this hypothesis; and Kaiser disposes far too rapidly of the chronological objections
against an identification with Hezekiah. If we follow 2 Kings 18:13, against 18:1,
Hezekiah came to the throne in or near 715. If he was conceived in 734, the year
of the Syro-Ephraimite crisis, he would then be eighteen or nineteen at his accession. At least in this respect, therefore, Hezekiah is a serious candidate.

69. H. Barth, *Die Jesaja-Worte in der Josiazeit* (see bibliography) identifies precisely the Josian redaction down to sections of verses. See also G. T. Sheppard,
"The Anti-Assyrian Redaction and the Canonical Context of Isaiah 1—39," *JBL*
104 (1985): 193–216.

70. On the "hardening" (literally, "fattening") of hearts, see E. Jenni, "Jesajas
Berufung in der neueren Forschung," *TZ* 15 (1959): 321–39 and O. Kaiser, *Isaiah 1—12,* 82–83. It can best be understood as arising out of the need to explain
the failure of Isaiah's mission in 734 B.C.E.

71. On Isaiah 6 see, in addition to the commentaries, M. M. Kaplan, "Isaiah
6:1–11," *JBL* 45 (1926): 251–59; I. Engnell, *The Call of Isaiah* (Uppsala: Lundquist,
1949); L. J. Liebreich, "The Position of Chapter Six in the Book of Isaiah," *HUCA*
25 (1954): 37–40; R. Knierim, "The Vocation of Isaiah," *VT* 18 (1968): 47–68;
O. H. Steck, "Bemerkungen zu Jesaja 6," *BZ* 16 (1972): 188–206. The position of
this chapter in the unit to which it belongs (6:1–9:1a [MT 6:1–8:23a]), rather
than at the beginning of the book, may be explained in the sense that it describes
Isaiah's commissioning for a specific task, not necessarily the absolute beginning
of his prophetic activity. J. Milgrom, "Did Isaiah Prophesy During the Reign of
Uzziah?" *VT* 14 (1964): 164–82, may therefore be right in arguing that Isaiah was
active before Uzziah, and wrong in assuming that chapters 1—5 contain the sayings from that time.

72. On the prophetess (*hannᵉbîʿâ*) of Isa. 8:3 see the commentaries and
A. Jepsen, "Die Nebiah in Jes 8:3," *ZAW* 72 (1960): 267–68. It has been suggested
that if she was not a prophetic figure in her own right, she may have been a temple singer. We simply do not know, and it is perhaps prudent to add that we are
not told that she was Isaiah's wife.

73. K. Budde, "Zu Jesaja 8, Vers 9 und 10," *JBL* 49 (1930): 423–28; K. Galling,
"Ein Stück judäischen Bodenrechts in Jes. 8," *ZDPV* 56 (1933): 209–18; T. Lescow, "Jesajas Denkschrift aus der Zeit des syrisch-ephraimitischen Krieges," *ZAW*
85 (1973): 315–31; H.-P. Müller, "Glauben und Bleiben: Zur Denkschrift Jesajas
Kapitel 6:1–8:18," *SVT* 26 (1974): 25–54.

74. See also "your anger has turned away" (*yāšōb ʿappᵉkā,* Isa. 12:1), and cf. the
refrain of the poem in 5:24–25 plus 9:8–10:4, "his anger is not turned away"
(*loʾ šāb ʿappô*).

75. On the lexical and thematic links between chapters 1 and 65—66 see

L. J. Liebreich, "The Compilation of the Book of Isaiah," *JQR* 46 (1955–1956): 259–77; 47 (1956–1957) 114–38; R. Lack, *La Symbolique du livre d'Isaïe* (Rome: Biblical Institute Press, 1973), 139–41; A. J. Tomasino, "Isaiah 1:1–2:4 and 63—66 and the Composition of the Isaianic Corpus," *JSOT* 57 (1993): 81–98.

76. The most recent study is J. Blenkinsopp, "Fragments of Ancient Exegesis in an Isaian Poem (Jes 2:6–22)," *ZAW* 93 (1981): 51–62.

77. G. von Rad, "Die Stadt auf dem Berge," *EvTh* 8, (1948–49) 439–47 (= "The City on the Hill," *The Problem of the Hexateuch and Other Essays* [London: Oliver & Boyd, 1965], 232–42); H. Wildberger, "Die Völkerwallfahrt zum Zion," *VT* 7 (1957): 62–81. On the preceding title, see P. R. Ackroyd, "A Note on Isaiah 2:1," *ZAW* 75 (1963): 320–21.

78. That is, *lo'-šāb 'appô* ("his anger is not turned away," Isa. 9:11 [MT 9:12], etc.); cf. *lo' ʾᵃšîbennû* ("I will not cause it to turn back," Amos 1:3, etc.); the implicit object of the verb is probably *'ap*, the divine anger, as argued by R. P. Knierim, in G. W. Coats and B. O. Long, eds., *Canon and Authority*, 163–75.

79. J. Fichtner, "Jesaja unter den Weisen," *TLZ* 74 (1949): 75–80; R. T. Anderson, "Was Isaiah a Scribe?" *JBL* 79 (1960): 57–58; J. W. Whedbee, *Isaiah and Wisdom* (Nashville: Abingdon Press, 1971).

80. Some refer the saying to the death of Sargon II in 705 and the accession of Sennacherib, who would thus be the serpent and the adder respectively (Isa. 14:29). In that case the most recent "smiting" that we know of would be Sargon's campaign in 712 against Ashdod (*ANET*, 286).

81. Isaiah 1:4; 5:19, 24; 10:20; 12:6; 17:7; 29:19; 30:11, 12, 15; 31:1. ("The Holy One of Jacob" [29:23] occurs in a passage [29:22–24] that is not Isaian.) Compare "the Holy God" 5:16; "the Holy One," 5:19; 10:17. On God's holiness see W. Eichrodt, *Theology of the Old Testament*, vol. 1 (Philadelphia: Westminster Press, 1961), 270–82.

82. This interpretation of Isa. 31:4 is not entirely secure, however, since the metaphor could mean that the lion (Yahweh) fights against (*'al*) Mount Zion and will not surrender his prey (Jerusalem) to the shepherds (Egyptians) who have come out to rescue it; see O. Kaiser, *Isaiah 13—39*, 315–17, who, however, comes out in favor of a different meaning.

83. In addition to the commentaries, see M. B. Crook, "A Suggested Occasion for Isaiah 9:2–7 and 11:1–9," *JBL* 68 (1949): 213–24; A. Alt, "Jesaja 8:23–9:6: Befreiungsnacht und Krönungstag," *Kleine Schriften*, vol. 2, 1953, 206–25; S. Mowinckel, *He That Cometh* (Oxford: Basil Blackwell, 1959), 102–10; H. von Reventlow, "A Syncretistic Enthronement Hymn in Isa. 9:1–6," *UF* 3 (1971): 321–25; O. Kaiser, *Isaiah 1—12*, 123–30, 156–62.

NOTES TO PART IV: THE END OF NATIONAL INDEPENDENCE

1. Cushi is certainly a proper name (cf. Jer. 36:14), but since it is also a gentilic it could have appeared problematic; cf. the problem of Moses' Cushite wife (Num. 12:1), a subject of protracted discussion in the Midrash, and Amos 9:7, where *kušiyyîm* are the foreigners par excellence. It is perhaps worth noting that

the short book of Zephaniah mentions the Cushite people or the land of Cush twice (2:12; 3:10). See the commentaries and J. Heller, "Zephanjas Ahnenreihe," *VT* 21 (1971): 102–4.

2. The causal connection between Zeph. 2:1–3 and 2:4 indicated by *kî* suggests that inhabitants of the Philistine cities are being addressed throughout.

3. Compare Isa. 2:1–4; 4:2–6; 11:10–16; 14:1–2; 18:7; 19:18–24; 27:12–13; 60–61; 65:17–25; 66:18–24.

4. "From this place" (*min-hammāqôm hazzeh*, Zeph. 1:4) looks like a Deuteronomic addition, and in the same verse the phrase "with the priests" (*'im hakkōhⁿnîm*) has been added by a glossator unaware that Zephaniah was using the term *kᵉmārîm* (pagan priests) deliberately and disparagingly for the Jerusalem priesthood.

5. See K. Elliger, "Das Ende der 'Abendwölfe,'" in W. Baumgartner et al., eds., *Festschrift Alfred Bertholet zum 80. Geburtstag* (Tübingen: J.C.B. Mohr [Paul Siebeck], 1950), 158–75; M. Stenzel, "Zum Verständnis von Zeph. 3: 3b," *VT* 1 (1951): 303–5.

6. Especially the Day of Yahweh (Amos 5:18–20; 8:9–14; cf. Zeph. 1:14–18), represented as a day of battle (Zeph. 1:16), the use of a standard form of the curse (Amos 5:11; cf. Zeph. 1:13), and the theme of seeking Yahweh in the hope of salvation (Amos 5:4–7, 14–15; cf. Zeph. 2:3). The juxtaposition of the woe on Jerusalem (3:1–7) with the anti-Assyrian oracle (2:13–15) is also reminiscent of Amos 1:3–2:8.

7. It would be hazardous to conclude from these topographical allusions that the inhabitants of the city were anticipating the (alleged) Scythian invasion of ca. 630 B.C.E. Quite apart from the mythological undertones of such references as these, it would be natural for *any* real or anticipated invasion to approach the city from the north. On the "Scythian question" in Jeremiah, see below, p. 140.

8. The parallelism between the three divine requirements of Micah 6:8 and the three imperatives addressed to the "humble of the land" in Zeph. 2:3 is quite close; and especially interesting is the use of verbal forms *p'l* and *'sh* with *mišpāt*.

9. See A.D.H. Mayes, *Deuteronomy* (London: Oliphants, 1979), 81–103.

10. The connection is seen most clearly in the abolition of non-Yahwistic cult centers, that is, the "high places" (Deut. 12:2–3) and proscription of Canaanite-type cults in general (Deut. 12:29–31; 16:21–22; 18:9–14; 20:18). However, none of the social legislation in Deuteronomy is featured in the account of the reform. See Mayes (previous note) and M. Weinfeld, *Deuteronomy 1—11: A New Translation with Introduction and Commentary* (New York: Doubleday, 1991), 65–77.

11. Confirmation of two stages of religious reform, attributed to Hezekiah and Josiah, respectively, has been proposed based on the excavation of a sanctuary in the citadel of Arad. Constructed in the late tenth century B.C.E., its inner sanctum was found to contain two incense altars, a sacrificial altar, and a *massēbâ* (cult stela). The excavator (Y. Aharoni) claimed that the sacrificial altar went out of use in the eighth century, following on Hezekiah's reforms, and the sanctuary itself in the following century, following on those of Josiah. As established by Aharoni, the stratigraphy allows for but does not compel acceptance of his conclusion; for example, stratum VII, when the sanctuary went out of use, cor-

responds to the entire seventh century B.C.E. See Y. Aharoni in M. Avi-Yonah, ed., *Encyclopedia of Archaeological Excavations in the Holy Land,* vol. 1, (Englewood Cliffs: Prentice-Hall, 1975), 82–89; Miriam Aharoni, *The New Encyclopedia of Archaeological Excavations in the Holy Land,* vol. 1 (New York & London: Simon & Schuster, 1993), 82–85. However, D. Ussishkin, one of the most cautious and sophisticated of Syro-Palestinian archaeologists, rejects Aharoni's stratigraphy, dates the shrine's existence from the seventh to the early sixth century B.C.E., and rejects any connection with either Hezekiah's or Josiah's reforms; see his "The Date of the Judaean Shrine at Arad," *IEJ* 38 (1988): 142–57.

12. First Kings 14:18; 15:29; 18:36; 2 Kings 9:7, 36; 10:10; 14:25; 17:13, 23; 21:10; 24:2.

13. Among recent restatements see E. W. Nicholson, *Deuteronomy and Tradition* (Philadelphia: Fortress Press, 1967, and A. W. Jenks, *The Elohist and North Israelite Traditions* (Missoula, Mont.: Scholars Press, 1977).

14. Of a quite general nature are Hos. 4:1–3 (reminiscent of the Decalogue) and the allusions to murder, villainy, and robbery at 6:9 and 7:1.

15. A. Bentzen, *Die josianische Reform und ihre Voraussetzungen* (Copenhagen: G.E.C. Gadd, 1926); G. von Rad, *Studies in Deuteronomy* (London: SCM Press, 1953), especially 66–68.

16. With the exception of one reference in a late editorial strand (Deut. 27:14), Levites as second-order clergy are not attested in Deuteronomy, and allusions to such Levites in Dtr are among the clearest instances of late editing (Josh. 3:3; 1 Sam. 6:15; 2 Sam. 15:24; 1 Kings 8:4).

17. See especially G. von Rad, "The Levitical Sermon in 1 and 2 Chronicles," in *The Problem of the Hexateuch and Other Essays* (Edinburgh: Oliver & Boyd, 1965), 267–80.

18. Amos 7:1, 6; Micah 2:6, 11; Ezek. 21:1, 7. In spite of ntp = drip, the verb does not carry a pejorative connotation; hence the NEB "go drivelling on" at Amos 7:16 was unjustified and wisely changed in the REB (Revised English Bible).

19. Removing landmarks (Deut. 19:14; Micah 2:2), usury and abusive debt collection (Deut. 24:6, 10–13, 17; Micah 2:8, 9a), defense of the poor (Deut. 15:4; 14:28–29, etc.; Micah 3:1–2; 6:10), maintenance of process of justice (Deut. 16:18–20; Micah 3:9), condemnation of bribery (Deut. 16:18–20; Micah 3:11), correct weights and measures (Deut. 25:13–16; Micah 6:10–11).

20. The most detailed presentation is that of M. Weinfeld, *Deuteronomy and the Deuteronomic School* (Oxford: Clarendon Press, 1972).

21. Prov. 25:1; Jer. 2:8; 8:8–9. In *b. B. Bat.* 15a Proverbs, Ecclesiastes, Song of Songs, and Isaiah are attributed to Hezekiah and his men, which at least testifies to the persistence of a tradition of literary activity.

22. Max Weber, *The Sociology of Religion,* 51.

23. The Qumran commentary on Nahum (4Q169) is translated by G. Vermes, *The Dead Sea Scrolls in English* (Sheffield: JSOT Press, 1987³), 279–82.

24. On the disputed date of Nahum see J.J.M. Roberts, *Nahum, Habakkuk and Zephaniah,* 38–39, who opts for 640–630 B.C.E.

25. See P.A.H. de Boer, "An Inquiry into the Meaning of the Term *maśśā'*,"

OTS 5 (1948): 197–214; R. R. Wilson, *Prophecy and Society in Ancient Israel*, 257–59. The term is used generally by Judean prophets and in most cases for oracles against foreign nations. If *śar hammaśśā'* (or *b'maśśā'*) at 1 Chron. 15:22, 27 is a liturgical title meaning "master of the oracle," as suggested by S. Mowinckel, *The Psalms in Israel's Worship*, vol. 2, 56, we would have confirmation of the cultic setting of this type of saying.

26. Nahum 1:3a, which contradicts the preceding verse, is an explanatory gloss explaining God's anger as the result of God's refusal to condone immorality. In 4b a word beginning with *daleth* is required in place of *'umlal*, and in 6a *l'pānāyw* (for *lipnê*) should come after *ya'ᵃmôd*. On acrostic psalms see W. Soll, "Acrostic," *ABD* 1:58–60; and on the Nahum acrostic, in addition to the commentaries, P. Humbert, "Essai d'analyse de Nahoum 1:2–2:3," *ZAW* 44 (1926): 266–80; J. de Vries, "The Acrostic of Nahum in the Jerusalem Liturgy," *VT* 16 (1966): 476–81; D. L. Christensen, "The Acrostic of Nahum Reconsidered," *ZAW* 87 (1975): 17–30.

27. Since the identity of Elkosh is unknown, arguments for the non-Judean origin of Nahum are bound to be speculative even when as ingenious as that of A. S. van der Woude, "The Book of Nahum: A Letter Written in Exile," *OTS* 20 (1977): 108–26.

28. By emending the last word of Nahum 3:17, *'ayyām*, to *'ôy lāhem* (MT has *'ôy mah*), and joining it to the following verse, some commentators identify vv. 18–19 as a separate woe saying, a very brief one by comparison with vv. 1–17.

29. P. Humbert, "Le Problème du livre de Nahoum," *RHPR* 12 (1932): 1–15; J. Lindblom, *Prophecy in Ancient Israel*, 253.

30. See 2 Kings 23:4; 2 Chron. 34:6–7. For archaeological confirmation, see J. H. Hayes and J. M. Miller, eds., *Israelite and Judaean History*, 465. According to Albrecht Alt, "Judas Gaue unter Josia," *PJB* 21 (1925): 100–16, the city lists in Joshua 15 and 19 derive from an administrative document of Josiah's reign.

31. The exact sequence of events is unclear. See Hayes and Miller, 471, and bibliography, 469.

32. B. Duhm, *Das Buch Habakuk: Text, Übersetzung und Erklärung* (Tübingen: J.C.B. Mohr, 1906), 19–23; and, in favor of the text as it stands, P. Humbert, *Problèmes du livre d'Habacuc*, 34.

33. In addition to the works cited in the bibliography, see P. Humbert, "Essai d'analyse de Nahoum 1:2–2:3," *ZAW* 44 (1926): 266–80; M. J. Guenthaner, "Chaldeans or Macedonians?" *Bib* 8 (1927): 129–60, 257–89; W. Staerk, "Zu Habakuk 1:5–11: Geschichte oder Mythos?" *ZAW* 51 (1933): 1–28.

34. E. Nielsen, "The Righteous and the Wicked in Habaqquq," *StTh* 6 (1953): 54–78. See also the perceptive comments of M. A. Sweeney, "Habakkuk," in J. L. Mays, ed., *Harper's Bible Commentary* (San Francisco: Harper & Row, 1988), 739–41.

35. Here (Hab. 2:1) we should perhaps read *miṣpeh* for *māṣôr*, parallel with *mišmeret*, as at Isa. 21:8; cf. the designation *ṣōpeh*, watchman, for prophet (e.g., Ezek. 3:17) and the frequent use of *ṣph* in association with prophecy (Isa. 21:6; 52:8; 56:10; Jer. 6:17; Ezek. 3:17; 33:1–9; Hos. 9:8; Micah 7:7).

36. Other aspects of this important text are discussed by M. Stenzel,

"Habakuk 2:1–4, 5a," *Bib* 33 (1952): 506–10; S. Schreiner, "Erwägungen zum Text von Hab. 2:4–5," *ZAW* 86 (1974): 538–42; J. A. Emerton, "The Textual and Linguistic Problems of Habakkuk 2:4–5," *JTS* 28 (1977): 1–18; J. G. Janzen, "Hab. 2:2–4 in the Light of Recent Philological Advances," *HTR* 73 (1980): 53–78.

37. See M. Stenzel, "Habakuk 2:15–16," *VT* 3 (1953): 97–99; E. Otto, "Die Stellung der Wehe-Worte in der Verkündigung des Propheten Habakuk," *ZAW* 89 (1977): 73–107.

38. Among the many studies that have pursued the implications of Mowinckel's C source should be mentioned J. P. Hyatt, "Jeremiah and Deuteronomy," *JNES* 1 (1942): 156–73; "The Deuteronomic Edition of Jeremiah," in *Vanderbilt Studies in the Humanities*, vol. 1 (Nashville: Vanderbilt University Press, 1951), 71–95; H. H. Rowley, "The Prophet Jeremiah and the Book of Deuteronomy," in H. H. Rowley, ed., *Studies in Old Testament Prophecy* (Edinburgh: T. & T. Clark, 1950), 157–74; H. Cazelles, "Jérémie et le Deutéronome," *RSR* 38 (1951): 5–36; E. Nicholson, *Preaching to the Exiles*, especially 20–32; Hyatt (1942), Rowley, and Cazelles deal with the related question of Jeremiah's attitude to the Josian (Deuteronomic) reform.

39. Nicholson, *Preaching to the Exiles*, 39–40; M. Kessler, "Form-Critical Suggestions on Jer. 36," *CBQ* 28 (1966): 389–401; R. P. Carroll, *Jeremiah: A Commentary*, 656–58 provides an outstanding commentary on this chapter.

40. T. H. Robinson, "Baruch's Roll," *ZAW* 42 (1924): 209–21; G. Wanke, *Untersuchungen zur sogenannten Baruchschrift* (Berlin: de Gruyter, 1971; only Jer. 26—28 and 36 could have been written by Baruch); W. L. Holladay, "A Fresh Look at 'Source B' and 'Source C' in Jeremiah," *VT* 25 (1975): 394–412.

41. While few conclusions of this kind will pass unchallenged, there must be substantial doubt about the Jeremian origins of the following: Jer. 3:6–10, 11–14, 15–18, 24–25; 5:18–19; 9:12–16, 23–26; 10:1–16 (10:11 is an Aramaic gloss within this editorial expansion); 12:7–13, 14–17; 15:5–9; 22:8–9. In addition, most, if not all of the following, are Deuteronomic reworkings of Jeremian sayings: Jer. 7:1–8:3; 11:1–17; 16:1–21; 17:19–27; 18:1–12; 19:1–20:6; 21:1–10; 22:1–5; 23:1–8; 25:1–14.

42. Similar prophetic discourses in Dtr are: 1 Kings 11:29–39 (Ahijah); 2 Kings 22:14–20 (Huldah). Among those who have argued against the Deuteronomic origin of Mowinckel's C source, which includes the prose paraphrases, Helga Weippert, *Die Prosareden des Jeremiabuches*, believes they could have been composed by Jeremiah himself, while W. Thiel, *Die deuteronomistische Redaktion von Jeremia 1—25*, assigns them to disciples of the prophet during the exilic period.

43. See G. von Rad, "Die Konfessionen Jeremias," *EvTh* 3 (1936): 265–70; S. H. Blank, "The Confessions of Jeremiah and the Meaning of Prayer," *HUCA* 21 (1948): 331–54; J. Bright, "Jeremiah's Complaints: Liturgy or Expressions of Personal Distress?" in J. I. Durham and J. R. Porter, eds., *Proclamation and Presence* (London: SCM Press, 1970), 189–214 (Bright accepts the latter alternative against H. Reventlow); A.H.J. Gunneweg, "Konfession oder Interpretation im Jeremiabuch," *ZTK* 67 (1970): 395–416; R. P. Carroll, *From Chaos to Covenant*, 107–35; *Jeremiah: A Commentary*, 275–79.

44. H. Reventlow, *Liturgie und prophetisches Ich bei Jeremia* (Gütersloh:

Gütersloher Verlagshaus/Gerd Mohn, 1963), while failing to establish this hypothesis, provided a focus for discussion.

45. An accessible account of relevant archaeological data is P. King, *Jeremiah: An Archaeological Companion* (Louisville: Westminster/John Knox Press, 1993).

46. K. Baltzer, *Die Biographie der Propheten* (Neukirchen-Vluyn: Neukirchener Verlag, 1975).

47. For a different view see J. Bright, *Jeremiah*, 276–87, questioned by R. P. Carroll, *From Chaos to Covenant*, 204–25.

48. Servant (*'ebed*) is a synonym for prophet in Deuteronom(ist)ic writings (e.g., Josh. 1:1–2; 1 Kings 14:18; 15:29; 18:36; 2 Kings 9:36; 10:10; 14:25), and the term *'ªbādāyw hannᵉbī'īm*, "his servants the prophets," is used of the prophetic succession as a whole (see n. 12 and cf. Jer. 7:25; 25:4; 26:5; 29:19; 35:15; 44:4; Amos 3:7).

49. See the remarks of E. Nicholson, *Preaching to the Exiles*, 45–58, and W. L. Holladay, "The Background of Jeremiah's Self-Understanding," *JBL* 83 (1964): 153–64.

50. On Jeremiah and the "false prophets," see T. W. Overholt, *The Threat of Falsehood: A Study in the Theology of the Book of Jeremiah* (London: SCM Press, 1970); J. L. Crenshaw, *Prophetic Conflict* (Berlin: de Gruyter, 1971), especially 49–61; I. Meyer, *Jeremia und die falschen Propheten* (Freiburg: Universitätsverlag, 1977).

51. The structure of these and similar passages has been analyzed by N. Habel, "The Form and Significance of the Call Narratives," *ZAW* 77 (1965): 301–23.

52. It is of course conceivable that the narrative in Ex. 3:1–4:17 draws on accounts of prophetic commissioning including that of Jeremiah, especially if one accepts a Deuteronomic contribution to the call of Moses; see J. Blenkinsopp, *The Pentateuch: An Introduction to the First Five Books of the Bible* (New York: Doubleday, 1992), 148–51. In comparing the two accounts we are speaking of the *Deuteronomic Moses*.

53. Jeremiah 3:6–10 is not an exception; cf. the allegory of the two sisters who were prostitutes in Ezekiel 23.

54. Much has been written on the date of Jeremiah's call, so that it is possible to mention only some of the more significant contributions: F. Horst, "Die Anfänge des Propheten Jeremia," *ZAW* 41 (1923): 94–153; T. C. Gordon, "A New Date for Jeremiah," *ExpT* 44 (1932–33) 562–565; H. Bardtke, "Jeremia der Fremdvölkerprophet," *ZAW* 53 (1935): 218–19 ("thirteenth" is a scribal error for "twenty-third"); J. Milgrom, "The Date of Jeremiah, Chapter 2," *JNES* 14 (1955): 65–69 (from the period 627–616 B.C.E.); P. E. Broughton, "The Call of Jeremiah," *Australian Biblical Review* 6 (1958): 41–43; H. H. Rowley, "The Early Prophecies of Jeremiah in Their Setting," *BJRL* 45 (1962–63): 198–234 (= *Men of God* [London: Thomas Nelson & Sons, 1963], 133–68); C. F. Whitley, "The Date of Jeremiah's Call," *VT* 14 (1964): 467–83; J. P. Hyatt, "The Beginnings of Jeremiah's Prophecy," *ZAW* 78 (1966): 204–14 (rejects his own earlier arguments for late years of Josiah's reign, *JBL* 59 [1940]: 509, and supports Whitley's arguments for the year of Jehoiakim's accession).

55. Typically Deuteronomic phrases are: "to command the covenant," "the iron furnace" (referring to slavery in Egypt), "fulfil the oath which I swore to your

fathers," "walk in the stubbornness of his [evil] heart," "bring upon them [you] the words of this covenant."

56. Shaphan, who functioned as a kind of Secretary of State (*sōpēr*) during the reign of Josiah, seems to have exercised some jurisdiction over the temple, received the newly discovered book from Hilkiah, and decided what to do with it (2 Kings 22:3–10). He and his son Ahikam were members of the delegation sent to consult with the prophetess Huldah (22:11–14). Ahikam protected Jeremiah at the time of his trial (Jer. 26:24). Another son of Shaphan, Elasah, bore Jeremiah's letter to the Babylonian diaspora (Jer. 29:3), while yet another son, Gemariah, had a room in one of the temple gatehouses in which Baruch read the scroll (Jer. 36:10). He was one of those who urged the king not to burn it (36:25). His son, Micaiah, was also active at that time (36:11–13) while another grandson of Shaphan, Gedaliah, was made governor, and probably puppet king, of the province after the fall of Jerusalem and took it on himself to protect Jeremiah (Jer. 39–41; 2 Kings 25:22–25).

57. On the tension between legal experts and prophets see J. Blenkinsopp, *Prophecy and Canon* (Notre Dame: University of Notre Dame Press, 1977), 24–53.

58. B. S. Childs, "The Enemy from the North and the Chaos Tradition," *JBL* 78 (1959): 187–98; B. T. Arnold, "North Country, The," *ABD*, 4:1136.

59. It is worth noting how much of Jeremiah's activity took place in the temple. The oracle accompanying the jar-breaking was repeated in the temple court (Jer. 19:14), where the confrontations with Pashhur and Hananiah also took place (chaps. 20; 28:1, 5). The "temple sermon" also, of course, was delivered there (26:2, 7; cf. 7:2) and the trial followed at the New Gate of the temple (26:10). There also the Rechabites were offered wine (chap. 35) and the scroll was read by Baruch, again at the New Gate (36:10). In his letter to the authorities Shemaiah simply assumed that Jeremiah, as a prophet, was under temple jurisdiction (29:24–28).

60. Several passages appear to refer to a drought (Jer. 8:14–15, 20; 9:10, 12, 15 [MT 9:9, 11, 14]; 9:20–22 [MT 9:19–21], reinforced by the allusion to Mot, bringer of aridity and death in the Baal cycle, from Ugarit (9:21). The liturgical character of the language in 14:1–15:3 has often been noted.

61. On the basis of Jer. 16:1–9 it has been widely assumed that Jeremiah was celibate by choice, but this is by no means assured. R. P. Carroll, *Jeremiah: A Commentary*, 338–42, warns against taking this passage as "the unmediated record of somebody's life" and the perils of psychologizing should likewise not be neglected (Jeremiah as "time's eunuch," as a Kierkegaardian or Kafkaesque figure, etc). W. McKane, *A Critical and Exegetical Commentary on Jeremiah*, 366–68, also questions the autobiographical bearing of the passage.

62. A little later the pro-Egyptian party demanded the death penalty on the grounds that he was "weakening the hands of the soldiers" (Jer. 38:4); cf. the same phrase used in Lachish ostracon 6 (*ANET*, 322).

63. R. R. Wilson, *Prophecy and Society in Ancient Israel*, 231–51.

64. G. von Rad, *Old Testament Theology*, vol. 2, 274–77; *The Message of the Prophets*, 162, 167.

65. The filthy loincloth (Jer. 13:1–11), refusal to marry and have children

(16:1–9), visit to the potter (18:1–11), public smashing of a pot (19:1–15), wooden and iron yoke-bars (27:1–28:17), purchase of land at Anathoth (32:1–44), offering wine to the Rechabites (35:1–11), hiding stones in the palace courtyard in Egypt (43:8–13).

NOTES TO PART V: BETWEEN THE OLD ORDER AND THE NEW

1. See the remarks of C. F. Whitley, *The Exilic Age* (London: Longmans, Green & Co., 1957), 1–28.

2. James Barr, "Le Judaïsme postbiblique et la théologie de l'Ancien Testament," *RTP* 18 (1968): 209–17; J. Blenkinsopp, *Prophecy and Canon*, 17–23; "Tanakh and the New Testament," in L. Boadt et al., eds., *Biblical Studies: Meeting Ground of Jews and Christians* (New York: Paulist Press, 1980), 96–119.

3. J. H. Hayes and J. M. Miller, eds., *Israelite and Judaean History*, 475. An inscribed ostracon, found at Arad about thirty kilometers south of Beersheba, dates from this time and seems to refer to an Edomite attack; see Y. Aharoni, in M. Avi-Yonah, ed., *Encyclopedia of Archaeological Excavations in the Holy Land*, vol. 1 (Englewood Cliffs: Prentice-Hall, 1975), 87; B. MacDonald, "Archaeology of Edom," *ABD* 2:295–301.

4. Amos 1:11–12; Isa. 21:11–12; 34:5–7; 63:1–6; Jer. 49:7–22; Ezek. 25:12–14; 35:1–15; Mal. 1:3–5; Ps. 137; Lam. 4:21–22. See J. R. Bartlett, "Edom," *ABD* 2:287–95.

5. Sepharad (v. 20), the word for Spain in later Hebrew, could refer to Sardis in Lydia, site of an impressive synagogue, or Saparda, a city in Media. See the commentaries and J. Gray, "The Diaspora of Israel and Judah in Obadiah v. 20," *ZAW* 65 (1965): 53–59; D. Neiman, "Sepharad: The Name of Spain," *JNES* 22 (1963): 128–32.

6. Gedaliah was the son of Ahikam, who protected Jeremiah when he was accused of treason (Jer. 26:24; 40:6), and grandson of Shaphan. A seal impression found at Lachish (Tell ed-Duweir) inscribed *lgdlyhw [']šr 'l hbyt* (to Gedaliah who is over the house) probably refers to the same person in his capacity as majordomo of the palace; see O. Tufnell, ed., *Lachish*, vol. 3, *The Iron Age* (London: Oxford University Press, 1953), 348. N. Avigad, *Hebrew Bullae from the Time of Jeremiah* (Jerusalem: Israel Exploration Society, 1986), 24–25, suggests that another bulla inscribed *lgdlyhw 'bd hmlk* may refer to the same person since the script is identical. The odd absence of a title in the relevant texts, supplied gratuitously in the RSV and other modern versions, may be due to embarrassment at a non-Davidite as ruler.

7. R. P. Carroll, "The Myth of the Empty Land," *Semeia* 9 (1992): 79–93.

8. Jeremiah 41:5 tells of a group of eighty pious Northerners bringing offerings to the temple of Yahweh who were murdered at Mizpah by the Ishmael faction. It is generally assumed that they were on their way to Jerusalem, but it is also possible that a sanctuary of however modest dimensions was attached to the Neo-Babylonian capital at or near Mizpah, and that this was their destination; cf. Mizpah as religious center in the (late) narrative in Judges 20—21. On sanctuaries

outside Jerusalem see Morton Smith, *Palestinian Parties and Politics that Shaped the Old Testament* (New York: Columbia University Press, 1971), 82–98.

9. On the arguments of Noth and Janssen for a Palestinian origin of Dtr see P. R. Ackroyd, *Exile and Restoration,* 29–30, 65–68. On the Judean rather than Babylonian origin of Isaiah 40—55, see below p. 184.

10. The fifth-century records of the trading house of Murashu (*ANET,* 221–22) contain a significant percentage of Jewish names, for example, Tobiah (cf. Ezra 2:60).

11. Frequent allusion to "the place Casiphia" in Ezra 8:15–20 has attracted attention because "place" (*māqôm*) can serve as a synonym for "temple." Furthermore, Iddo is often attested as a priestly name (e.g., Ezra 5:1; 6:14; Neh. 12:16). Note also in this respect the vision of Zechariah (5:5–11) in which the woman whose name is Wickedness is transported to Babylon where a house (temple) is to be built for her. It has been suggested that this refers to a Canaanite goddess worshiped at a syncretist shrine that may have been built by a group opposed to the resumption of the Jerusalem cult; see M. Smith, *Parties and Politics,* 90–91.

12. For examples of Babylonian magic see *ANET,* 309–10; also H. Ringgren, *Religions of the Ancient Near East* (London: SPCK, 1973), 89–99; H.W.F. Saggs, *The Encounter with the Divine in Mesopotamia and Israel* (London: Athlone Press, 1978), 125–52.

13. See my *Prophecy and Canon,* 73–79.

14. See *ANET,* 308, and E. F. Weidner, "Jojachin König von Juda, in babylonischen Keilinschriften," *Mélanges syriens offerts à M. René Dussaud,* vol. 2 (Paris: Paul Geuthner, 1939), 923–35; W. F. Albright, "King Jehoiachin in Exile," *BA* 5 (1942): 49–55; D. J. Wiseman, *Nebuchadrezzar and Babylon* (Oxford: Oxford University Press, 1983), 81–84.

15. Second Samuel 3:18; 1 Kings 8:24–26; 2 Kings 19:34 (= Isa. 37:35); Jer. 33:21–22, 26.

16. Jeremiah 6:13; 8:10; 14:13–16; 20:6; 23:5–6, 16, 32; 27:9–10, 14–16; 28:15; 29:8–9, 31; Ezek. 13:2–8; 22:28.

17. Jeremiah 14:13, 15; 37:19; *šālôm:* 4:10; 5:12; 6:14; 8:11; cf. Ezek. 13:10, 16.

18. Amos 2:12; Isa. 30:9–10; Micah 2:6–11; Jer. 11:21; 20:1–6, 26. See T. Overholt, "Commanding the Prophets: Amos and the Problem of Prophetic Authority," *CBQ* 41 (1979): 517–32.

19. This is a major point in Josephus's explanation of the fall of Jerusalem in A.D. 70. Josephus liked to think of himself as in the same situation as Jeremiah (*War* 5:391, 393; 6:103) in that both he and Jeremiah warned their contemporaries against the danger of the false prophets (*Ant* 10:103–7), but they chose not to listen (*War* 6:285–87).

20. On the tradition history of the passage and the Deuteronomic additions to it see J. Gray, *1 and 2 Kings: A Commentary* (Philadelphia: Westminster Press, 1970[2]), 318–23; also J. L. Crenshaw, *Prophetic Conflict,* 41–42, and R. R. Wilson, *Prophecy and Society in Ancient Israel,* 187–91.

21. J. Blenkinsopp, "Abraham and the Righteous of Sodom," *JJS* 33 (1982): 119–32; "The Judge of All the Earth: Theodicy in the Midrash on Genesis 18:22–33," *JJS* 41 (1990): 1–12.

22. See my *Prophecy and Canon*, 85–95.

23. That is, Deut. 4:27–31; 30:1–3; 1 Kings 8:33–34, 46–53, to which we may add certain passages in Jeremiah that are probably of Deuteronomic origin, especially Jer. 24:7; 29:10–14. See E. W. Nicholson, *Preaching to the Exiles: A Study of the Prose Tradition in the Book of Jeremiah* (Oxford: Basil Blackwell, 1970), passim.

24. On the proposed Josian redactional strand in Isaiah see above p. 102.

25. The kind of homiletic material well represented in Deuteronomy may have originated, or at least been delivered in a liturgical, synagogue-type setting after the fall of Jerusalem.

26. Ezekiel 1:1–2; 8:1; 20:1; 24:1; 26:1; 29:1; 29:17; 30:20; 31:1; 32:1, 17; 33:21; 40:1.

27. K. Jaspers, "Der Prophet Ezechiel: Eine pathographische Studie," in *Arbeiten zur Psychiatrie, Neurologie und ihren Grenzbebieten: Festschrift K. Schneider* (Heidelberg: L. Schneider, 1947), 77–85; see also E. C. Broome, Jr., "Ezekiel's Abnormal Personality," *JBL* 65 (1946): 277–92.

28. On the work of Torrey, Herntrich, Berry, and others, see H. H. Rowley, *Men of God*, 175–84.

29. On the school of Ezekiel, see Zimmerli, *Ezekiel*, 68–74.

30. Compare H. G. May, "The Departure of the Glory of Yahweh," *JBL* 56 (1937): 309–21; J. Blenkinsopp, *Ezekiel*, 18–23, 59–60.

31. On the date of Ezekiel's call, see Rowley, *Men of God*, 198–203; Zimmerli, *Ezekiel*, 112–15.

32. Argued more fully in my paper "The Structure of P," *CBQ* 138 (1976): 275–92, and *Prophecy and Canon*, 59–69.

33. J. Bowman, "Ezekiel and the Zadokite Priesthood," *TGUOS* 16 (1955–56): 1–14; M. Haran, "Ezekiel's Code (Ezek. 40—48) and Its Relation to the Priestly School," *Tarbiz* 44 (1974–75): 30–53 (Hebrew); J. D. Levenson, *Theology of the Program of Restoration of Ezekiel 40—48* (Missoula, Mont.: Scholars Press, 1976).

34. In addition to the commentaries, see M. Greenberg, "On Ezekiel's Dumbness," *JBL* 77 (1958): 101–5; R. R. Wilson, "An Interpretation of Ezekiel's Dumbness," *VT* 22 (1972): 91–104.

35. Job 1—2 illustrates this point, to prove that Job's family, retainers, and many others in the land of Uz had to die.

36. A. Malamat, *SVT* 28 (1975): 130, suggests Hananiah's prophecy in Jer. 28:1–4.

37. W. Zimmerli, "The Word of God in the Book of Ezekiel," in R. W. Funk, ed., *History and Hermeneutic* (New York: Harper & Row, 1967), 13.

38. H. J. van Dijk, *Ezekiel's Prophecy on Tyre* (Rome: Biblical Institute Press, 1968).

39. Zimmerli, *VT* 15 (1965): 516–21.

40. C. G. Howie, "Gog and Magog," *IDB* 2 (1962): 436–37, 67; M. C. Astour, "Gog and Magog," *ABD* 2:1056–7.

41. In addition to the commentaries, see H. G. May, "The King in the Garden of Eden: A Study of Ezekiel 28:12–19," in B. W. Anderson and W. Harrelson, eds., *Israel's Prophetic Heritage*, 166–76.

42. Isaiah 13:1–22; 14:3–11, 12–21; 21:1–10; Jer. 25:12–14.

43. Isaiah 4:2; 11:1–10; 32:1–8; Jer. 23:5–6; 30:8–9; 33:14–22; Ezek. 34:23–24; 37:24–25; Amos 9:11–15; Micah 5:2–5a [MT 5:1–4a].

44. For example, closure at 48:22 and 57:21 is suggested by the repetition of the phrase *'ēn šālôm . . . lārešā'îm* ("there is no peace for the wicked"); or the third large section could begin at 55:1 as well as at 56:1, especially since *lō' yikkārēt* ("will not be cut off") occurs at 55:13 and 56:5.

45. J. D. Smart, *History and Theology in Second Isaiah* (Philadelphia: Westminster Press, 1965), 20–23; H. M. Barstad, "Lebte Deuterojesaja in Judäa?" in S. A. Christoffersen and H. M. Barstad, eds., *Veterotestamentica: Donum natalicium Arvido S. Kapelrud a collegis et amicis 14 lustra complenti* (Oslo: Oslo University Press, 1982), 77–87; "On the So-Called Babylonian Literary Influence in Second Isaiah," *SJOT* 2 (1987): 90–110.

46. C. R. North, *The Suffering Servant*, 89–90.

47. F. M. Cross, "The Council of Yahweh in Second Isaiah," *JNES* 12 (1953): 274–78; C. Westermann, *Isaiah 40—66*, 32—46 (who, however, deemphasizes the call).

48. *mebaśśeret* may therefore be taken as a *nomen officii;* cf. *sōperet* (Ezra 2:55) and *qōhelet;* on which see Gesenius-Kautzsch, *Hebrew Grammar*, §122r.

49. G. S. Kirk and J. E. Raven, *The Presocratic Philosophers: A Critical History with a Selection of Texts* (Cambridge: Cambridge University Press, 1962), 163–81.

50. Compare Gen. 1:1–2:4 (P); Amos 4:13; 5:8–9; 9:5–6; Job 38; etc. The theme is dealt with by C. Stuhlmueller, *Creative Redemption in Deutero-Isaiah* (Rome: Biblical Institute Press, 1970).

51. The theme is dealt with at greater length in my "The Unknown Prophet of the Exile," *Scripture* 14 (1962): 81–90, 109–18.

52. In the Bronze Age Baal cycle from Ugarit, Yamm is defeated by Baal. The references are given in E. R. Follis, "Sea," *ABD*, 5:1058–59.

53. Compare the use of rhetorical questions (e.g., in Isa. 40:12–31), forensic terminology (e.g., Isa. 41:21), and a wide range of rhetorical figures, especially in the polemic against idolatry (Isa. 40:18–20; 41:6–7; 44:9–20; 45:20–21; 46:1–7); cf. Hag. 1:4–11; 2:3, 11–19; Zech. 1:3–6; 7:5–7; Mal. 1:2–14; 2:10–17; 3:6–8, 13–15.

54. In Isa. 40–48: 41:8, 9; 43:10; 44:1, 2, 21 (twice); 45:4; 48:20; parallelism with "messenger(s)" in 42:19 and 44:26 render the collective meaning less certain, while 42:1 almost certainly alludes to an individual. Apart from "servants of rulers" (49:7, and 54:17 in the plural), all occurrences in chaps. 49—55 refer to an individual (49:3, 5, 6; 50:10; 52:13; 53:11). See W. Zimmerli, *TDNT*, vol. 4, 654–77, and *The Servant of God* (Naperville, Ill.: Alec R. Allenson, 1965²).

55. J. Blenkinsopp, "A Jewish Sect in the Persian Period," *CBQ* 52 (1990): 11–14.

56. Individual prophetic servants: 1 Kings 15:29; 2 Kings 9:36; 10:10; 14:25; the prophets as a whole: 2 Kings 9:7; 17:13, 23; 21:10; 24:2, etc.

57. For example, 2 Sam. 3:18; 1 Kings 8:24–26; 11:13.

58. Jeremiah 23:5–6; 30:8–9; 33:14–26; Ezek. 34:23–24; 37:24–25; cf. Hag. 2:23; Zech. 3:8 (Zerubbabel).

59. Duhm referred to the passages in question as *Dichtungen*, claiming that they stood out by virtue of their literary quality, "durch die ruhige Sprache, durch das Ebenmass der Stichen und Strophen," *Das Buch Jesaja*, 311.

60. See further below, pp. 216–22.

61. The textual condition of Isa. 53:11 does not permit a precise and certain distinction between speakers.

62. R. N. Whybray, *Thanksgiving for a Liberated Prophet,* 92–106, presents the most thorough arguments for the view that the Servant was not put to death. If, however, he was, we may raise the question whether Isa. 30:20–21, which alludes to a teacher now hidden who will be seen once again and his message heard, does not refer to the prophetic leader and teacher of Isaiah 52—53 who lives on through his disciples. O. Kaiser, *Isaiah 13—39,* 301, believes the passage may come from as late as the Seleucid period and, specifically, from the scribal and apocalyptic milieu of Daniel.

NOTES TO PART VI: PROPHECY IN THE SECOND COMMONWEALTH

1. *yᵉhûdîm,* meaning "Jews" rather than "Judeans" (as, for example, in 2 Kings 16:6, when the Northern Kingdom was still in existence), is perhaps first attested in Jeremiah (32:12; 34:9; 40:11–12; 41:3; cf. 38:19) and 2 Kings (25:25; 43:9; 44:1; 52:28, 30). Following Josephus (*Ant,* 11:173), however, we should trace the origins of Judaism to the community formed of the descendants of the preexilic Judeans that took shape in and around Jerusalem in the early Persian period. Nehemiah 4:1–2 (MT 3:33–34) suggests that at the time of Nehemiah's governorship the inhabitants of Samaria did not think of themselves as Jews even if they worshiped Yahweh.

2. Morton Smith, *Parties and Politics,* 193–201, argues against Alt's thesis that Judah was under the jurisdiction of Samaria. See further G. Widengren in Hayes and Miller, *Israelite and Judaean History,* 509–11.

3. For the Cyrus cylinder, see *ANET,* 315–16.

4. For the "Passover Papyrus," see A. Cowley, *Aramaic Papyri of the Fifth Century B.C.* (Osnabrück: Otto Zeller, 1967 [1923]), 60–65; B. Porten, *Archives from Elephantine* (Berkeley, Calif.: University of California Press, 1967, 128–33); *ANET,* 491.

5. This does not imply that the Pentateuch was in final form by the early Persian period or even by the time of Ezra, whose "law of the God of heaven" (Ezra 7:12) cannot simply be equated with it. On the Pentateuchal laws as the civil constitution of the Jewish ethnos see E. Blum, *Studien zur Komposition des Pentateuch* (Berlin: de Gruyter, 1990), 333–60; J. Blenkinsopp, *The Pentateuch,* 239–42.

6. Originally, perhaps, a kind of dice for giving simple yes or no answers, Urim and Thummim were incorporated into the high priest's vestments (Ex. 28:30; Lev. 8:8); see I. Mendelsohn, "Urim and Thummim," *IDB,* 4:739–40; E. Lipiński, "Urim and Thummim," *VT* 20 (1970): 495–96.

7. The different editorial strata in Deuteronomy 27 can be discerned by the quite distinct allusions to Levi as a tribe (v. 12), the Levitical priests (v. 9), and Levites as distinct from priests (v. 14). In Deuteronomy all "Levitical priests," whether engaged in cult at the central sanctuary or not, have in principle the same status (Deut. 18:6–8). The Deuteronomic history does not attest to the existence of Levites as distinct from priests either. First Kings 8:4 ("the priests and

the Levites brought them up") is absent from some of the best manuscripts of the LXX, and is almost certainly a gloss, the purpose of which is to correct the previous statement; elsewhere in this record we hear only of priests (1 Kings 8:3, 6, 10–11). Second Kings 23:4 appears to speak of the high priests and the priests of the second order, but we should read the singular, *kōhēn mišneh*, as at 2 Kings 25:18. No preexilic prophet mentions Levites, and even the term "Levitical priests" occurs only in the Deuteronomistic stratum of Jeremiah (33:17–22).

8. It is defended by E. J. Bickermann, "The Edict of Cyrus in Ezra 1," *JBL* 65 (1946): 249–75; G. Widengren, in Hayes and Miller, eds., *Israelite and Judaean History*, 498–99, and R. de Vaux, "The Decrees of Cyrus and Darius on the Rebuilding of the Temple," *The Bible and the Ancient Near East* (London: Darton, Longman & Todd, 1972), 61–96. We must at least admit significant editing by the Chronicler, as de Vaux and others admit.

9. A.T.E. Olmstead, *History of the Persian Empire*, 107–18; for contrasting interpretations of Darius' account of these events see J. M. Cook, *The Persian Empire* (London: J. M. Dent & Sons, 1983), 49–55 and R. N. Frye, *The History of Ancient Iran* (Munich: C. H. Beck, 1984), 96–106.

10. See the commentaries and R. A. Mason, "The Purpose of the 'Editorial Framework' of the Book of Haggai," *VT* 27 (1977): 415–21.

11. It is generally assumed that the sanctuary in question was on the site of the Jerusalem temple, but the natural sense of Zech. 7:2–3, unamended, is that the destination of the delegation was Bethel, which may have supplanted Jerusalem as the religious center during the Neo-Babylonian period, located close to the administrative center of Mizpah as it was.

12. K. Koch, "Haggais unreines Volk," *ZAW* 79 (1967): 52–66; H. G. May, "'This People' and 'This Nation' in Haggai," *VT* 18 (1968): 190–97; D. R. Hildebrand, "Temple Ritual: A Paradigm for Moral Holiness in Haggai 2:10–19," *VT* 39 (1989): 154–68.

13. In that case, however, it is difficult to see how they reached such a conclusion. Calculated from 586, the seventy years would then have been only four years short of completion, while seventy-eight years would have passed since the first deportation. The probability that the Jeremian prophecy nevertheless lies behind the urgent preaching of Haggai is increased by the fact that (according to Ezra 6:15) the temple actually was rebuilt four years later. We recall that Jeremiah promised that in seventy years Yahweh would bring them back "to this place," at which time they would seek him and their prayers would be heard (Jer. 29:10, 12–13).

14. For Darius' Behistun (Behistan, Bisitun) inscription see R. G. Kent, *Old Persian* (New Haven: American Oriental Society, 1953[2]), 116–36.

15. R. P. Carroll, *When Prophecy Failed,* 157–83.

16. The Satan (Adversary) appears elsewhere as fulfilling a specific function only at 1 Chron. 21:1 and Job 1—2. Functionally similar is "the Spirit" who volunteers to deceive Ahab in Micaiah's vision, 1 Kings 22:21–22.

17. M. Barker, "The Two Figures in Zechariah," *HeyJ* 18 (1977): 38–46, suggests that the two "sons of oil" in Zech. 4:14 represent two branches of the priesthood that had reached, or were being urged to reach, a negotiated settlement.

18. Morton Smith, *Palestinian Parties and Politics*, 90–91. For a different interpretation, emphasizing the economic ills of the time, see Margaret Barker, "The Evil in Zechariah," *HeyJ* 19 (1978): 20–26. The unusual form *hāriš'ā* (the Wickedness, Zech. 5:8) suggests, by assonance, the goddess Asherah.

19. On the social background see the commentaries and J. L. Berquist, "The Social Setting of Malachi," *BTB* 19 (1989): 121–26; P. L. Redditt, "The Book of Malachi in Its Social Setting," *CBQ* 56 (1994): 240–55; also E. Stern, *The Material Culture of the Land of the Bible*, 158–95.

20. E. Pfeiffer, "Die Disputationsworte im buche Maleachi," *EvTh* 19 (1959): 546–68; H.-J. Boecker, "Bemerkungen zur formgeschichtlichen Terminologie des Buches Maleachi," *ZAW* 78 (1966): 78–80; J. A. Fischer, "Notes on the Literary Form and Message of Malachi," *CBQ* 34 (1972): 315–20.

21. They are known as Yahweh-fearers (*yir'ē YHWH*), servers of God (*'ōbēd 'elōhîm*), righteous (*saddîq*) as distinct from the wicked; they give special attention to the divine Name (*hōš'bē š'mô*). The language is therefore strongly reminiscent of the different ways in which the prophetic group attested in the last chapters of Isaiah is described. They too are servants of Yahweh (Isa. 65:8–9, 13–16; 66:14) who venerate his Name (59:19; cf. 65:15–16) and await the final judgment that will vindicate the righteous (65:13–14; 66:5, 24). Malachi 3:16–18 either anticipates, or is of the same kind as, or is perhaps even identical with Nehemiah's covenant.

22. In addition to the commentaries see B. V. Malchow, "The Messenger of the Covenant in Mal. 3:1," *JBL* 103 (1984): 252–55.

23. Reading *mal'ākî* for the MT *mal'āk* with the OG, *Sam. Pent.*, and Vulgate.

24. 1QS 9:11; 4QTestim; John 1:21, 25; 6:14; 7:40; Acts 3:22.

25. Neither Deuteronomy nor Dtr refers to priests as Aaronite or to Aaron as discharging priestly functions. Apart from allusion to Aaron's death (Deut. 10:6; 32:50), of P origin, Deuteronomy refers to Aaron only once, a disparaging allusion (Deut. 9:20). The almost total silence of both pre- and postexilic sources prior to Chronicles, with the exception of P, on Aaron qua priest and priests as Aaronite still awaits a satisfactory explanation.

26. See, for example, R. P. Carroll, "Twilight of Prophecy or Dawn of Apocalyptic?" *JSOT* 14 (1979): 3–35; M. A. Knibb, "Prophecy and the emergence of the Jewish Apocalypses," in R. Coggins et al., eds., *Israel's Prophetic Tradition*, 169–76.

27. On the basis of his reading of Ezra 4:3 (*kî 'anahnû yahad nibneh*), Talmon had earlier argued that the *gōlâ*-community referred to itself as a *yahad* or conventicle, the term later used of themselves by the Qumran sectarians; see his "The Sectarian YHD—A Biblical Noun," *VT* 3 (1953): 133–40.

28. We are assuming that the chronological order presupposed by the biblical editor, though not without its difficulties, is defensible and should be maintained. The interminable debate on this issue is summarized in P. R. Ackroyd, *Israel under Babylonia and Persia*, 191–96, and again in G. W. Anderson, ed., *Tradition and Interpretation*, 333–34. Ackroyd makes out a cautious case for 398 B.C.E., the seventh year of Artaxerxes II Mnemon, while Morton Smith, *Palestinian Parties and Politics*, 120–23, vigorously defends the earlier date. See also J. Blenkinsopp, *Ezra-Nehemiah: A Commentary* (Philadelphia: Westminster Press, 1988), 139–44.

29. There is no indication that Nehemiah was of Davidic descent, pace U. Kellermann, *Nehemia: Quellen, Überlieferung und Geschichte* (Berlin: de Gruyter, 1967), 21–23, 154–59, and there is no reason to believe that, as cupbearer or wine steward at the royal court in Susa (Neh. 1:11b), he was a eunuch; see J. Blenkinsopp, *Ezra-Nehemiah*, 213.

30. The miserable social and economic conditions in Judah are reflected in Hag. 1:6, 8–11; 2:16–17; Zech. 8:10; Isa. 58:3–4; 59:6, 9–15; Joel 1—2; Neh. 5:1–5.

31. First Maccabees 2:42–48; 7:13. These *asidaioi* ($h^a sîdîm$) are described as "mighty warriors of Israel" (2:42) and therefore presumably were not "pacifists." The "many who were seeking righteousness and justice," who went down into the wilderness, refused to fight on the Sabbath and were slaughtered (2:29–38) are not identified with the Asidaeans, and there is nothing to suggest that they would not have fought on the other six days of the week.

32. Isaiah 55:3–4 refers to the Davidic covenant but without a promise of its restoration.

33. See above pp. 182–83.

34. *pōš^e'îm bî* (66:24); cf. *pāš^e'û bî* (1:2). This and other verbal links between the last and the first chapter of the book of Isaiah are listed by L. J. Liebreich, "The Compilation of the Book of Isaiah," *JQR* 46 (1955/1956): 259–71; 47 (1956/1957): 114–38, and especially pp. 276–77.

35. *ṣōpîm*, synonymous with *n^e bî'îm;* cf. Ezek. 3:17; 33:7; Jer. 6:17; Isa. 52:8. In Isa. 62:6 the similar term *šōm^e rîm*, "watchmen" or "guardians," is used.

36. The designation "mourners" (*'a bē lîm, mit'abbelîm*, Isa. 57:18; 61:2–3; 66:10; cf. Ezra 10:6; Neh. 1:4; Dan. 10:2–3) functions in a way comparable with "servants" and "quakers."

37. P. D. Hanson, *The Dawn of Apocalyptic*, 92–93, takes this verse to indicate a rift between what he calls "the central Israelite community," that is, the Zadokite priests and their allies, and the group represented by the speaker. The context, however, makes it quite clear that the prayer is in the name of the community as a whole, the "holy people" that once possessed and now has lost its sanctuary (v. 18). This is not the language of a group ostracized by the temple authorities.

38. Hanson, *The Dawn of Apocalyptic*, 146–50, argues at length that the seer is denouncing the Zadokite priesthood, but in order to do so he must interpret the abuses symbolically, which is quite unnecessary. The reproach is explicitly addressed to a nation (*gôy*) and people (*'am*). Use of cultic terminology does not imply that priests are being addressed, and *kî q^e daštîkā* cannot be translated "or I will communicate holiness to you."

39. The verbs used are strong: "hate" involves active dissociation as in the divorce formula; *niddāh* (piel), "cast out," occurs only here and at Amos 6:3 where it has the sense of "conjuring up," "setting aside," probably by magical means. At Isa. 66:5 we are approaching the meaning "excommunicate" that the verb has in Mishnaic Hebrew.

40. Isaiah 65:15–16 is difficult. "The Lord YHWH will put you to death" is probably a later insertion. Verse 16a reads: "he who blesses himself in the land will bless himself by the God Amen, and he who takes an oath in the land will

swear by the God Amen." Since this sounds strange, most commentators take it on themselves to emend MT *'āmēn* to *'emet, 'omen,* or *'ēmûn*. The MT is, however, textually unassailable and makes sense. If we retain it, it follows from the logical connection of v. 15 with v. 16 that this is to be the new name of the faithful community, a community which, in other words, says yes to God. This, incidentally, seems to be the way the text was understood by Paul (2 Cor. 1:17–20) and the author of Revelation (3:14). Isaiah 62:1–5 provides another example of eschatological name-giving.

41. Very common in the older commentators, for example, Wellhausen, Budde, Gressmann, Torrey; for a survey of opinions see Muilenburg, *IB* 5:758–60. Muilenburg's own opinion, that the seer is opposing the view that limits salvation to the cult, is shared by Westermann, *Isaiah 40—66,* 412–14, and Whybray, *Isaiah 40—66,* 279–80.

42. The verb *ḥrd* is attested frequently with the sense of fearing, shaking, trembling; less frequently with the more specific connotation of numinous fear and trembling (Ex. 19:16; 1 Sam. 14:15). In the participial form the only occurrences are 1 Sam. 4:13 (*hāyāh libbô ḥārēd 'al 'ǎrôn hā'ĕlohîm'*); Isa. 66:2, 5; Ezra 9:4; 10:3. The close similarity between the last four suggests not a title but a designation that has attained a certain fixity.

43. It seems, in other words, that Ezra overstepped the terms of his commission in forcing community leaders to divorce their foreign (i.e., non-Judean) wives, certainly not mandated by any law Israelite or Persian. The same conclusion is suggested by the abrupt ending of the Ezra story (Ezra 10:44).

44. In a famous rabbinic story concerning the ritual status of the oven of Akhnai (*b. B. Meṣi'a* 59b), a *bat qôl* was disregarded in favor of appeal to scripture. On the *bat qôl* in general see A. Rothkoff, "Bat Kol," *EJ* 4:324–25.

45. See the classic treatment of charismatic authority in Max Weber, *The Theory of Social and Economic Organization* (New York: Free Press, 1964), 324–423.

46. Ahlström, *Joel and the Temple Cult of Jerusalem,* 129, decides for 515–500 B.C.E. but it is doubtful whether one can be so precise.

47. This is more or less identical with the conclusion reached by H.G.M. Williamson, *Israel in the Book of Chronicles,* 83–86, and *1 and 2 Chronicles,* 15–17, even though he detaches Ezra-Nehemiah from the Chronicler. D. L. Petersen, *Late Israelite Prophecy,* 57–60, follows F. M. Cross and D. N. Freedman in dating the nucleus of the work to the early sixth century, with later expansions. Sara Japhet, *1 and 2 Chronicles: A Commentary* (Louisville: Westminster/John Knox Press, 1993), 23–28, opts for the early Hellenistic period, the end of the fourth century B.C.

48. See J. A. Sanders, *Discoveries in the Judaean Desert of Jordan,* vol. 4, *The Psalms Scroll of Qumrân Cave 11 (11QPsᵃ)* (Oxford: Oxford University Press, 1965), 137–39.

49. Mowinckel, *The Psalms in Israel's Worship* 2:56, reads *śar hammaśśā'* as a title meaning "master of the oracle." While the meaning "precentor" or "director of music" seems more likely, the use of *maśśā'* in this context is nonetheless interesting.

50. See, for example, the Qumran *Hôdāyôth* (1QH); Luke 1:67–69; 1 Cor. 14;

and the remarks of W. H. Brownlee, *The Meaning of the Qumran Scrolls for the Bible* (New York: Oxford University Press, 1964), 271–73, on liturgical prophecy at Qumran. M. Gertner, "The Masorah and the Levites: An Essay in the History of a Concept," *VT* 10 (1960): 241–84, argues for a connection between Second Temple Levites and the Masoretes.

51. See my "Prophecy and Priesthood in Josephus," *JJS* 25 (1974): 239–62.

52. A. Lods, *The Prophets and the Rise of Judaism*, 153, 205.

53. J. A. Bewer in J.M.P. Smith et al., *A Critical and Exegetical Commentary on Micah, Zephaniah, Nahum, Habakkuk, Obadiah and Joel* (Edinburgh: T.& T. Clark, 1912), 61 (between 352 and 348 B.C.E.); H. W. Wolff, *Joel and Amos*, 77–78.

54. The problem is different for those who regard Joel as a unity; for example, J. A. Thompson, *IB* 6:732–34; A. S. Kapelrud, *Joel Studies*, 193–95, who records without criticism Engnell's view of the book as a liturgical, preexilic unity. For the problem of dating in general, see Wolff, *Joel and Amos*, 4–6, 60–61.

55. Josephus, *Ant.* 11:317–47; *b. Yoma* 69a.

56. R. C. Dentan, *IB* 6:1102–5; M. Delcor, "Deux passages difficiles: Zacharie 12:11 et 11:13," *VT* 3 (1953): 67–77; D. R. Jones, "A Fresh Interpretation of Zechariah 9—11," *VT* 12 (1962): 241–59; M. Treves, "Conjectures Concerning the Date and Authorship of Zech. 9—14," *VT* 13 (1963): 196–207; R. Mason, *The Books of Haggai, Zechariah and Malachi*, 103–10; R. L. Smith, *Micah-Malachi* (Waco, Tex.: Word Books, 1984), 267–72; R. Albertz, *A History of Israelite Religion in the Old Testament Period*, vol. 2, *From the Exile to the Maccabees* (Louisville: Westminster/John Knox Press, 1994 [1992]), 568–70.

57. The Samaritans of a later day used a double entendre in referring to themselves as *šōmᵉrîm*, the observant ones.

58. Some aspects of this enigmatic narrative fit surprisingly well with what we know about Nehemiah. He is appointed to a position of authority over Judah when the province was in terrible shape (Neh. 1:3 etc.), the ruling elite was being enriched at the expense of the poor, some of whom were being sold into indentured service (Neh. 5:1–5); he took action against some of these members of the elite, both lay and clerical (Neh. 6:16–19; 13:4–9, 28–29); and he broke definitively with "Israel," that is, the opposition in Samaria under Sanballat.

59. See Mason, *The Books of Haggai, Zechariah and Malachi*, 117–20.

60. On the identity of the city, see H. Wildberger, *Jesaja*, 893–96, 905–6; O. Kaiser, *Isaiah 13–39*, 173–79; W. R. Millar, *Isaiah 24—27*, 15–21.

61. Note the change to the first-person plural and singular at 24:16; the individual speaker's lament about treacherous behavior would most naturally allude to those who were rejoicing. The preceding exclamation *rāzî-lî, rāzî-lî* ("I have my secret! I have my secret!") should not be emended; *raz* with this meaning occurs at Sir. 8:18 and the Aramaic equivalent (*rāzāh*) in Daniel (2:18 etc.). It can have the meaning of a divine plan for the future communicated in cryptic, symbolic fashion and requiring divine illumination for its decipherment. See J. Niehaus, "*raz-pᵉšar* in Isaiah 24," *VT* 31 (1981): 376–78.

62. Literary studies on Jonah abound, no doubt because of the preference for narrative among biblical literary critics. In my view Sasson (1990) is the best of the recent commentaries on the text.

INDEX OF ANCIENT SOURCES

EARLY JEWISH WRITINGS

JOSEPHUS

QUMRAN

RABBINIC TEXTS

NEW TESTAMENT

CPSIA information can be obtained
at www.ICGtesting.com
Printed in the USA
LVOW11s1415100817
544514LV00003B/127/P

9 780664 256395